METHOD

FOR PRAYER

METHOD

FOR PRAYER

Freedom in the face of God

Matthew Henry

CHRISTIAN HERITAGE

Ligon Duncan, is the Senior Minister of the historic First Presbyterian Church (PCA), Jackson, Mississippi. He is now Adjunct Professor of Theology at the Reformed Theological Seminary (RTS), where he was formerly the John R. Richardson Professor of Systematic Theology. He is Convener of the Twin Lakes Fellowship, a Council Member of the Alliance of Confessing Evangelicals, Chairman of the Council on Biblical Manhood and Womanhood, and Secretary of the Board of Belhaven College. He is currently editor of a multi-volume set on the Westminster Assembly entitled *The Westminster Confession into the 21st. Century* (Volume 1 ISBN 1-85792-862-8, Volume 2 1-85792-878-4, Volumes 3 & 4 forthcoming).

© J. Ligon Duncan III
ISBN 1-85792-068-6
ISBN 978-1-85792-068-0

10 9 8 7 6 5 4 3 2 1

Published in 1994
Reprinted in 1998, 2006 and 2007
by
Christian Focus Publications Ltd.
Geanies House, Fearn, Ross-shire
Scotland, IV20 1TW, UK

You can now buy online at
www.christianfocus.com

Cover design by Danie Van Straaten

Printed by Color House Graphics, Inc. USA

CONTENTS

EDITOR'S INTRODUCTION

Matthew Henry (1662-1714), beloved commentator on the Scriptures, was born near Whitchurch (Salop), England.[1] He began preaching at the age of 23 and spent most of his ministry as pastor of a church in Chester (1687-1712). He was a prolific writer, most famous for his *Commentary on the Whole Bible* which he began in November of 1704 and left incomplete upon his death. Ministerial colleagues concluded the work with reference to his notes and writings (Henry had finished the commentary from Genesis through Acts).

Throughout his life as a minister, Henry was a diligent student of the word, sometimes rising as early as 4 o'clock in the morning and often spending eight hours a day in his study in addition to his pastoral labors. He was also, however, a man of prayer. His life-long concern for prayer is said to have originated with his recovery from a potentially terminal illness at the age of 10. Whatever the case, the whole of his labors is marked by the wisdom which only those who are habitually dependent upon the Almighty in prayer may hope to attain.

Henry completed a book on prayer in March of 1712, just two months before leaving Chester (where he had served for twenty-five years) to pastor a church in London. Hence, it reflects a lifetime of prayer, ministry and Christian experience. Its full title was *A Method for Prayer with Scripture Expressions proper to be used under each head*. In it, Henry lays down an outline of a plan for prayer (Adoration, Confession, Petition, Thanksgiving, Intercession, and Conclusion) and supplies the contents of prayer from the Scriptures themselves.

The editor's acquaintance with Matthew Henry's book on prayer dates to a suggestion of one of his seminary professors, O. Palmer Robertson. Some of the students, appreciative of Dr. Robertson's peculiar power in public prayer, inquired as to what he would suggest to us for becoming more proficient in leading in congregational prayer. Beside the cultivation of the habit of regular private prayer, he recommended one book: Matthew Henry's *Method for Prayer*.

---

[1] For those unfamiliar with English geography, Whitchurch (Salop) is about 18 miles south, south-east of Chester, not too far from the border with Wales, and located in the area today known as Shropshire.

A Press, Inc. of Greenville, South Carolina, USA, eventually reprinted a copy of the 1819, Berwick edition. Having recommended the book to many friends who greatly benefitted from their reading of *Method for Prayer,* it seemed appropriate to prepare the book for reintroduction to the broader Christian community. Various editions were compared, in the process of which numerous errors were discovered. And since the most recent editions of the work were typeset in the nineteenth century, it was decided to completely re-typeset and edit the volume. Henry's numbering system for the outline has been modified to make it easier to follow. A few footnotes have been added. Incorrect Scripture references have been rectified. Latin and Greek phrases have been translated. Three of Henry's sermons on prayer have been included. And three appendices by the editor have been attached.

The aim of the republication of this old work is to assist and encourage modern Christians in both public and private prayer. Surely we all recognize that the Church of our day, at least in the West, is weak in the way of prayer. Few of us, perhaps, understand what prayer really is. We do not pray often. We do not pray with Scriptural proportion, nor does our prayer much reflect the language and thought of the Bible. We do not pray fervently. Maybe we really do not believe in prayer.

Resorting to a more Scriptural pattern of prayer may be a simple (but profound) answer to many problems in our practice of prayer. Praying Scripturally will teach us what prayer is, even while we do it. It will correct 'shopping list' views of prayer which abound in the Christian community. It will begin to solve in our own minds the question of 'unanswered prayer'. It will remind us of just how much there is to pray about day by day. It will teach us of the extreme urgency of prayer. It will return proportion to prayers long on petition, but short on adoration, confession, and thanksgiving. It will instruct us how best to pray for ministers, missionaries, and one another. It will show us the proper way to approach God in prayer. It will remind us of the good things that God does for us (which we, more often than not, take for granted). It will remind us to always give thanks to God (which, paradoxically, is so important for our own assurance of His faithfulness in answering prayer). It will begin to engrave in our minds Biblical patterns of thought which can help immunize us from the enticing folly of the world's view of life. It will force us to rehearse the solemn warnings and precious promises of God (which will do eternal good to our souls). And it will move us from our inherent man-centeredness in prayer to a Biblical, God-centered way of praying.

For those who are called upon to lead the Church in public prayer, or who simply desire to be more faithful and competent in their own private petitions, a Scriptural manner of praying provides the order, proportion, and variety which should characterize all our prayers. We have attached a number of helps to assist the reader in achieving this end. Part one of this volume contains the entire text of Matthew Henry's *Method for Prayer*. Reading and re-reading through it will train the Christian in the use of Biblical truth and language in prayer. Part two comprises three of Henry's sermons on prayer given shortly after Henry had arrived in London, in late August and early September of 1712. They concern how a Christian may start, spend, and close the day in prayer. They are included as an encouragement to regular private devotions. Finally, we have affixed three appendices. The first is a complete outline of Henry's plan for prayer. The reader may find it helpful to refer to in calling to mind subject matter for prayer. The second provides some guidelines for public prayer, drawn from Samuel Miller's excellent book, *Thoughts on Public Prayer.*[2] It is designed to help those who pray in public regularly or occasionally better prepare themselves for the task. The final appendix is an abbreviated version of Henry's outline, designed to be referred to at one's convenience.

My thanks to my student assistants, Michael Andres, Rob Bailey, David Mikkelson, and Scott Moore, for their help in the task of editing, and to my youngest brother, Melton Ledford Duncan, and my mother, Shirley Duncan, who did the proof-reading. My appreciation is also extended to Christian Focus Publications for their interest in the project and willingness to bring it to fruition.

Ligon Duncan
Jackson, Mississippi
June 1993

---

[2] Miller's book is highly recommended and may be obtained from Sprinkle Publications, P.O. Box 1094, Harrisonburg, VA, 22801.

To The
READER

Religion is so much the business of our lives, and the worship of God so much the business of our religion, that what hath a sincere intention, and probable tendency, to promote and assist the acts of religious worship, I think, cannot be unacceptable to any that heartily wish well to the interests of God's kingdom among men: For if we have spiritual senses exercised, true devotion, that aspiring flame of pious affections to God, as far as in a judgment of charity we discern it in *others* (though in different shapes and dresses, which may seem *uncouth* to one another) cannot but appear *beautiful and amiable,* and as far as we feel it in *our own breasts,* cannot but be found very *pleasant* and *comfortable.*

Prayer is a principal branch of religious worship, which we are moved to by the very light of nature, and obliged to by some of its fundamental laws. *Pythagoras'* golden verses begin with this precept, Whatever men made a God of, they prayed to, *Deliver me, for thou art my God* (Isa. 44: 17). Nay, whatever they prayed to they made a God of — *Deos qui rogat ille facit.*[1] It is a piece of respect and homage so exactly consonant to the natural ideas which all men have of God, that it is certain those that *live without prayer, live without God in the world.*

Prayer is the solemn and religious offering up of devout acknowledgments and desires to God, or a sincere representation of holy affections, with a design to give unto God the glory due unto his Name thereby, and to obtain from him promised favours, and both through the Mediator. Our *English* word *Prayer* is too strait, for that properly signifies *Petition,* or *Request;* whereas humble adorations of God, and thanksgivings to him, are as necessary in Prayer, as any other part of it. The *Greek* word means a *Vow directed to God.* The *Latin* word *Votum* is used for Prayer: *Jonah's* mariners with their sacrifices *made vows;* for prayer is to *move* and *oblige* ourselves, not to *move or oblige* God.

Clement of Alexandria (in *The Stromata,* 7, Ante-Nicene Christian Library, 534) calls Prayer (with an excuse for the boldness

---

1. An allusion to Pythagoras' Rules of Conduct; "Begin your work first having prayed for the Gods to accomplish it.

of the expression) *conversing with God:* And it is the scope of a long discourse of his there, to shew that his *Believer* lives a life of communion with God, and so is praying always; that he studies by his prayers continually to converse with God. Some (saith he) had their stated hours of prayer, but he *prays all his life long.* The scripture describes prayer to be our *drawing near to God, lifting up our souls* to him, *pouring out our hearts* before him.

This is the life and soul of prayer; but this soul in the present state must have a body, and that body must be such as becomes the soul, and is suited and adapted to it. Some words there must be of the mind at least, in which as in the smoke, this incense must ascend; not that God may *understand us,* for our *thoughts afar off* are known to him, but that we may the better *understand ourselves.*

A golden thread of heart-prayer must run through the web of the whole Christian life; we must be frequently addressing ourselves to God in short and sudden *Ejaculations,* by which we must keep up our communion with God in providences and common actions, as well as in ordinances and religious services, Thus prayer must be *sparsim* (a sprinkling of it) in every duty, and *our Eyes* must be *ever towards the Lord.*

In *mental* prayer thoughts are words, and they are the *Firstborn* of the soul, which are to be consecrated to God. But if when we pray alone we see cause for the better fixing of our minds, and exciting of our devotions, to clothe our conceptions with words; if the conceptions be the genuine products of the new nature, one would think words should not be far to seek. Nay, if the *groanings* be such *as cannot be uttered,* he *that searcheth the heart* knows them to be *the mind of the Spirit,* and will accept of them (Rom. 8:26, 27) and answer the *Voice of our breathing* (Lam. 3:56). Yet through the infirmity of the flesh, and the aptness of our hearts to wander and trifle, it is often necessary that words should go *first,* and be kept in mind for the directing and exciting of devout actions, and in order thereunto, the assistance here offered I hope will be of some use.

When we join with others in prayer, who are our mouth to God, our minds must attend *them,* by an intelligent believing concurrence with that which is the sense and scope, and substance of what they say, and affections working in us suitable thereunto: And this the scripture directs us to signify, by saying *Amen,* mentally if not vocally, *at their giving of Thanks* (I Cor. 14:16). And as far as our joining with them will permit, we may intermix pious ejaculations of our own, with their addresses, provided they be pertinent, that not the least fragment of praying time may be lost.

But he that is the mouth of others in prayer, whether in public or private, and therein useth that *freedom of speech,* that holy liberty of prayer which is allowed us (and which we are sure many good Christians have found by experience to be very comfortable and advantageous in this duty) ought not only to consult the workings of his own heart (though them principally, as putting most life and spirit into the performance) but the edification also of those that join with him; and both in matter and words should have an eye to that; and for service in that case I principally design this endeavour.

That bright ornament of the Church, the learned Dr. *Wilkins,* bishop of *Chester,* hath left us an excellent performance much of the same nature with this, in his *discourse concerning the gift of prayer;* which, some may think, makes this of mine unnecessary: But the multiplying of books of devotion is what few serious Christians will complain of: And as on the one hand I am sure those that have *this* poor essay of mine will still find great advantage by *that;* so on the other hand I think those who have *that* may yet find some further assistance by this.

It is desirable that our prayers should be *copious* and *full;* our burthens, cares, and wants are many, so are our sins and mercies. The promises are numerous and very rich, our God gives liberally, and hath bid us *open our mouths wide,* and he will *fill them,* will *satisfy them with good things.*

We are not straitened in him, why then should we be stinted and straitened in our own bosoms! Christ had taught his disciples the Lord's prayer, and yet tells them (John 16:24) that *hitherto they had asked nothing, i.e.* nothing in comparison with what they should ask when the *Spirit* should be *poured out,* to *abide* with the church *for ever;* and they should *see greater things than these.* Then *ask, and ye shall receive, that your joy may be full.* We are encouraged to be *particular* in prayer, and in *every thing to make our requests known to God,* as we ought also to be particular in the adoration of the divine perfections, in the confession of our sins, and our thankful acknowledgments of God's mercies.

But since at the same time we cannot go over the tenth part of the particulars which are fit to be the matter of prayer, without making the duty burthensome to the flesh which is weak, even where the spirit is willing (an extreme which ought carefully to be avoided) and without danger of intrenching upon other religious exercises, it will be requisite that what is but *briefly touched upon* at one time, should be *enlarged upon* at another time: And herein this storehouse of materials for prayer may be of use to put us in remembrance of our several errands at the throne of grace, that none may be quite forgotten.

And it is requisite to the decent performance of the duty, that some proper *method* be observed, not only that what is said be *good,* but that it be said in its proper place and time; and that we offer not any thing to the glorious Majesty of heaven and earth, which is confused, impertinent, and indigested. Care must be taken, than more than ever, that we be not *rash with our mouth, nor hasty to utter any thing before God;* that we say not what comes uppermost, nor use such repetitions as evidence not the fervency, but the barrenness and slightness of our spirits; but that the matters we are dealing with God about being of such vast importance, we observe a decorum in our words, that they be well chosen, well weighed, and well placed.

And as it is good to be *methodical* in prayer, so it is good to be *sententious:* The Lord's prayer is remarkably so; and *David's* psalms, and many of St. *Paul's* prayers which we have in his epistles: We must consider that the greatest part of those that join with us in prayer will be in danger of losing or mistaking the sense, if the period be long, and the parenthesis many, and in this as in other things, they that are strong ought to bear the infirmities of the weak: *Jacob* must lead as the children and flock can follow.

As to the words and expressions we use in prayer, though I have here in my enlargements upon the several heads of prayer confined myself almost wholly to scripture language, because I would give an instance of the sufficiency of the scripture to furnish us for every good work, yet I am far from thinking but that it is convenient and often necessary to use other expressions in prayer besides those that are purely scriptural; only I would advise that the *sacred* dialect be most used, and made familiar to us and others in our dealing about *sacred* things; that language Christian people are most accustomed to, most affected with, and will most readily agree to; and where the scriptures are opened and explained to the people in the ministry of the word, scripture language will be most intelligible, and the sense of it best apprehended. This is *sound speech that cannot be condemned.* And those that are able to do it may do well to enlarge by way of descant or paraphrase upon the scriptures they make use of; still speaking according to that rule, and comparing spiritual things with spiritual, that they may illustrate each other.

And it is not to be reckoned a perverting of scripture, but is agreeable to the usage of many divines, especially the Fathers, and I think is warranted by divers quotations in the New Testament out of the Old, to *allude* to a scripture phrase, and to make use of it by way of accommodation to another sense than what was the first intendment of it, provided it agree with the analogy of faith. As for instance, those words, (Ps. 87:7), *All my springs are in thee,* may very fitly be applied to God, though there it appears by the feminine article in the original, to be meant of *Sion;* nor has it ever been thought any wrong to the scripture phrase, to pray for the blessings of *the upper springs and the nether springs,* though the expression from whence it is borrowed (Judg. 1:15). hath no reference at all to what we mean; but by common use every one knows the signification, and many are pleased with the significancy of it.

Divers heads of prayer may no doubt be added to those which I have here put together, and many scripture expressions too, under each head (for I have only set down such as first occurred to my thoughts) and many other expressions too, not in scripture words, which may be very comprehensive and emphatical, and apt to excite devotion. And perhaps those who covet earnestly this excellent gift, and covet to excel in it, may find it of use to them to have such a book as this interleaved, in which to insert such other heads and expressions as they think will be most agreeable to them, and are wanting here.

And though I have here recommended a good method for prayer, and that which has been generally approved, yet I am far from thinking we should always tie ourselves to it; that may be varied as well as the expression: Thanksgiving may very aptly be put some-times before confession or petition, or our intercessions for others before our petitions for ourselves, as in the Lord's Prayer. Sometimes one of these parts of prayer may be enlarged upon much more than another; or they may be decently interwoven in some other method; *Ars est celaree artem.*[2]

There are those (I doubt not) who at some times have their hearts so wonderfully elevated and enlarged in prayer, above themselves; at

---

2. The quote is from Ovid, *The Art of Love.* It reads literally: 'it is art to conceal art.' Henry thus warns that whatever form of prayer we choose, method should not attract attention to itself and thus detract from the content of prayer.

other times, such a fixedness and fulness of thought, such a fervour of pious and devout affections, the product of which is such a fluency and variety of pertinent and moving expressions, and in such a just and natural method, that then to have an eye to such a scheme as this, would be a hindrance to them, and would be in danger to cramp and straiten them: If the *Heart* be full of its *good matter,* it may make *the tongue as the pen of a ready Writer.* But this is a case that rarely happens, and ordinarily there is need of proposing to ourselves a certain method to go by in prayer, that the service may be performed decently and in order; in which yet one would avoid that which looks too formal. A man may write straight without having his paper ruled.

Some few forms of Prayer I have added in the last Chapter, for the use of those who need such helps, and that know not how to do as well or better without them; and therefore I have calculated them for families. If any think them too long, let them observe that they are divided into many paragraphs, and those mostly independent, so that when brevity is necessary some paragraphs may be omitted.

But after all, the intention and close application of the mind, the lively exercises of Faith and Love, and the outgoings of holy desire towards God, are so essentially necessary to Prayer, that without these in sincerity, the best and most proper language is but a lifeless image. If we had the tongue of men and angels, and have not the heart of humble serious Christians in Prayer, we are but as a sounding brass and a tinkling cymbal. It is only the *effectual fervent prayer,* the *in-wrought in-laid* Prayer that *avails much.* Thus therefore we ought to approve ourselves to God in the integrity of our hearts, whether we pray by, or without a pre-composed Form.

When I had finished the third Volume of Expositions of the Bible, which is now in the press; before I proceed, as I intend, in an humble dependence on the divine Providence and Grace, to the fourth volume, I was willing to take a little time from that work to this poor performance, in hopes it might be of some service to the generation of them that seek God, that seek the face of the God of *Jacob:* And if any good Christians receive assistance from it in their devotions, I hope they will not deny me one request, which is, that they will pray for me, that I may obtain mercy of the Lord to be found among the faithful watchmen on *Jerusalem's* walls, who never hold their peace day or night, but give themselves to the word and prayer, that at length I may finish my course with joy.

CHAPTER 1

*Of the first part of PRAYER, which is Address to God,
Adoration of him, with suitable Acknowledgments,
Professions, and preparatory Requests.*

Our spirits being composed into a very reverent serious frame, our thoughts gathered in, and all that is within us, charged in the Name of the great God, carefully to attend the solemn and awful service that lies before us, and to keep close to it, we must with a fixed attention and application of mind, and an active lively faith, set the Lord before us, see his eye upon us, and set ourselves in his special presence, presenting ourselves to him as living sacrifices, which we desire may be holy and acceptable, and a reasonable service;[1] and then bind these sacrifices with cords to the horns of the altar.[2] in such thoughts as these;

Let us now lift up our hearts[3] with our eyes and hands, unto God in the heavens.[4]

Let us stir up ourselves to take hold on God,[5] to seek his face, and to give him the glory due unto his Name.[6]

Unto thee, O Lord, do we lift up our souls.[7]

Let us now with humble boldness, enter into the holiest by the blood of Jesus, in the new and living way, which he hath consecrated for us through the veil.[8]

Let us now attend upon the Lord without distraction,[9] and let not our hearts be far from him when we draw nigh to him with our mouths, and honour him with our lips.[10]

Let us now worship God, who is a Spirit, in spirit and in truth; For such the Father seeks to worship him.[11]

Having thus engaged our hearts to approach unto God.[12]

1. We must solemnly address ourselves to that infinitely great and glorious Being with whom we have to do, as those that are possessed with a full belief of his presence, and a holy awe and reverence of his Majesty; which we may do in such expressions as these.

Holy, holy, holy Lord God Almighty, which art, and wast, and art to come.[13]

O thou whose name alone is Jehovah, and who art the most High over all the earth![14]

O God, thou art our God, early will we seek thee;[15] our God, and we will praise thee; our fathers' God, and we will exalt thee.[16]

O thou who art the true God, the living God, the one only living and true God, and the everlasting King,[17] The Lord our God, who is one Lord.[18]

And we may thus distinguish ourselves from the worshippers of false gods.

The idols of the heathens are silver and gold, they are vanity and a lie, the work of men's hands; they that make them are like unto them, and so is every one that trusteth in them.[19] But the portion of Jacob is not like unto them, for he is the former of all things, and Israel is the rod of his inheritance; the Lord of hosts is his name;[20] God over all, blessed for evermore.[21]

Their rock is not our Rock, even the enemies themselves being judges; for he is the Rock of ages,[22] the Lord Jehovah, with whom is everlasting strength;[23] Whose name shall endure for ever, and his memorial unto all generations,[24] when the gods that have not made the heavens and the earth, shall perish from off the earth, and from under these heavens.[25]

2. We must reverently adore God, as a Being transcendently bright and blessed, self-existent, and self-sufficient, an infinite and eternal Spirit that has all perfections in himself, and give him the glory of his titles and attributes.

O Lord our God, thou art very great, thou art clothed with honour and majesty, thou coverest thyself with light as with a garment,[26] and yet as to us makest darkness thy pavilion;[27] for we cannot order our speech by reason of darkness.[28]

This is the message which we have heard of thee, and we set to our seal that it is true, that God is light, and in him is no darkness at all:[29] And that God is love, and they that dwell in love, dwell in God and God in them.[30]

Thou art the Father of light, with whom is no variableness or shadow of turning, and from whom proceedeth every good and perfect gift.[31]

Thou art the blessed and only Potentate; the King of kings, and Lord of lords, who only hast immortality, dwelling in the light, which no man can approach unto, whom no man hath seen or can see.[32]

We must acknowledge his Being to be unquestionable and past dispute.

The heavens declare thy glory, O God, and the firmament sheweth thy handy-work,[33] and by the things that are made is clearly seen and understood thine eternal power and Godhead.[34] So that they are fools without excuse, who say there is no God;[35] for verily there is a reward for the righteous, verily there is a God that judgeth in the earth, and in heaven too.[36]

We therefore come to thee believing, that thou art, and that thou art the powerful and bountiful rewarder of them that diligently seek thee.[37]

Yet we must own his nature to be incomprehensible.

We cannot by searching find out God, we cannot find out the Almighty unto perfection.[38]

Great is the Lord and greatly to be praised, and his greatness is unsearchable.[39]

Who can utter the mighty acts of the Lord? who can shew forth all his praise?[40]

— And his perfections to be matchless, and without compare.

Who is a God like unto thee, glorious in holiness, fearful in praises, doing wonders?[41]

Who in the heaven can be compared unto the Lord? Who among the sons of the mighty can be likened unto the Lord? O Lord God of hosts, who is a strong Lord like unto thee, or to thy faithfulness round about thee.[42]

Among the gods there is none like unto thee, O Lord, neither are there any works like unto thy works; for thou art great, and dost wondrous things; thou art God alone.[43]

There is not any creature that has an arm like God, or can thunder with a voice like him.[44]

And that he is infinitely above us and all other beings.

Thou art God, and not man; hast not eyes of flesh, nor seest thou as man seeth;[45] Thy days are not as the days of man, nor thy years as man's days.[46]

As heaven is high above the earth, so are thy thoughts above our thoughts, and thy ways above our ways.[47]

All nations before thee are as a drop of the bucket, or the small dust of the balance, and thou takest up the isles as a very little thing;

they are as nothing, and are counted to thee less than nothing, and vanity.[48]

Particularly in our adorations we must acknowledge

2.1. That he is an eternal God, immutable, without beginning of days or end of life, or change of time.

Thou art the King eternal, immortal, invisible.[49] Before the mountains were brought forth, or ever thou hadst formed the earth and the world, from everlasting to everlasting thou art God;[50] the same yesterday, to-day, and for ever.[51]

Of old hast thou laid the foundation of the earth, and the heavens are the works of thy hands: they shall perish, but thou shalt endure; yea, all of them shall wax old like a garment, as a vesture shalt thou change them, and they shall be changed; but thou art the same, and thy years shall have no end.[52]

Thou art God and changest not; therefore is it that we are not consumed.[53] Art thou not from everlasting, O Lord our God, our holy one?[54] The everlasting God, even the Lord the Creator of the ends of the earth, who faintest not, neither art weary; there is no searching out of thine understanding.[55]

2.2. That he is present in all places, and there is no place in which he is included, or out of which he is excluded.

Thou art a God at hand, and not a God afar off; none can hide himself in secret places that thou canst not see him, for thou fillest heaven and earth.[56]

Thou art not far from every one of us.[57]

We cannot go any whither from thy presence, or fly from thy Spirit: If we ascend into heaven, thou art there; if we make our bed in hell, in the depths of the earth, behold thou art there; if we take the wings of the morning, and dwell in the uttermost parts of the sea, even there shall thy hand lead us, and thy right-hand shall hold us, that we cannot outrun thee.[58]

2.3. That he hath a perfect knowledge of all persons and things, and sees them all, even that which is most secret, at one clear, certain, and unerring view.

All things are naked and open before the eyes of him with whom we have to do; even the thoughts and intents of the heart.[59]

Thine eyes are in every place beholding the evil and the good:[60] they run to and fro through the earth, that thou mayest shew thyself strong on the behalf of those whose hearts are upright with thee.[61]

Thou searchest the heart, and triest the reins, that thou mayest give to every man according to his ways, and according to the fruit of his doings.[62]

O God, thou hast searched us, and known us, thou knowest our down-sitting, and our up-rising, and understandest our thoughts afar off: Thou compassest our path and our lying down, and art acquainted with all our ways: There is not a word in our tongue, but lo, O Lord, thou knowest it altogether. Such knowledge is too wonderful for us, it is high, we cannot attain unto it.

Darkness and light are both alike to thee.[63]

2.4. That his wisdom is unsearchable, and the counsels and designs of it cannot be fathomed.

Thine understanding, O Lord, is infinite, for thou tellest the number of the stars, and callest them all by their names.[64]

Thou art wonderful in counsel, and excellent in working.[65] Wise in heart, and mighty in strength.[66]

O Lord, how manifold are thy works! in wisdom hast thou made them all;[67] all according to the counsel of thine own will.[68]

O the depth of the wisdom and knowledge of God! how unsearchable are his judgments, and his ways past finding out.[69]

2.5. That his sovereignty is incontestible, and he is the owner and absolute Lord of all.

The heavens, even the heavens are thine, and all the hosts of them. The earth is thine, and the fullness thereof; the world, and they that dwell therein.[70] In thy hand are the deep places of the earth, and the strength of the hills are thine also: The sea is thine, for thou madest it, and thy hands formed the dry land;[71] All the beasts of the forest are thine, and the cattle upon a thousand hills;[72] Thou art therefore a great God, and a great King above all gods.

In thy hand is the soul of every living thing, and the breath of all mankind.[73]

Thy dominion is an everlasting dominion, and thy kingdom is from generation to generation: Thou dost according to thy will in the armies of heaven, and among the inhabitants of the earth, and none can stay thy hand, or say unto thee, What dost thou? or Why dost thou so?[74]

2.6 That his power is irresistible, and the operations of it cannot be controlled.

We know, O God, that thou canst do every thing, and that no thought can be with-holden from thee;[75] Power belongs to thee;[76] and with thee nothing is impossible.[77]

All power is thine, both in heaven and earth.[78]

Thou killest and thou makest alive, thou woundest and thou healest, neither is there any that can deliver out of thy hand.[79]

What thou hast promised thou art able also to perform.[80]

2.7. That he is a God of unspotted purity and perfect rectitude.

Thou art holy, O thou that inhabitest the praises of Israel:[81] Holy and reverend is thy name;[82] and we give thanks at the remembrance of thy holiness.[83]

Thou art of purer eyes than to behold iniquity,[84] neither shall evil dwell with thee.[85]

Thou art the Rock, thy work is perfect, all thy ways are truth and judgment; a God of truth, and in whom is no iniquity.[86] Thou art our Rock, and there is no unrighteousness in thee.[87]

Thou art holy in all thy works,[88] and holiness becomes thy house, O Lord, for ever.[89]

2.8. That he is just in the administration of his government; and never did, nor ever will do wrong to any of his creatures.

Righteous art thou, O God, when we plead with thee:[90] and wilt be justified when thou speakest, and clear when thou judgest.[91]

Far be it from God that he should do wickedness, and from the Almighty that he should commit iniquity: for the work of a man shall he render unto him.[92]

Thy righteousness is as the great mountains, even then when thy judgments are a great deep![93] And though clouds and darkness are round about thee, yet judgment and justice are the habitation of thy throne.[94]

2.9. That his truth is invariable, and the treasures of his goodness inexhaustible.

Thou art good, and thy mercy endureth for ever.[95] Thy loving kindness is great toward us,[96] and thy truth endureth to all generations.[97]

Thou hast proclaimed thy name, The Lord, the Lord God, merciful, and gracious, slow to anger, abundant in goodness and truth: keeping mercy for thousands, forgiving iniquity, transgression and sin.[98] And this name of thine is our strong tower.[99]

Thou art good, and doest good;[100] good to all, and thy tender mercies is over all thy works. But truly God is in a special manner good to Israel, even to them that are of a clean heart.[101]

O that thou wouldest cause thy goodness to pass before us,[102] that we may taste and see that the Lord is good; and his loving kindness may be always before our eyes.[103]

J. Lastly, That when we have said all we can of the glorious perfections of the Divine nature, we fall infinitely short of the merit of the subject.

No, these are but parts of his ways, and how little a portion is heard of God? But the thunder of his power who can undersand?[104]

Touching the Almighty, we cannot find him out; he is excellent in power and in judgment, and in plenty of justice,[105] he is exalted far above all blessing and praise.[106]

3. We must give to God the praise of that splendor and glory wherein he is pleased to manifest himself, in the upper world.

Thou hast prepared thy throne in the heavens;[107] and it is a throne of glory, high and lifted up; and before thee the seraphims cover their faces.[108] And it is in compassion to us that thou holdest back the face of that throne, and spreadest a cloud upon it.[109]

Thou makest thine angels spirits, and thy ministers a flame of fire.[110] Thousand thousands of them minister unto thee, and ten thousand times ten thousand stand before thee, to do thy pleasure.[111] They excel in strength, and hearken to the voice of thy word.[112] And we are come by faith and hope, and holy love, into a spiritual communion with that innumerable company of angels, and the spirits of just men made perfect, even to the general assembly and church of the first born, in the heavenly Jerusalem.[113]

4. We must give glory to him as the Creator of the world, and the great Protector, Benefactor, and Ruler of the whole creation.

Thou art worthy O Lord, to receive blessing, and honour, and glory, and power; for thou hast created all things, and for thy pleasure, and for thy praise, they are and were created.[114]

We worship him that made the heaven and the earth, the sea and the fountains of waters;[115] who spake, and it was done; who commanded, and it stood fast;[116] who said, let there be light, and there was light, let there be a firmament, and he made the firmament; and he made all very good;[117] and they continue this day according to his ordinance, for all are his servants.[118]

The day is thine, the night also is thine; thou hast prepared the light and the sun: Thou hast set all the borders of the earth, thou hast made the summer and winter.[119]

Thou upholdest all things by the word of thy power,[120] and by thee all things consist.[121]

The earth is full of thy riches, so is the great and wide sea also.[122] The eyes of all wait upon thee, and thou givest them their meat in due season: Thou openest thy hand, and satisfiest the desires of every living thing.[123] Thou preservest man and beast, and givest food to all flesh.[124]

Thou, even thou art Lord alone; thou hast made heaven, the heaven of heavens, with all their host, the earth and all things that are therein, the sea, and all that is therein, and thou preservest them all; And the host of heaven worshippeth thee,[125] whose kingdom ruleth over all.[126]

A sparrow falls not to the ground without thee.[127]

Thou madest man at first of the dust of the ground, and breathest into him the breath of life, and so he became a living soul.[128]

And thou hast made of that one blood all nations of men, to dwell on all the face of the earth, and hast determined the times before appointed, and the bounds of their habitation.[129]

Thou art the most High who ruleth in the kingdom of men, and givest it to whomsoever thou wilt;[130] for from thee every man's judgment proceeds.[131]

Hallelujah, the Lord God omnipotent reigns,[132] and doth all according to the counsel of his own will, to the praise of his own glory.[133]

5. We must give honour to the three persons in the Godhead distinctly, to the Father, the Son, and the Holy Ghost, that great and sacred Name, into which we were baptized, and in which we assemble for religious worship, in communion with the universal church.

We pay our homage to three that bear record in heaven, the Father, the Word, and the Holy Ghost: for these three are one.[134]

We adore thee, O Father, Lord of heaven and earth;[135] and the eternal Word, who was in the beginning with God, and was God, by whom all things were made, and without whom was not any thing made that was made, and who in the fulness of time was made flesh, and dwelt among us, and shewed his glory, the glory as of the only begotten of the Father, full of grace and truth.[136]

And since it is the will of God, that all men should honour the Son, as they honour the Father,[137] we adore him as the brightness of his Father's glory, and the express image of his person; herein joining with the angels of God, who were all bid to worship him.[138]

We pay homage to the exalted Redeemer, who is the faithful witness, the first begotten from the dead, and the Prince of the kings of the earth[139] confessing that Jesus Christ is Lord, to the glory of God the Father.[140]

We also worship the Holy Ghost, the Comforter, whom the Son hath sent from the Father, even the Spirit of truth, who proceedeth from the Father,[141] and who is sent to teach us all things, and to bring all things to our remembrance;[142] who indited the scriptures, holy men of God writing them, as they were moved by the Holy Ghost.[143]

6. We must acknowledge our dependance upon God, and our obligations to him, as our Creator, Preserver, and Benefactor.

Thou, O God, madest us, and not we ourselves, and therefore we are not our own but thine; thy people, and the sheep of thy pasture;[144] Let us therefore worship, and fall down, and kneel before the Lord our Maker.[145]

Thou Lord art the former of our bodies, and they are fearfully and wonderfully made, and curiously wrought. Thine eye did see our substance yet being unperfect, and in thy book all our members were written, which in continuance were fashioned, when as yet there was none of them.[146]

Thou hast clothed us with skin and flesh, thou hast fenced us with bones and sinews: thou hast granted us life and favour, and thy visitation preserves our spirit.[147]

Thou art the Father of our spirits,[148] for thou formedst the spirit of man within him,[149] and madest us these souls.[150] The Spirit of God hath made us, and the breath of the Almighty hath given us life.[151] Thou puttest wisdom in the inward part, and giveth understanding to the heart.[152]

Thou art God our Maker, and teachest us more than the beasts of the earth, and makest us wiser than the fowls of heaven.[153]

We are the clay, and thou our potter; we are the work of thy hand.[154]

Thou art he that tookest us out of the womb, and keepest us in safety when we were at our mother's breasts; we have been cast upon thee from the womb,[155] and held up by thee: thou art our God from our mother's bowels, and therefore our praise shall be continually of thee.[156]

In thee, O God, we live and move, and have our being; for we are thine offspring.[157]

In thy hand our breath is, and thine are all our ways;[158] for the way of man is not in himself, neither is it in man that walketh to direct his steps;[159] but our times are in thy hand.[160]

Thou art the God that hath fed us all our life long unto this day, and redeemed us from all evil.[161]

It is of thy mercies that we are not consumed, even because thy compassions fail not; they are new every morning; great is thy faithfulness.[162]

If thou take away our breath we die, and return to the dust, out of which we were taken.[163]

Who is he that saith and it cometh to pass, if thou commandest it not? Out of thy mouth, O most High, both evil and good proceed.[164]

7. We must avouch this God to be our God, and own our relation to him, his dominion over us, and propriety in us.

Our souls have said unto the Lord, thou art our God, though our goodness extendeth not unto thee,[165] neither if we are righteous art thou the better.[166]

Thou art our King, O God:[167] Other lords besides thee have had dominion over us, but from henceforth by thee only will we make mention of thy name.[168]

We avouch the Lord this day to be our God, to walk in his ways, and to keep his statutes, and commandments, and his judgments, and to hearken to his voice, and give ourselves unto him, to be his peculiar people, as he hath promised, that we may be a holy people unto the Lord our God:[169] and may be unto him for a name, and for a praise, and for a glory.[170]

O Lord, truly we are thy servants, we are thy servants born in thy house, and thou hast loosed our bonds:[171] we are bought with a price, and therefore we are not our own;[172] but yield ourselves unto the Lord,[173] and join ourselves unto him in an everlasting covenant, that shall never be forgotten.[174]

We are thine, save us, for we seek thy precepts;[175] It is thine own, Lord, that we give thee, and that which cometh of thine hand.[176]

8. We must acknowledge it an unspeakable favour, and an inestimable privilege, that we are not only admitted, but invited and encouraged to draw nigh to God in prayer.

Thou hast commanded us to pray always, with all prayer and supplication with thanksgiving, and to watch thereunto with all perseverance and supplication for all saints.[177] To continue in prayer; and in every thing with prayer and supplication to make our request known to God.[178]

Thou hast directed us to ask, and seek, and knock, and hast promised that we shall receive, we shall find, and it shall be opened to us.[179]

Thou hast appointed us a great high-priest, in whose name we may come boldly to the throne of grace, that we may find mercy and grace to help in time of need.[180]

Thou hast assured us, that while the sacrifice of the wicked is an abomination to the Lord, the prayer of the upright is his delight;[181]

And that he that offers praise glorifies thee,[182] and the sacrifice of thanksgiving shall please the Lord better than that of an ox or bullock that has horns and hoofs.[183]

Thou art he that hearest prayer, and therefore unto thee shall all flesh come.

Thou sayest, Seek ye my face, and our hearts answer, thy face, Lord, will we seek.[184] For should not a people seek unto their God?[185] Whither shall we go but to thee? Thou hast the words of eternal life.[186]

9. We must express the sense we have of our own meanness and unworthiness to draw near to God, and speak to him.

But will God in very deed dwell with man upon the earth, that God whom the heaven of heavens cannot contain,[187] with man that is a worm, and the son of man that is a worm?[188]

Who are we, O Lord God, and what is our father's house, that thou hast brought us hitherto, to present ourselves before the Lord, that we have through Christ an access by one Spirit unto the Father?[189] And yet as if this had been a small thing in thy sight, thou hast spoken concerning thy servants for a great while to come, and is this the manner of men, O Lord God.[190]

What is man that thou art thus mindful of him, and the son of man that thou visitest him,[191] and dost thus magnify him?

O Let not the Lord be angry, if we that are but dust and ashes take upon us to speak unto the Lord of glory.[192]

We are not worthy of the least of all the mercies, and of all the truth which thou hast shewed unto thy servants;[193] nor is it meet to take the children's bread, and cast it to such as we are; yet the dogs eat of the crumbs that fall from their master's table;[194] and thou art rich in mercy to all that call upon thee.[195]

10. We must humbly profess the desire of our hearts towards God, as our felicity and portion, and fountain of life and all good to us.

Whom have we in heaven but thee; and there is none upon earth that we desire besides thee, or in comparison of thee: When our flesh and our heart fail, be thou the strength of our heart, and our portion for ever;[196] the portion of our inheritance in the other world, and of our cup in this, and then we will say that the lines are fallen unto us in pleasant places, and that we have a goodly heritage.[197]

The desire of our souls is to thy Name, and to the remembrance of thee; with our souls have we desired thee in the night, and with our spirits within us will we seek thee only.[198]

As the hart panteth after the water brook, so panteth our soul after thee, O God; our soul thirsteth for God, for the living God, who will command his loving-kindness in the day time, and in the night, his song shall be with us, and our prayer to the God of our life.[199]

O that we may come hungering and thirsting after righteousness;[200] for thou fillest the hungry with good things, but the rich thou sendest empty away.[201]

O that our souls may thirst for thee, and our flesh long for thee in a dry and thirsty land, where no water is, that we may see thy power and thy glory, as we have seen thee in the sanctuary. Thy loving kindness is better than life; our souls shall be satisfied with that as with marrow and fatness, and then our mouths shall praise thee with joyful lips.[202]

11. We must likewise profess our believing hope and confidence in God, and his all-suffiency, in his power, providence, and promise.

In thee, O God, do we put our trust, let us never be ashamed;[203] yea, let none that wait on thee be ashamed.[204]

Truly our souls wait upon God; from him cometh our salvation: He only is our Rock and our salvation; in him is our glory, our strength, and our refuge, and from him is our expectation.[205]

When refuge fails us, and none cares for our souls, we cry unto thee, O Lord; thou art our refuge, and our portion, in the land of the living.[206]

Some trust in chariots, and some in horses, but we will remember the name of the Lord our God.[207] We will trust in thy mercy, O God, for ever and ever, and will wait on thy name, for it is good before thy saints.[208]

We have hoped in thy word; O remember thy word unto thy servants, upon which thou hast caused us to hope.[209]

12. We must intreat God's favourable acceptance of us, and our poor performances.

There be many that say, who will shew us any good? but this we say, Lord, lift up the light of thy countenance upon us; and that shall put gladness into our hearts, more than they have whose corn and wine increaseth.[210]

We entreat thy favour with our whole heart,[211] for in this we labour, that whether present or absent we may be accepted of the Lord.[212]

Hear our prayer, O Lord, give ear to our supplications; in thy faithfulness answer us.[213] And be nigh unto us in all that which we call upon thee for;[214] for thou never saidst to the seed of Jacob, seek ye me in vain.[215]

Thou that hearest the young ravens which cry,[216] be not silent to us, lest if thou be silent to us, we be like them that go down to the pit.[217]

Let our prayer be set forth before thee as incense, and the lifting up of our hands be acceptable in thy sight as the evening sacrifice.[218]

13. We must beg for the powerful assistance and influence of the blessed Spirit of grace in our prayers.

Lord, we know not what to pray for as we ought, but let thy Spirit help our infirmities, and make intercession for us.[219]

O pour upon us the Spirit of grace and supplication;[220] the Spirit of adoption teaching us to cry, Abba, Father;[221] that we may find in our hearts to pray this prayer.

O send out thy light and thy truth; let them lead us, let them guide us to thy holy hill and thy tabernacles; to God, our exceeding joy.[222]

O Lord, open thou our lips, and our mouth shall shew forth thy praise.[223]

14. We must make the glory of God our highest end in all our prayers.

This is that which thou, O Lord, hast said, that thou wilt be sanctified in them that come nigh unto thee, and before all the people thou wilt be glorified;[224] we therefore worship before thee, O Lord, that we may glorify thy name;[225] and therefore we call upon thee, that thou mayest deliver us, and we may glorify thee.[226]

For of thee, and through thee, and to thee, are all things.[227]

15. We must profess our entire reliance on the Lord Jesus Christ alone for acceptance with God, and come in his name.

We do not present our supplication before thee for our righteousness;[228] for we are before thee in our trespasses,[229] and cannot stand before thee because of them:[230] But we make mention of Christ's righteousness, even of his only, who is the Lord our righteousness.[231]

We know that even spiritual sacrifices are acceptable to God only through Christ Jesus,[232] nor can we hope to receive any thing but what we ask of thee in his name,[233] and therefore make us accepted in the beloved,[234] that other angel, who put much incense to the prayers of saints, and offers them up upon the golden altar before the throne.[235]

We come in the name of the great High Priest, who is passed into the heavens, Jesus the Son of God, who was touched with the feeling of our infirmities, and is therefore able to save to the uttermost all those that come to God by him,[236] because he ever lives, making intercession.[237]

Behold, O God, our shield, and look upon the face of thine anointed,[238] in whom thou hast by a voice from heaven declared thyself to be well pleased; Lord, be well pleased with us in him.[239]

References

[1] Rom. 12:1.
[2] Ps. 118:27.
[3] Lam. 3:41.
[4] John 17:1.
[5] Isa. 64:7.
[6] Ps. 27:8; 29:2.
[7] Ps. 25:1.
[8] Heb. 10: 19-20.
[9] 1 Cor. 7:35.
[10] Matt. 15:8.
[11] John 4:23-24.
[12] Jer. 30:21.
[13] Rev. 4:8.
[14] Ps. 83:18.
[15] Ps. 63:1.
[16] Exod. 15:2.
[17] Jer. 10:10.
[18] Deut. 6:4.
[19] Ps. 115:4, 8.
[20] Jer. 10:16.
[21] Rom. 9:5.
[22] Deut. 32:31.
[23] Isa. 26:4.
[24] Ps. 135:13.
[25] Jer. 10:11.
[26] Ps. 104:1-2.
[27] Psal 18:11.
[28] Job 37:19.
[29] 1 John 1:5.
[30] 1 John 4:16.
[31] James 1:17.
[32] 1 Tim. 6:15-16.
[33] Ps. 19:1.
[34] Rom. 1:19.
[35] Ps. 14:1
[36] Ps. 58:11.
[37] Heb. 11:6.
[38] Job 11:7.

[39] Ps. 145: 3.
[40] Ps. 106:2.
[41] Exod. 15:11.
[42] Ps. 89:6, 8.
[43] Ps. 86:8, 10.
[44] Job 40:9.
[45] Job 10:4-5.
[46] Job 10:4-5.
[47] Isa. 55:9.
[48] Isa. 40:15, 17.
[49] 1 Tim. 1:17.
[50] Ps. 90:2.
[51] Heb 13:8.
[52] Ps. 102:25-27.
[53] Mal. 3:6.
[54] Hab. 1:12.
[55] Isa. 40:28.
[56] Jer. 23:23-24.
[57] Acts 17:27.
[58] Ps. 139:7-10.
[59] Heb. 4:12-13.
[60] Prov. 15:3.
[61] 2 Chron. 16:9.
[62] Jer. 17:10.
[63] Ps. 139:1-4, 6, 12.
[64] Ps. 147:4-5.
[65] Isa. 28:29.
[66] Job 9:4.
[67] Ps. 104:24.
[68] Eph. 1:11.
[69] Rom. 11:33.
[70] Ps. 115:16, 24:1.
[71] Ps. 95:3-5.
[72] Ps. 50:10
[73] Job 12:10.
[74] Dan. 4:34-35.
[75] Job 13:2.
[76] Ps. 62:11.

[77] Luke 1:37.
[78] Matt. 28:18.
[79] Deut. 32:39.
[80] Rom. 4:21.
[81] Ps. 22:3.
[82] Ps. 111:9.
[83] Ps. 30:4.
[84] Hab. 1:13.
[85] Ps. 5:4.
[86] Deut. 32:4.
[87] Ps. 92:15.
[88] Ps. 145:17.
[89] Ps. 93:5.
[90] Jer. 12:1.
[91] Ps. 51:4
[92] Job 34:10-11.
[93] Ps. 36:6.
[94] Ps. 97:2.
[95] Ps. 136:1.
[96] Ps. 117:2.
[97] Ps. 100:5.
[98] Ex. 34:6-7.
[99] Prov. 18:10.
[100] Ps. 119:68.
[101] Ps. 73:1.
[102] Exod. 33:19.
[103] Ps. 34:8, 26:3.
[104] Job 26:14.
[105] Job 37:23.
[106] Neh. 9:5.
[107] Ps. 103:19.
[108] Isa. 6:1-2.
[109] Job 26:9.
[110] Ps. 104:4.
[111] Rev. 5:11.
[112] Ps. 103:20-21.
[113] Heb. 12:22-23.
[114] Rev. 4:11.

115 Rev. 14:7.
116 Ps. 33:9.
117 Gen. 1:3, 6-7.
118 Ps. 119:91.
119 Ps. 74:16-17.
120 Heb. 1:3.
121 Col. 1:17.
122 Ps. 104:24-25.
123 Ps. 145:15-16.
124 Ps. 36:6.
125 Neh. 9:6.
126 Ps. 103:19.
127 Matt. 10:29.
128 Gen. 2:7.
129 Acts 17:26.
130 Dan. 4:25.
131 Prov. 29:26.
132 Rev. 19:6.
133 Eph. 1:11-12.
134 1 John 5:7.
135 Matt. 11:25.
136 John 1:1-2, 8, 14.
137 John 5:23.
138 Heb. 1:3, 6.
139 Rev. 1:5.
140 Phil. 2:11.
141 John 15:26.
142 John 14:26.
143 2 Pet. 1:21.
144 Ps. 100:3.
145 Ps. 95:6.
146 Ps. 139:14-16.
147 Job 10:11-12.
148 Heb. 12:9.
149 Zech. 12:1.
150 Jer. 38:16.
151 Job 33:4.
152 Job 38:36.
153 Job 35:10-11.
154 Isa. 64:8.
155 Ps. 22:9-10.
156 Ps. 71:6.

157 Acts 17:28.
158 Dan. 5:23.
159 Jer. 10:23.
160 Ps. 31:15-16.
161 Gen. 48:15.
162 Lam. 3:22-23.
163 Ps. 104:29.
164 Lam. 3:37-38.
165 Ps. 16:2.
166 Job 35:7.
167 Ps. 44:4.
168 Isa. 26:13.
169 Deut. 26:17-19.
170 Jer. 13:11.
171 Ps. 116:16.
172 1 Cor. 6:20.
173 2 Chron. 30:8.
174 1 Jer. 50:5.
175 Ps. 119:94.
176 1 Chron. 29:16.
177 Phil. 4:6.
178 Eph. 6:18.
179 Matt. 7:7.
180 Heb. 4:16.
181 Prov 15:8.
182 Ps. 50:23.
183 Ps. 69:31.
184 Ps. 65:2, 27:8.
185 Isa. 8:19.
186 John 6:68.
187 2 Chron. 6:18.
188 Job 25:6.
189 Eph 2:18.
190 2 Sam. 7:18-19.
191 Ps. 8:4.
192 Gen. 18:27, 30.
193 Gen. 32:10.
194 Matt. 15:26-27.
195 Rom. 10:12.
196 Ps. 73:25-26.
197 Ps. 16:5-6.
198 Isa. 26:8-9.

199 Ps. 42:1-2, 8.
200 Matt. 5:6.
201 Luke 1:53.
202 Ps. 63:1-3, 5.
203 Ps. 31:1.
204 Ps. 25:3.
205 Ps. 62:1-2, 5-7.
206 Ps. 142:4-5.
207 Ps. 20:7.
208 Ps. 52:8-9.
209 Ps. 119:81, 49.
210 Ps. 4:6-7.
211 Ps. 119:58.
212 2 Cor. 5:9.
213 Ps. 143:1.
214 Deut. 4:7.
215 Isa. 45:19.
216 Ps. 147:9.
217 Ps. 28:1.
218 Ps. 141:2.
219 Rom. 8:26.
220 Zech. 12:10.
221 Rom. 8:15.
222 Ps. 43:3.
223 Ps. 51:15.
224 Lev 10:3.
225 Ps. 86:9.
226 Ps. 50:15.
227 Rom. 11:36.
228 Dan. 9:18.
229 Ezra 9:15.
230 Ps. 130:3.
231 Jer. 23:6.
232 I Pet. 2:5.
233 John 16:23.
234 Eph. 1:6.
235 Rev. 8:3.
236 Heb. 4:14-15.
237 Heb. 7:25.
238 Ps. 84:9.
239 Matt. 3:17.

CHAPTER 2

Of the second part of PRAYER,
which is Confession of Sin, Complaints of ourselves,
and humble Professions of Repentance.

Having given glory to God which is his due, we must next take shame to ourselves, which is our due, and humble ourselves before him in the sense of our own sinfulness and vileness; and herein also we must give glory to him, as our Judge by whom we deserve to be condemned, and yet hope, through Christ, to be acquitted and absolved.[1]

In this part of our work,

1. We must acknowledge the great reason we have to lie very low before God, and to be ashamed of ourselves when we come into his presence, and to be afraid of his wrath, having made ourselves both odious to his holiness, and obnoxious to his justice.

O our God! we are ashamed, and blush to lift up our faces before thee, our God; for our iniquities are increased over our head, and our trespass is grown up into the heavens.[2]

To us belong shame and confusion of face, because we have sinned against thee.[3]

Behold we are vile, what shall we answer thee? we will lay our hand upon our mouth,[4] and put our mouth in the dust, if so be there may be hope,[5] crying with the convicted leper under the law, Unclean, unclean.[6]

Thou puttest no trust in thy saints, and the heavens are not clean in thy sight; How much more abominable and filthy is man, who drinketh iniquity like water.[7]

When our eyes have seen the King, the Lord of hosts, we have reason to cry out, Woe unto us, for we are undone.[8]

Dominion and fear are with thee, thou makest peace in thy high places: There is not any number of thine armies, and upon whom doth not thy light arise? How then can man be justified with God, or how can he be clean, that is born of a woman?[9]

Thou, even thou art to be feared, and who may stand in thy sight when once thou art angry?[10] Even thou, our God, art a consuming fire,[11] and who knows the power of thine anger?[12]

If we justify ourselves, our own mouth shall condemn us, if we say we are perfect, that also shall prove us perverse; for if thou contend with us, we are not able to answer thee for one of a thousand.[13]

If we knew nothing by ourselves, yet were we not thereby justified, for he that judgeth us is the Lord;[14] who is greater than our hearts, and knows all things.[15] But we ourselves know that we have sinned, Father, against heaven, and before thee, and are no more worthy to be called thy children.[16]

2. We must take hold of the great encouragement God hath given us to humble ourselves before him with sorrow, and shame, and to confess our sins.

If thou, Lord, shouldst mark iniquities, O Lord who should stand! But there is forgiveness with thee, that thou mayest be feared; with thee there is mercy, yea, with our God there is plenteous redemption, and he shall redeem Israel from all his iniquities.[17]

Thy sacrifices, O God, are a broken spirit; a broken and a contrite heart, O God, thou wilt not despise;[18] Nay, though thou art the high and lofty One that inhabitest eternity, whose name is holy;[19] though the heaven be thy throne and the earth thy footstool, yet to this man wilt thou look, that is poor and humble, of a broken and a contrite spirit, and that trembleth at thy word,[20] to revive the spirit of the humble, and to revive the heart of the contrite ones.

Thou hast graciously assured us, though they that cover their sins shall not prosper, yet those that confess and forsake them shall find mercy.[21] And when a poor penitent said, I will confess my transgression unto the Lord, thou forgavest the iniquity of his sin, for this shall every one that is godly, in like manner, pray unto thee in a time when thou mayest be found.[22]

We know, that if we say we have no sin, we deceive ourselves, and the truth is not in us; but thou hast said that if we confess our sins, thou art faithful and just to forgive us our sins, and to cleanse us from all unrighteousness.[23]

3. We must therefore confess and bewail our original corruption in the first place, that we were the children of apostate and rebellious parents, and the nature of man is depraved and wretchedly degenerated from its primitive purity and rectitude, and our nature is so.

Lord, thou madest man upright, but they have sought out many inventions;[24] And being in honour did not understand, and therefore abode not, but became like the beasts that perish.[25]

By one man sin entered into the world, and death by sin, and so death passed upon all men, for that all have sinned: By that one man's disobedience many were made sinners, and we among the rest.[26]

We are a seed of evil doers;[27] our father was an Amorite, and our mother a Hittite,[28] and we ourselves were called (and not miscalled) transgressors from the womb, and thou knewest we would deal very treacherously.[29]

The nature of man was planted a choice and noble vine, wholly a right seed, but it is become the degenerate plant of a strange vine;[30] producing the grapes of Sodom, and the clusters of Gomorrah.[31] How is the gold become dim, and the most fine gold changed![32]

Behold, we were shapen in iniquity, and in sin did our mothers conceive us.[33] For, who can bring a clean thing out of an unclean? Not one.[34] We are by nature children of wrath, because children of disobedience even as others.[35]

All flesh hath corrupted their way,[36] we are all gone aside, we are altogether become filthy, there is none that doth good, no, not one.[37]

4. We must lament our present corrupt dispositions to that which is evil, and our indisposedness to, and impotency in, that which is good. We must look into our own hearts, and confess with holy blushing.

4.1. The blindness of our understandings, and their unaptness to admit the rays of the divine light.

By nature our understandings are darkened, being alienated from the life of God through the ignorance that is in us, because of the blindness of our hearts.[38]

The things of the Spirit of God are foolishness to the natural man, neither can we know them, because they are spiritually discerned.[39]

We are wise to do evil, but to do good we have no knowledge.[40] We know not, neither do we understand, we walk on in darkness.[41]

God speaketh once, yea, twice, but we perceive it not;[42] but hearing, we hear, and do not understand,[43] and we see men as trees walking.[44]

4.2. The stubbornness of our wills, and their unaptness to submit to the rules of the divine law.

We have within us a carnal mind, which is enmity against God, and is not in subjection to the law of God, neither indeed can be.[45]

Thou hast written to us the great things of thy law, but they have been accounted by us a strange thing, and our corrupt hearts have been sometimes ready to say,[46] what is the Almighty that we should serve him?[47] And that we would certainly do whatsoever thing goeth forth out of our own mouth.[48] For we have walked in the way of our own heart, and in the sight of our eyes,[49] fulfilling the desires of the flesh, and of the mind.[50]

Our neck hath been an iron sinew,[51] and we have made our hearts as an adamant stone; we have refused to hearken, have pulled away the shoulder,[52] and stopped our ears like the deaf adder, that will not hearken to the voice of the charmer, charm he never so wisely.[53]

How have we hated instruction, and our heart despised reproof, and have not obeyed the voice of our teachers, nor inclined our ear to them that instructed us.[54]

4.3. The vanity of our thoughts, their neglect of those things which they ought to be conversant with, and dwelling upon those things that are unworthy of them and tend to corrupt our minds.

Every imagination of the thoughts of our heart is evil, only evil, and that continually, and it has been so from our youth.[55]

O how long have those vain thoughts lodged within us![56] those thoughts of foolishness which are sin.[57] From within, out of the heart proceed evil thoughts;[58] which devise mischief upon the bed,[59] and carry the heart with the fool's eyes into the ends of the earth.[60]

But God is not in all our thoughts, it is well if he be in any:[61] Of the Rock that begat us, we have been unmindful, and have forgotten the God that formed us;[62] We have forgotten him days without number, and our hearts have walked after vanity, and become vain.[63] Their inward thought having been, that our houses should continue for ever; this our way is our folly.[64]

4.4. The carnality of our affections, their being placed upon wrong objects, and carried beyond due bounds.

We have set those affections on things beneath, which should have been set on things above, where our treasure is, and where Christ sits on the right hand of God,[65] the things which we should seek.[66]

We have followed after lying vanities, and forsaken our own mercies;[67] have forsaken the fountain of living waters, for cisterns, broken cisterns that can hold no water.[68]

We have panted after the dust of the earth, and have been full of care what we shall eat, and what we shall drink, and wherewithal we shall be clothed, the things after which the Gentiles seek, and the righteousness thereof.[69]

We have lifted up our souls unto vanity,[70] and set our eyes upon that which is not; have looked at the things that are seen, which are temporal; but the things that are eternal, have been forgotten and postponed.[71]

4.5. The corruption of the whole man: Irregular appetites towards those things that are pleasing to sense, and inordinate passions against those things that are displeasing, and an alienation of the mind from the principles, powers, and pleasures of the spiritual and divine life.

We are born of the flesh, and we are flesh:[72] Dust we are;[73] We have borne the image of the earthy;[74] and in us, that is, in our flesh dwells no good thing; For if to will is present to us, yet how to perform that which is good, we find not; for the good which we would do, we do it not; and the evil which we would not do, that we do.[75]

We have a law in our members warring against the law of our mind, and bringing us into captivity to the law of sin that is in our members: So that when we would do good, evil is present with us.[76]

The whole head is sick, the whole heart is faint, from the sole of the foot, even unto the head, there is no soundness in us, but wounds, and bruises, and putrifying sores.[77]

There is in us a bent to backslide from the living God:[78] Our hearts are deceitful above all things, and desperately wicked; who can know them?[79] They start aside like a broken bow.[80]

5. We must lament and confess our omissions of our duty, our neglect of it, and triflings in it, and that we have done so little since we came into the world, of the great work we were sent into the world about; so very little to answer the end of our creation, or of our redemption, of our birth and of our baptism; and that we have profited no more by the means of grace.

We have been as fig-trees planted in the vineyard, and thou hast come many years seeking fruit from us, but hast found none;[81] and therefore we might justly be cut down, and cast into the fire for cumbering the ground:[82] Thou hast come looking for grapes, but behold wild grapes: for we have been empty vines bringing forth fruit unto ourselves.[83]

We have known to do good, but have not done it:[84] We have hid our Lord's money, and therefore deserve the doom of the wicked and slothful servant.[85]

We have been unfaithful stewards, that have wasted our Lord's goods;[86] for one sinner destroys much good.[87]

Many a price hath been put into our hands to get wisdom, which we have had no heart to;[88] or our heart hath been at our left hand.[89]

Our childhood and youth were vanity,[90] and we have brought our years to an end, as a tale that is told.[91]

We have not known, or improved the day of our visitation;[92] have not provided meat in summer, nor gathered food in harvest, though we have had guides, overseers, and rulers.[93]

We are slow of heart to understand and believez: and whereas for the time we might have been teachers of others, we are yet to learn the first principles of the oracles of God: have need of milk, and cannot bear strong meat.[94]

We have cast off fear, and restrained prayer before God;[95] have not called upon thy name, nor stirred up ourselves to take hold on thee.[96]

We have come before thee as thy people come, and have sat before thee as thy people sit, and have heard thy words, when our hearts at the same time have been going after our covetousness.[97] And thus have we brought the torn, and the lame, and the sick for sacrifice, have offered that to our God, which we would not have offered to our governor; and have vowed and sacrificed to the Lord a corrupt thing, when we had in our flock a male.[98]

6. We must likewise bewail our many actual transgressions, in thought, word, and deed.

We have sinned, Father, against heaven and before thee:[99] we have all sinned, and come short of the glory of Godg; for the God in whose hand our breath is, and whose are all our ways, have we not glorified.[100]

Against thee, thee only, have we sinned, and have done much evil in thy sight:[101] neither have we obeyed the voice of the Lord our God, to walk in his laws which he hath set before us;[102] though they are holy, just, and good.[103]

Who can understand his errors? Cleanse thou us from secret faults.[104]

In many things we all offend;[105] and our iniquities are more than the hairs of our head.[106]

As a fountain casteth out her waters, so do our hearts cast out wickedness;[107] and this hath been our manner from our youth up, that we have not obeyed thy voice.[108]

Out of the evil treasure of our hearts we have brought forth many evil things.[109]

6.1. We must confess and bewail the workings of pride in us.

We have all reason to be humbled for the pride of our hearts,[110] that we have thought of ourselves above what hath been meet,[111] and have not thought soberly, nor walked humbly with our God.[112]

We have leaned to our own understanding,[113] and trusted in our own hearts;[114] and have sacrificed to our own net.[115]

We have sought our own glory more than the glory of him that sent us,[116]and have been puffed up for that which we should have mourned.[117]

6.2. The breaking out of passion and rash anger.

We have not had the rule which we ought to have had over our own spirits, which have therefore been as a city that is broken down, and has no walls.[118]

We have been soon angry, and anger hath rested in our bosoms.[119] And when our spirits have been provoked, we have spoken unadvisedly with our lipse: and have been guilty of that clamour and bitterness, which should have been put far from us.[120]

6.3. Our covetousness and love of the world.

Our conversation has not been without covetousness,[121] nor have we learned in every state to be content with such things as we have.[122]

Who can say that he is clean from that love of money which is the root of all,[123] that covetousness which is idolatry?[124]

We have sought great things to ourselves, when thou hast said, Seek them not.[125]

6.4. Our sensuality and flesh-pleasing.

We have minded the things of the flesh more than the things of the Spirit,[126] and have lived in pleasure in the earth, and have been wanton, and have nourished our hearts as in a day of slaughter.[127]

We have made provision for the flesh, to fulfil the lusts of it:[128] even those lusts which war against our souls;[129] and in many instances, have acted, as if we had been lovers of pleasure more than lovers of God.[130]

When we did eat, and when we did drink, did we not eat to ourselves, and drink to ourselves?[131]

6.5. *Our security and unmindfulness of the changes we are liable to in this world.*

We have put far from us the evil day,[132] and in our prosperity have said, we should never be moved,[133] as if to-morrow must needs be as this day, and much more abundant.[134]

We have encouraged our souls to take their ease, to eat and drink, and be merry, as if we had goods laid up for many years, when perhaps this night our souls may be required of us.[135]

We have been ready to trust in uncertain riches, more than in the living God;[136] to say to the gold, Thou art our hope, and to the fine gold, Thou art our confidence.[137]

6.6. *Our fretfulness and impatience, and murmuring under our afflictions, our inordinate dejection and distrust of God and his providence.*

When thou chastisedst us, and we were chastised, we have been as a bullock unaccustomed to the yoke;[138] and though our own foolishness hath perverted our way, yet our heart hath fretted against the Lord;[139] and thus in our distress, we have trespassed yet more against the Lord.[140]

We have either despised the chastening of the Lord, or fainted when we have been rebuked of him;[141] and if we faint in the day of adversity, our strength is small.[142]

We have said in our haste, We are cast off from before thine eyes;[143] and that the Lord hath forsaken us, our God hath forgotten us, as if God would be favourable no more;[144] as if he had forgotten to be gracious, and had in anger shut up his tender mercies. This has been our infirmity.[145]

6.7. *Our uncharitableness towards our brethren, and unpeaceableness with our relations, neighbours, and friends, and perhaps injustice towards them.*

We have been very guilty concerning our brother:[146] for we have not studied the things that make for peace, nor things wherewith we might edify one another.[147]

We have been ready to judge our brother, and to set at nought our brother, forgetting that we must all shortly stand before the judgment seat of Christ.[148]

Contrary to the royal law of charity, we have vaunted ourselves and been puffed up, have behaved ourselves unseemly and sought our own, have been easily provoked, have rejoiced in iniquity,[149] and been secretly glad at calamities.[150]

We have been desirous of vain glory, provoking one another, envying one another:[151] when we should have considered one another, to provoke to love, and to good works.[152]

The bowels of our compassion have been shut up from those that are in need;[153] and we have hidden ourselves from our own flesh.[154] Nay, perhaps our eye has been evil against our poor brother,[155] and we have despised the poor.[156]

And if in any thing we have gone beyond and defrauded our brother,[157] if we have walked with vanity, and our foot hath hasted to deceit, and any blot hath cleaved to our hands,[158] Lord, discover it to us, that if we have done iniquity, we may do so no more.[159]

6.8. *Our tongue sins.*

In the multitude of our words there wanteth not sin,[160] nor can a man full of talk be justified.[161]

While the lips of the righteous feed many, our lips have poured out foolishness, and spoken frowardness.[162] Much corrupt communication hath proceeded out of our mouths; that foolish talking and jesting which is not convenient, and little of that which is good, and to the use of edifying, and which might minister grace unto the hearers.[163]

If for every idle word that men speak they must give an account, and if by our words we must be justified, and if by our words we must be condemned;[164] woe unto us, for we are undone; for we are of unclean lips, and dwell in the midst of a people of unclean lips.[165]

What would become of us, if God should make our own tongues to fall upon us?[166]

6.9. *Our spiritual slothfulness and decay.*

We have been slothful in the business of religion, and not fervent in spirit, serving the Lord.[167]

The things which remain are ready to die, and our works have not been found perfect before God.[168]

We have observed the winds, and therefore have not sown, have regarded the clouds, and therefore have not reaped,[169] and with the sluggard have frighted ourselves with the fancy of a lion in the way, a lion in the streets, and have turned on our bed as the door on the hinges;[170] still crying, Yet a little sleep, and a little slumber.[171]

We have lost our first love;[172] and where is now the blessedness we sometimes spake of?[173]

Our goodness hath been as the morning cloud, and the early dew which soon passeth away.[174]

And that which is at the bottom of all, is the evil heart of unbelief in us which inclines us to depart from the living God.[175]

7. We must acknowledge the great evil that there is in sin, and in our sin; the malignity of its nature, and its mischievousness to us.

7.1. The sinfulness of sin.

O that sin may appear sin to us, may appear in its own colours, and that by the commandment we may see it to be exceeding sinful,[176] because it is the transgression of the law.[177]

By every willful sin we have in effect said, we will not have this man to reign over us.[178] And who is the Lord, that we should obey his voice?[179] And thus have we reproached the Lord,[180] and cast his laws behind our back.[181]

7.2. The foolishness of sin.

O God, thou knowest our foolishness, and our sins are not hid from thee:[182] we were foolish in being disobedient:[183] and our lusts are foolish and hurtful.[184]

Foolishness was bound up in our hearts when we were children;[185] for though vain man would be wise, he is born like the wild ass's colt.[186]

Our way hath been our folly,[187] and in many instances we have done foolishly.[188] So foolish have we been and ignorant, and even as beasts before God.[189]

7.3. The unprofitableness of sin.

We have sinned and perverted that which was right, and it profited us not.[190]

What fruit have we now in these things whereof we have cause to be ashamed, seeing the end of those things is death?[191] And what are we profited, if we should gain the whole world, and lose our own souls?[192]

7.4. The deceitfulness of sin.

Sin hath deceived us, and by it slain us,[193] for our hearts have been hardened through the deceitfulness of sin:[194] and we have been drawn away of our own lust, and enticed.[195]

It has promised us liberty, but has made us the servants of corruption;[196] hath promised, that we shall not surely die, and that we shall be as gods;[197] but it has flattered us, and spread a net for our feet.[198]

The pride of our heart particularly has deceived us.[199]

7.5. The offence which by sin we have given to the holy God.

By breaking the law we have dishonoured God,[200] and have provoked the Holy One of Israel to anger most bitterly.[201, 202] And many a thing that we have done hath displeased the Lord.[203]

God has been broken by our whorish heart, and our eyes that have gone a whoring after our idols.[204]

We have tempted him, and proved him, and grieved him, in the wilderness,[205] have rebelled and vexed his holy Spirit,[206] and pressed him with our iniquities, as a cart is pressed that is full of sheaves.[207]

We have grieved the Holy Spirit of God, by whom we are sealed to the day of redemption.[208]

7.6. The damage which by sin we have done to our own souls, and their great interests.

By our iniquities we have sold ourselves,[209] and in sinning against thee, we have wronged our own souls.[210] Our sins have separated between us and God,[211] and have kept good things from us; and by them our minds and consciences have been defiled.[212]

Our own wickedness hath corrected us, and backslidings have reproved us, and we cannot but know and see, that it is an evil thing, and bitter, that we have forsaken the Lord our God, and that his fear hath not been in us.[213]

O what fools are they that make a mock at sin?[214]

8. We must aggravate[215] our sins, and take notice of those things which make them more heinous in the sight of God, and more dangerous to ourselves.

We bewail before thee all our sins, and all our transgressions in all our sins.[216]

8.1. The more knowledge we have of good and evil, the greater is our sin.

We have known our master's will, but have not done it, and therefore deserve to be beaten with many stripes.[217]

We have known the way of the Lord, and the judgments of our God, and yet have altogether broken the yoke, and burst the bonds.[218]

We have known the judgment of God, that they which do such things are worthy of death, and yet have done them, and have had pleasure in them that do them.[219]

We have taught others, and yet have not taught ourselves;[220] and while we profess to know God, we have in works denied him.[221]

8.2. The greater profession we have made of religion, the greater hath been our sin.

We call ourselves of the holy city, and stay ourselves upon the God of Israel, and make mention of his name, but not in truth and in righteousness.[222] For we have dishonoured that worthy name by which we are called,[223] and given great occasion to the enemies of the Lord to blaspheme.[224]

We have named the name of Christ, and yet have not departed from iniquity.[225]

8.3. The more mercies we have received from God, the greater has been our sin.

Thou hast nourished and brought us up as children, but we have rebelled against thee.[226]

We have ill requited thee, O Lord, as foolish people and unwise: Thou art our father that made us, and bought us, and established us, yet our spot has not been the spot of thy children.[227]

We have not rendered again, according to the benefit done unto us.[228]

8.4. The fairer warning we have had from the word of God, and from our own consciences concerning our danger of sin, and danger by sin, the greater is the sin, if we go on in it.

We have been often reproved, and yet have hardened our neck,[229] and have gone on frowardly in the way of our heart.[230]

Thou hast sent to us, saying, O do not this abominable thing which I hate; but we have not hearkened, nor inclined our ear.[231]

The word of God hath been to us precept upon precept, and line upon line;[232] and though we have beheld our natural faces in the glass, yet we have gone away, and straightway forgot what manner of men we were.[233]

8.5. The greater afflictions we have been under for sin, the greater is the sin if we go on in it.

Thou hast stricken us, but we have not grieved; we have refused to receive correction, and have made our faces harder than a rock;[234] and the rod hath not driven the foolishness out of our hearts.[235]

Thou hast chastened us with the rod of men, and with the stripes of the children of men,[236] yet we have not turned to him that smiteth us, nor have we sought the Lord of hosts.[237]

When some have been overthrown as *Sodom* and *Gomorrah* were, we have been as brands plucked out of the fire, yet have we not returned unto thee, O Lord.[238] And when thy hand has been lifted up, we have not seen it.[239]

8.6. The more vows and promises we have made of better obedience, the greater has our sin been.

We have not performed the words of the covenant which we have made before thee,[240] but as treacherous dealers we have dealt treacherously.[241]

Did we not say we would not transgress, we would not offend any more?[242] We did, and yet we have returned with the dog to his vomit,[243] we have returned to folly after God hath spoken peace.[244]

9. We must judge and condemn ourselves for our sins, and own ourselves liable to punishment.

And now, O our God, what shall we say after this, for we have forsaken thy commandments?[245] We have sinned, what shall we do unto thee, O thou preserver of man?[246]

We know that the law curseth every one that continues not in all things that are written in the book of the law, to do them;[247] that the wages of every sin is death;[248] and that for these things sake the wrath of God cometh upon the children of disobedience.[249]

And we are all guilty before God;[250] the scripture hath concluded us all under sin;[251] and therefore thou mightest justly be angry with us, till thou hadst consumed us, so that there should be no remnant nor escaping.[252]

If thou shouldest lay righteousness to the line, and judgment to the plummet,[253] thou mightest justly separate us unto all evil, according to all the curses of the covenant, and blot out our names from under heaven.[254]

Thou mightest justly swear in thy wrath that we should never enter into thy rest;[255] mightest justly set us naked and bare, and take away our corn in the season thereof,[256] and put into our hands the cup of trembling, and make us drink even the dregs of that cup.[257]

Thou art just in whatever thou art pleased to lay upon us; for thou hast done right, but we have done wickedly.[258] Nay, that our God has punished us less than our iniquities have deserved.[259]

Thou therefore shalt be justified when thou speakest, and clear when thou judgest;[260] and we will accept of the punishment of our iniquity;[261] and humble ourselves under thy mighty hand,[262] and say that the Lord is righteous.[263]

Wherefore should a living man complain, a man for the punishment of his sins?[264] No; we will bear the indignation of the Lord because we have sinned against him.[265]

10. We must give to God the glory of his patience and long-suffering towards us, and his willingness to be reconciled.

O the riches of the patience and forbearance of God![266] how long-suffering is he to us-ward, not willing that any should perish, but that all should come to repentance.[267]

Thou hast not dealt with us according to our sin, nor rewarded us after our iniquities,[268] but thou waitest to be gracious to us.[269]

Sentence against our evil works has not been executed speedily,[270] but thou hast given us space to repent, and make our peace with thee;[271] and callest even backsliding children to return to thee, and hast promised to heal their backslidings; and therefore, behold we come unto thee, for thou art the Lord our God.[272]

Surely the long-suffering of our Lord is salvation;[273] and if the Lord had been pleased to kill us, he would not at this time have showed us such things as these.[274]

And O that this goodness of God might lead us to repentance![275] for though we have trespassed against our God, yet now there is hope in Israel concerning this thing.[276]

Thou hast said it, and hast confirmed it with an oath, that thou hast no pleasure in the death of sinners, but rather that we should turn and live:[277] Therefore will we rend our hearts, and not our garments, and turn to the Lord our God; for he is gracious and merciful, slow to anger, and of great kindness. Who knows if he will return, and repent, and leave a blessing behind him?[278]

11. We must humbly profess our sorrow and shame for sin, and humbly engage ourselves in the strength of divine grace, that we will be better, and do better for the future.

Lord, we repent, for the kingdom of heaven is at hand;[279] to which thou hast exalted thy Son Christ Jesus, to give repentance and remission of sins.[280]

We have heard of thee by the hearing of the ear, but now our eyes see thee; wherefore we abhor ourselves, and repent in dust and ashes;[281] therefore will we be like the doves of the valleys, every one mourning for his iniquites.[282]

O that our heads were waters, and our eyes fountains of tears, that we might weep day and night for our transgressions,[283] and might in such a manner sow in those tears as that at last we may reap in joy; may now go forth weeping, bearing precious seed, and may in due time come again with rejoicing, bringing in our sheaves with us.[284]

Our iniquities are gone over our heads as a heavy burden, they are too heavy for us;[285] but weary and heavy laden under this burden we come to Christ, who has promised that in him we shall find rest to our souls.[286]

O that knowing every man the plague of his own heart,[287] we may look unto him whom we have pierced and may mourn, and be in bitterness for him, as one that is in bitterness for a first-born.[288] That we may sorrow after a godly sort, with that sorrow which worketh repentance unto salvation, not to be repented of;[289] and that we may remember, and be confounded, and never open our mouth any more, because of our shame when thou art pacified toward us.[290]

And, O that we may bring forth fruits meet for repentance![291] and may never return again to folly;[292] for what have we to do any more with idols?[293] sin shall not have dominion over us, for we are not under the law, but under grace.[294]

We have gone astray like lost sheep; seek thy servants, for we do not forget thy commandments.[295]

References

1 Josh. 7:19.
2 Ezra 9:6.
3 Dan. 9:8.
4 Job 40:4.
5 Lam. 3:29.
6 Lev. 13:45.
7 Job 15:15-16.
8 Isa. 6:5.
9 Job 25:2-4.
10 Ps. 76:7.
11 Heb. 12:29.
12 Ps. 90:11.
13 Job 9:3, 20.
14 I Cor. 4:4.
15 1 John 3:20.
16 Luke 15:21.
17 Ps. 130:3-4, 7-8.
18 Ps. 51:17.
19 Isa. 57:15.
20 Isa. 66:1-2.
21 Prov. 28:13.
22 Ps. 32:5-6.
23 1 John 1:8-9.
24 Eccles. 7:29.
25 Ps. 49:12.
26 Rom. 5:12, 19.

27 Isa. 1:4.
28 Ezek. 16:3.
29 Isa. 48:8.
30 Jer. 2:21.
31 Deut. 32:32.
32 Lam. 4:1.
33 Ps. 51:5.
34 Job 14:4.
35 Eph. 2:2-3.
36 Gen. 6:12.
37 Ps. 14:3.
38 Eph. 4:18.
39 1 Cor. 2:14.
40 Jer. 4:22.
41 Ps. 82:5.
42 Job 33:14.
43 Matt. 13:14.
44 Mark 8:24.
45 Rom. 8:7.
46 Hosea 8:12.
47 Job 21:15.
48 Jer. 44:17.
49 Eccles. 11:9-10.
50 Eph. 2:3.
51 Isa. 48:4.
52 Zech. 7:11-12.

53 Ps. 58:4-5.
54 Prov. 5:12-13.
55 Gen. 6:5, 8:21.
56 Jer. 4:14.
57 Prov. 24:9.
58 Matt. 15:19.
59 Mic. 2:1.
60 Prov. 17:24.
61 Ps. 10:4.
62 Deut. 32:18.
63 Jer. 2:32, 2:5.
64 Ps. 49:11, 13.
65 Col. 3:1-2.
66 Matt. 6:21.
67 Jonah 2:8.
68 Jer. 2:13.
69 Matt. 6:32-33.
70 Ps. 24:4.
71 2 Cor. 4:18.
72 John 3:6.
73 Gen. 3:19.
74 1 Cor. 15:49.
75 Rom. 7:18-19.
76 Rom. 7:21, 23.
77 Isa. 1:6.
78 Hos 11:7.

79 Jer. 17:9.
80 Hosea 7:16.
81 Luke 13:6-7.
82 Matt. 3:10.
83 Isa. 5:4.
84 James 4:17.
85 Matt. 25:18, 26.
86 Luke 16:1.
87 Eccles. 9:18.
88 Prov. 17:16.
89 Eccles. 10:2.
90 Eccles. 11:10.
91 Ps.90:9.
92 Luke 19:44.
93 Prov. 6:7-8.
94 Luke 24:25.
95 Heb. 5:12.
96 Job 15:4.
97 Isa. 64:7.
98 Ezek. 33:31.
99 Mal. 1:8, 14.
100 Luke 15:18.
101 Rom. 3:23.
102 Dan. 5:23.
103 Ps. 51:4.
104 Dan. 9:10.
105 Rom. 7:12.
106 Ps. 19:12.
107 James 3:2.
108 Ps. 40:12.
109 Jer. 6:7.
110 Jer. 22:21.
111 Matt. 12:35.
112 2 Chron. 32:26.
113 Rom. 12:3.
114 Micah 6:8.
115 Prov. 3:5.
116 Prov. 28:26.
117 Hab. 1:16.
118 John 7:18.
119 1 Cor. 5:2.
120 Prov. 25:28.
121 Eccles. 7:9.
122 Ps. 106:33.
123 Eph. 4:31.
124 Heb 13:5.
125 Phil. 4:11.
126 1 Tim. 6:10.
127 Col. 3:5.
128 Jer. 45:5.
129 Rom. 8:5.
130 James 5:5.
131 Rom. 13:14.
132 1 Pet. 2:11.
133 2 Tim. 3:4.
134 Zech. 7:6.
135 Amos 6:3.
136 Ps. 30:6.
137 Isa. 56:12.
138 Luke 12:19-20.
139 1 Tim 6:17.
140 Job 31:24.
141 Jer. 31:18.
142 Prov. 19:3.
143 2 Chron. 28:22.
144 Prov. 24:10.
145 Ps. 31:22.
146 Isa. 49:14.
147 Ps. 77:9-10.
148 Gen. 42:21.
149 Rom. 14:19.
150 Rom. 14:10.
151 1 Cor. 13:4-6.
152 Prov. 17:5.
153 Gal. 5:26.
154 Heb. 10:24.
155 1 John 3:17.
156 Isa. 58:7.
157 Deut. 15:9.
158 James 2:6.
159 1 Thess. 4:6.
160 Job 31:5, 7.
161 Job 34:32.
162 Prov. 10:19.
163 Job 11:2.
164 Prov. 10:21, 32.
165 Eph. 4:29, 5:4.
166 Matt. 12:36-37.
167 Isa. 6:5.
168 Ps. 64:8.
169 Rom. 12:11.
170 Rev. 3:2.
171 Eccles. 11:4.
172 Prov. 26:13-14.
173 Prov. 6:10.
174 Rev 2:4.
175 Gal. 4:15.
176 Hosea 6:4.
177 Heb. 3:12.
178 Rom. 7:13.
179 1 John 3:4.
180 Luke 19:14.
181 Exod. 5:2.
182 Numb. 15:30.
183 Neh. 9:26.
184 Ps. 69:5.
185 Titus 3:3.
186 1 Tim. 6:9.
187 Prov. 22:15.
188 Job 11:12.
189 Ps. 49:13.
190 2 Sam. 24:10.
191 Ps. 73:22.
192 Job 33:27.
193 Rom. 6:21.
194 Matt. 16:26.
195 Rom. 7:11.
196 Heb. 3:13.
197 James 1:14.
198 2 Pet. 2:19.
199 Gen. 3:4-5.
200 Prov. 29:5.
201 Obad. 3.
202 Rom. 2:23.
203 Isa. 1:4.
204 Hosea 12:14.
205 2 Sam. 11:27.
206 Ezek. 6:9.
207 Ps. 95:9-10.
208 Isa. 63:10.
209 Amos 2:13.
210 Eph. 4:30.
211 Isa. 50:1.
212 Prov. 8:36.
213 Isa. 59:2.

214 The Author means that we must look at our sins in the worst light, to see just how evil we are taking into account the persons we have offended, the nature of the offense,

the circumstances of our sin.

See The Westminster Larger Catechism, Questions 150 and 151.

215 Titus 1:15.
216 Jer. 2:19.
217 Prov 14:9.
218 Lev. 16:21.
219 Luke 12:47.
220 Jer. 5:4-5.
221 Rom. 1:32.
222 Rom. 2:21.
223 Tit. 1:16.
224 Isa. 48:1-2.
225 James 2:7.
226 2 Sam. 12-14.
227 2 Tim 2:19.
228 Isa. 1:2.
229 Deut. 32:5,6, 9.
230 2 Chron. 32:25.
231 Prov. 29:1.
232 Isa. 57:17.
233 Jer. 44:4-5.
234 Isa. 28:13.
235 James 1:23-24.
236 Jer. 5:3.
237 Prov. 22:15.
238 2 Sam. 7:14.
239 Isa. 9:13.
240 Amos 4:11.
241 Isa. 26:11.
242 Jer. 34:18.
243 Isa. 24:16.
244 Jer. 2:20.
245 2 Pet. 2:22.
246 Ps. 85:8.
247 Ezra 9:10.
248 Job 7:20.
249 Gal. 3:10.
250 Rom 6:23.
251 Eph. 5:6.
252 Rom. 3:19.
253 Gal. 3:22.
254 Ezra 9:14.
255 Isa. 28:17.
256 Deut. 28:17.
257 Ps. 95:11.
258 Hosea 2:3, 9.
259 Isa. 51:17.
260 Neh. 9:33.
261 Ezra 9:13.
262 Ps. 51:4.
263 Lev. 26:43.
264 1 Pet. 5:6.
265 2 Chron. 12:6.
266 Lam. 3:39.
267 Micah 7:9.
268 Rom. 2:4.
269 2 Pet. 3:9.
270 Ps. 103:10.
271 Isa. 30:18.
272 Eccles. 8:11.
273 Rev. 2:21.
274 Jer. 3:23.
275 2 Pet. 3:15.
276 Judg. 13:23.
277 Rom. 2:4.
278 Ezra 10:2.
279 Ezek. 33:11.
280 Joel 2:13-14.
281 Matt. 3:2.
282 Acts 5:31.
283 Job 42:5-6.
284 Ezek. 7:16.
285 Jer. 9:1.
286 Ps. 126:5-6.
287 Ps. 38:4.
288 Matt. 11:28.
289 1 Kings 8:38.
290 Zech. 12:10.
291 2 Cor. 7:10.
292 Ezek. 16:63.
293 Matt. 3:8.
294 Ps. 85:8.
295 Hosea 14:8.

CHAPTER 3

Of the third part of PRAYER,
which is Petition and Supplication for the good things
which we stand in need of.

Having opened the wounds of sin, both the guilt of it, and the power of it, and its remainders in us, we must next seek unto God for the remedy, for healing and help, for from him alone it is to be expected, and he will for this be inquired of by us.[1] And now we must affect our hearts with a deep sense of the need we have of those mercies which we pray for, that we are undone, for ever undone, without them; and with a high esteem and value for them, that we are happy, we are made for ever, if we obtain them; that we may like Jacob, wrestle with him in prayer, as for our lives, and the lives of our souls.

But we must not think in our prayers to prescribe to him, or by our importunity to move him. He knows us better than we know ourselves, and knows what he will do.[2] But thus we open our wants and our desires, and then refer ourselves to his wisdom and goodness; and hereby we give honour to him as our protector and benefactor, and take the way which he himself hath appointed, of fetching in mercy from him, and by faith plead his promise with him, and if we are sincere herein, we are, through his grace, qualified according to the tenor of the new covenant, to receive his favours, and are to be assured that we do, and shall receive them.[3]

And now, Lord, what wait we for? Truly our hope is even in thee; deliver us from all our transgressions, that we may no more be the reproach of the foolish.[4]

Lord, all our desire is before thee, and our groaning is not hid from thee;[5] even the groanings which cannot be uttered: for he that searcheth the heart, knows what is the mind of the Spirit.[6]

We do not think that we shall be heard for our much speaking; for our Father knows what things we have need of,[7] before we ask him;

but our Master hath told us, that whatsoever we ask the Father in his name, he will give it us. And he hath said, Ask, and ye shall receive, that your joy may be full.[8]

And this is the confidence that we have in him that if we ask any thing according to his will, he heareth us; And if we know that he hear us, whatsoever we ask, we know that we have the petitions we desired of him.[9]

1. We must earnestly pray for the pardon and forgiveness of all our sins.

Lord, we come to thee, as the poor publican that stood afar off, and would not so much as lift up his eyes to heaven, but smote upon his breast; and we pray his prayer, God be merciful to us sinners.[10] The God of infinite mercy be merciful to us.

O wash us thoroughly from our iniquity, and cleanse us from our sin, for we acknowledge our transgressions, and our sin is ever before us. O purge us with hyssop and we shall be clean, wash us and we shall be whiter than snow; hide thy face from our sins, and blot out our iniquities.[11]

Be thou merciful to our unrighteousness, and our sins and our iniquities do thou remember no more.[12] O forgive us that great debt.[13]

Let us be justified freely by thy grace,[14] through the redemption that is in Jesus from all those things from which we could not be justified by the law of Moses.[15]

O let not our iniquity be our ruin;[16] but let the Lord take away our sin, that we may not die,[17] not die eternally; that we may not be hurt of the second death.[18]

Blot out as a cloud our transgressions, and as a thick cloud our sins; for we return unto thee, because thou hast redeemed us.[19]

Enter not into judgment with thy servants, O Lord, for in thy sight shall no flesh living be justified.[20]

Take away all iniquity, and receive us graciously; heal our backslidings, and love us freely, and let thine anger be turned away from us; for in thee the fatherless findeth mercy.[21]

Though our sins have been as scarlet, let them be as white as snow, and though they have been red like crimson, let them be as wool, that being willing and obedient, we may eat the good of the land.[22]

We will say unto God, Do not condemn us,[23] but deliver us from going down to the pit, for thou hast found the ransom.[24]

For the encouraging of our faith, and the exciting of our fervency in this petition for the pardon of sin, we may plead with God,

1.1. The infinite goodness of his nature, his readiness to forgive sin, and his glorying in it.

Thou, Lord, art good, and ready to forgive; and rich in mercy to all them that call upon thee. Thou art a God full of compassion, and gracious, long-suffering, and plenteous in mercy and truth.[25]

Thou art a God of pardon, merciful, slow to anger, and of great kindness[26] that dost not always chide, nor keep thine anger for ever.[27]

Thou, even thou, art he that blottest out our transgressions for thine own sake, and wilt not remember our sins, which we are here to put thee in remembrance of, to plead with thee, and to declare that we may be justified.[28]

And now, we beseech thee, let the power of our Lord be great, according as thou hast spoken, saying, the Lord is long-suffering, and of great mercy, forgiving iniquity and transgression. Pardon, we beseech thee, the iniquity of thy people according unto the greatness of thy mercy: and as thou hast forgiven even until now.[29]

For who is a God like unto thee, that pardonest iniquity, and passest by the transgression of the remnant of thine heritage; who retainest not thine anger for ever, because thou delightest in mercy. O that thou wouldest have compassion upon us, and subdue our iniquities, and cast all our sins into the depths of the sea.[30]

1.2. The merit and righteousness of our Lord Jesus Christ, which we rely upon as our main plea in our petition for the pardon of sin.

We know that as thou art gracious and merciful, so thou art the righteous God that loveth righteousness,[31] and wilt by no means clear the guilty.[32] We cannot say, Have patience with us and we will pay thee all;[33] for we are all as an unclean thing, and all our righteousnesses are as filthy rags.[34] But Jesus Christ is made of God to us righteousness;[35] being made sin for us, though he knew no sin, that we might be made the righteousness of God in him.[36]

We have sinned, but we have an advocate with the Father, Jesus Christ the righteous, who is the propitiation for our sins, and not for ours only, but for the sins of the whole world.[37]

It is God that justifieth, who is he that shall condemn? It is Christ that died, yea, rather that is risen again, and now is even at the right hand of God, who also maketh intercession for us,[38] and whose blood speaks better things than that of Abel.[39]

We desire to count every thing loss for Christ, and dung that we may win Christ, and be found in him, not having any righteousness of our own, but that which is through the faith of Christ.[40]

This is the name whereby we will call him, THE LORD OUR RIGH-TEOUSNESS.[41] In him, Lord, we believe, help thou our own unbelief.[42]

Lord, remember David and all his troubles;[43] the son of David, remember all his offerings, and accept his burnt sacrifice;[44] and turn not away the face of thine anointed,[45] who by his own blood is entered into heaven itself, now to appear in the presence of God for us.[46]

Hast not thou thyself set forth thy Son Christ Jesus, to be a propitiation for sin through faith in his blood, to declare thy righteousness for the remission of sins, to declare at this time thy righteousness, that thou mayest be just, and the justifier of him that believeth in Jesus?[47] And we now receive the atonement.[48]

1.3. The promises God hath made in his word to pardon and absolve all them that truly repent, and unfeignedly believe his holy gospel.

Lord, is not this the word which thou hast spoken, That if the wicked forsake his way, and the unrighteous man his thoughts, and return unto the Lord, even to our God, that thou wilt abundantly pardon, wilt multiply to pardon?[49]

To thee the Lord our God belong mercies and forgivenesses, though we have rebelled against thee.[50]

Is not this the covenant which thou hast made with the house of Israel, that thou wilt take away their sins;[51] that thou wilt forgive their iniquity, and remember their sin no more;[52] that the iniquity of Israel shall be sought for, and there shall be none; and the sins of Judah, and they shall not be found?[53]

Hast thou not said, that if the wicked will turn from all his sins which he hath committed, and keep thy statutes he shall live, he shall not die, all his transgressions shall not be mentioned unto him?[54]

Hast thou not appointed that repentance and remission of sins should be preached in Christ's name, unto all nations?[55]

Didst thou not promise that when the sins of Israel were put upon the head of the scape-goat, they should be sent away into the wilderness, into a land not inhabited?[56] And as far as the east is from the west, so far dost thou remove our transgressions from us.[57]

O remember these words unto thy servants, upon which thou hast caused us to hope.[58]

1.4. Our own misery and danger because of sin.

For thy Name's sake, O Lord, pardon our iniquity, for it is great;[59] for innumerable evils have compassed us about, our iniquities have taken hold upon us, so that we are not able to look up. Be pleased, O Lord, to deliver us; O Lord, make haste to help us.[60]

O remember not against us former iniquities, let thy tender mercy speedily prevent us, for we are brought very low. Help us, O God of our salvation, for the glory of thy name; deliver us and purge away our sins for thy name's sake.[61]

Remember not the sins of our youth, nor our transgressions, according to thy mercy remember thou us, for thy goodness' sake, O Lord.[62]

1.5. The blessed condition which they are in whose sins are pardoned.

O let us have the blessedness of those whose transgression is forgiven, and whose sin is covered; of that man unto whom the Lord imputeth not iniquity, and in whose spirit there is no guile.[63]

O let us have redemption through Christ's blood, even the forgiveness of sins, according to the riches of thy grace, wherein thou hast abounded towards us in all wisdom and prudence.[64] That being in Christ Jesus, there may be no condemnation to us.[65]

That our sins, which are many, being forgiven us, we may go in peace:[66] And the inhabitant shall not say, I am sick, if the people that dwell therein be forgiven their iniquity.[67]

2. We must likewise pray that God will be reconciled to us, that we may obtain his favour and blessing, and gracious acceptance.

2.1. That we may be at peace with God, and his anger may be turned away from us.

Being justified by faith, let us have peace with God, through our Lord Jesus Christ, and through him let us have access into that grace wherein believers stand, and rejoice in hope of the glory of God.[68]

Be not thou a terror to us, for thou art our hope in the day of evil.[69]

In Christ Jesus let us, who sometimes were afar off, be made nigh by the blood of Christ;[70] for he is our peace, who hath broken down the middle wall of partition between us; and that he might reconcile us to God by his cross, hath slain the enmity thereby, so making peace. Through him therefore let us, who have made ourselves strangers and foreigners, become fellow-citizens with the saints, and of the household of God.[71]

Fury is not in thee; who would set the briars and thorns against thee in battle? thou wouldest burn them together; but thou hast encouraged us to take hold on thy strength, that we make peace, and hast promised that we shall make peace.[72] O let us therefore acquaint ourselves with thee, and be at peace, that thereby good may come unto us.[73]

Heal us, and we shall be healed; save us, and we shall be saved; for thou art our praise.[74] Be not angry with us for ever, but revive us again, that thy people may rejoice in thee. Shew us thy mercy, O Lord, and grant us thy salvation.[75]

2.2. That we may be taken into covenant with God, and admitted into a relation to him.

Be thou to us as a God, and take us to be to thee a people,[76] and make us a willing people in the day of thy power.[77]

Though we are no more worthy to be called thy children,[78] for how shouldest thou put us, that have been rebellious, among the children, and give us the pleasant land? but thou hast said, That we shall call thee our Father, and not turn away from thee. Shall we not therefore from this time cry into thee, our Father, thou art the guide of our youth.[79]

Lord, we take hold of thy covenant,[80] to thee we join ourselves in a perpetual covenant;[81] O that thou wouldest cause us to pass under the rod, and bring us into the bond of the covenant,[82] that we may become thine.[83]

Make with us an everlasting covenant, even the sure mercies of David.[84]

2.3. That we may have the favour of God, and an interest in his special love.

We intreat thy favour, O God, with our whole hearts; be merciful to us according to thy word,[85] for in thy favour is life,[86] yea, thy loving kindness is better than life itself.[87] Lord, make thy face to shine upon us, and be gracious unto us; Lord, lift up the light of thy countenance upon us, and give us peace.[88]

Remember us, O Lord, with the favour that thou bearest unto thy people: O visit us with thy salvation that we may see the good of thy chosen, and may rejoice in the goodness of thy nation, and may glory with thine inheritance.[89]

2.4. That we may have the blessing of God.

O God, be merciful to us, and bless us, and cause thy face to shine on us; yea, let God, even our God give us his blessing.[90]

The Lord that made heaven and earth, bless us out of Zion;[91] bless us with all spiritual blessings in heavenly things, by Christ Jesus.[92]

O that thou wouldest bless us indeed![93] Command the blessing upon us, even life for evermore:[94] for thou blessest, O Lord, and it shall be blessed.[95]

Let us receive the blessing from the Lord, even the righteousness from the God of our salvation.[96]

Hast thou but one blessing! Yea, thou hast many blessing; Bless us, even us also, O our Father;[97] yea, let the blessing of Abraham come upon us, which comes upon the Gentiles through faith.[98] And the blessing of Jacob, for we would not let thee go, except thou bless us.[99]

2.5. That we may have the presence of God with us.
If thy presence go not up with us, carry us not up hence;[100] never leave us, nor forsake us.[101]

O cast us not away from thy presence, nor ever take thy holy Spirit away from us;[102] but let us always dwell with the upright in thy presence.[103]

3. We must pray for the comfortable sense of our reconciliation to God, and our acceptance with him.

3.1. That we may have some evidence of the pardon of our sins, and of our adoption.
O make us to hear joy and gladness, that the bones which sin hath broken may rejoice.[104]

Say unto each of us, Son, Daughter be of good cheer, thy sins are forgiven thee.[105]

Let the blood of Christ, who through the eternal Spirit offered himself without spot to God, purge our conscience from dead works, to serve thee the living God.[106]

Let thy Spirit witness with our spirit, that we are the children of God, and if children, then heirs, heirs of God, and joint heirs with Christ.[107] Say unto our souls, that thou art our salvation.[108]

3.2. That we may have a well-grounded peace of conscience; a holy security and serenity of mind arising from a sense of our justification before God, and a good work wrought in us.
The Lord of peace himself gives us peace, all peace, always, by all means;[109] that peace which Jesus Christ hath left with us, which he gives to us, such a peace as the world can neither give nor take away; such a peace as that our hearts may not be troubled nor afraid.[110]

Let the work of righteousness in our souls be peace, and the effect of righteousness quietness and assurance for ever.[111]

Speak peace unto thy people, and to thy saints, and let not them turn again to folly.[112]

O create the fruit of the lips, peace, peace to them that are afar off, and to them that are nigh, and restore comfort to thy mourners.[113]

Where the sons of peace are, let thy peace find them out, and rest upon them.[114]

Cause us to hear thy loving-kindness,[115] and to taste that thou art gracious, for in thee do we trust.[116]

Let the peace of God, which passeth all understanding, keep our hearts and minds, through Christ Jesus;[117] and let that peace rule in our hearts, unto which we are called.[118]

Now the God of hope fill us with all joy and peace in believing, that we may abound in hope, through the power of the Holy Ghost.[119]

4. We must pray for the grace of God, and all the kind and powerful influences and operations of that grace.

We come to the throne of grace, that we may obtain not only mercy to pardon, but grace to help in every time of need; grace for seasonable help.[120]

From the fulness that is in Jesus Christ,[121] (in whom it pleased the Father, that all fulness should dwell)[122] let every one of us receive, and grace for grace.

4.1. We must pray for grace to fortify us against every evil thought, word, and work. Having been earnest for the removing of the guilt of sin, that we may not die for it as a crime, we must be no less earnest for the breaking of the power of sin, that we may not die by it as a disease, but that it may be mortified in us.

O let no iniquity have dominion over us, because we are not under the law, but under grace.[123]

Let the flesh be crucified in us, with its affections and lusts; that walking in the Spirit we may not fulfill the lusts of the flesh.[124]

Let our old man be crucified with Christ, that the body of sin may be destroyed, that henceforth we may not serve sin: and let not sin reign in our mortal bodies (in our immortal souls) that we should obey it in the lusts thereof. But being made free from sin, let us become the servants of righteousness.[125]

Let the law of the spirit of life, which is in Christ Jesus, make us free from the law of sin and death.[126]

Give us grace to put off the old man which is corrupt according to the deceitful lusts, that we may put on the new man, which after God is created in righteousness and true holiness.[127] That the world may be crucified to us, and we to the world by the cross of Christ.[128]

And that the temptations of Satan may not overcome us.

We pray that we may not enter into temptation.[129] Or however, that no temptation may take us, but such as is common to men, and let the faithful God never suffer us to be tempted above what we are able, but with the temptation make way for us to escape.[130]

Put upon us the whole armour of God, that we may be able to stand against the wiles of the devil, to withstand in the evil day, and having done all to stand; let our loins be girt about with truth, put on us the breast-plate of righteousness, and let our feet be shod with the preparation of the gospel of peace. Give us the shield of faith, wherewith we may quench all the fiery darts of the wicked, and the helmet of salvation; and let the sword of the Spirit, which is the word of God, be always ready to us.[131]

Enable us to resist the devil,[132] as that he may fly from us; to resist him stedfast in the faith.[133] And the God of peace tread Satan under our feet, and do it shortly.[134]

4.2. We must pray for grace to furnish us for every good thought, word, and work; that we may not only be kept from sin, but may be in every thing as we should be, and do as we should do.

Let Christ be made of God to us, not only righteousness, but wisdom, sanctification, and redemption.[135]

Let us be planted together in the likeness of Christ's death and resurrection, that as he was raised from the dead by the glory of the Father, so we also may walk in newness of life.[136]

4.2.1. That the work of grace may be wrought there where it is not yet begun.

Lord, teach transgressors thy ways, and let sinners be converted unto thee;[137] and let the disobedient be turned to the wisdom of the just, and make ready a people prepared for the Lord.[138]

Let those be quickened that are yet dead in trespasses and sins;[139] Say unto them, Live; yea, say unto them, Live; and the time shall be a time of love.[140]

Open their eyes, and turn them from darkness to light, and from the power of Satan unto God, that they may receive forgiveness of sins, and an inheritance among them who are sanctified.[141]

By the blood of the covenant send forth the prisoners out of the pit, in which is no water, that we may turn to the strong-hold, as prisoners of hope.[142] Let the word of God prevail to the pulling down of strong-holds, and the casting down of the imaginations, and every high thing that exalteth itself against the knowledge of God, and let every thought be brought in obedience to Christ.[143]

4.2.2 That where it is begun it may be carried on, and at length perfected, and the foundation that is well laid may be happily built upon.

Fulfill in us all the good pleasure of thy goodness, and the work of faith with power.[144]

Let the God that has begun a good work in us, perform it unto the day of Christ.[145]

Perfect, O God, that which concerns us: Thy mercy, O Lord, endures for ever; forsake not the work of thine own hands.[146]

Lord, let thy grace be sufficient for us, and let thy strength be made perfect in weakness, that where we are weak, there we may be strong,[147] strong in the Lord, and the power of his might.[148]

4.3. More particularly we must pray for grace.

4.3.1. To teach and instruct us, and make us knowing and intelligent in the things of God.

Give us so to cry after knowledge, and to lift up our voice for understanding, to seek for it as silver, and to search for it as for hid treasure, that we may understand the fear of the Lord, and find the knowledge of God.[149]

Give us all to know thee, from the least even to the greatest,[150] and to follow on to know thee;[151] and so to know thee, the only true God, and Jesus Christ, whom thou hast sent, as may be life eternal to us.[152]

Give us the spirit of wisdom and revelation in the knowledge of Christ, that the eyes of our understanding being enlightened, we may know what is the hope of his calling, and what the riches of the glory of his inheritance in the saints, and may experience what is the exceeding greatness of his power to us-ward who believe according to the working of his mighty power.[153]

Open thou our eyes, that we may see the wondrous things of thy law and gospel.[154]

Give us to know the certainty of those things wherein we have been instructed;[155] and let our knowledge grow up to all riches of the full assurance of understanding, to the acknowledgment of the mystery of God, even of the Father and of Christ.

Deal with thy servants according to thy mercy, and teach us thy statutes; we are thy servants, give us understanding that we may know thy testimonies. Let our cry come before thee, O Lord; give us understanding, according to thy word,[156] that good understanding which they have that do thy commandments, whose praise endureth for ever.[157]

4.3.2. To lead us into, and keep us in the way of truth; and if in any thing we be in an error to rectify our mistake.

Let the Spirit of truth guide us unto all truth,[158] and cause us to understand wherein we have erred.[159]

That which we see not teach thou us,[160] and enable us to prove all things, as to hold fast that which is good.[161]

Lord, grant that we may not be as children, tossed to and fro, and carried about with every wind of doctrine by the slight of men, but speaking the truth in love, may grow up into Christ in all things, who is the head.[162]

Lord give us so to do thy will, as that we may know of the doctrine whether it be of God;[163] and so to know the truth, as that the truth may make us free, may make us free indeed.[164]

Enable us, we pray thee, to hold fast the form of sound words, which we have heard in faith and love which is in Christ Jesus,[165] and to continue in the things which we have learned and been assured of.[166]

4.3.3. To help our memories, that the truths of God may be ready to us, whenever we have occasion to use them.

Lord, let thy spirit teach us all things, and bring all things to our remembrance, whatsoever thou hast said unto us;[167] that the word of Christ may dwell richly in us in all wisdom and spiritual understanding.[168]

Lord, grant that we may give a more earnest heed to the things which we have heard, lest at any time we let them slip, and may keep in memory what hath been preached to us, and may not believe in vain.[169]

Lord, make us ready and mighty in the scriptures, that we may be perfect, thoroughly furnished unto all good works,[170] and being well instructed into the kingdom of heaven, may, as the good householder, bring out of our treasure things new and old.[171]

4.3.4. To direct our consciences, to shew us the way of our duty, and to make us wise, knowing, judicious Christians.

Lord, give us a wise and understanding heart,[172] that wisdom which in all cases is profitable to direct;[173] that wisdom of the prudent which is to understand his way.[174]

This we pray, that our love may abound yet more and more in knowledge, and in all judgment, that we may discern things that differ, and may approve things that are excellent; that we may be sincere, and without offence unto the day of Christ, and may be filled with the fruits of righteousness, which are by Jesus Christ unto the glory and praise of God.[175]

O that we may be filled with the knowledge of thy will in all wisdom and spiritual understanding; that we may walk worthy of God unto all-pleasing, being fruitful in every good work, and increasing in the knowledge of God.[176]

Teach us thy way, O God, and lead us in a plain path, because of our observers.[177]

When we know not what to do, our eyes are up unto thee:[178] Then let us hear the Lord behind us, saying, this is the way, walk in it, that we turn not to the right hand nor to the left.[179]

Order our steps in thy word, and let no iniquity have dominion over us.[180]

4.3.5. To sanctify our nature, to plant in us all holy principles and dispositions, and to increase every grace in us.

The very God of peace sanctify us wholly; and we pray God, our whole spirit, and soul, and body, may be preserved blameless unto the coming of our Lord Jesus Christ; for faithful is he that calleth, who also will do it.[181]

Create in us a clean heart, O God, and renew a right spirit within us: and cast us not away from thy presence, and take not thy holy Spirit away from us; restore unto us the joy of thy salvation, and uphold us with thy free Spirit.[182]

Write thy law in our hearts, and put it in our inward part,[183] that we may be the epistles of Christ, written by the Spirit of the living God, not in tables of stone, but in fleshly tables of the heart,[184] that the law of our God being in our heart, none of our steps may slide,[185] and we may delight to do thy will, O God,[186] may delight in the law of God after the inward man.[187]

O that we may obey from the heart that form of doctrine into which we desire to be delivered,[188] as into a mould, that our whole souls may be leavened by it;[189] and that we may not be conformed to this world, but transformed by the renewing of our mind;[190] may not fashion ourselves after our former lusts in our ignorance,[191] but as obedient children, may be holy in all manner of conversation, as he who hath called us is holy.[192]

4.3.5.1. We must pray for faith.

Unto us (Lord) let it be given to believe;[193] for the faith by which we are saved is not of ourselves, it is the gift of God.[194]

Lord, increase our faith[y], and perfect what is lacking in it,[195] that we may be strong in faith, giving glory to God.[196]

Lord, give us so to be crucified with Christ, as that the life we may live in the flesh, we may live by the faith of the Son of God, who loved us, and gave himself for us;[197] and so to bear about with us continually the dying of the Lord Jesus, as that the life also of Jesus may be manifested in our mortal bodies.[198]

As we have received Christ Jesus, the Lord enable us so to walk in him, rooted and built up in him, and established in the faith as we have been taught, abounding therein with thanksgiving.[199]

Let every word of thine profit us,[200] being mixed with faith, by which we receive thy testimony, and set to our seal that God is true.[201]

We beseech thee work in us that faith which is the substance of things hoped for, and the evidence of things not seen,[202] by which we may look above the things that are seen, that are temporal, and may look at the things that are not seen, that are eternal.[203]

Enable us by faith to set the Lord always before us,[204] and to have our eyes ever towards him,[205] that we may act in every thing, as seeing him that is invisible, and having a respect to the recompense of reward.[206]

Let our hearts be purified by faith,[207] and let it be our victory overcoming the world.[208] And let us be kept from fainting, by believing that we shall see the goodness of the Lord in the land of the living.[209]

4.3.5.2. We must pray for the fear of God.

Lord, work in us that fear of thee, which is the beginning of wisdom,[210] which is the instruction of wisdom,[211] and which is a fountain of life, to depart from the snares of death.[212]

Unite our hearts to fear thy name,[213] that we may keep thy commandment, which is the whole duty of man.[214]

O put thy fear into our hearts, that we may never depart from thee.[215] Let us all be devoted to thy fear:[216] And let us be in the fear of the Lord every day, and all the day long.[217]

4.3.5.3. We must pray that the love of God and Christ may be rooted in us, and in order thereunto, that the love of the world may be rooted out of us.

Give us grace, we beseech thee, to love thee the Lord our God, with all our heart, and soul, and mind, and might, which is the first and great commandment;[218] to set our love upon thee, and to delight ourselves always in thee;[219] and therein we shall have the desire of our hearts.[220]

Circumcise our hearts to love the Lord our God with all our heart, and with all our soul, that we may live.[221]

O that the love of God may be shed abroad in our hearts by the Holy Ghost.[222]

O that Jesus Christ may be very precious to us, as he is to all that believe,[223] that he may be in our account the chiefest of ten thousands, and altogether lovely; and that he may be our beloved and our friend:[224] That though we have not seen him yet we may love him; and though we now see him not, yet believing we may rejoice with joy unspeakable, and full of glory.[225]

Let the love of Christ to us constrain us to live, not to ourselves, but to him that died for us and rose again.[226] And, Lord, grant that we may not love the world, nor the things that are in the world, because if any man love the world, the love of the Father is not in him;[227] that we may set our affections on things above, and not on things that are on the earth.[228]

4.3.5.4. We must pray that our consciences may be always tender, and that we may live a life of repentance.

Lord, take away the stony heart out of our flesh, and give us a heart of flesh.[229]

Make us afraid of all appearances of evil,[230] and careful not to give Satan advantage against us, as being not ignorant of his devices.[231]

Lord, give us the happiness which they have that fear always, that when we think we stand, we may take heed lest we fall.[232]

4.3.5.5. We must pray to God to work in us charity and brotherly love.

Lord, put upon us that charity which is the bond of perfectness,[233] that we may keep the unity of the Spirit in the bond of peace,[234] and may live in love of peace, that the God of love and peace may be with us.[235]

Lord, give us to love our neighbour as ourselves, with that love which is the fulfilling of the law,[236] to love one another with a pure heart fervently,[237] that hereby all men may know that we are Christ's disciples.[238]

And as we are taught of God to love one another, give us to abound therein more and more,[239] and as we have an opportunity, to do good to all men,[240] and as much as in us lies to live peaceably with all men,[241] always following after the things which make for peace,[242] and things wherewith one may edify another.[243]

Lord, make us able to love our enemies, to bless them that curse us, and to pray for them that despitefully use us, and to do good to them that hate us,[244] forbearing one another, and forgiving one another in love, as Christ forgave us.[245]

4.3.5.6. *We must pray for the grace of self-denial.*

Lord, give us grace to deny ourselves, to take up our cross daily, and to follow Christ,[246] to keep under the body, and bring it into subjection.[247]

Lord, keep us from being lovers of our ownselves,[248] from being wise in our own conceit, and leaning to our own understanding.[249]

Lord, give us to seek not our own only, but every one his brother's welfare.[250]

And grant that none of us may live to ourselves, or die to ourselves, but whether we live or die we may be the Lord's, and may live and die to him.[251]

4.3.5.7. *We must pray for humility and meekness.*

Lord, give us all to learn of Christ to be meek and lowly in heart, that we may find rest to our souls;[252] and that herein the same mind be in us that was also in Christ Jesus.[253]

Lord, hide pride from us, and clothe us with humility,[254] and put upon us the ornament of a meek and quiet spirit, which in thy sight is of great price.[255]

Lord, give us grace to walk worthy of the vocation wherewith we are called, with all lowliness and meekness, with long-suffering, forbearing one another in love.[256]

Let anger never rest in our bosoms,[257] nor the sun ever go down upon our wrath;[258] but enable us to shew all meekness towards all men, because we ourselves also were sometimes foolish and disobedient.[259]

Let us be clothed as becomes the elect of God, holy and beloved, with bowels of mercies, kindness, humbleness of mind, meekness, and long-suffering,[260] that being merciful, as our Father which is in heaven is merciful,[261] we may be perfect as he is perfect.[262]

4.3.5.8. *We must pray for the graces of contentment and patience, and a holy indifferency to all the things of sense and time.*

Lord, teach us whatsoever state we are in, therewith to be content; let us know how to be abased, and how to abound; every where, and in all things, let us be instructed both to be full and to be hungry, both to abound and to suffer need.[263] And let godliness with contentment be great gain to us,[264] and a little with the fear of the Lord and quietness, is better than a great treasure and trouble therewith.[265]

Lord, grant that our conversation may be without covetousness, and we may always be content with such things as we have;[266] still saying, The will of the Lord be done.[267]

Enable us in our patience to possess our own souls;[268] and let patience always have its perfect work, that we may be perfect and entire, wanting nothing.[269]

Lord, give us grace to weep as though we wept not, and to rejoice as though we rejoiced not, and to possess as though we possessed not, and to use the world as not abusing it, because the time is short, and the fashion of this world passeth away.[270]

4.3.5.9. We must pray for the grace of hope; a hope in God and Christ, and a hope of eternal life.

Let patience work experience in us, and experience hope, such a hope as maketh not ashamed.[271] Through patience and comfort of the scriptures,[272] let us have hope, and be saved by hope.[273]

Let the God of Jacob be our help, and our hope always be in the Lord our God.[274]

Let us be begotten again to a lively hope by the resurrection of Jesus Christ,[275] and let that hope be to us as an anchor of the soul, sure and stedfast, entering into that within the veil, whither the forerunner is for us entered.[276]

Let us have Christ in us the hope of glory, and never be moved away from that hope of the gospel;[277] but enable us to give diligence unto the full assurance of hope unto the end.[278]

4.3.5.10. We must pray for grace to preserve us from sin, and all appearances of it, and approaches towards it.

Now we pray to God that we may do no evil,[279] but may be blameless and harmless, as the children of God, without rebuke, in the midst of a crooked and perverse generation.[280]

Turn away our eyes from beholding vanity, and quicken thou us in thy way:[281] Remove from us the way of lying, and grant us thy law graciously.[282]

Incline not our hearts to any evil thing, to practise wicked works with them that work iniquity, and let us not eat of their dainties.[283]

O cleanse us from our secret faults, keep back thy servant also from presumptuous sins: let not them have dominion over us, but let us be upright, and innocent from the great trangressions:[284] and grant that hereby we may prove ourselves upright before thee, by keeping ourselves from our own iniquity.[285]

Let thy word be hid in our hearts, that we may not sin against thee,[286] and thy grace be at all times sufficient for us, ready to us, and mighty in us,[287] and never give us up to our own heart's lust, to walk in our own counsels.[288]

Enable us to walk circumspectly, not as fools, but as wise,[289] so circumspectly, that we may cut off occasion from them which desire occasion[290] to blaspheme that worthy name by which we are called,[291] and with well-doing may put to silence the ignorance of foolish men,[292] and may adorn the doctrine of God our Saviour in all things.[293]

4.4. We must pray for grace to enable us both to govern our tongues well, and to use them well.

Lord, enable us to take heed to our ways, that we offend not with our tongue, and to keep our mouth as it were with a bridle,[294] that it may not be hasty to utter any thing.[295]

Set a watch, O Lord, before our mouth, keep the door of our lips,[296] that we may not offend in word.[297]

Let our speech be always with grace, seasoned with salt,[298] and enable us always out of the good treasure of our heart to bring forth good things.[299] Let our mouth speak wisdom, and our tongue talk judgment;[300] and let not thy words depart out of our mouth, nor out of the mouth of our seed, or our seed's seed, from henceforth and for ever.[301]

Enable us always to open our mouth with wisdom, and let the law of kindness be in our tongue:[302] Give us to know what is acceptable,[303] that our tongue may be as choice silver, and our lips may feed many.[304]

4.5. We must pray for grace to direct and quicken us to, and to strengthen and assist us in our duty, in the whole course of our conversation.

Let the grace of God, which hath appeared to us, and to all men, bringing salvation, effectually teach us to deny all ungodliness and worldly fleshly lusts, and to live soberly, righteously, and godly in this present world, looking for the blessed hope, and the glorious appearing to the great God, and our Saviour Jesus Christ, who gave himself for us, that he might redeem us from all iniquity, and purify unto himself a peculiar people, zealous of good works.[305]

4.5.1. That we may be prudent and discreet in our duty.

Thou hast said, If any man lack wisdom, he must ask it of God, who gives to all men liberally, and upbraideth not, and it shall be given him.[306] Lord, we want wisdom, make us wise as serpents, and harmless as doves,[307] that wisdom may make our face to shine,[308] and may be better to us than weapons of war.[309]

Enable us to walk in wisdom towards them that are without, redeeming the time.[310]

Give us to order all our affairs with discretion, and to behave ourselves wisely in a perfect way, with a perfect heart.[311]

4.5.2. That we may be honest and sincere in our duty.

Let our wisdom be not that from beneath, which is earthly, sensual, devilish; but wisdom from above, which is first pure, than peaceable, gentle, and easy to be intreated, full of mercy and good fruits, without partiality, and without hypocrisy.[312]

O that we may always have our conversation in the world, in simplicity and godly sincerity, not with fleshly wisdom, but by the grace of God.[313]

Lord, uphold us in our integrity, and set us before thy face for ever,[314] and let integrity and uprightness preserve us, for we wait on thee.[315]

Let our hearts be found in thy statutes, that we be not ashamed,[316] and let our eye be single, that our whole body may be full of light.[317]

4.5.3. That we may be active and diligent in our duty.

Lord, quicken us to work the works of him that sent us while it is day, because the night comes wherein no man can work;[318] and what good our hands find to do, to do it with all our might, because there is no work or knowledge in the grave whither we are going.[319]

Lord, grant that we may never be slothful in any good business, but fervent in spirit, serving the Lord;[320] stedfast and unmoveable, always abounding in the work of the Lord, forasmuch as we know that our labour is not in vain in the Lord.[321]

Lord, make us zealously affected in every good work,[322] and what we do, enable us to do it heartily, as unto the Lord, and not unto men.[323]

Lord, enable us to do the work of every day in its day, according as the duty of the day requires,[324] redeeming the time, because the days are evil,[325] that when our Lord comes he may find us so doing.[326]

4.5.4. That we may be resolute and courageous in our duty, as those that know that though we may be losers for Christ, we shall not be losers by him in the end.

Lord, teach us to endure hardness, as good soldiers of Jesus Christ,[327] that we may not fear the reproach of men,[328] or their revilings, nor be ashamed of Christ, or of his words,[329] knowing whom we have believed, even one who is able to keep what we have committed to him against that day.[330]

Though bonds and afflictions should abide us, Lord, grant that none of these things may move us, and that we may not count life itself dear to us, so we may finish our course with joy.[331]

Enable us in all things to approve ourselves to God, and then to pass by honour and dishonour, by evil report and good report, clad with the armour of righteousness on the right hand, and on the left,[332] as those that account it a very small thing to be judged of man's judgment, for he that judgeth us is the Lord.[333]

4.5.5. *That we may be pleasant and cheerful in our duty.*

Lord, enable us to rejoice evermore,[334] to rejoice in the Lord always,[335] because he hath again said unto us, Rejoice; that we may go on our way rejoicing, may eat our bread with joy, and drink our wine with a merry heart, as we shall have reason to do if God now accepteth our works.[336]

Give us grace to serve thee the Lord our God with joyfulness and gladness of heart in the abundance of all things;[337] and to sing in the ways of the Lord, because great is the glory of our God.[338]

Let us have that cheerfulness of heart which doth good like a medicine,[339] and deliver us from that heaviness which maketh the heart stoop,[340] and that sorrow of the world which worketh death.[341]

4.5.6. *That we may do the duty of every condition of life, every event of providence, and every relation wherein we stand.*

Lord, enable us in a day of prosperity to be joyful, and in a day of adversity to consider, because God hath set the one over against the other,[342] to add to our knowledge temperance, and to temperance patience.[343]

Give us grace to abide with thee in the calling wherein we are called:[344] and in all our ways to acknowledge thee, and be thou pleased to direct our steps.[345]

Let those that are called, being servants, be the Lord's freemen; and those that are called, being free, be Christ's servants.[346]

Let all in every relation dwell together in unity, that it may be as the dew of Hermon, and as the dew that descends upon the mountains of Zion.[347] O that we may dwell together as joint-heirs of the grace of life, that our prayers may not be hindered.[348]

Give us grace to honour all men, to love the brotherhood, to fear God,[349] and to be subject to the higher powers, not only for wrath, but also for conscience sake.[350]

4.5.7. *That we may be universally conscientious.*

O that we may stand perfect and complete in all the will of God.[351]

O that our ways were directed to keep thy commandments. And then shall we not be ashamed when we have respect to them all.[352]

Teach us, O Lord, the way of thy statutes, and we shall keep it unto the end. Give us understanding, and we shall keep thy law, yea, we shall observe it with our whole heart. Make us to go in the path of thy commandments, for therein do we delight. Incline our hearts unto thy testimonies, and not to covetousness.[353]

Grant us, we pray thee, according to the riches of thy glory, that we may be strengthened with all might by the Spirit in the inward man: That Christ may dwell in our hearts by faith, and that we being rooted and grounded in love, may be able to comprehend with all saints, what is the breadth, and length, and depth, and height, and may know the love of Christ, which passeth knowledge, and be filled with a divine fulness,[354] and may partake of a divine nature.

And let the love of Christ constrain us to live not to ourselves, but to him that died for us and rose again.[355]

4.6. We must pray for grace to make us wiser and better every day than another.

Lord, give us to increase with the increases of God;[356] to grow in grace and in the knowledge of our Lord and Saviour Jesus Christ;[357] to hold on our way, and having clean hands, to grow stronger and stronger.[358]

Let our path be as the shining light, which shines more and more unto the perfect day.[359]

We have not yet attained, nor are we already perfect; Lord, grant that therefore, forgetting the things that are behind, we may reach forth to those things that are before, for the prize of the high calling of God in Christ Jesus.[360]

Be thou as the dew unto us, that we may grow as the lily, and cast forth our roots as Lebanon; that our branches may spread, and our beauty be as the olive-tree.[361] And let the Sun of righteousness arise upon us with healing under his wings, that we may go forth and grow up as calves of the stall.[362]

4.7. We must pray for the effectual support and comfort under all the crosses and afflictions that we meet with in this world.

We know that we are born to trouble as the sparks fly upward! but in six troubles be thou pleased to deliver us, and in seven let no evil touch us.[363]

Let the eternal God be our refuge, and underneath be the everlasting arms,[364] that the spirit thou hast made may not fail before thee, nor the soul that thou hast redeemed.[365]

Let us be strengthened with all might, according to thy glorious power, unto all patience and long-suffering with joyfulness.[366]

Let thy statutes be our songs in the house of our pilgrimage; and let thy testimonies, which we have taken as a heritage for ever, be always the rejoicing of our hearts.[367]

When we are troubled on every side, yet let us not be distressed, and when we are perplexed, let us not be in despair,[368] but as sorrowful, and yet always rejoicing; as having nothing, and yet possessing all things.[369]

4.8. We must pray for grace to preserve us to the end, and to fit us for whatever lies before us betwixt this and the grave.

Lord, deliver us from every evil work, and preserve us to thy heavenly kingdom,[370] being kept from falling, that we may be presented faultless, at the coming of thy glory with exceeding joy.[371]

Lord, make us to increase and abound in love, one towards another, and towards all men, that our hearts may be established unblameable in holiness, before God even our Father, at the coming of our Lord Jesus Christ with all his saints.[372]

If Satan desire to have us that he may sift us as wheat, yet let Christ's intercession prevail for us, that our faith fail not.[373]

Till we are taken out of the world, let us be kept from the evil, and sanctified through thy truth: thy word is truth.[374]

Build us up, we pray thee, in our most holy faith, and keep us in the love of God, looking for the mercy of our Lord Jesus Christ unto eternal life.[375]

Grant that we may continue to call upon thee as long as we live,[376] and till we die may never remove our integrity from us: and that our righteousness we may hold fast, and never let it go, and our hearts may not reproach us so long as we live.[377]

4.9. We must pray for grace to deliver us from death,[378] and to carry us well through our dying moments.

Lord, make us to know our end, and the measure of our days, what it is, that we may know and consider how frail we are; and that our days are as a hand-breadth, and that every man at his best state is altogether vanity,[379] and our days upon earth are as a shadow, and there is no abiding.[380]

Lord, teach us so to number our days, that we may apply our hearts unto wisdom,[381] and make us to consider our latter end.[382]

Lord, make us always ready, with our loins girded about, and our lights burning, because the Son of man comes in an hour that we think not.[383]

Keep us all the days of our appointed time, waiting till our change comes; and then shalt thou call, and we will answer.[384]

Bring us to our grave as a shock of corn in its season;[385] satisfy us with life, whether it be longer or shorter, and shew us thy salvation.[386]

And when we walk through the valley of the shadow of death, be thou with us, that we may fear no evil, let thy rod and thy staff comfort us.[387]

Let goodness and mercy follow us all the days of our life, and let us dwell in the house of the Lord for ever.[388] Mercy and truth be with us.[389]

Redeem our souls from the power of the grave, and receive us:[390] Guide us by thy counsel, and afterward receive us into glory.[391]

4.10. We must pray for grace to fit us for heaven, and that we may at length be put in possession of eternal life.

Lord, make us meet to partake of the inheritance of the saints in light;[408] let God himself work us to the self-same thing, and give us the earnest of the Spirit in our hearts.[392]

O that we may now have our conversation in heaven, that we may from thence with comfort look for the Saviour, the Lord Jesus, who shall change our vile bodies, that they may be fashioned like unto his glorious body.[393]

O that we may set our affections on things that are above, and that our life may be hid with Christ in God, that when Christ, who is our life, shall appear, we also may appear with him in glory;[394] that when he shall appear, we may be like him, may see him as he is,[395] may behold his face in righteousness, and when we awake may be satisfied with his likeness.[396]

When we fail, let us be received into everlasting habitations, in the city that hath habitations, whose builder and maker is God,[397] that we may be together for ever with the Lord, to see as we are seen, and know as we are known. And in the mean time help us to comfort ourselves and one another with these words;[398] and having this hope in us, to purify ourselves, even as Christ is pure.[399]

And now, our Lord Jesus Christ himself, and God even our Father, who hath loved us, and hath given us everlasting consolation and good hope through grace, comfort our hearts and stablish us in every good word and work.[400]

4.11. We must pray for the good things of life, with an humble submission to the will of God.

Lord, thou hast told us that godliness hath the promise of the life that now is, as well as of that which is to come;[401] and that if we seek first the kingdom of God and the righteousness thereof, other things shall be added to us;[402] and therefore we cast all our care about these things upon thee,[403] who carest for us; for our heavenly Father knows that we have need of all these things.[404]

4.11.1. We must pray to be preserved from the calamities to which we are exposed.

Thou, Lord, art our refuge and our fortress, and under thy wings will we trust, thy truth shall be our shield and buckler: Let us therefore not be afraid for the terror by night, nor for the arrow that flieth by day. Having made the Lord our refuge, and the Most High our habitation, let no evil befall us, nor any plague come high our dwelling.[405]

Let the Lord be our keeper, even he that keepeth Israel, and neither slumbers nor sleeps. Let the Lord be our shade on our right hand, that the sun may not smite us by day, nor the moon by night; let the Lord preserve us from all evil; the Lord preserve our souls; the Lord preserve our going out and coming in, from this time forth, and even for evermore.[406]

Lord, make a hedge about us, about our houses, and about all that we have round about;[407] and take sickness away from the midst of us.[408]

4.11.2. We must pray to be supplied with the comforts and supports we daily stand in need of.

O that the beauty of the Lord our God may be upon us; prosper thou the work of our hands upon us, yea, the work of our hands establish thou it:[409] Save now, we beseech thee, O Lord: O Lord, we beseech thee, send now prosperity.[410]

Let our sons be as plants grown up in their youth, and our daughters as corner stones polished after the similitude of a palace: Let our garners be full, affording all manner of store; and let there be no breaking in or going out, no complaining in our streets: Happy is the people that is in such a case, yea rather, happy is the people whose God is the Lord.[411]

Let us be blessed in the city, and blessed in the field, let our basket and our store be blessed, let us be blessed when we come in, and when we go out.[412] Let thy good providence so order all events concerning us, that they may be made to work for good to us, as thou hast promised they shall to all that love thee, and are called according to thy purpose.[413]

Give us to trust in the Lord, and do good, and then we shall dwell in the land, and verily we shall be fed; and be thou pleased to bring forth our righteousness as the light, and our judgment as the noonday.[414]

Let us be hid from the scourge of the tongue, and not be afraid of destruction when it cometh: let us be in league with the stones of the field, and let the beasts of the field be at peace with us; let us know that our tabernacle is in peace, and let us visit our habitation and not sin.[415]

And if God will be with us, and will keep us in the way that we go, during our pilgrimage in this world, and will give us bread to eat, and raiment to put on, so that we may come to our heavenly Father's house in peace, then the Lord shall be our God.[416]

4.12. We must plead the promises of God for the enforcing of all our petitions, put these promises in suit, and refer ourselves to them.

Lord, thou hast given us many exceeding great and precious promises,[417] which are all yea and amen in Christ.[418] Now be it unto thy servants according to the word which thou hast spoken.[419]

Give us to draw water with joy out of these wells of salvation,[420] to suck and be satisfied from those breasts of consolation;[421] and now, O Lord God, let the word which thou hast spoken concerning they servants be established for ever, and do as thou hast said.[422]

Deal with us according to the tenor of the everlasting covenant, which is well ordered in all things and sure, and which is all our salvation, and all our desire.[423]

Look upon us and be merciful to us, as thou usest to do unto those that love thy name,[424] and do more for us than we are able to ask or think,[425] and supply all our needs according to thy riches in glory by Christ Jesus.[426]

References

[1] Ezek. 36:37.
[2] John 6:6.
[3] Mark 11:24.
[4] Ps. 39:7-8.
[5] Ps. 38:9.
[6] Rom. 8:26-27.
[7] Matt. 6:7-8.
[8] John 16:23- 25.
[9] 1 John 5:14-15.
[10] Luke 18:13.
[11] Ps. 51:2-3, 7.
[12] Heb. 8:12.
[13] Matt. 18:32.
[14] Rom. 3:24.
[15] Acts 13:39.
[16] Ezek. 18:30.
[17] 2 Sam. 12:13.

[18] Rev. 2:11.
[19] Isa. 44:22.
[20] Ps. 143:2.
[21] Hosea 14:2-4.
[22] Isa. 1:18-19.
[23] Job 10:2.
[24] Job 33:24.
[25] Ps. 86:5, 15.
[26] Neh. 9:17.
[27] Ps. 103:9.
[28] Isa. 43:25-26.
[29] Numb. 14:17-19.
[30] Micah 7:18-19.
[31] Ps. 11:7.
[32] Exod. 34:7.
[33] Matt. 18:26.
[34] Isa 64:6.

[35] 1 Cor. 1:30.
[36] 2 Cor. 5:21.
[37] 1 John 2:1-2.
[38] Rom. 8:33-34.
[39] Heb. 12:24.
[40] Phil. 3:7-9.
[41] Jer. 23:6.
[42] Mark 9:24.
[43] Ps. 132:1.
[44] Ps. 20:3.
[45] Ps. 132:10.
[46] Heb 9:24.
[47] Rom 3:25-26.
[48] Rom. 5:11.
[49] Isa. 55:7.
[50] Dan. 9:9.
[51] Rom. 11:27.

52 Jer. 31:34.
53 Jer. 50:20.
54 Ezek. 33:15-16.
55 Luke 24:47.
56 Lev. 16:22.
57 Ps. 103:12.
58 Ps. 119:49.
59 Ps. 25:11.
60 Ps. 40:12-13.
61 Ps. 79:8-9.
62 Ps. 25:7.
63 Ps. 32:1-2.
64 Eph. 1:7-8.
65 Rom. 8:1.
66 Luke 7:47, 50.
67 Isa. 33:24.
68 Rom. 5:1-2.
69 Jer. 17:17.
70 Eph. 2:13.
71 Eph. 2:14-19.
72 Isa. 27:4-5.
73 Job 22:21.
74 Jer. 17:14.
75 Ps. 85:5-7.
76 Heb. 8:10.
77 Ps. 110:3.
78 Luke 15:19.
79 Jer. 3:19.
80 Jer. 3:4.
81 Isa. 56:4.
82 Jer. 50:5.
83 Ezek. 20:37.
84 Ezek. 16:8.
85 Isa. 55:3.
86 Ps. 119:58.
87 Ps. 30:5.
88 Ps. 63:3.
89 Num. 6:25-26.
90 Ps. 106:4-5.
91 Ps. 67:1, 6.
92 Ps. 134:3.
93 Eph. 1:3.
94 1 Chron. 4:10.
95 Ps. 133:3.
96 1 Chron. 17:27.
97 Ps.24:5.
98 Gen. 27:38.
99 Gal. 3:14.
100 Gen. 32:26.
101 Ex. 33:15.
102 Heb 13:5.
103 Ps. 51:11.
104 Ps. 140:13.
105 Ps. 51:8.
106 Matt. 9:2.
107 Heb. 9:14.
108 Rom. 8:16-17.
109 Ps. 35:3.
110 2 Thess. 3:16.
111 John 14:27.
112 Isa. 32:17.
113 Ps. 85:8.
114 Isa. 57:18-19.
115 Luke 10:6.
116 Ps. 143:8.
117 1 Pet. 2:3.
118 Phil. 4:7.
119 Col. 3:15.
120 Rom. 15:13.
121 Heb. 4:16.
122 John 1:16.
123 Col. 1:19.
124 Rom. 6:14.
125 Gal. 5:16, 24.
126 Rom. 6:6, 12, 18.
127 Rom. 8:2.
128 Eph. 4:22, 24.
129 Gal. 6:14.
130 Matt. 26:41.
131 1 Cor. 10:13.
132 Eph. 6:12-17.
133 James 4:7.
134 1 Pet. 5:9.
135 Rom. 16:20.
136 1 Cor. 1:30.
137 Rom. 6:4.
138 Ps. 51:13.
139 Luke 1:17.
140 Eph. 2:1.
141 Ezek. 16:6, 8.
142 Acts 26:18.
143 Zech. 9:11-12.
144 2 Cor. 10:5.
145 2 Thes. 1:11.
146 Phil. 1:6.
147 Ps. 138:8.
148 2 Cor. 12:9-10.
149 Eph. 6:10.
150 Prov. 2:3-5.
151 Heb 8:11.
152 Hosea 6:3.
153 John 17:3.
154 Eph. 1:17-19.
155 Ps. 119:18.
156 Luke 1:4.
157 Ps. 119:124-125, 169.
158 Ps. 111:10.
159 John 16:13.
160 Job 6:24.
161 Job 34:32.
162 I Thes. 5:21.
163 Eph. 4:14-15.
164 John 7:17.
165 John 8:32, 36.
166 2 Tim. 1:13.
167 2 Tim. 3:14.
168 John 14:26.
169 Col. 3:16.
170 Heb. 2:1.
171 2 Tim. 3:17.
172 Matt. 13:52.
173 1 Kings 3:9.
174 Eccles. 10:10.
175 Prov. 14:8.
176 Phil. 1:9-11.
177 Col. 1:9-10.
178 Ps. 27:11.
179 2 Chron. 20:12.
180 Isa. 30:21.
181 Ps. 119:133.
182 1 Thess. 5:23-24.
183 Ps. 51:10-12.
184 Heb. 8:10.
185 2 Cor. 3:3.
186 Ps. 37:31.
187 Ps. 40:8.
188 Rom. 7:22.
189 Rom. 6:17.
190 Matt. 13:33.
191 Rom. 12:2.
192 1 Pet. 1:14.
193 1 Pet. 1:15.
194 John 3:27.
195 Eph. 2:8.

196 Luke 17:5.
197 1 Thess. 3:10.
198 Rom. 4:20.
199 Gal. 2:20.
200 2 Cor. 4:10.
201 Col. 2:6-7.
202 Heb. 4:2.
203 John 3:33.
204 Heb. 11:1.
205 2 Cor. 4:18.
206 Ps. 16:8.
207 Ps. 25:15.
208 Heb. 11:26-27.
209 Acts 15:9.
210 1 John 5:4.
211 Ps. 27:13.
212 Prov. 1:7.
213 Prov. 15:33.
214 Prov. 14:27.
215 Ps. 86:11.
216 Eccles. 12:13.
217 Jer. 32:40.
218 Ps. 119:38.
219 Prov. 23:17.
220 Matt. 22:37-38.
221 Ps. 91:14.
222 Ps. 37:4.
223 Deut. 30:6.
224 Rom. 5:5.
225 1 Pet. 2:7.
226 Dan. 5:10, 16.
227 1 Pet. 1:7-8.
228 2 Cor. 5:14.
229 1 John 2:15.
230 Col. 3:2.
231 Ezek. 11:19.
232 1 Thess. 5:22.
233 2 Cor. 2:11.
234 1 Cor. 10:12.
235 Col. 3:14.
236 Eph. 4:3.
237 2 Cor. 13:11.
238 Rom. 13:9-10.
239 1 Pet. 1:22.
240 John 13:35.
241 1 Thess. 4:9-10.
242 Gal. 6:10.
243 Rom. 12:18.
244 Rom. 14:19.
245 Matt. 5:44.
246 Col. 3:13.
247 Matt. 16:24.
248 1 Cor. 9:27.
249 2 Tim. 3:2.
250 Prov. 3:5, 7.
251 1 Cor. 10:24.
252 Rom. 14:6-7.
253 Matt. 11:29.
254 Phil. 2:5.
255 Job 33:17.
256 1 Pet. 3:4-5.
257 Eph. 4:1-2.
258 Eccles. 7:9.
259 Eph. 4:26.
260 Titus 3:2-3.
261 Col. 3:12.
262 Luke 6:36.
263 Matt. 5:48.
264 Phil. 4:11-12.
265 1 Tim. 6:6.
266 Prov. 15:16.
267 Heb. 13:5.
268 Acts 21:14.
269 Luke 21:19.
270 James 1:4.
271 1 Cor. 7:29-31.
272 Rom. 5:4-5.
273 Rom. 15:4.
274 Rom. 8:24.
275 Ps. 146:5.
276 1 Pet. 1:3.
277 Heb. 6:19-20.
278 Col. 1:23, 27.
279 Heb. 6:11.
280 2 Cor. 13:7.
281 Phil. 2:15.
282 Ps. 119:37.
283 Ps. 119:29.
284 Ps. 141:4.
285 Ps. 19:12-13.
286 Ps. 18:23.
287 Ps. 119:11.
288 2 Cor. 12:9.
289 Jer. 7:24.
290 Eph. 5:15.
291 2 Cor. 11:12.
292 James 2:7.
293 1 Pet. 2:15.
294 Titus 2:10.
295 Ps. 39:1.
296 Eccles. 5:2.
297 Ps. 141:3.
298 James 3:2.
299 Col. 4:6.
300 Matt. 12:35.
301 Ps. 37:30.
302 Isa. 59:21.
303 Prov. 31:26.
304 Prov. 10:32.
305 Prov. 10:21.
306 Titus 2:11-14.
307 James 1:5.
308 Matt. 10:16.
309 Eccles. 8:1.
310 Eccles. 9:18.
311 Col. 4:5.
312 Ps. 101:2.
313 James 3:15, 17.
314 2 Cor. 1:12.
315 Ps. 41:10.
316 Ps. 25:21.
317 Ps. 119:80.
318 Matt. 6:22.
319 John 9:4.
320 Eccles. 9:10.
321 Rom. 12:11.
322 1 Cor. 15:58.
323 Gal. 4:18.
324 Col. 3:23.
325 Ezra 3:4.
326 Eph. 5:16.
327 Luke 12:43.
328 2 Tim. 2:3.
329 Isa. 51:7.
330 Mark 8:38.
331 2 Tim. 1:12.
332 Acts. 20:23-24.
333 2 Cor. 6:4, 7-8.
334 1 Cor. 4:3-4.
335 1 Thess. 5:16.
336 Phil. 4:4.
337 Eccles. 9:7.
338 Deut. 28:47.
339 Ps. 138:5.

340 Prov. 17:22.
341 Prov. 12:25.
342 2 Cor. 7:10.
343 Eccles. 7:14.
344 2 Peter 1:6.
345 1 Cor. 7:24.
346 Prov. 3:6.
347 1 Cor. 7:22.
348 Ps. 133:1, 3.
349 1 Pet. 3:7.
350 1 Peter 2:17.
351 Rom. 13:1, 5.
352 Col. 4:12.
353 Ps. 119:5-6.
354 Ps. 119:33-36.
355 Eph. 3:16-20.
356 2 Cor. 5:14-15.
357 Col. 2:19.
358 2 Pet. 3:18.
359 Job 17:9.
360 Prov. 4:18.
361 Phil. 3:12-14.
362 Hosea 14:5-6.
363 Mal. 4:2.
364 Job 5:7, 19.
365 Deut. 33:27.
366 Isa. 57:16.
367 Col. 1:11.
368 Ps. 119:54, 111.
369 2 Cor. 4:8.
370 2 Cor. 6:10.
371 2 Tim 4:18.
372 Jude 24.
373 1 Thess. 3:13.
374 Luke 22:31-32.
375 John 17:15, 17.
376 Jude 20-21.
377 Ps. 116: 2.
378 Job 27:5-6.
379 Ps. 39:4-5.
380 Job 8:9.
381 Ps. 90:12.
382 Deut. 32:29.
383 Luke 12:35, 40.
384 Job 14:14-15.
385 Job 5:26.
386 Ps. 91:16.
387 Ps. 23:4.
388 Ps. 23:6.
389 2 Sam. 15:20.
390 Ps. 49:15.
391 Ps. 73:24.
392 Col. 1:12.
393 2 Cor. 5:5.
394 Phil. 3:20-21.
395 Col. 3:2-4.
396 1 John 3:2.
397 Ps. 17:15.
398 Heb. 11:10.
399 1 Thess. 4:17-18.
400 1 John 3:3.
401 2 Thess. 2:16-17.
402 I Tim. 4:8.
403 Matt. 6:33.
404 1 Peter 5:7.
405 Matt. 6:32.
406 Ps. 91:2, 4-5, 9-10.
407 Ps. 121:4-8.
408 Job 1:10.
409 Exod. 23:25.
410 Ps. 90:17.
411 Ps. 118:25.
412 Ps. 144:12-15.
413 Deut. 28:3, 5, 6.
414 Rom. 8:28.
415 Ps. 37:3, 6.
416 Job 5:21, 23-24.
417 Gen. 28:20-21.
418 2 Pet. 1:4.
419 2 Cor. 1:20.
420 Luke 1:38.
421 Isa. 12:3.
422 Isa. 66:11.
423 2 Sam. 7:25.
424 2 Sam. 23:5.
425 Ps. 119:132.
426 Eph. 3:20.

CHAPTER 4

**Of the fourth part of PRAYER
which is Thanksgivings for the mercies we have received
from God, and the many Favours of his we are interested
in and have, and hope for Benefit by.**

Our errand at the throne of grace is not only to seek the favour of God, but to give unto him the glory due unto his name, and that not only by an awful adoration of his infinite perfections, but by a grateful acknowledgment of his goodness to us, which cannot indeed add any thing to his glory, but he is pleased to accept of it, and to reckon himself glorified by it, if it comes from a heart that is humbly sensible of its own unworthiness to receive any favour from God, that values the gifts, and loves the giver of them.

1. We must stir up ourselves to praise God with the consideration both of the reason and of the encouragement we have to praise him.

Unto thee, O God, do we give thanks, unto thee do we give thanks; for that thy name is near, thy wondrous works declare.[1]

Let our souls bless the Lord, and let all that is within us bless his holy name; yea let our souls bless the Lord, and not forget any of his benefits.[2]

We will praise the Lord, for it is good, it is pleasant; and praise is comely for the upright, yea, it is a good thing to give thanks unto the Lord,[3] and to sing praises unto thy name, O most High, and to show forth thy loving-kindness in the morning, and thy faithfulness every night.[4]

We will extol thee, our God O King, and will bless thy name for ever and ever: every day will we bless thee, and will praise thy name for ever and ever; we will abundantly utter the memory of thy great goodness, and sing of thy righteousness.[5]

We will sing unto the Lord a new song, and his praise in the congregation of saints; O let Israel rejoice in him that made him, let the children of Zion be joyful in their King: Let the saints be joyful in glory, and let the high-praises of God be in their hearts, and in their mouths.[6]

While we live we will bless the Lord, and will sing praise unto our God while we have any being,[7] and when we have no being on earth, we hope to have a being in heaven to be doing it better.

We are here through Jesus Christ to offer the sacrifice of praise to thee, which we desire to do continually, that is, the fruit of our lips, giving thanks to thy name.[8] And thou hast said that he that offers praise glorifies thee,[9] and that this also shall please the Lord better that an ox or bullock that hath horns or hoofs.[10]

We will mention the loving-kindness of the Lord, and the praises of the Lord, according to all that the Lord hath bestowed on us, and the great goodness towards the house of Israel, which he hath bestowed on them, according to his mercies, and according to the multitude of his loving-kindness.[11]

2. We must be particular in our thanksgivings to God,

2.1. For the discoveries which he hath made to us in his word of the goodness of his nature.

We give thanks unto the God of gods, unto the Lord of lords, for his mercy endures for ever.[12]

Thy goodness is thy glory,[13] and it is for that which all thy works do praise thee, and thy saints do bless thee.[14]

Thou art gracious and full of compassion, slow to anger, and of great mercy,[15] and hast told us, that thou dost not afflict willingly, or grieve the children of men,[16] but though thou cause grief, yet thou wilt have compassion according to the multitude of thy mercies.[17]

Thou takest pleasure in them that fear thee, in them that hope in thy mercy.[18]

2.2. For the many instances of his goodness.

2.2.1. The goodness of his providence relating to our bodies, and the life that now is; and this,

2.2.1.1. 1st, With reference to all the creatures, and the world of mankind in general.

Thou hast stretched out the heavens like a curtain,[19] and in them thou hast set a tabernacle for the sun, which is as a bridegroom coming out of his chamber, and rejoiceth as a strong man,[20] to shine on the evil, and on the good; and sendest rain on the just and on the unjust.[21]

When we consider the heavens, the work of thy fingers, the sun, the moon and the stars which thou hast ordained; Lord, what is man that thou thus visitest him?[22] For truly the light is sweet, and a pleasant thing it is for the eyes to behold the sun:[23] All the glory be to the Father of light,[24] who commandeth the morning, and causeth the day spring to know his place.[25]

Thou didst not leave thyself without witness among the heathen in that thou didst good, and gavest them rain from heaven, and fruitful seasons, filling their hearts with food and gladness.[26]

Thou coverest the heavens with clouds, and preparest rain for the earth, and makest grass to grow upon the mountains: Thou givest to the beast his food, and to the young ravens which cry.[27]

Thou causest it to rain on the wilderness, where there is no man, to satisfy the desolate and waste ground.[28]

Thou visitest the earth, and waterest it, thou greatly enrichest it with the river of God, which is full of water; thou preparest them corn, when thou hast so provided for it: Thou waterest the ridges thereof abundantly, thou settlest the furrows thereof; thou makest it soft with showers, thou blessest the springing thereof: thou crownest the year with thy goodness, and thy paths drop fatness.[29]

Thou sendest the springs into the valleys, which run among the hills; and they give drink to every beast of the field: and by them the fowls of the heavens have their habitation, which sing among the branches.[30]

Thou hast laid the foundation of the earth, that it should not be removed for ever, and settest bounds to the waters of the sea, that they turn not again to cover the earth.[31] Thou hast shut up the sea with doors, and broken up for it thy decreed place, saying, Hitherto shalt thou come, but no farther, here shall thy proud waves be stayed.[32] And thou hast made good what thou hast sworn, that the waters of Noah shall no more go over the earth.[33]

Thy covenant of the day and of the night is not broken,[34] but still thou givest the sun for a light by day, and the ordinances of the moon and of the stars for a light by night;[35] and art faithful to that covenant of providence, that while the earth remains, seed-time and harvest-time, cold and heat, summer and winter, day and night shall not cease.[36]

The heaven, even the heavens are thine, but the earth thou hast given to the children of men,[37] and thou hast put all things under their feet, and made them to have dominion over the works of thy hands;[38] so that the fear of man, and the dread of man is upon every beast of the earth, and upon the fowl of the air and into his hand they are delivered, because thou hadst a favour to him,[39] and thy delights were with the sons of men.[40]

Thou causest the grass to grow for the cattle, and herb for the service of man, that thou mayest bring forth food out of the earth; wine that makes glad the heart of man, and oil to make his face to shine, and bread which strengthens man's heart.[41]

Thou givest to all life and breath,[42] and all things on the earth, O Lord, are full of thy mercy.[43]

All the creatures wait upon thee, that thou mayest give them their meat in due season; that thou givest them they gather: thou openest thy hand, they are filled with good; Thou sendest forth thy Spirit, they are created; thou renewest the face of the earth. This thy glory shall endure forever, and thou rejoicest in these works.[44]

It is through thy goodness, O Lord, that as one generation of mankind passeth away, another generation comes,[45] and that thou hast not blotted out the name of that corrupt and guilty race from under heaven.[46]

2.2.1.2. 2ndly, With reference to us in particular.

2.2.1.2.1. We must give thanks that he has made us reasonable creatures, capable of knowing, loving, serving, and enjoying him, and that he hath not made us like the beasts that perish.

We will praise thee, for we are fearfully and wonderfully made, and that our souls, our nobler part, know right well;[47] for no man knows the things of a man, save the spirit of man, which is in him.[48]

Thou hast made us of that rank of beings which is a little lower than the angels, and is crowned with glory and honour;[49] for there is a spirit in man, and the inspiration of the Almighty giveth them understanding.[50] And the spirit of a man is the candle of the Lord.[51] Our bodies are capable of being the temples of the Holy Ghost, and our souls of having the Spirit of God dwell in them;[52] we therefore glorify thee with our bodies, and with our spirits, which are thine.[53]

Thou, Lord, hast formed us for thyself, that we might shew forth thy praise.[54]

2.2.1.2.2. We must give thanks for our preservation, that our lives are prolonged, and the use of our reason and understanding, our limbs and senses are continued to us.

It was owning to thy good providence that we died not from the womb, and did not give up the ghost when we came out of the belly, that the knees prevented us, and the breast that we should suck.[55]

Though we were called transgressors from the womb,[56] yet by thy power we have been born from the belly, and carried from the womb,[57] and thou holdest our souls in life, and sufferest not our foot to be moved.[58]

All our bones shall say, Lord, who is like unto thee![59] for thou keepest the bones, and not one of them is broken.[60]

We lay us down and sleep, for thou, Lord, makest us to dwell in safety.[61]

Thou hast given thine angels a charge concerning us, to keep us in all our ways, to bear us up in their hands, lest we dash our foot against a stone.[62] And they are all ministering spirits, sent forth to minister for the good of them that shall be heirs of salvation.[63]

2.2.1.2.3. For signal recoveries from danger by sickness or otherwise.

When perhaps there has been but a step between us and death,[64] and when we have received a sentence of death within ourselves,[65] and have been ready to say in the cutting off of our days, we should go to the gates of the grave, and were deprived of the residue of our years, yet thou hast in love to our souls delivered them from the pit of corruption, and cast all our sins behind thy back.[66]

When the sorrows of death have compassed us, and the pains of hell have got hold upon us, we have called upon the name of the Lord and have found that gracious is the Lord, and righteous, yea, our God is merciful; we have been brought low, and he hath helped us, and hath delivered our souls from death, our eyes from tears, and our feet from falling. We will therefore walk before the Lord in the land of the living.[67]

2.2.1.2.4. For the supports and comforts of this life, which have hitherto made the land of our pilgrimage easy and pleasant to us.

Blessed be the Lord, who daily loads us with his benefits, even the God of our salvation.[68]

Thou makest us to lie down in green pastures, thou feedest us beside the still waters: Thou preparest a table for us in the presence of our enemies, thou anointest our head, and our cup runs over.[69]

It may be we were sent forth without purse or scrip, but lacked we any thing? Nothing, Lord.[70]

The candle of God hath shined upon our head, and by his light we have walked through darkness, and the secret of God has been in our tabernacle.[71]

Thou hast given us all things richly to enjoy,[72] and into our hands hast brought plentifully.[73]

Many a time we have eaten and been filled, and have delighted ourselves in thy great goodness.[74]

When we remember all the ways which the Lord our God, hath led us for so many years in this wilderness,[75] we must here set up a stone and call it Ebenezer, for hitherto the Lord hath helped us.[76]

2.2.1.2.5. For success in our callings and affairs, comfort in relations, and comfortable places of abode.

It is God that girdeth us with strength, and maketh our way perfectly: that hath blessed the work of our hands,[77] and it may be so that though our beginning was small, yet our latter end hath greatly increased.[78]

Our houses have been safe from fear, and there hath been no rod of God upon us;[79] so that the voice of rejoicing and salvation hath been our tabernacle from day to day.[80]

With our staff it may be we have passed over this Jordan, and now we are become two bands,[81] and it is God that setteth the solitary in families.[82]

If we have lived joyfully with our relations,[83] and they have been to us as the loving hind, and as the pleasant roe, we must give thee thanks for it, for every creature is that to us, and no more, that thou makest it to be.[84]

2.2.1.2.6. For our own share in the public plenty, peace, and tranquillity.
When we have eaten and are full, we have reason to bless thee for the good land which thou hast given us;[85] A land which the eyes of the Lord our God are always upon, from the beginning of the year even to the end of the year.[86]

Thou makest peace in our borders, and fillest us with the finest of the wheat:[87] We are delivered from the noise of the archers at the place of drawing water; there therefore will we rehearse the righteous acts of the Lord, even his righteous acts toward the inhabitants of his villages.[88]

We thank thee that the powers that are set over us are ministers of God to us for good,[89] that they seek the welfare of our people, speaking peace to all their seed.[90]

2.2.2 The goodness of his grace relating to our souls and the life that is come.

But especially blessed be the God and Father of our Lord Jesus Christ, who hath blessed us with all spiritual blessings in heavenly things in Christ.[91]

2.2.2.1. 1st, We must give God thanks for his kindnesses to the children of men, relating to their better part, and their future state, and his favours to the church in general.

2.2.2.1.1. We must give thanks for his gracious design and contrivance of man's redemption and salvation, when he was lost and undone by sin.

O how wonderfully did the kindness and love of God our Savior towards man appear, not by any works of righteousness which we had done, but according to his mercy he saved us:[92] We had destroyed ourselves, but in thee, and thee only, was our help.[93]

When we were cast out in the open field, and no eye pitied us, thou sawest us polluted in our own blood, and thou saidest unto us, Live; yea, thou saidest unto us, Live; and the time was a time of love.[94]

When the redemption of the soul was so precious, as that it must have ceased for ever, and no man could by any means redeem his brother, or give to God a ransom for hims, then thou wast pleased to find a ransom, that we might be delivered from going down to the pit.[95]

When we must needs die, and were as water spilt on the ground, which cannot be gathered up again, then didst thou devise means that the banished might not be for ever expelled from him.[96]

When thou sparedst not the angels that sinned, but didst cast them down to hell;[97] thou saidst concerning the rage of mankind, destroy it not for a blessing is in it.[98]

Herein appears the wisdom of God in a mystery, even the hidden wisdom, which God ordained before the world for our glory.[99]

2.2.2.1.2. For the eternal purposes and counsels of God concerning man's redemption.

We are bound to give thanks always to thee, O God, because thou hast from the beginning chosen some to salvation through sanctification of the Spirit:[100] That there is a remnant according to the election of grace,[101] whom God hath chosen in Christ before the foundation of the world, that they should be holy and without blame before thee in love, having predestinated them to the adoption of children by Jesus Christ unto thyself, according to the good pleasure of thy will, to the praise of the glory of thy grace.[102]

Thine they were, and thou gavest them to Christ, and this is thy will, that of all that thou hast given him he should lose nothing, but should raise it up at the last day.[103]

2.2.2.1.3. For the appointing of the Redeemer, and God's gracious condescension to deal with men upon new terms, receding from the demands of the broken covenant of innocency.

We bless thee, that when sacrifice and offering thou wouldst not, and in it hadst no pleasure,[104] that then the eternal Son of God said, Lo,

I come to do thy will, O God, and a body hast thou prepared me: And that as in the volume of the book it was written of him, he did delight to do thy will, O God, yea, thy law was within his heart.[105]

Thou hast laid help upon one that is mighty, one chosen out of the people: Thou hast found David thy servant, with the holy oil thou hast anointed him, even with the oil of gladness above his fellows, and didst promise that with him thy hand should be established, and thy arm should strengthen him, and that thou wouldest make him thy first-born, higher that the kings of the earth.[106]

We bless thee, that the Father now judgeth no man, but hath committed all judgment to the Son: That as he has life in himself, so he hath given to the Son to have life in himself, and hath given him authority to execute judgment also, because he is the Son of man.[107] That the Father loved the Son, and hath given all things into his hand;[108] and that the counsel of peace is between them both.[109]

That he is thy servant, whom thou dost uphold, thine elect in whom thy soul delighteth,[110] thy beloved Son in whom thou art well pleased:[111] That thou hast given him for a covenant of the people,[112] and that through him we are not under the law, but under grace.[113]

That God so loved the world, as to give his only begotton Son, that whosoever believes in him should not perish, but have everlasting life.[114]

2.2.2.1.4. For the early and ancient indication of the gracious design concerning fallen man.

We bless thee, that as soon as ever man had sinned, it was graciously promised that the seed of the woman should break the serpent's head;[115] and that in the Old Testament sacrifices, Jesus Christ was the lamb slain from the foundation of the world.[116]

And that by faith the elders, though they received not the promise, yet obtained a good report, for they obtained witness that they were righteous.[117]

We bless thee for the promise made to Abraham, that in his seed all the families of the earth should be blessedr; and to Jacob, that the Shiloh should come, and to him should the gathering of the people be;[118] and that the Patriarchs rejoiced to see Christ's day, and they saw it and were glad.[119]

2.2.2.1.5. For the many glorious instances of God's favour to the Old Testament church.

We adore that wisdom, peace and goodness with which thou broughtest the vine out of Egypt, didst cast out the heathen and plant it; thou preparedst room before it, and didst cause it to take deep root, and it filled the land.[120]

And they got not the land in possession by their own sword, neither did their own arm save them, but thy right hand, and thine arm, and the light of thy countenance, because thou hadst a favour to them.[121]

We bless thee that to the Jews were committed the oracles of God,[122] that they had the adoption and the glory, and the covenant, the giving of the law, and the service of God, and the promises?[123] And that there did not fail one word of all thy good promise, which thou promisedst by the hand of Moses thy servant.[124]

We bless thee for all that, which thou didst at sundry times and in divers manners speak in times past unto the fathers by the prophets,[125] these holy men of God, who spake as they were moved by the Holy Ghost,[126] and prophesied of the grace that should come unto us, testifying beforehand the suffering of Christ, and the glory that should follow, and that not to themselves only, but to us they ministered those great things, things which the angels themselves desire to look into.[127]

And especially we bless thee, that thou hast provided some better things for us, that they without us should not be made perfect.[128]

2.2.2.1.6 For the wonderful and mysterious incarnation of the son of God, and his coming into the world.

We bless thee, that when the fulness of time was come, thou didst send forth thy Son, made of a woman, made under the law, to redeem them that were under the law, that we might receive the adoption of sons.[129]

That the eternal Word was made flesh, and dwelt among us, and there were those who saw his glory, the glory as of the only begotten of the Father, full of grace and truth.[130] And without controversy, great is the mystery of godliness, that God was manifested in the flesh.

We bless thee, that to this end he was born, and for this cause he came into the world, that he might bear witness of the truth;[131] and we believe, and are sure, that he is that Christ, the Son of the living God; that it is he that should come, and we are to look for no other.[132]

We bless thee, that the Son of man is come to seek and to save that which was lost;[133] that he is come that we might have life, and that we might have it more abundantly,[134] and that for this purpose the Son of God was manifested that he might destroy the works of the devil.[135]

Lord, we receive it as a faithful saying, and well worthy of all acceptation, that Christ Jesus came into the world to save sinners, even the chief.[136]

We bless thee, that forasmuch as the children are partakers of flesh and blood, he also himself likewise took part of the same; That he took not on him the nature of angels, but our nature, and was in all things made like unto his brethren, that he might be a merciful and faithful High Priest in things pertaining to God, to make reconciliation for the sins of the people: and that he is not ashamed to call them brethren.[137]

And that the first-begotton was brought into the world with a charge given to all the angels of God to worship him.[138]

2.2.2.1.7. For God's gracious owning of him in his undertaking, and in the carrying of it on.

We bless thee, that thou wast in Christ, reconciling the world to thyself, not imputing their trespasses unto them, and that thou hast committed unto us the word of reconciliation.[139]

That thou hast thyself given him for a witness to the people, a leader and commander to the people. That he was sanctified and sealed and sent into the world, and that the Father who sent him did not leave him alone, for he always did those things that pleased himt.

Glory be to God in the highest, for in and through Jesus Christ there is on earth peace, and good-will towards men.[140]

In this was manifested the love of God towards us, because that God sent his only begotton Son into the world, that we might live through him.[141]

We thank thee for the power thou hast given him over all flesh, that he should give eternal life to as many as were given him.[142]

2.2.2.1.8. For his holy life, his excellent doctrine, and the glorious miracles he wrought to confirm his doctrine.

We bless thee for the assurance we have, that he is a teacher come from God, since no man could do those miracles which he did, except God were with him.[143]

That thou hast in these last days spoken unto us by thy Son,[144] whose doctrine was not his,[145] but his that sent him, and he spake as one having authority;[146] and that we are encouraged to come and learn of him, because he is meek and lowly in heart, and in learning of him we shall find rest to our souls.[147]

We bless thee that he hath left us an example, that we should follow his steps, in that he did not sin, neither was guile found in his mouth, and when he was reviled, he reviled not again;[148] and his meat and drink was to do the will of his Father;[149] in that he was holy, harmless, undefiled, separate from sinners.[150] O that we may be armed with the same mind, and that as he was, so we may be in this world;[151] and that we may so walk even as he walked.[152]

We bless thee, that the works which he did, the same bore witness of him, that the Father had sent him,[153] that by his power the blind received their sight, the lame walked, the lepers were cleansed, the deaf heard, the dead were raised up, and the poor had the gospel preached to them;[154] and even the winds and the sea obeyed himl, for which we glorify the God of Israel.[155] Doubtless this was the Son of God.[156]

2.2.2.1.9. For the great encouragement Christ gave to poor sinners to come to him.

We bless thee that Jesus Christ came to call not the righteous, but sinners (such as we are) to repentance, and had power on earth to forgive sin;[157] that he came to save his people from their sins;[158] and is the Lamb of God that takes away the sin of the world,[159] and that he is (to his honour, not to his reproach) a friend to publicans and sinners.[160]

We thank thee for the gracious invitation he gave to those who are weary and heavy laden to come to him for rest:[161] and for the assurance he hath given, that whosoever comes unto him, he will in nowise cast him out.[162]

That he made a gracious offer, that whosoever thirst might come unto him and drink.[163]

2.2.2.1.10. For the full satisfaction which he made to the justice of God for the sin of man by the blood of his cross, for the purchases, victories, and triumphs of the cross, and for all the precious benefits which flow to us from the dying of the Lord Jesus.

Herein indeed God commendeth his love to us, in that while we were yet sinners, Christ died for us,[164] that we might be reconciled to him by the death of his Son. Herein is love, not that we loved God, but that he loved us, and sent his son to be the propitiation for our sins,[165] and not for ours only, but for the sins of the whole world;[166] that he tasted death for every man, that through death he might destroy him that had the power of death, that is the devil.[167]

We bless thee, that by one offering he hath perfected for ever them that are sanctified,[168] that he hath finished transgression, made an end of sin, made re-conciliation for iniquity, and hath brought in an everlasting righteousness.[169]

That he hath redeemed us from the curse of the law, by being made a curse for us.[170]

That what the law could not do, in that it was weak through the flesh, God hath done by sending his own Son in the likeness of flesh, who by a sacrifice for sin, condemned sin in the flesh.[171]

That he was wounded for our transgressions, and bruised for our iniquities, and that the chastisement of our peace was upon him, and by his stripes we are healed; and that the Lord having laid upon him the iniquity of us all, it pleased the Lord to bruise him, and put him to grief.[172]

That appearing to put away sin by the sacrifice of himself, he did by the eternal Spirit offer himself without spot unto God, and by his own blood entered in once into the holy place, having obtained eternal redemption for us.[173]

That he hath spoiled principalities and powers, and made a show of them openly, triumphing over them in his cross, and hath blotted out the hand-writing of ordinances which was against us, which was contrary to us, taking it out of the way, by nailing it to his cross.[174]

That he is our peace, who, having broken down the middle wall of partition between Jew and Gentile, hath made himself of twain one new man, hath reconciled both unto God in one body, by the cross, having slain the enmity thereby.[175]

That he hath loved us, and washed us from our sins in his own blood, and hath made us unto our God kings and priests.[176]

O the height, and depth, and length and breadth of that love of Christ which passeth knowledge![177] that great love wherewith he loved us![178]

Worthy is the Lamb that was slain, to receive power, and riches, and wisdom, and strength, and honour, and glory, and blessing; for he was slain, and hath redeemed us to God by his blood.[179]

2.2.2.1.11. For his resurrection from the dead on the third day.

We thank thee, that as he was delivered for our offences, so he arose again for our justification,[180] and was declared to be the Son of God with power, by the resurrection from the dead.[181]

That though he was dead, yet he is alive, and lives forevermore, and hath the keys of hell and death,[182] and being raised from the dead, he dies no more, death hath no more dominion over him.[183]

That now is Christ risen from the dead, and is become the first fruits of them that slept, that as in Adam all died, so in Christ all might be made alive, and every one in his own order.[184]

That God suffered not his holy One to see corruption, but loosed the pains of death, because it was impossible he should be holden of them, and so declared to all the house of Israel, that the same Jesus whom they crucified is both Lord and Christ.[185]

And that for this end Christ both died, and rose, and revived, that he might be Lord both of the dead and living,[186] and that whether we wake or sleep, we might live together with him.[187]

2.2.2.1.12 For his ascension into heaven, and his sitting at God's right hand there.

We bless thee that our Lord Jesus has ascended to his Father and our Father, to his God and our God;[188] is ascended up on high, having led captivity captive, and hath received gifts from men, yea, even for the rebellious also, that the Lord God might dwell among them.[189]

That as the forerunner he is for us entered into heaven itself,[190] now to appear in the presence of God for us,[191] a Lamb, as it had been slain, standing in the midst of the throne.[192]

That he is set on the right hand of the throne of the majesty in the heavens,[193] angels and authorities and powers being made subject to him.[194]

That he is gone before, to prepare a place for us in his Father's house, where there are many mansions, and though whither he is gone we cannot follow him now, yet we hope to follow him hereafter,[195] when he shall come again to receive us to himself, that where he is, there we may be also.[196]

2.2.2.1.13. For the intercession which he ever lives to make, in the virtue of his satisfaction.

We thank thee, that having borne the sins of many, he makes intercession for transgressors;[197] and prays not for those only that were given him when he was upon earth, but for all that shall believe on him through their word; that they all may be one.[198]

That we have an Advocate with the Father, even Jesus Christ the righteous,[199] who is therefore able to save to the uttermost all those that come to God as a Father by making him as a Mediator, seeing he ever lives making intercession.[200]

That we have a High Priest taken from among men, and ordained for men in things pertaining to God, that he may offer both gifts and sacrifice for sin, who can have compassion on the ignorant, and on them who are out of the way, and that he is become the author of eternal salvation to all them that obey him.[201]

2.2.2.1.14. For the dominion and sovereignty, to which the Redeemer is exalted.

We thank thee, that because our Lord Jesus humbled himself, and became obedient unto death, even the death of the cross, therefore God hath highly exalted him, and given him a name above every name, that at the name of JESUS every knee shall bow, and every tongue confess (as we do at this time) that Jesus Christ is Lord, to the glory of God the Father.[202] That all power is given unto him both in heaven and in earth, that thou hast set him over the works of thy hands,[203] and hast put all things in subjection under his feet, and so hast crowned him with glory and honour.[204]

That he is King of kings, and Lord of lords,[205] that the Ancient of days hath given him dominion, and glory, and a kingdom, an everlasting dominion, and a kingdom which shall not be destroyed.[206]

That the government is upon his shoulders, and that his name is called Wonderful, Counsellor, the mighty God, the everlasting Father, and the Prince of peace: and of the increase of his government and peace there shall be no end.[207]

That thou hast set him as a King upon thy holy hill of Zionr, and that he shall reign over the house of Jacob for ever,[208] shall reign till he has put down all opposing rule, principality, and power, till all his enemies are made his footstool, and then he shall deliver up the kingdom to God, even the Father, that God may be all in all.[209]

2.2.2.1.15 For the assurance we have of his second coming to judge to world.

We bless thee that thou hast appointed a day in which thou wilt judge the world in righteousness, by that man whom thou hast ordained, whereof thou hast given assurance unto all men, in that thou hast raised him from the dead.[210]

That in that day the Lord Jesus shall be revealed from heaven with his mighty angels, in flaming fire, taking vengeance on them that know not God, and that obey not the gospel of our Lord Jesus Christ:[211] And shall come to be glorified in his saints, and admired in all them that believe; for them that sleep in Jesus he will bring with him.[212]

That he shall then send forth his angels to gather out of his kingdom all things that offend, and them which do iniquity,[213] and to gather together his elect from the four winds,[214] and then shall the righteous shine forth as the sun in the kingdom of their Father.[215]

And we then, according to thy promise, look for new heavens, and a new earth, wherein dwells righteousness: Lord, grant that, seeing we look for such things, we may give diligence to be found of him in peace, without spot, and blameless.[216] And then come Lord Jesus, come quickly.[217]

2.2.2.1.16. For the sending of the Holy Spirit to supply the want of Christ's bodily presense, to carry on his undertaking, and to prepare things for his second coming.

We bless thee, that when our Lord Jesus went away, he sent us another comforter to abide with us for ever, even the Spirit of truthc, who shall glorify the Son, for he shall take of his, and shall show it unto us.[218]

That being by the right hand of God exaltede, and having received of the Father the promise of the Holy Ghost, he poured it forth as rivers of living water.[219]

Blessed be God for the signs and wonders, and divers miracles and gifts of the Holy Ghost, with which God bare witness to the great salvation.[220] And blessed be God for the promise, that as earthly parents, though evil, know how to give good gifts to their children, so our heavenly Father will give the Holy Spirit to them that ask him,[221] that Holy Spirit of promise which is the earnest of our inheritance until the redemption of the purchased possession.[222]

2.2.2.1.17. For the covenant of grace made with us in Jesus Christ, and all the exceeding great and precious privileges of that covenant, and for the seals of it.

We thank thee, that in Jesus Christ thou hast made an everlasting covenant with us, even the sure mercies of David,[223] and that though the mountains may depart, and the hills be removed, yet this covenant of thy peace shall never be removed.[224]

That thou hast given unto us exceeding great and precious promises, that by these we might be partakers of a divine nature:[225] and that Jesus Christ is the Mediator of this better covenant, which is established upon better promises.[226]

That though thou chasten our transgression with the rod, and our iniquity with stripes, yet thy lovingkindness thou wilt not utterly take away, nor cause thy faithfulness to fail, thy covenant thou wilt not break, nor alter the thing that is gone out of thy lips.[227]

That being willing more abundantly to show to the heirs of promise the immutability of thy counsel, thou hast confirmed it by an oath, that by two immutable things, in which it was impossible for God to lie, we might have strong consolation, who have fled for refuge to lay hold on the hope set before us.[228]

That baptism is appointed to be a seal of the righteousness which is by faith, as circumcision was;[229] that it assures us of the remission of sins, and the gift of the Holy Ghost; and that this promise is to us and our childrenr. And that the cup in the Lord's Supper is the blood of the New Testament, which was shed for many, for the remission of sins.[230]

2.2.2.1.18. For the writing of the scriptures, and the preserving of them pure and entire to our day.

We thank thee, that we have the scriptures to search, and that in them we have eternal life, and that they testify of Christ,[231] and that all scripture is given by inspiration of God, and is profitable for doctrine, for reproof, for correction, and for instruction in righteousness.[232]

That whatsoever things were written aforetime, were written for our learning, that we through patience and comfort of the scripture might have hope;[233] And that we have this most sure word of prophecy, as a light shining in a dark place.[234]

That the vision is not become to us as the words of a book that is sealed,[235] but that we hear in our own tongue the wonderful works of God.[236]

We thank thee, O Father, Lord of heaven and earth, that the things which were hid from the wise and prudent, and which many prophets and kings desired to see, and might not, are revealed to us babes: Even so, Father, for so it seemed good in thy sight.[237]

2.2.2.1.19. For the institution of ordinances, and particularly that of the ministry.

We thank thee, that thou hast not only shewed thy word unto Jacob, but thy statutes and judgments unto Israel, unto us; Thou hast not dealt so with other nations, and as for thy judgments, they have not known them.

That the tabernacle of God is with men, and he will dwell with them,[238] and that he hath set his sanctuary in the midst of them for evermore,[239] and there will meet with the children of Israel.[240]

We thank thee, that thou hast made known unto us thy holy Sabbaths,[241] and that still there remains the keeping of a Sabbath to the people of God.[242] And that when the Lord Jesus ascended up on high he gave gifts unto men, not only prophets, apostles, and evangelists, but pastors and teachers, for the perfecting of the saints, for the work of the ministry, for the edifying of the body of Christ, till we all come in the unity of the faith, and of the knowledge of the Son of God, unto a perfect man, unto the measure of the stature of the fulness of

Christ.[243] And that while they teach us to observe all things which Christ hath commanded, he hath promised to be with them always, even unto the end of the world.[244]

2.2.2.1.20. For the planting of the Christian religion in the world, and the setting up of the gospel church, in despite of all the opposition of the powers of darkness.

We thank thee, that the preaching of Jesus Christ, according to the commandment of the everlasting God, and the gospel which was made known to all nations for the obedience of faith,[245] was mighty through God to the pulling down of the strong holds,[246] that the Lord wrought with it, and confirmed the word by signs following,[247] so that Satan fell as lightning from heaven.[248]

That though the gospel was preached in much contention,[249] yet it grew and prevailed mightily,[250] and multitudes turned to God from idols, to serve the living and true God, and to wait for his Son from heaven.[251]

Now came salvation and strength, and the kingdom of our God, and the power of his Christ.[252] And the exalted Redeemer rode forth with his bow, and with his crown, conquering and to conquer,[253] and nations were born at once.[254]

2.2.2.1.21. For the preservation of Christianity in the world unto this day.

We bless thee, that though the enemies of Israel have afflicted them from their youth up, have many a time afflicted them, yet they have not prevailed against them; though the plowers have plowed on their back, yet the righteous Lord has cut asunder the cords of the wicked.[255]

That Jesus Christ hath built his church upon a rock, which the gates of hell cannot prevail against,[256] but his seed shall endure for ever, and his throne as the days of heaven.[257]

2.2.2.1.22 For the martyrs and confessors, the lights of the church, and the good examples of those that are gone before us to heaven.

We bless thee for all those who have been enabled to approve themselves to God in much patience, in afflictions, in distresses,[258] who when they have been brought before governors and kings for Christ's sake, it has turned to them for a testimony, and God has given them a mouth and wisdom, which all their adversaries were not able to gainsay or resist.[259]

That those who for Christ's sake were killed all the day long, and accounted as sheep for the slaughter, yet in all these things we are more than conquerors, through him that loved us.[260]

That they overcame the accuser of the brethren by the blood of the Lamb, and by the word of their testimony, and not by loving their lives unto the death.[261]

We bless thee for the cloud of witnesses with which we are encompassed about,[262] for the footsteps of the flock,[263] for the elders that have obtained a good report,[264] and are now through faith and patience, inheriting the promises.[265] Lord, give us to follow them, as they followed Christ.[266]

2.2.2.1.23. For the communion of saints, that spiritual communion which we have in faith and hope, and holy love, and in prayers and praises with all good Christians.

We bless thee, that if we walk in the light, we have fellowship one with another,[267] even with all that in every place call on the name of Jesus Christ our Lord, both theirs and ours.[268]

That we, being many, are one bread and one body,[269] and that though there are diversities of gifts and administrations, and operations, yet there is the same Spirit, the same Lord, and the same God, which worketh in all.[270]

We thank thee, that all the children of God which were scattered abroad,[271] are united in him who is the head of the body, the church;[272] so they are all our brethren and companions in tribulation, and in the kingdom and patience of Jesus Christ.[273]

2.2.2.1.24 For the prospect and hope of eternal life, when time shall be no more.

We thank thee for the crown of life which the Lord hath promised to them that love him;[274] the inheritance incorruptible, undefiled, and that fadeth not away, reserved in heaven for us.[275]

That having here no continuing city,[276] we are encouraged to seek the better country, that is, the heavenly, the city that hath foundations, whose builder and maker is God.[277]

That we are in hope of eternal life, which God, that cannot lie, hath promised,[278] And that all true believers, through grace, have eternal life abiding in them.[279]

2.2.2.2. 2ndly, We must give God thanks for the spiritual mercies bestowed upon us in particular, especially if we are called with an effectual call, and have a good work of grace begun in us.

2.2.2.2.1. We must bless God for the striving of his Spirit with us, and the admonitions and checks of our own consciences.

We bless thee, that thou hast not given us over to a reprobate mind,[280] that our consciences are not seared,[281] that thou hast not said concerning us, They are joined to idols, let them alone,[282] but that thy Spirit is yet striving with us.[283]

We thank thee for the work of the law written in our hearts, our own consciences also bearing witness, and our own thoughts between themselves accusing or excusing one another.[284]

2.2.2.2.2. We must bless God if there be a saving change wrought in us by his blessed Spirit.

And hath God by his grace translated us out of the kingdom of darkness into the kingdom of his dear Son?[285] Hath he called us into fellowship of Jesus Christ,[286] and made us nigh by his blood, who by nature were afar off?[287] Not unto us, O Lord, not unto us, but unto thy name we give glory.[288]

We give thanks to God always for those to whom the gospel is come, not in word only, but in power, and the Holy Ghost, and in much assurance.[289]

Thou hast loved us with an everlasting love, and therefore with loving kindness thou hast drawn us,[290] drawn us with the cords of a man, and the bands of love.[291]

When the strong man armed kept his palace in our hearts, and his goods were in peace, it was a stronger than he that came upon him, and took from him all his armour wherein he trusted, and divided the spoil.[292]

2.2.2.2.3. We must give thanks for the remission of our sins, and the peace of our consciences.

We bless thee for the redemption we have through Christ's blood, even the forgiveness of sins, according to the riches of thy grace, wherein thou hast abounded towards us.[293]

That thou hast forgiven all our iniquities, and healed all our diseases;[294] and hast in love to our souls delivered them from the pit of corruption: For thou hast cast all our sins behind thy back.[295]

When thou broughtest us into the wilderness, yet there thou spakest comfortably to us, and gavest us our vineyards from thence; and the valley of Achor for a door of hope.[296]

2.2.2.2.4. For the powerful influences of the divine grace to sanctify and preserve us, to prevent our falling into sin, and to strengthen us in doing our duty.

Thou hast not quenched the smoking flax, nor broke the bruised reed,[297] nor despised the day of small things,[298] but having obtained help of God, we continue hitherto.[299]

In the day when we cried thou answered us, and hast strengthened us with strength in our souls.[300]

We have been continually with thee, thou hast holden us by the right hand, when our feet were almost gone, and our steps had well nigh slipt.[301]

We have reason never to forget thy precepts, for by them thou hast quickened us; and unless thy law had been our delight, we should many a time have perished in our affliction;[302] for thy statutes have been our songs in the house of our pilgrimage.[303]

Unless the Lord had been our help our souls had almost dwelt in silence; but when we said, Our foot slippeth, thy mercy, O Lord, held us up: and in the multitude of our thoughts within us, thy comforts have been the delight of our souls.[304]

2.2.2.2.5. *For sweet communion with God in holy ordinances, and the communications of his favour.*

We have been abundantly satisfied with the fatness of thy house, and thou hast made us drink of the river of thy pleasures. For with thee is the fountain of life, in thy light we shall see light.[305]

Thou hast brought us to thy holy mountain, and made us joyful in thy house of prayer,[306] and we found it good for us to draw near to God.[307]

We have reason to say, That a day in thy courts is better than a thousand, and that it is better to be door-keepers in the house of our God, than to dwell in the tents of wickedness; for the Lord God is a sun and shield, he will give grace and glory, and no good thing will he withhold from them that walk uprightly: O Lord of hosts, blessed is the man that trusteth in thee.[308]

We have sitten down under thy shadow with delight, and thy fruit hath been sweet unto our taste, thou hast brought us into the banqueting house, and thy banner over us has been love.[309]

2.2.2.2.6. *For gracious answers to our prayers.*

We have reason to love thee, O Lord, because thou hast heard the voice of our supplications, and because thou hast inclined thine ear unto us; we will therefore call upon thee as long as we live.[310]

Out of the depths we have called unto thee, O Lord,[311] and thou hast heard our vows, and given us the heritage of those that fear thy name.[312]

Nay, before we have called, thou hast answered, and while we have been yet speaking, thou hast heard and hast said,[313] Here I am,[314] and hast been nigh unto us in all that which we call unto thee for.[315]

Lord, thou hast heard the desire of the humble, thou wilt prepare their heart, and cause thine ear to hear.[316]

Blessed be God, who hath not turned away our prayer, or his mercy from us;[317] for we have prayed, and have gone away, and our countenance has been no more sad.[318]

2.2.2.2.7. *For support under our afflictions, and spiritual benefit and advantage by them.*

Thou hast comforted us in all our tribulation,[319] hast considered our trouble, and known our souls in adversity, and shewed us thy marvellous kindness, as in a strong city.[320]

When afflictions have abounded, consolations have much more abounded.[321] Though no afflictions for the present have been joyous, but grievous, nevertheless, afterwards it hath yielded the peaceable fruit of righteousness; and hath proved to be for our profit, that we might be partakers of thy holiness.[322]

We have had reason to say, that it was good for us we were afflicted, that we might learn thy commandments; for before we were afflicted we went astray, but afterwards have kept thy word.[323]

It has been but for a season, and when there was need, that we were in heaviness, through manifold temptations; and we beg that all the trials of our faith may be found unto praise, and honour and glory, at the appearing of Jesus Christ, whom having not seen we love, in whom, though we now see him not, yet believing, we rejoice, with joy unspeakable, and full of glory; are longing to receive the end of our faith, even the salvation of our souls.[324]

2.2.2.2.8. *For the performances of God's promises.*

Thou hast dealt well with thy servants, O Lord, according to thy word,[325] and thou hast been ever mindful of thy covenant, the word which thou hast commanded to a thousand generations.[326]

There hath not failed one word of all the good promise which thou hast promised to David thy servant, and Israel thy people.[327]

And now, what shall we render unto the Lord for all his benefits towards us? Let our souls return to him and repose in him, as their rest, because he hath dealt bountifully with us; we will take the cup of our salvation, and call upon the name of the Lord;[328] for the Lord is good, his mercy is everlasting,and his truth endureth to all generations.[329]

We will bless the Lord at all times, yea, his praise shall continually be in our mouths,[330] we will sing unto the Lord as long as we live;[331] and we hope to be shortly with those blessed ones who dwell in his house above, and are still praising him, and who rest not day or night, from saying, Holy, holy, holy, Lord God Almighty.[332]

References

1 Ps. 75:1.
2 Ps. 103:1-2.
3 Ps. 92:1.
4 Ps. 92:1-2.
5 Ps. 145:1-2, 7.
6 Ps. 149:1-2, 5-6.
7 Ps. 146:2.
8 Heb. 13:15.
9 Ps. 50:23.
10 Ps. 69:31.
11 Isa. 63:7.
12 Ps. 136:2-3.
13 Exod. 33:19.
14 Ps. 145:10.
15 Ps. 145:8.
16 Lam. 3:33.
17 Lam. 3:32-33.
18 Ps. 147:11.
19 Ps. 104:2.
20 Psal 19:4-5.
21 Matt. 5:45.
22 Ps. 8:3-4.
23 Eccles. 11:7.
24 James 1:17.
25 Job 38:12.
26 Acts 14:17.
27 Ps. 147:8-9.
28 Job 38:26-27.
29 Ps. 65:9-11.
30 Ps. 104:10-12.
31 Ps. 104:5, 9.
32 Job 38:9, 11.
33 Isa. 54:9.
34 Jer. 33:20.
35 Jer. 31:35.
36 Gen. 8:22.
37 Ps. 115:16.
38 Ps. 8:6.
39 Gen. 9:2.
40 Prov. 8:31.
41 Ps. 104:14-15.
42 Acts 17:25.
43 Ps. 119:64.
44 Ps. 104:27-28, 30-31.
45 Eccles. 1:4.
46 Deut. 29:20.
47 Ps. 139:14.
48 1 Cor. 2:11.
49 Ps. 8:5.
50 Job 32:8.
51 Prov. 20:27.
52 1 Cor. 6:19, 3:16.
53 1 Cor. 6:20.
54 Isa. 43:21.
55 Job 3:11-12.
56 Isa. 48:8.
57 Isa. 46:3.
58 Ps. 66:9.
59 Ps. 35:10.
60 Ps. 34:20.
61 Ps. 3:5.
62 Ps. 91:11-12.
63 Heb. 1:14.
64 1 Sam. 20:3.
65 2 Cor. 1:9.
66 Isa. 38:10, 17.
67 Ps. 116:3-6, 8-9.
68 Ps. 68:19.
69 Ps. 23:2, 5.
70 Luke 22:35.
71 Job 29:3-4.
72 1 Tim. 6:17.
73 Job 12:6.
74 Neh. 9:25.
75 Deut. 8:2.
76 1 Sam. 7:12.
77 Ps. 18:32.
78 Job 1:10.
79 Job 8:7.
80 Job 21:9.
81 Ps. 118:15.
82 Gen. 32:10.
83 Ps. 68:6.
84 Eccles. 9:9.
85 Prov. 5:19.
86 Deut. 8:10.
87 Deut. 11:12.
88 Ps. 147:14.
89 Judg. 5: 11.
90 Rom. 13:4.
91 Esther 10:3.
92 Eph. 1:3.
93 Titus 3:4-5.
94 Hosea 13:9.
95 Ezek. 16:5-6, 8.
96 Ps. 49:7.
97 Job 33:24.
98 2 Sam. 14:14.
99 2 Pet. 2:4.
100 Isa. 65:8.
101 1 Cor. 2:7.
102 2 Thess. 2:13.
103 Rom. 11:5.
104 Eph. 1:4-6.
105 John 17:6, 6:39.
106 Heb. 10:5-7.
107 Ps. 40:7-8.
108 Ps. 89:19-21, 27.
109 John 5:22, 26-27
110 John 3:35.
111 Zech. 6:13.
112 Isa. 42:1.
113 Matt. 17:5.
114 Isa. 49:8.
115 Rom. 6:14.
116 John 3:16.
117 Gen. 3:15.
118 Rev. 13:8.
119 Heb. 11:2, 4, 39.
120 Gen. 12:3.
121 Gen. 49:10.
122 John 8:56.
123 Ps. 80:8-9.
124 Ps. 44:3.
125 Rom. 3:2.
126 Rom. 9:4.

127 1 Kings 8:56.
128 Heb. 1:1.
129 2 Pet. 1:21.
130 1 Pet. 1:10-12.
131 Heb. 11:40.
132 Gel. 4:4-5.
133 John 1:14.
134 John 18:37.
135 John 6:69.
136 Luke 19:10.
137 John 10:10.
138 1 John 3:8.
139 1 Tim. 1:15.
140 Heb. 2:11, 14, 16-17.
141 Heb. 1:6.
142 2 Cor. 5:19.
143 John 8:29.
144 Luke 2:14.
145 1 John 4:9.
146 John 17:2.
147 John 3:2.
148 Heb. 1:2.
149 John 7:16.
150 Matt. 7:29.
151 Matt. 11:29.
152 1 Pet. 2:21-23.
153 John 4:34.
154 Heb. 7:26.
155 1 Pet. 4:1.
156 1 John 4:17.
157 John 5:36.
158 Matt. 11:5.
159 Matt. 8:27.
160 Matt. 15:31.
161 Matt. 27:54.
162 Matt. 9:6, 13.
163 Matt. 1:21.
164 John 1:29.
165 Matt. 11:19.
166 Matt. 11:28.
167 John 6:37.
168 John 7:37.
169 Rom. 5:8.
170 1 John 4:10.
171 1 John 2:2.
172 Heb. 2:9, 14.
173 Heb. 10:14.
174 Dan. 9:24.
175 Gal. 3:13.
176 Rom. 8:3.
177 Isa. 53:5-6, 10.
178 Heb. 9:12, 14, 26.
179 Col. 2:14-15.
180 Eph. 2:14-16.
181 Rev. 1:5-6.
182 Eph. 3:18-19.
183 Eph. 2:4.
184 Rev. 5:9-12.
185 Rom. 4:25.
186 Rom. 1:4.
187 Rev. 1:18.
188 Rom. 6:9.
189 1 Cor. 15:20, 22-23.
190 Acts 2:24, 31, 36.
191 Rom. 14:9.
192 1 Thess. 5:10.
193 John 20:17.
194 Ps. 68:18.
195 Heb. 6:20.
196 Heb. 9:24.
197 Rev. 5:6.
198 Heb. 8:1.
199 1 Pet. 3:22.
200 John 14:2-3.
201 John 13:36.
202 Isa. 53:12.
203 John 17:20-21.
204 1 John 2:1.
205 Heb. 7:25.
206 Heb. 5:1-2, 9.
207 Phil. 2:8-10.
208 Matt. 28:18.
209 Heb. 2:7-9.
210 Rev. 19:16.
211 Dan. 7:14.
212 Isa. 9:6-7.
213 Ps. 2:6.
214 Luke 1:33.
215 1 Cor. 15:24-25, 28.
216 Acts 17:31.
217 2 Thess. 1:7-8.
218 1 Thess. 4:14.
219 Matt. 13:41, 43.
220 Matt. 24:31.
221 2 Pet. 3:13-14.
222 Rev. 22:20.
224 John 16:14.
225 Acts 2:33.
226 John 7:38.
227 Heb. 2:4.
228 Luke 11:13.
229 Eph. 1:13-14.
230 Isa. 55:3.
231 Isa. 54:10.
232 2 Pet. 1:4.
233 Heb. 8:6.
234 Ps. 89:32-34.
235 Heb. 6:17-18.
236 Rom. 4:11.
237 Acts 2:38-39.
238 Matt. 26:28.
239 John 5:39.
240 2 Tim. 3:16.
241 Rom. 15:4.
242 2 Pet. 1:19.
243 Isa. 29:11.
244 Acts 2:11.
245 Luke 10:21, 24.
246 Ps. 147:19-20.
247 Rev. 21:3.
248 Ezek. 37:26.
249 Exod. 29:43.
250 Neh. 9:14.
251 Heb. 4:9.
252 Eph. 4:8, 11-13.
253 Matt. 28:20.
254 Rom. 16:25-26.
255 2 Cor. 10:4.
256 Mark 16:20.
257 Luke 10:18.
258 1 Thess. 2:2.
259 Acts 19:20.
260 1 Thess. 1:9-10.
261 Rev. 12:10.
262 Rev. 6:2.
263 Isa. 66:8.
264 Ps. 129:1-4.
265 Matt. 16:18.
266 Ps. 89:29.
267 2 Cor. 6:4.
268 Luke 21:12-13, 15.
269 Rom. 8:36-37.
270 Rev. 12:11.
271 Heb. 12:1.

272 Song. 1:8.
273 Heb. 11:2.
274 Heb. 6:12.
275 1 Cor. 11:1.
276 1 John 1:7.
277 1 Cor. 1:2.
278 1 Cor. 10:17.
279 1 Cor. 12:4-6.
280 John 11:52.
281 Col. 1:18.
282 Rev. 1:9.
283 James 1:12.
284 I Peter 1:4.
285 Heb. 13:14.
286 Heb. 11:10, 16.
287 Titus 1:2.
288 1 John 5:13.
289 Rom. 1:28.
290 1 Tim. 4:2.
291 Hosea 4:17.
292 Gen. 6:3.
293 Rom. 2:15.
294 Col. 1:13.
295 1 Cor. 1:9.
296 Eph. 2:13.
297 Ps. 115:1.
298 1 Thess. 1:2, 5.
299 Jer. 31:3.
300 Hosea 11:4.
301 Luke 11:21-22.
302 Eph. 1:7.
303 Ps. 103:3-4.
304 Isa. 38:17.
305 Hosea 2:14-15.
306 Matt. 12:20.
307 Zech. 4:10.
308 Acts. 26:22.
309 Ps. 73:2-3.
310 Ps. 119:92-93.
311 Ps. 119:54.
312 Ps. 36:8-9.
313 Isa. 56:7.
314 Ps. 73:28.
315 Ps. 84:10-12.
316 Song. 2:3-4.
317 Ps. 116:1-2.
318 Ps. 130:1.
320 Ps. 61:5.
321 Isa. 65:24.
323 Isa. 58:9.
327 Deut. 4:7.
325 Ps. 10:17.
326 Ps. 66:20.
327 1 Sam. 1:18.
328 2 Cor. 1:4.
329 Ps. 31:7, 21.
330 2 Cor. 1:5.
331 Heb. 12:10-11.
332 Ps. 119:67, 71.

CHAPTER 5

Of the fifth part of PRAYER,
which is Intercession, or Address
and Supplication to God for others.

Our Lord Jesus hath taught us to pray, not only with, but for others:
And the apostle hath appointed us to make supplication for all saints:
and many of his prayers in his epistles are for his friends: And we
must not think that when we are in this part of prayer, we may let fall
our fervency, and be more indifferent, because we ourselves are not
immediately concerned in it, but rather let a holy fire of love, both to
God and man here, make our devotions yet more warm and lively.[1]

*1. We must pray for the whole world of mankind, the lost world; and
thus we must honour all men,[2] and according to our capacity do good
to all men.[3]*

We pray, as we are taught, for all men, believing that this is good
and acceptable in the sight of God our Saviour, who will have all men
to be saved, and to come unto the knowledge of the truth, and of Jesus
Christ, who gave himself a ransom for all.[4]

O look with compassion upon the world that lies in wickedness,[5] and
let the prince of this world be cast out,[8] that has blinded their minds.[7]

O let thy way be known upon earth, that barbarous nations may be
civilized,[8] and those that live without God in the world may be brought
to the service of the living God;[9] and thus let thy saving health be known
unto all nations: Let the people praise thee, O God, yea, let all the people
praise thee: O let the nations be glad and sing for joy, for thou shalt
judge the people righteously, and govern the nations upon earth.[10]

O let thy salvation and thy righteousness be openly shewed in the
sight of the heathen, and let all the ends of the earth see the salvation
of our God.[11]

O give thy Son the heathen for his inheritance, and the uttermost parts of the earth for his possession:[12] For thou hast said, It is a light thing for him to raise up the tribes of Jacob, and to restore the preserved of Israel, but thou wilt give him for a light to the Gentiles.[13]

Let all the kingdoms of this world become the kingdoms of the Lord, and of his Christ.[14]

2. For the propagating of the gospel in foreign parts, and the enlargement of the church, by the bringing in of many to it.

O let the gospel be preached unto every creature;[15] for how shall men believe in him of whom they have not heard; and how shall they hear without preachers? and how shall they preach except they be sent?[16] and who shall send forth labourers but the Lord of the harvest?[17]

Let the people which sit in darkness see a great light, and to them which sit in the regions and shadow of death, let light spring up.[18]

Add unto thy church daily such as shall be saved;[19] enlarge the place of its tents, lengthen its cords and strengthen its stakes.[20]

Bring thy seed from the east, and gather them from the west, say to the north, Give up; and to the south, Keep not back; Bring thy sons from far, and thy daughters from the ends of the earth.[21] Let them come with acceptance to thine altar, and glorify the house of thy glory; let them fly as a cloud, and as the doves to their windows.[22]

In every place let incense be offered to thy name, and pure offerings; and from the rising of the sun to the going down of the same, let thy name be great among the Gentiles;[23] and let the offering up of the Gentiles be acceptable, being sanctified by the Holy Ghost.[24] O let the earth be full of the knowledge of the Lord, as the waters cover the sea.[25]

3. For the conversion of the Jews.

Let the branches which are broken off not abide still in unbelief, but be grafted in again into their own olive-tree. And though blindness is in part happened to Israel, yet let the fulness of the Gentiles come in, and let all Israel be saved.[26]

Let them be made to look upon him whom they have pierced,[27] and that they turn to the Lord, let the veil which is upon their hearts be taken away.[28]

4. For the eastern churches that are groaning under the yoke of Mahometan tyranny.

Let the churches of Asia, that were golden candlesticks,[29] which the Lord Jesus delighted to walk in the midst of, be again made so.[30]

Restore unto them their liberties as at first, and their privileges as at the beginning; purely purge away their dross, and take away all their tin,[31] and turn again their captivity, as streams in the south.[32]

5. For the churches in the plantations.

Be thou the confidence of all the ends of the earth, and of those that are afar off beyond the sea;[33] And let them have the blessing which came upon the head of Joseph, and upon the crown of the head of him that was separated from his brethren, even to the utmost bound of the everlasting hills.[34]

Create peace to those that are afar off, as well as to those that are nigh.[35]

And let those that suck of the abundance of the seas, and of treasures hid in the sand, call the people to the mountain, that they may offer sacrifices of righteousness.[36]

6. For the universal church, wherever dispersed, and for all the interests of it.

Our hearts desire and prayer to God for the gospel-Israel, is, that it may be saved.[37]

Do good, in thy good pleasure, unto Zion, build the walls of Jerusalem.[38] Peace be within her walls, and prosperity within her palaces: for our brethren and companions' sake, we will now say, Peace be within her.[39] O that we may see the good of the gospel-Jerusalem all the days of our life, and peace upon Israel;[40]

And that thus we may have reason to answer the messengers of the nations, that the Lord hath founded Zion, and the poor of his people shall trust to that.[41]

Save thy people, O Lord, and bless thine heritage; Feed them also, and lift them up for ever.[42] Give strength unto thy people, and bless thy people with peace:[43] with thy favour do thou compass them as with a shield.[44]

Grace be with all them that love the Lord Jesus Christ in sincerity;[45] for thou knowest them that are thine: and give to all that name the name of Christ to depart from iniquity.[46]

We pray for all that believe in Christ, that they all may be one;[47] and since there is one body, and one Spirit, and one hope of our calling, one lord, one faith, one baptism and one God and Father of all,[48] give to all Christians to be of one heart, and one way.[49]

Let the word of the Lord in all places, have a free course, and let it be glorified.[50]

7. For the conviction and conversion of atheists, deists and infidels, and of all that are out of the way of truth, and of profane scoffers, and those that disgrace Christianity by their vicious and immoral lives.

O teach transgressors thy ways, and let sinners be converted unto thee.[51]

O give them repentance to the acknowledging of the truth,[52] the truth as it is in Jesus,[53] the truth which is according to godliness,[54] that they may recover themselves out of the snare of the devil.[55]

Let those that are as sheep going astray return to Jesus Christ, the Shepherd and Bishop of our souls.[56]

Show those fools their folly and misery, that have said in their hearts, there is no God, and that are corrupt and have done abominable work.[57]

Lord, maintain the honour of the scripture, the law and the testimony, and convince those who speak not according to that word, that it is because there is no light in them:[58] magnify that word above all thy name;[59] magnify the law, magnify the gospel, and make both honourable.[60]

Let those that will not be won by the word, be won by the conversation of Christians, which we beg may be such in every thing, that they who believe not may be convinced of all,[61] and judged of all, may be brought to worship God, and to report that God is with them of a truth.[62]

8. For the amending of every thing that is amiss in the church, the reviving of primitive Christianity, and the power of godliness, and in order thereunto, the pouring out of the Spirit.

Lord, let thy Spirit be poured out upon thy churches from on high, and then the wilderness shall become a fruitful field,[63] then judgment shall return unto righteousness, and all the upright in heart shall follow it.[64]

Let what is wanting be set in order,[65] and let every plant that is not of our heavenly Father's planting be plucked up.[66]

Let the Lord whom we seek come to his temple like a refiner's fire, and fuller's soap, and let him purify the sons of Levi, and all the seed of Israel, and purge them as gold and silver, that they may offer unto the Lord an offering unto righteousness, pleasant to the Lord, as in the days of old, as in former years.[67]

Let pure religion and undefiled before God and the Father, flourish and prevail every where,[68] that kingdom of God among men, which is not meat and drink, but righteousness, and peace, and joy in the Holy Ghost.[69] O revive this work in the midst of the years, in the midst of the years make known,[70] and let our times be times of reformation.[71]

9. For the breaking of the power of all the enemies of the church, and the defeating of all their designs against her.

Let all that set themselves, and take counsel together against the Lord, and against his anointed, that would break their bands asunder, and cast away their cords from them, imagine a vain thing. Let him that sits in heaven laugh at them, and have them in derision; speak unto them in thy wrath, and vex them in thy sore displeasure.[72] Give them, O Lord what thou wilt give them; give them a miscarrying womb, and dry breasts.[73]

O our God, make them like a wheel and as stubble before the wind: Fill their faces with shame, that they may seek thy name, O Lord, and that men may know, thou whose name is JEHOVAH, art the most High over all the earth.[74]

Put them in fear, O Lord, that the nations may know themselves to be but men,[75] and wherein the proud enemies of thy church deal proudly, make it to appear that thou art above them.[76]

Let them be confounded and turned back that hate Zion, and be as the grass upon the house tops, which withereth before it grow up.[77]

Let no weapon formed against thy church prosper, and let every tongue that riseth against it in judgment be condemned.[78]

Make Jerusalem a burdensome stone for all people, and let all that burden themselves with it be cut in pieces, though all the people of the earth should be gathered together against it;[79] so let all thy enemies perish, O Lord, but let them that love thee be as the sun when he goes forth in his strength.[80]

Lord, let the man of sin be consumed with the Spirit of thy mouth, and destroyed with the brightness of thy coming: And let those be undeceived that have been long under the power of strong delusions to believe a lie, and let them receive the truth in the love of it.[81]

Let Babylon fall, and sink like a millstone into the sea,[82] and let the kings of the earth, that have given their power and honour to the beast,[83] be wrought upon at length to bring it into the new Jerusalem.[84]

10. For the relief of suffering churches, and the support, comfort, and deliverance of all that are persecuted for righteousness' sake.

We desire in our prayers to remember them that are in bonds for the testimony of Jesus, as bound with them, and them which suffer adversity, as being ourselves also in the body.[85] O send from above, and deliver them from those that hate them, and bring them forth into a large place.[86]

O let not the rod of the wicked rest upon the lot of the righteous, lest the righteous should put forth their hands unto iniquity.[87]

Awake, awake, put on strength, O arm of the Lord: awake as in the ancient days, as in the generations of old, and make the depths of the sea a way for the ransomed of the Lord to pass over.[88]

For the oppression of the poor, and the sighing of the needy, now do arise, O Lord, and set them in safety from them that puff at them.[89]

O strengthen the patience and faith of thy suffering saints, that they may hope and quietly wait for the salvation of the Lord.[90]

O let the year of thy redeemed come,[91] and the year of recompenses for the controversy of Zion.[92]

O that the salvation of Israel were come out of Zion: And when the Lord bringeth back the captivity of his people, Jacob shall rejoice, and Israel shall be glad.[93]

O let not the oppressed return ashamed, but let the poor and needy praise thy name.[94]

Lord, arise, and have mercy upon Zion, and let the time to favour her, yea, the set time come; yea, let the Lord build up Zion, and appear in his glory, Lord, regard the prayer of the destitute, and do not despise their prayer.[95]

O Lord God, cease, we beseech thee; by whom shall Jacob arise, for he is small?[96] O cause thy face to shine upon that part of thy sanctuary that is desolate for the Lord's sake.[97]

Let the sorrowful sighing of the prisoners come before thee, and according to the greatness of thy power preserve thou those that for thy name's sake are appointed to die.[98]

Let those whose teachers are removed into corners, again see their teachers, though they have the bread of adversity, and the water of affliction.[99]

11. For the nations of Europe and the countries about us.

Thou Lord, art the governor among the nations.[100] Who shall not fear thee, O King of nations?[101] Thou sittest in the throne judging right; judge the world therefore in righteousness, and minister judgment to the people in uprightness.[103]

Lord, hasten the time when thou wilt make wars to cease to the ends of the earth,[103] when nation shall no more lift up sword against nation, nor kingdom against kingdom, but swords shall be beaten into plough-shares, and spears into pruning-hooks, and they shall not learn war any more.[104]

Make kings nursing fathers, and their queens nursing mothers to the Israel of God.[105]

And in the days of these kings let the God of heaven set up a kingdom which shall never be destroyed, even the kingdom of the Redeemer.[106] And whatever counsels there are in men's hearts, Lord, let thy counsels stand,[107] and do thou fulfil the thoughts of thy heart unto all generations.[108]

12. For our own land and nation, the happy islands of Great Britain and Ireland, which we ought in a special manner to seek the welfare of, that in the peace thereof we may have peace.

12.1. We must be thankful to God for his mercies to our land.

We bless thee that thou hast planted us in a very fruitful hill,[109] and hast not made the wilderness our habitation, or the barren land our dwelling,[110] but our land yields her increase.[111]

Lord, thou hast dealt favourably with our land;[112] we have heard with our ears, and our fathers have told us, what work thou didst for us in their days, and in the times of old;[113] And as we have heard, so have we seen; for we have thought of thy loving-kindness, O God, in the midst of thy temple.[114]

Thou hast given us a pleasant land,[115] it is Immanuel's land,[116] it is a valley of vision,[117] thou hast set up thy tabernacle among us, and thy sanctuary is in the midst of us.[118]

We dwell safely under our own vines and fig-tree,[119] and there is peace to him that goeth out, and to him that comes in.[120]

And because the Lord loved our people, therefore he hath set a good government over us, to do judgment and justice;[121] to be a terror to evil doers, and a protection and praise to them that do well.[122]

12.2. We must be humbled before God for our national sins and provocations.

But we are a sinful people, a people laden with iniquity, a seed of evil doers:[123] And a great deal of reason we have to sigh and cry for the abominations that are committed among us.[124]

Iniquity abounds among us, and the love of many is waxen cold.[125]

We have not been forsaken, nor forgotten of our God, though our land be full of sin against the Holy One of Israel.[126]

12.3. We must pray earnestly for national mercies.

12.3.1. For the favours of God to us, and the tokens of his presence among us, as that in which the happiness of our nation is bound up.

O the hope of Israel, the Saviour thereof in time of trouble: Be not thou a stranger in our land, or a wayfaring man that turns aside to tarry but for a night, but be thou always in the midst of us; we are called by thy name, O leave us not: Though our iniquities testify against us, yet do thou it for thy name's sake; though our backslidings are many, and we have sinned against thee.[127]

Turn us to thee, O Lord God of hosts, and then cause thy face to shine, and we shall be saved. O stir up thy strength, and come and save us.[128]

Show us thy mercy, O Lord, and grant us thy salvation, yea, let that salvation be nigh them that fear thee, that glory may dwell in our land. Let mercy and truth meet together, righteousness and peace kiss each other: Let truth spring out of the earth, and righteousness look down from heaven; yea, let the Lord give that which is good: Let righteousness go before him, and set us in the way of his steps.[129]

12.3.2. For the continuance of the gospel among us, and the means of grace, and a national profession of Christ's holy religion.

O let the throne of Christ endure for ever among us,[130] even the place of thy sanctuary, that glorious high throne from the beginning.[131]

Let our candlestick never be removed out of his place, though we have deserved it should, because we have left our first love.[132] Never do to us as thou didst to thy place which was in Shiloh, where thou didst set thy name at the first.[133]

Let us never know what a famine of the word means; nor ever be put to wander from sea to sea, and from the river to the ends of the earth, to seek the word of God.[134]

Let wisdom and knowledge be the stability of our times, and strength of salvation, and let the fear of the Lord be our treasure:[135] Let the righteous flourish among us, and let there be those that shall fear thee in our land, as long as the sun and moon endure, throughout all generations,[136] that there may be abundance of peace, and the children which shall be created may praise the Lord.[137]

12.3.3. For the continuance of our outward peace and tranquillity, our liberty and plenty, for the prosperity of our trade, and a blessing upon the fruits of the earth.

Let God himself be a wall of fire round about us, and the glory in the midst of us,[138] yea, let his gospel be our glory, and upon all that glory let there be a defence; and create upon every dwelling place of Mount Zion, and upon her assemblies, a cloud and smoke by day, and the shining of a flaming fire by night.[139]

Peace be within our borders, and prosperity within our palaces, the prosperity both of merchandise, and husbandry,[140] that Zebulun may rejoice in his going out, and Issachar in his tents.[141] Appoint salvation to us for walls and bulwarks, and in order to that let the gates be opened, that the righteous nation which keepeth the truth may enter in.[142]

Make our officers peace, and our exactors righteousness; let violence never be heard in our gates, wasting or destruction in our borders, but let our walls be called Salvation, and our gates Praise:[143] Never let our land be termed forsaken and desolate, but let the Lord delight in us, and let our land be married to him.[144]

Let our peace be as a river, and in order to that, our righteousness as the waves of the sea:[145] Let that righteousness abound among us, which exalteth a nation, and deliver us from sin, which is a reproach to any people.[146]

Never make our heavens as brass, and our earth as iron,[147] nor take away thy corn in the season thereof, and thy wine in the season thereof,[148] but give us rain moderately, the former and the latter rain in due sea-son,[149] and reserve unto us the appointed weeks of the harvest,[150] giving us fair weather also in its season. Let our land yield her increase, and the trees their fruit, that we may eat bread and be full, and dwell in our land safely.[151]

Abundantly bless our provision, and satisfy our poor with bread,[152] that they which have gathered it may eat and praise the Lord.[153] Blow not thou upon it, for then when we look for much it will come to little,[154] but bless our blessings, that all nations may call us blessed, and a delightsome land.[155]

12.3.4 For the success of all endeavors for the reformation of manners, the suppression of vice and profaneness, and support of religion and virtue, and the bringing of them into reputation.

O let the wickedness of the wicked come to an end, but establish thou the just, O thou righteous God that triest the hearts and reins.[156] Spirit many to rise up for thee against the evil doers, and to stand up for thee against the workers of iniquity.[157]

Let the Redeemer come to Zion, and turn away ungodliness from Jacob;[158] And let the filth of Jerusalem be purged from the midst thereof, by the spirit of judgment, and the spirit of burning.[159]

Let all iniquity stop her mouth,[160] and let the infection of that plague be stayed, by executing judgement.[161]

Let those that are striving against sin, never be weary or faint in their minds.[162]

Cause the unclean spirit to pass out of the land,[163] and turn to the people a pure language, that they may call on the name of the Lord.[164]

Make us high above all nations in praise, and in name, and in honour, by making us a holy people unto the Lord our God.[165]

12.3.5. For the healing of our unhappy divisions, and the making up of our breaches.

For the divisions that are among us, there are great searchings of heart;[166] for there are three against two, and two against three in a house.[167] But is the breach wide as the sea, which cannot be healed?[168]

Is there no balm in Gilead? Is there no physician there? Why then is not the health of the daughter of our people recovered?[169] Lord, heal the breaches of our land, for because of them it shaketh.[170]

We beg in the name of the Lord Jesus Christ that there may be no divisions among us, but that we may be perfectly joined together in the same mind, and in the same judgment.[171]

Now the God of patience and consolation grant us to be like-minded one towards another, according to Christ Jesus, that we may with one mind and one mouth glorify God,[172] even the Father of our Lord Jesus Christ, and promote the common salvation.[173]

Lord, keep us from judging one another, and despising one another, and give us to follow after the things which make for peace, and things wherewith one may edify another;[174] that living in love and peace, the God of love and peace may be with us.[175]

Let nothing be done through strife or vain glory, but every thing in lowliness of mind,[176] and grant that our moderation may be known unto all men, because the Lord is at hand.[177]

12.3.6 For victory and success against our enemies abroad, that seek our ruin.

Rise, Lord, and let thine enemies be scattered, and let those that hate thee flee before thee, but return, O Lord, to the many thousands of thine Israel.[178]

Give us help from trouble, for vain is the help of man; through God let our forces do valiantly;[179] yea, let God himself tread down our enemies; and give them as dust to our sword, and as driven stubble to our bow.[180]

Let us be a people saved by the Lord, as the shield of our help, and the sword of our excellency;[181] and make our enemies sensible that the Lord fighteth for us against them.[182]

Those who jeopard their lives for us in the high places of the field,[183] teach their hands to war, and their fingers to fight,[184] give them the shield of thy salvation, and let thy right hand hold them up,[185] and cover their heads in the day of battle.[186]

12.3.7 For all orders and degrees of men among us, and all we stand in any relation to.

12.3.7.1 For our sovereign Lord the king, that God will protect his person, preserve his health, and continue his life and government long a public blessing.

Give the king thy judgments, O God, and thy righteousness, that he may judge the poor of the people, may save the children of the needy, and may break in pieces the oppressor.[187]

Let his throne be established with righteousness,[188] and upheld with mercy;[189] Give him long life and length of days for ever and ever, and let his glory be great in thy salvation; and make him exceeding glad with thy countenance: Through the tender mercy of the Most High let him not be moved.[190]

Clothe his enemies with shame, but upon himself let the crown flourish,[191] and continue him long, very long, a nursing Father to thine Israel.[192]

12.3.7.2. For the succession in the Protestant line, that a blessing may attend it, that the entail of the crown may prove a successful expedient for the establishing of peace and truth in our days, the securing of them to posterity, and the extinguishing the hopes of our Popish adversaries, and all their aiders and abettors.

Lord, preserve to us the lamp which thou hast ordained for thine annointed,[193] that the generation to come may know thee, even the children which shall be born, that they may set their hope in God, and keep his commandments.[194]

Let the Protestant succession abide before God for ever; O prepare mercy and truth which may preserve it, so we will sing praise unto thy name for ever.[195] Thus let the Lord save Zion, and build the cities of

Judah, and the seed of thy servants shall inherit it, and they that love thy name shall dwell therein.[196]

Let their design who would make a captain to return into Egypt,[197] be again defeated, and let not the deadly wound that hath been given to the beast be healed any more.[198]

Let our eyes see Jerusalem, the city of our solemnities, a quiet habitation, a tabernacle that shall not be taken down: Let none of the stakes thereof be removed, nor any of the cords thereof be broken, but let the glorious Lord be to us a place of broad waters and streams; for the Lord is our judge, the Lord is our law-giver, the Lord is our king, he will save us.[199]

12.3.7.3. For the privy counsellors, the ministers of state, the members of Parliament, the ambassadors and envoys abroad, and all that are employed in the conduct of public affairs.

Counsel our counsellors, and teach our senators wisdom:[200] O give them a spirit of wisdom and understanding, a spirit of counsel and might, a spirit of knowledge, and of the fear of the Lord, to make them of quick understanding in the fear of the Lord.[201]

O remove not the speech of the trusty, nor take away the understanding of the aged,[202] nor ever let the things that belong to the nation's peace be hid from the eyes of those that are instructed with the nation's counsels.[203]

Make it to appear that thou standest in the congregation of the mighty, and judgest among the gods,[204] and that when the princes of the people are gathered together, even the people of the God of Abraham, the God of Abraham himself is among them; and let the shields of the earth belong unto the Lord, that he may be greatly exalted.[205]

Let those that be of us build the old waste places, and raise up the foundations of many generations, that they may be called the repairers of the breaches, and restorers of paths to dwell in.[206]

12.3.7.4. For the magistrates, the judges, and justices of peace in the several counties and corporations.

Make those that rule over us just, ruling in the fear of God;[207] and let those that judge remember that they judge not for man, but for the Lord, who is with them in the judgment, that therefore the fear of the Lord may be upon them.[208]

Make them able men, and men of truth, fearing God, and hating covetousness,[209] that judgment may run down like a river, and righteousness as a mighty stream.[210]

Enable our magistrates to defend the poor and fatherless, to do justice for the afflicted and needy, to deliver the poor and needy, and to rid them out of the hand of the wicked,[211] and let rulers never be a terror to good works, but to the evil.[212]

12.3.7.5. For all the ministers of God's holy word and sacraments, the masters of assemblies.

Teach thy ministers how they ought to behave themselves in the house of God, which is the church of the living God,[213] that they may not preach themselves, but Christ Jesus the Lord,[214] and may study to shew themselves approved to God, workmen that need not to be ashamed, rightly dividing the word of truth.[215]

Make them mighty in the scriptures,[216] that from thence they may be thoroughly furnished for every good work,[217] in doctrine shewing uncorruptness, gravity, and sincerity, and sound speech, which cannot be condemned.[218] Enable them to give attendance to reading, to exhortation, to doctrine, to meditate upon these things,[219] to give themselves to prayer, and to the ministry of the word,[220] to give themselves wholly to them; and to continue in them, that they may both save themselves and those that hear them.[221]

Let utterance be given to them, that they may open their mouths boldly, to make known the mystery of the gospel, that thereof they may speak, as they ought to speak,[222] as able ministers of the New Testament, not of the letter, but of the Spirit,[223] and let them obtain mercy of the Lord to be faithful.[224]

Let the arms of their hands be made strong by the hands of the mighty God of Jacob;[225] and let them be full of power by the Spirit of the Lord of hosts,[226] to show thy people their transgressions, and the house of Jacob their sins.[227]

Make them sound in the faith, and enable them always to speak the things which become sound doctrine,[228] with meekness instructing those that oppose themselves; and let not the servants of the Lord strive, but be gentle to all men, apt to teach.[229]

Make them good examples to the believers, in word, in conversation, in charity, in spirit, in faith, and in purity;[230] and let them be clean that bear the vessels of the Lord,[231] and let Holiness to the Lord be written upon their foreheads.[232]

Lord, grant that they may not labour in vain, or spend their strength for nought, and in vain,[233] but let the hand of the Lord be with them, that many may believe, and turn to the Lord.[234]

12.3.7.6. For all the universities, schools, and nurseries of learning.

Let the schools of the prophets be replenished with every good gift and every perfect gift from above, from the Father of lights.[235]

Cast salt into these fountains, and heal the waters thereof,[236] that from thence may issue streams, which shall make glad the city of our God, the holy place of the tabernacles of the most high.[237]

12.3.7.7. For the common people of the land.

Give grace to all the subjects of this land, that they may, under the government God hath set over us, live quiet and peaceable lives, in all godliness and honesty,[238] dwelling together in unity, that the Lord may command a blessing upon us, even life for evermore.[239]

Let all of every denomination that fear God and work righteousness, be accepted of him;[240] yea, let such as love thy salvation say continually, The Lord be magnified, that hath pleasure in the prosperity of his servants.[241]

12.3.7.8. For the several ages and conditions of men, as they stand in need of mercy and grace.

12.3.7.8.1. For those that are young and setting out in the world.

Lord, give to those that are young to remember their Creator in the days of their youth, that thereby they may be kept from the vanity which childhood and youth are subject to, and may be restrained from walking in the way of their heart, and in the sight of their eyes, by considering, that for all these things God will bring them into judgment.[242]

Lord, make young people sober-minded,[243] and let the word of God abide in them, that they may be strong, and may overcome the wicked one.[244]

From the womb of the morning let Christ have the dew of thy youth,[245] and let him be formed in the hearts of those that are young.[246]

Keep those that are setting out in the world from the corruption that is in the world through lust;[247] and give to those that have been well educated, to hold fast the form of sound words,[248] and to continue in the things which they have learned.[249]

12.3.7.8.2 For those that are old, and of long standing in profession.

There are some that are old disciples of Jesus Christ,[250] Lord, give them still to bring forth fruit in old age, to shew that the Lord is upright, that he is their rock, and there is no unrighteousness in him.[251]

Now the evil days are come, and the years of which they say there is no pleasure in them,[252] let thy comforts delight their souls.[253]

Even to their old age be thou he, and to the hoary hairs do thou carry them thou hast made; we beseech thee bear, yea, do thou carry and deliver them.[254]

Those whom thou hast taught from their youth up, and have hitherto declared all thy wondrous work, now also when they are old and grey-headed, leave them not, cast them not off in their old age, fail them not when their strength fails.[255] Let every hoary head be a crown of glory to those that have it, being found in the way of righteousness,[256] and give them to know whom they have believed.[257]

12.3.7.8.3. For those that are rich and prosperous in the world, some of whom perhaps need prayers as much as those that request them.

Lord, keep those that are rich in the world from being high-minded, and trusting in uncertain riches, and give them to trust in the living God, who giveth us richly all things to enjoy: That they may do good, and be rich in good works, ready to distribute, willing to communicate, that they may lay up in store for themselves a good security for the time to come.[258]

Though it is hard for those that are rich to enter into the kingdom of heaven, yet with thee this is possible.[259]

12.3.7.8.4. For those that are poor and in affliction, for such we have always with us.

Lord, make those that are poor in the world rich in faith, and heirs of the kingdom, and give to them to receive the gospel.[260]

O that the poor of the flock may wait upon thee, and may know the word of the Lord.[261]

Many are the troubles of the righteous, good Lord deliver them out of them all;[262] and though no affliction for the present seems to be joyous, but grievous, nevertheless, afterward let it yield the peaceable fruit of righteousness to them that are exercised thereby.[263]

12.3.7.8.5 For our enemies, and those that hate us.

Lord, give us to love our enemies, to bless them that curse us, and to pray for them that despitefully use us, and persecute us.[264]

Father, forgive them, for they know not what they do;[265] and lay not their malice against us to their charge,[266] and work in us a disposition to forbear and forgive in love,[267] as thou requirest we should, when we pray.[268]

And grant that our ways may so please the Lord, that even our enemies may be at peace with us.[269]

Let the wolf and the lamb lie down together, and let there be none to hurt and destroy in all thy holy mountain: let not Ephraim envy Judah, nor Judah vex Ephraim.[270]

12.3.7.8.6. *For our friends and those that love us.*

And we wish for all those whom we love in truth, that they may prosper, and be in health, especially that their souls may prosper.[271]

The grace of the Lord Jesus Christ be with their spirits.[272]

References

[1] Ps. 116:7, 12, 13.
[2] 1 Pet. 2:17.
[3] Gal. 6:10.
[4] 1 Tim. 2:3-4, 6.
[5] 1 John 5:19.
[6] John 12:31.
[7] 2 Cor. 4:4.
[8] Ps. 67:2.
[9] Eph. 2:12.
[10] Ps. 67:2-4.
[11] Ps. 98:2-3.
[12] Ps. 2:8.
[13] Isa. 49:6.
[14] Rev. 11:15.
[15] Mark 16:15.
[16] Rom. 10:14-15.
[17] Matt. 9:38.
[18] Matt. 4:16.
[19] Acts 2:47.
[20] Isa. 54:2.
[21] Isa. 43:5-6.
[22] Isa. 60:7-8.
[23] Mal. 1:11.
[24] Rom. 15:16.
[25] Isa. 11:9.
[26] Rom. 11:23-26.
[27] Zech. 12:10.
[28] 2 Cor. 3:16.
[29] Rev. 1:11-12.
[30] Rev. 2:1.
[31] Isa. 1:25-26.
[32] Ps. 126:4.
[33] Ps. 65:5.
[34] Gen. 49:26.
[35] Isa. 57:19.
[36] Deut. 33:19.
[37] Rom. 10:1.
[38] Ps. 51:18.
[39] Ps. 122:7-8.
[40] Ps. 128:5-6.
[41] Isa. 14:32.
[42] Ps. 28:9.
[43] Ps. 29:11.
[44] Ps. 5:12.
[45] Eph. 6:24.
[46] 2 Tim. 2:19.
[47] John 17:20-21.
[48] Eph. 4:4-6.
[49] Jer. 32:39.
[50] 2 Thess. 3:1.
[51] Ps. 51:13.
[52] 2 Tim. 2:25.
[53] Eph. 4:21.
[54] Titus 1:1.
[55] 2 Tim. 2:26.
[56] 1 Pet. 2:25.
[57] Ps. 14:1.
[58] Isa. 8:20.
[59] Ps. 138:2.
[60] Isa. 42:21.
[61] 1 Pet. 3:1.
[62] 1 Cor. 14:24-25.
[63] Isa. 32:15.
[64] Ps. 94:15.
[65] Titus 1:5.
[66] Matt. 15:13.
[67] Mal. 3:3-4.
[68] James 1:27.
[69] Rom. 14:17.
[70] Hab. 3:2.
[71] Heb. 9:10.
[72] Ps. 2:1-5.
[73] Hosea 9:14.
[74] Ps. 83:13, 16, 18.
[75] Ps. 9:20.
[76] Exod. 18:11.
[77] Ps. 129:5-6.
[78] Isa. 54:17.
[79] Zech. 12:3.
[80] Judg. 5:31.
[81] 2 Thess. 2:2-3, 8, 10-11.
[82] Rev. 18:2, 21.
[83] Rev. 17:12-13.
[84] Rev. 21:2.
[85] Heb.13:3.
[86] Ps. 18:16-17, 19.
[87] Ps. 125:3.
[88] Isa. 51:9-10.
[89] Ps. 12:5.
[90] Rev. 13:10.
[91] Lam. 3:26.
[92] Isa. 63:4.
[93] Isa. 34:8.
[94] Ps. 14:7.
[95] Ps. 74:21.
[96] Ps. 102:13, 16-17.
[97] Amos 7:5.
[98] Dan. 9:17.
[99] Ps. 79:11.
[100] Isa. 30:20.
[101] Ps. 22:28.
[102] Jer. 10:7.
[103] Ps. 9:4, 8.
[104] Ps. 46:9.
[105] Isa. 2:4.
[106] Isa. 49:23.
[107] Dan. 2:44.
[108] Prov. 19:21.
[109] Ps. 33:11.
[110] Isa. 5:1.
[111] Job 39:6.
[112] Ps. 85:12.
[113] Ps. 85:1.
[114] Ps. 44:1.
[115] Ps. 48:8-9.
[116] Jer. 3:19.
[117] Isa. 8:8.
[118] Isa. 22:1.
[119] Ezek. 37:26-27.
[120] 1 Kings 4:25.

121 2 Chron 15:5.
122 1 Kings 10:9.
123 Rom. 13:3.
124 Isa. 1:4.
125 Ezek. 9:4.
126 Matt. 24:12.
127 Jer. 51:5.
128 Jer. 14:7-9.
129 Ps. 80:2-3.
130 Ps. 85:7, 9-13.
131 Ps. 45:6.
132 Jer. 17:12.
133 Rev. 2:4-5.
134 Jer. 7:12.
135 Amos 8:11-12.
136 Ps. 33:6.
137 Ps. 72:5, 7.
138 Ps. 102:18.
139 Zech. 2:5.
140 Isa. 4:5.
141 Ps. 122:7.
142 Deut. 33:18.
143 Isa. 26:1-2.
144 Isa. 60:17-18.
145 Isa. 62:4.
146 Isa. 48:18.
147 Prov. 14:34.
148 Deut. 28:23.
149 Hosea 2:9.
150 Joel 2:23.
151 Jer. 5:24.
152 Lev. 26:4-5.
153 Ps. 132:15.
154 Isa. 62:9.
155 Hag. 1:9.
156 Mal. 3:10, 12.
157 Ps. 7:9.
158 Ps. 94:16.
159 Rom. 11:26.
160 Isa. 4:4.
161 Ps. 107:42.
162 Ps. 106:30.
163 Heb. 12:3-4.
164 Zech 13:2.
165 Zeph. 3:9.
166 Deut. 26:19.
167 Zech 13:2.
168 Zeph. 3:9.

169 Deut. 26:19.
170 Luke 12:52.
171 Lam. 2:13.
172 Jer. 8:22.
173 Ps. 60:2.
174 1 Cor. 1:10.
175 Rom. 15:5-6.
176 Jude 3.
177 2 Cor. 13:11.
178 Phil. 2:3.
179 Phil. 4:5.
180 Numb. 10:35-36.
181 Ps. 60:11-12.
182 Isa. 41:2.
183 Deut. 33:29.
184 Exod. 14:25.
185 Judg. 5:18.
186 Ps. 144:1.
187 Ps. 18:34-35.
188 Ps. 140:7.
189 Ps. 72:1, 4.
190 Prov. 16:12.
191 Prov. 20:28.
192 Ps. 21:4-7.
193 Ps. 132:18.
194 Isa. 49:23.
195 Ps. 132:17.
196 Ps. 78:6-7.
197 Ps. 61:7-8.
198 Ps. 69:35-36.
199 Num. 14:4.
200 Isa. 33:20-22.
201 Ps. 105:22.
202 Isa. 11:2-3.
203 Job 12:20.
204 Luke 19:42.
205 Ps. 82:1.
206 Ps. 47:9.
207 Isa. 58:2.
208 2 Sam. 23:3.
209 2 Chron. 19:6-7.
210 Exod. 18:21.
211 Amos 5:24.
212 Ps. 82:3-4.
213 Rom. 13:3.
214 1 Tim. 3:15.
215 2 Cor. 4:5.
216 2 Tim. 2:15.

217 Acts. 18:24.
218 2 Tim. 3:17.
219 Titus 2:7.
220 1 Tim. 4:13, 15.
221 Acts 6:4.
222 1 Tim. 4:15.
223 Eph. 6:19-20.
224 2 Cor 3:6.
225 1 Cor. 7:25.
226 Gen. 49:24.
227 Micah 3:8.
228 Isa. 58:1.
232 Titus 1:13, 2:1.
233 2 Tim. 2:24-25.
234 1 Tim. 4:12.
235 Isa. 52:11.
236 Exod. 28:36.
237 Isa. 49:4.
238 Acts 11:21.
239 James 1:17.
240 2 Kings 2:21.
241 Ps. 46:4.
242 1 Tim. 2:2.
243 Ps. 133:1, 3.
244 Acts 10:35.
245 Ps. 35:27.
246 Eccles. 12:1, 14.
247 Titus 2:6.
248 1 John 2:14.
249 Ps. 110:3.
250 Gal. 4:19.
251 2 Pet. 1:4.
252 2 Tim. 1:13-14.
253 2 Tim. 3:14.
254 Acts 21:16.
255 Ps. 92:14-15.
256 Eccles. 12:1.
257 Ps. 94:19.
258 Isa. 46:4.
259 Ps. 71:6, 17-18.
260 Prov. 16:31.
261 2 Tim. 1:12.
262 1 Tim. 6:17, 19.
263 Matt. 19:24, 26.
264 James 2:5.
265 Zech. 11:11.
266 Ps. 34:19.
267 Heb. 12:11.

[268] Matt. 5:44.
[269] Luke 23:34.
[270] Acts 7:60.

[271] Col. 3:13.
[272] Mark 11:25.
[273] Prov. 16:7.

[274] Isa. 11:6, 9, 13.
[275] 3 John 2.
[276] Philem. 25.

CHAPTER 6

Of Addresses to God upon particular Occasions, whether Domestic or Public.

It is made our duty, and prescribed as a remedy against disquieting care, that in every thing, by prayer and supplication, with thanksgiving, we should make our requests known to God.[1] And it is part of the Parrhsia, the boldness, the liberty of speech, (so the word signifies) which is allowed us in our access to God,[2] that we may be particular in opening our case, and seeking to him for relief; that, according as the sore and the grief is, accordingly the prayer and the supplication may be by any man, or by the people of Israel.[3] Not that God needs to be particularly informed of our condition; he knows it better than we ourselves do, and our souls too in our adversity; but it is his will that we should thus acknowledge him in all our ways,[4] and wait upon him for the direction of every step,[5] not prescribing, but subscribing to infinite wisdom, humbly showing him our wants, burdens, and desires, and then referring ourselves to him, to do for us as he thinks fit.

We shall instance some of the occasions of particular address to God, more or less usual, which may either be the principal matter of a whole prayer, or inserted in our other prayers, and in some cases that are more peculiar to ministers, or others, in common to them with masters of families and private Christians. As there may be something particular.

1. In our morning prayers.

Our voice shalt thou hear in the morning, in the morning will we direct our prayer unto thee, and will look up;[6] for our souls wait for thee, O Lord, more than they that watch for the morning,[7] yea, more than they that watch for the morning; and we will sing aloud of thy mercy in the morning; for thou hast been our defence.[8]

It is thou, O God, that hast commanded the morning, and caused the day-spring to know its place, that it might take hold of the ends of the earth, and it is turned as clay to the seal.[9]

The day is thine, the night also is thine, thou hast prepared the light and the sun.[10]

With the light of the morning, let the day-spring from on high visit us, to give us the knowledge of salvation through the tender mercies of our God;[11] and let the Sun of righteousness arise upon our souls with healing under his wings;[12] and our path be as the shining light, which shines more and more to the perfect day.[13]

It is of thy mercy, O Lord, that we are not consumed, even because thy compassions fail not, they are new every morning, great is thy faithfulness;[14] and if weeping sometimes endures for a night, joy comes in the morning.[15]

We thank thee that we have laid us down;[16] have had where to lay our head,[17] and have not been wandering in deserts and mountains, in dens and caves of the earth:[18] And that we have slept, and have not been full of tossings to and fro till the dawning of the day, that wearisome nights are not appointed to us, and we are not saying at our lying down, When shall we arise, and the night be gone? But our bed comforts us, and our couch eases our complaints;[19] Thou givest us sleep as thou givest it to thy beloved.[20] And that having laid us down and slept, we have waked again; thou hast lightened our eyes, so that we have not slept the sleep of death.[21]

Thou hast preserved us from the pestilence that walketh in darkness,[22] and from the malice of the rulers of the darkness of this world,[23] the roaring lion that goes about seeking to devour:[24] He that keeps Israel, and neither slumbers nor sleeps,[25] has kept us, and so we have been safe.

But we cannot say with thy servant David, that when we awake we are still with thee,[26] or that our eyes have prevented the night-watches, that we might meditate on thy word;[27] but vain thoughts still lodge within us.[28] O pardon our sins, and cause us to hear thy loving-kindness this morning, for in thee do we trust; cause us to know the way, wherein we should walk, for we lift up our souls unto thee: Teach us to do thy will, for thou art our God, thy Spirit is good, lead us into the way and land of uprightness.[29]

And now let the Lord preserve and keep us from all evil this day, yea, let the Lord preserve our souls: Lord, preserve our going out; and coming in;[30] give thine angels charge concerning us, to bear us up in their hands, and keep us in all our ways.[31] And give us grace to do the work of the day in its day, as the duty of the day requires.[32]

2. In our evening prayers.

Thou, O God, makest the out-goings of the evening, as well as of the morning, to rejoice;[33] for thereby thou callest us from work and our labour, and biddest us rest a while.[34] And now let our souls return to thee,[35] and repose in thee as our rest, because thou hast dealt bountifully with us;[36] so shall our sleep be sweet to us.[37]

Blessed be the Lord, who daily loads us with his benefits, who hath this day preserved our going out and coming in:[38] And now we have received from thee our daily bread, we pray, Father, forgive us our trespasses.[39]

And we will lay us down and sleep; for thou, Lord, makest us to dwell in safety:[40] Make a hedge of protection (we pray thee) about us, and about our house, and about all that we have round about.[41] Let the angels of God encamp round about us, to deliver us;[42] that we may lie down, and none may make us afraid.[43]

Into thy hands we commit our spirits;[44] that in slumberings upon the bed, our ears may be opened and instructions sealed;[45] And let the Lord give us counsel, and let our reins instruct us in the night season:[46] Visit us in the night, and try us,[47] and enable us to commune with our own hearts upon our beds.[48]

Give us to remember thee upon our bed, and to meditate upon thee in the night watches,[49] with the saints that are joyful in glory, and that sing aloud upon their beds.[50]

3. In craving a blessing before meat.

Thou, O Lord, givest food to all flesh, for thy mercy endures for ever.[51] The eyes of all things wait on thee;[52] but especially thou givest meat to them that fear thee, being ever mindful of thy covenant.[53]

Thou art our life, and the length of our days,[54] the God that hast fed us all our life long unto this day:[55] Thou givest us all things richly to enjoy, though we serve thee but poorly.[56] Thou has not only given us every green herb, and the fruit of the trees, to be to us for meat,[57] but every moving thing that liveth, even as the green herb.[58]

And blessed be God that now under the gospel we are taught to call nothing common or unclean,[59] and that it is not that which goes into the man, that defiles the man,[60] but that every creature of God is good, and nothing to be refused; for God hath created it to be received with thanksgiving of them which believe and know the truth.[61]

We acknowledge we are not worthy of the least crumb that falls from the table of thy providence:[62] Thou mightest justly take away from us the stay of bread and the stay of water,[63] and make us to eat our bread by weight, and to drink our water by measure, and with astonishment:[64] because when we have been fed to the full, we have forgotten God our Maker.[65] But let our sins be pardoned, we pray thee, that our table may not become a snare before us, nor that be made a trap, which should have been for our welfare.[66]

We know that every thing is sanctified by the word of God and prayer;[67] and that man lives not by bread alone, but by every word that proceedeth out of the mouth of God,[68] and therefore, according to our Master's example we look up to heaven, and pray for a blessing upon our food;[69] abundantly bless our provision.[70]

Lord, grant that we may not feed ourselves without fear,[71] that we may not make a god of our belly,[72] that our hearts may never be overcharged with surfeiting or drunkenness,[73] but that whether we eat or drink, or whatever we do, we may do all to the glory of God.[74]

4. In returning thanks after our meat.

Now we have eaten and are full, we bless thee for the good land thou hast given us.[75] Thou preparest a table for us in the presence of our enemies, thou anointest our head, and our cup runs over.[76]

Thou, Lord, art the portion of our inheritance, and of our cup, thou maintainest our lot, so that we have reason to say, The lines are fallen to us in pleasant places, and we have a goodly heritage.[77]

Especially we bless thee for the bread of life, which came down from heaven, which was given for the life of the world. Lord, evermore give us that bread, and wisdom to labour less for the meat which perisheth, and more for that which endures to everlasting life.[78]

The Lord give food to the hungry,[79] and send portions to them for whom nothing is prepared.[80]

Let us be of those blessed ones that shall eat bread in the kingdom of God,[81] and shall eat of the hidden manna.[82]

5. When we are going on a journey.

Lord keep us in the way that we should go,[83] and let no evil thing befall us:[84] Let us have a prosperous journey by the will of God,[85] and with thy favour let us be compassed wherever we go as with a shield.[86]

Let us walk in our way safely,[87] and let not our foot stumble, or dash against a stone.[88]

Direct our way in every thing,[89] and enable us to order all our affairs with discretion,[90] and the Lord send us good speed, and shew kindness to us.[91]

And the Lord watch between us when we are absent the one from the other.[92]

6. *When we return from a journey.*

Blessed be the Lord God of Abraham, who hath not left us destitute of his mercy and his truth.[93]

All our bones shall say, Lord, who is like unto thee, for thou keepest all our bones.[94]

It is God that girdeth us with strength, and maketh our way perfect.[95]

7. *In the evening before the Lord's day.*

Now give us to remember, that to-morrow is the sabbath of the Lord,[96] and that it is a high day,[97] holy of the Lord and honourable,[98] and give us grace so to sanctify ourselves, that to-morrow the Lord may do wonders among us;[99] and to mind the work of our preparation, now the sabbath draws on.[100]

When thou sawest every thing that thou hadst made in six days, behold all was very good,[101] but in many things we have all offended.[102] O that by repentance and faith in Christ's blood, we may wash not only our feet, but also our hands, and our head, and our heart,[103] and so may compass thine altar, O Lord.[104]

Now give us to rest from all our own works,[105] and to leave all our worldly cares at the bottom of the hill, while we go up to the mount to worship God, and return again to them.[106]

8. *On the morning of the Lord's day.*

We bless thee, Lord, who hath shewed us light, and that the light we see is the Lord's;[107] that we see one more of the days of the Son of man,[108] a day to be spent in thy courts, which is better than a thousand elsewhere.[109]

We thank thee, Father, Lord of heaven and earth, that the things which were hid from the wise and prudent are revealed unto us babes, even so, Father, because it seemed good in thine eyes: That our eyes see, and our ears hear that which many prophets and kings desired to see, desired to hear and might not;[110] that life and immortality are brought to light by the gospel.[111]

And now, O that we may be in the Spirit on the Lord's day![112] that we may call the sabbath a delight,[113] and may honour the Son of man, who is the Lord also of the sabbath-day,[114] not doing our own ways, or finding our own pleasure, or speaking our own words.

9. *At the entrance upon the public worship on the Lord's day, by the master of the assemblies.*

Thou, O God, art greatly to be feared in the assembly of the saints, and to be had in reverence of all them that are about thee.[115] O give us grace to worship thee with reverence and godly fear, because thou our God art a consuming fire.[116]

That is that which thou hast said, that thou wilt be sanctified in them which come nigh unto thee; and before all the people thou wilt be glorified.[117] Thou art the Lord that sanctifiest us,[118] sanctify us by thy truth, that we may sanctify thee in our hearts,[119] and make thee our fear and our dread.[120]

We come together to give glory to the great Jehovah, who in six days made heaven and earth, the sea, and all that in them is, and rested the seventh day, and therefore blessed the sabbath day, and hallowed it.[121] And our help stands in the name of the Lord who made heaven and earth.[122]

O let us be new creatures,[123] thy workmanship, created in Christ Jesus unto good works.[124] And let that God, who on the first day of the world commanded the light to shine out of darkness, on this first day of the week shine in our hearts, to give us the light of the knowledge of the glory of God, in the face of Jesus Christ.[125]

We come together to give glory to the Lord Jesus Christ, and to sanctify this sabbath, to his honour, who was the stone that the builders refused, but now is become the head stone of the corner. This is the Lord's doing, it is marvellous in our eyes: This is the day which the Lord has made, we will rejoice and be glad in it:[126] He is the first and the last, who was dead and is alive.[127]

O that we may this day experience the power of Christ's resurrection,[128] and may be planted together in the likeness of it, that as Christ was raised up from the dead by the glory of the Father, so we also may walk in newness of life,[129] and may sit with him in heavenly places;[130] and by seeking the things that are above, may make it to appear that we are risen with him.[131]

We come together to give glory to the blessed Spirit of grace, and to celebrate the memorial of the giving of that promise of the Father, in whom the apostles received power on the first day of the week, as on that day Christ rose.[132]

O that we may this day be filled with the holy Ghost, and that the fruit of the Spirit in us may be in all goodness, and righteousness, and truth.[133]

We come together to testify our communion with the universal church, that though we are many, yet we are one; that we worship one and the same God the Father, of whom are all things, and we in him, in the name of one Lord Jesus Christ, by whom are all things, and we by him,[134] under the conduct of the same Spirit, one and the self-same Spirit, who divideth to every man severally as he will,[135] walking by the same rule,[136] looking for the same blessed hope, and the glorious appearing of the great God and our Saviour.[137]

10. In our preparation for the Lord's Supper.

Now we are invited to come eat of wisdom's bread, and drink of the wine that she has mingled,[138] give us to hunger and thirst after righteousness:[139] And being called to the marriage supper of the Lamb,[140] give us the wedding garment.[141]

Awake, O north wind, and come thou south, and blow upon our garden, that the spices thereof may flow forth; and then let our beloved come into his garden, and eat his pleasant fruits.[142]

Draw us, and we will run after thee; bring us into thy chambers, that there we may be glad and rejoice in thee, and may remember thy love more than wine. And when the king sits at his table, let our spikenard send forth the smell thereof.[143]

And the good Lord pardon every one that prepareth his heart to seek God, the Lord God of his fathers, though he be not cleansed according to the purification of the sanctuary: Hear our prayers, and heal the people.[144]

11. In the celebrating of the Lord's Supper.

O let this cup of blessing which we bless, be the communion of the blood of Christ,[145] let this bread which we break, be the communion of the body of Christ, and enable us herein to shew the Lord's death till he come.[146]

Now let us be joined to the Lord in an everlasting covenant;[147] so joined to the Lord, as to become one spirit with him.[148] Now let us be made partakers of Christ, by holding fast the beginning of our confidence steadfast unto the end.[149]

Let Christ's flesh be meat indeed to us, and his blood drink indeed: and give us so by faith to eat his flesh, and drink his blood, that he may dwell in us, and we in him, and we may live by him.[150]

Let the cross of Christ, which is to the Jews a stumbling block, and to the Greeks foolishness, be to us the wisdom of God, and the power of God.[151]

Seal to us the remission of sins, the gift of the Holy Ghost,[152] and the promise of eternal life,[153] and enable us to take this cup of salvation, and to call on the name of the Lord.[154]

12. After celebrating the Lord's Supper.

And now, Lord, give us to hold fast that which we have received, that no man take our crown:[155] And keep it always in the imaginations of the thoughts of our hearts, and prepare our hearts unto thee.[156]

Give us grace, as we have received Christ Jesus the Lord, so to walk in him,[157] that our conversation may be in every thing as becomes his gospel.[158]

O that we may now bear about with us continually the dying of our Lord Jesus, so as that the life also of Jesus may be manifested in our mortal bodies,[159] that to us to live may be Christ.[160]

Thy vows are upon us, O God.[161] O that we may be daily performing our vows.[162]

13. Upon occasion of the baptism of a child.

To thee, O God, whose all souls are, the souls of the parents, and the souls of the children,[163] we present this child a living sacrifice, which we desire may be holy and acceptable,[164] and that it may be given up and dedicated to the Father, Son, and Holy Ghost.[165]

It is conceived in sin,[166] but there is a fountain opened; O wash the soul of this child in that fountain,[167] now it is by thine appointment washed with pure water.[168]

It is one of the children of the covenant,[169] one of the children that is born unto thee,[170] it is thy servant, born in thy house;[171] O make good thy ancient covenant, that thou wilt be a God to believers, and to their seed;[172] for this blessing of Abraham comes upon the Gentiles,[173] and the promise is still to us, and to our children.[174]

Thou hast encouraged us to bring little children to thee; for thou hast said, that of such is the kingdom of God. Blessed Jesus, take up this child in the arms of thy power and grace, put thy hands upon it, and bless it;[175] let it be a vessel of honour sanctified, and meet for the master's use,[176] and owned as one of thine in that day when thou makest up thy jewels.[177]

O pour thy spirit upon our seed, thy blessing upon our offspring, that they may spring up as willows by the water-courses, and may come to subscribe with their own hands unto the Lord, and to sirname themselves by the name of Israel.[178]

14. Upon occasion of a funeral.

Lord, give it to us to find it good for us to go to the house of mourning, that we may be minded thereby of the end of all men, and may lay it to our heart,[179] and may be so wise as to consider our latter end;[180] for we must also be gathered to our people, as our neighbors and brethren are gathered;[181] and though whither those that are dead in Christ are gone, we cannot follow them now;[182] yet grant that we may follow them afterwards, every one in his own order.[183]

We know that thou wilt bring us to death, and to the house appointed for all living,[184] but let us not see death, till by faith we have seen the Lord Christ, and then let us depart in peace, according to thy word.[185] And when the earthly house of this tabernacle shall be dissolved, let us have a building of God, a house not made with hands, eternal in the heavens.[186]

And give us to know that our Redeemer liveth, and that though after our skins, worms destroy these bodies, yet in our flesh we shall see God, whom we shall see for ourselves, and our eyes shall behold, and not another.[187]

15. *Upon occasion of marriage.*

Give to those that marry, to marry in the Lord;[188] and let the Lord Jesus by his grace come to the marriage, and turn the water into wine.[189]

Make them helps meet for each other,[190] and instrumental to promote one anothers salvation,[191] and give them to live in holy love, that they may dwell in God, and God in them.[192]

Let the wife be as a fruitful vine by the side of the house,[193] and the husband dwell with the wife as a man of knowledge, and let them dwell together as joint heirs of the grace of life, that their prayers be not hindered,[194] and make us all meet for that world, where they neither marry nor are given in marriage.[195]

16. *Upon occasion of the ordaining of ministers.*

Let the things of God be committed to faithful men, who may be able also to teach others:[196] and make them such burning and shining lights,[197] at that it may appear that it was Christ Jesus who put them into the ministry;[198] and let not hands be suddenly laid on any.[199]

Give to those who are ordained, to take heed to the ministry which they have received of the Lord, that they fulfil it,[200] and to make full proof of it, by watching in all things.[201]

Let those who in Christ's name are to preach repentance and remission of sins, be endued with power from on high;[202] give them another spirit,[203] and make them good ministers of Jesus Christ, nourished up in the works of faith and good doctrine.[204]

17. *Upon occasion of the want of rain.*

Thou hast withholden the rain from us, and caused it to rain upon one city, and not upon another, yet have we not returned unto thee.[205]

But thou hast said, when heaven is shut up, that there is no rain, because we have sinned against thee: if we confess thy name, and turn from our sins, thou wilt hear from heaven, and forgive our sin, and give rain upon our land.[206]

We ask thee for the former and latter rain, and depend upon thee for it;[207] for there are not any of the vanities of the heathen that can give rain, nor can the heavens give showers, but we wait on thee, for thou hast made all these things.[208]

18. Upon occasion of excessive rain.

Let the rain thou sendest be in mercy to our land and not for correction,[209] not a sweeping rain, which leaveth no food.[210]

Thou hast sworn that the waters of Noah shall no more return to cover the earth;[211] let fair weather therefore come out of the north, for with thee is terrible majesty.[212]

19. Upon occasion of infectious diseases.

Take sickness away from the midst of us,[213] and deliver us from the noisome pestilence.[214]

Appoint the destroying angel to put up his sword into his sheath, and to stay his hand.[215]

20. Upon occasion of fire.

Thou callest to contend by fire,[216] we bewail the burning which the Lord hath kindled:[217] O Lord God, cease, we beseech thee,[218] and let the fire be quenched, as that kindled in Israel was at the prayer of Moses.[219]

21. Upon occasion of great storms.

Lord, thou hast the wind in thy hands,[220] and bringest them out of thy treasures,[221] even stormy winds fulfil thy word.[222] O preserve us and our habitations, that we be not buried in the ruins of them as Job's children were.[223]

22. Upon occasion of the cares, and burdens, and afflictions of particular persons: as,

22.1. When we pray with, or for those that are troubled in mind, and melancholy, and under doubts and fears about their spiritual state.

Lord, enable those that fear thee, and obey the voice of thy servant, but walk in darkness, and have no light, to trust in the name of the

Lord, and to stay themselves upon their God:[224] And at evening time let it be light.[225]

O strengthen the weak hands, confirm the feeble knees, say to them that are of a fearful heart, Be strong, fear not:[226] Answer them with good words, and comfortable words,[227] saying unto them, Be of good cheer, your sins are forgiven you:[228] Be of good cheer, it is I: be not afraid,[229] I am your salvation.[230] And make them to hear the voice of joy and gladness, that broken bones may rejoice.[231]

Let those who now remember God, and are troubled, whose spirits are overwhelmed, and whose souls refuse to be comforted,[232] be enabled to trust in thy mercy, so that at length they may rejoice in thy salvation;[233] though thou slay them, yet to trust in thee.[234]

Though deep calls unto deep, and all thy waves and thy billows go over them, yet do thou command thy loving-kindness for them in the day-time, and in the night let thy song be with them, and their prayer to the God of their life, though their souls are cast down and disquieted within them, give them hope in God, that they shall yet praise him, and let them find him the health of their countenance and their God.[235]

O renew a right spirit within them, cast them not away from thy presence, and take not thy Holy Spirit from them, but restore unto them the joy of thy salvation, and uphold them with thy free Spirit,[236] that their tongues may sing aloud of thy righteousness, and shew forth thy salvation.[237]

O bring them up out of this horrible pit, and this miry clay, and set their feet upon a rock, establishing their goings, and put a new song in their mouth, even praises to our God,[238] O comfort them again now after the time that thou hast afflicted them.[239]

Though for a small moment thou hast forsaken them, and hid thy face from them, yet gather them, and have mercy on them with everlasting kindness.[240]

O let thy Spirit witness with their spirits, that they are the children of God;[241] and by the blood of Christ let them be purged from an evil conscience.[242]

Lord, rebuke the tempter, even the accuser of the brethren, the Lord that hath chosen Jerusalem rebuke him, and let poor tempted troubled souls be as brands plucked out of the burning.[243]

22.2. Those that are under convictions of sin, and begin to be concerned about their souls and their salvation, and to inquire after Christ.

Those that are asking the way to Zion, with their faces thitherward,[244] that are lamenting after the Lord,[245] and are pricked to the heart for sin,[246] O show them the good and the right way, and lead them in it.[247]

To those that are asking what they shall do to inherit eternal life,[248] discover Christ as the way, the truth, and the life, the only true and living way.[249]

O do not quench the smoking flax, nor break the bruised reed, but bring forth judgment unto victory.[250] Let the great Shepherd of the sheep gather the lambs in his arms, and carry them in his bosom, and gently lead them,[251] and help them against their unbelief.[252]

Let not the red dragon devour the man-child, as soon as it is born, but let it be caught up to God, and to his throne.[253]

22.3. When we pray with, or for those that are sick and weak, and distempered in body, that those who are sick and in sin may be convinced, those who are sick and in Christ comforted.

Lord, thou hast appointed those that are sick to be prayed for, and prayed with, and hast promised that the prayer of faith shall save the sick; Lord, help us to pray in faith for the sick,[254] and as being ourselves also in the body.[255]

When our Lord Jesus was here upon earth, we find that they brought to him all sick people that were taken with divers diseases and torments, and he healed all manner of sicknesses, and all manner of diseases among the people: and he hath still the same power over bodily diseases that ever he had:[256] he saith to them, Go, and they go; Come, and they come; Do this, and they do it; and can speak the word, and they shall be healed.[257] And he is still touched with the feeling of our infirmities.[258] In the belief of this, we do by prayer bring our friends that are sick, and lay them before him.[259]

Lord, grant that those who are sick may neither despise the chastening of the Lord, nor faint when they are rebuked of him;[260] but that they may both hear the rod, and him that hath appointed it,[261] and may kiss the rod, and accept of the punishment of their iniquity.[262]

Give them to see that affliction cometh not forth out of the dust, nor springs out of the ground,[263] that they may therefore seek unto God, to the Lord more than to the physicians,[264] because unto God the Lord belong the issues of life and death.[265]

Lord, shew them wherefore thou contendest with them,[266] and give them in their affliction to humble themselves greatly before the God of their fathers,[267] and to repent and turn from every evil way, and make their ways and their doings good,[268] and being judged and being chastened of the Lord, they may not be condemned with the world.[269] By the sickness of the body, and the sadness of the countenance, let the heart be made better.[270]

O Lord, rebuke them not in thine anger, neither chasten in thy hot displeasure: Have mercy upon them, O Lord, for they are weak: Lord heal them, for their bones are vexed, their souls also are sore vexed: Return, O Lord, and deliver their souls, save them for thy mercy's sake:[271] and lay no more upon them than thou wilt enable them to bear, and enable them to bear what thou dost lay upon them.[272]

When thou with rebukes dost chasten man for sin, thou makest his beauty to consume away like a moth; surely every man is vanity. But remove thy stroke we pray thee, from those that are even consumed by the blow of thine hand. O spare a little, that they may recover strength before they go hence and be no more.[273]

Those that are chastened with pain upon their bed, and the multitude of their bones with strong pain, so that their life abhorreth bread, and their soul dainty meat, shew them thine uprightness, be gracious to them. Deliver them from going down to the pit, for thou hast found a ransom.[274]

Let the eternal God be their refuge, and underneath them be the everlasting arms,[275] consider their frame, remember that they are but dust.[276]

O deliver those that are thine in the time of trouble, preserve them and keep them alive: O strengthen them upon their bed of languishing, and make their bed in their sickness: Be merciful to them, and heal their souls, for they have sinned.[277]

O turn to them, and have mercy upon them, bring them out of their distresses, look upon their affliction and their pain, but especially forgive all their sin.[278]

Make thy face to shine upon them, save them for thy mercy's sake;[279] The God that comforteth them that are cast down, comfort them![280] and let the soul dwell at ease in thee,[281] when the body lies in pain.

(If it be the beginning of a distemper.) Lord set bounds to this sickness, and say, Hitherto shall it come, and no further;[282] let it not prevail to extremity, but in measure, when it shooteth forth, do thou debate, and stay thy rough wind in the day of thine east wind; and by this let iniquity be purged, and let this be all the fruit, even the taking away of sin.[283]

(If it have continued long.) Lord, let patience have her perfect work, even unto long-suffering, that those who have been long in the furnace,[284] may continue hoping,and quietly waiting for the salvation of the Lord;[285] Let tribulation work patience, and patience experience, and experience a hope that maketh not ashamed,[286] and enable them

to call even this affliction light, seeing it to work for them a far more exceeding and eternal weight of glory.[287]

(If there be hopes of recovery.) Lord, when thou hast tried, let them come forth like gold:[288] let their souls live and they shall praise thee, let thy judgments help them: O deal bountifully with them, that they may live and keep thy word.[289] In love to their souls deliver them from the pit of corruption, and cast all their sins behind thy back. Recover them, and make them to live.[290] Speak the word, and they shall be healed:[291] Say unto them, Live, yea, say unto them, Live, and the time shall be a time of love.[292]

Father, if it possible, let the cup pass away; however, not as we will, but as thou wilt:[293] The will of the Lord be done.[294] Perfect that which concerns them: thy mercy, O Lord, endures for ever, forsake not the work of thine own hands,[295] but whether they live or die, let them be the Lord's.[296]

(If they be in appearance at the point of death.)

Now the flesh and the heart are failing, Lord, be thou the strength of the heart, and an everlasting portion;[297] In the valley of the shadow of death, Lord be thou present, as the good Shepherd, with a guiding rod, and a supporting staff.[298] O do not fail them, nor forsake them now.[299] Be a very present help.[300] Into thy hands we commit the departing spirit,[301] as into the hands of a faithful Creator, by the hands of him who has redeemed it.[302] Let it be carried by the angels into Abraham's bosom.[303] Let it be presented to thee without spot, or wrinkle, or any such thing.[304] Lord Jesus, receive this precious soul,[305] let it come to the spirits of just men made perfect;[306] when it is absent from the body, let it be present with the Lord.[307] This day let it be with thee in paradise.[308] Now let it be for ever comforted,[309] and perfectly freed from sin,[310] and prepare us to draw after, as there are innumerable before,[311] that we may be together for ever with the Lord,[312] there where there shall be no more death, and where all tears shall be wiped away.[313]

22.4. When we pray with, or for those that are deprived of the use of their reason.

O look with pity upon those that are put out of possession of their own souls,[314] whose judgment is taken away,[315] so that their soul chooseth strangling and death rather than life.[316] O restore them to themselves, and their right mind.[317] Deliver them from doing themselves any harm.[318] And whatever afflictions thou layest upon any of us in this world, preserve to us the use of our reason, and the peace of our consciences.

22.5. When we pray with, or for sick children.

Lord, we see death reigning even over them that have not sinned after the similitude of Adam's transgression;[319] but Jesus Christ hath abolished death,[320] and admitted even little children into the kingdom of God.[321] O let sick children be pitied by thee, as they are by their earthly parents.[322] They are come forth like flowers, O let them not be cut down again: Turn from them, that they may rest till they shall have accomplished as a hireling their day.[323] Be gracious to us, and let the children live.[324] However, Father, thy will be done.[325] O let their spirits be saved in the day of the Lord Jesus.[326]

22.6. When we pray with or for families where death is, especially such as have lost their head.

Visit the houses of mourning, as our Saviour did, and comfort them, by assuring them that Christ is the resurrection and the life, that their relations which are removed from them,[327] are not dead, but sleep;[328] and that they shall rise again, that they may not sorrow as those that have no hope.[329] And enable them to trust in the living God,[330] the rock of ages, and enjoy the fountains of living waters, when creatures prove broken reeds and broken cisterns.[331]

Be a father to the fatherless, and a husband to the widows, O God, in thy holy habitation.[332] With thee let the fatherless find mercy,[333] keep them alive, and let the widows trust in thee,[334] that they may be widows indeed, who being desolate, trust in God, and continue instant in prayer night and day.[335] And where father and mother have forsaken, let the Lord take up the children,[336] and not leave them orphans, but come to them.[337]

22.7. When we pray with, or for those women that are near the time of travail, or in travail.

Lord, thou hast passed this sentence upon the woman that was first in the transgression,[338] that in sorrow she shall bring forth children.[339] But let this handmaid of thine be saved in child-bearing, and continue in faith, and charity, and holiness, with sobriety.[340] Enable her to cast her burden upon the Lord, and let the Lord sustain her;[341] and what time she is afraid, grant that she may trust in thee,[342] and may encourage herself in the Lord her God.[343] O let not the root be dried up from beneath, nor let the branch be withered, or cut off;[344] but let both live before thee. Be thou her strong habitation, her rock, and her fortress, give commandment to save her.[345] And when travail comes upon her, which she cannot escape, be pleased, O Lord, to deliver her:[346] O Lord, make haste to help her: Be thou thyself her help and deliverer, make no tarrying, O our God: Let her be safely delivered,[347] and remember the anguish no more, for joy that a child is born into the world, is born unto thee.[348]

22.8. When we pray with, or for those that are recovered from sickness, or are delivered in child-bearing, and desire to return thanks to God for his mercy.

We will extol thee, O Lord, upon the account of those whom thou hast lifted up, whose souls thou hast brought up from the grave, and kept them alive, that they should not go down to the pit.[349] Those that were brought low thou hast helped, hast delivered their souls from death, their eyes from tears, and their feet from falling. Now give them grace to walk before thee in the land of the living, to offer thee the sacrifices of thanksgiving, to call upon thy name, and to pay their vows unto the Lord.[350]

The grave cannot thus praise thee, death cannot celebrate thee, they that go down to the pit cannot hope for thy truth, but the living they shall praise thee, as we do this day.[351] Lord, grant that those who are delivered from death may not be as the nine lepers, who did not return to give thanks,[352] or as Hezekiah, who rendered not again according to the benefit done unto him;[353] but that they may so offer praise, as to glorify thee, and so order their conversation, as to see the salvation of God.[354]

Those whom the Lord has chastened sore, yet has not delivered over unto death; O that they may therefore praise him, who is become their salvation.[355]

22.9. When we pray with, or for those parents, whose children are a grief to them, or such as they are in fear about.

Lord, give to parents the desires of their soul's concerning their children, which is to see them walking in the truth;[356] form Christ in their souls.[357] O give them betimes to know the God of their fathers, and to serve him with a perfect heart, and a willing mind.[358] Let the children of youth, that are as arrows in the hand, be directed aright, that those parents may have reason to think themselves happy that have their quiver full of them,[359] and they may never be arrows in their hearts.

Let those foolish children, that are the grief of the father, and the heaviness of her that bare them, that mock at their parents, and despise to obey them,[360] be brought to repentance; and let those that have been unprofitable, now at length be made profitable.[361] O turn the hearts of the children to their fathers,[362] even the disobedient to the wisdom of the just, that they may be made ready a people prepared for the Lord.[363] O shew them their work, and their transgression, that they exceeded, and open their ear to discipline.[364]

22.10. When we pray with, or for those that are in prison.

Those that sit in darkness, and in the shadow of death, being bound in affliction and iron, because they rebelled against the word of God, and contemned the counsel of the Most High, give them grace to cry unto thee in their trouble,[365] and in a day of adversity to consider.[366]

In their captivity give them to bethink themselves to humble themselves, and pray, and seek thy face; to repent, saying, We have sinned, and have done perversely, and to return to thee with all their heart and with all their soul:[367] and bring their souls out of prison, that they may praise thy name:[368] Bring them into the glorious liberty of the children of God, out of the bondage of corruption.[369] Let the Son make them free, and then they shall be free indeed.[370]

Those that are wrongly imprisoned, be thou with them, as thou wast with Joseph in the prison, and show them mercy.[371] Hear the poor, and despise not thy prisoners,[372] but let their sorrowful sighing come before thee, and according to the greatness of thy power preserve those that are unjustly appointed to die.[373]

22.11 When we pray with, or for condemned malefactors, that have but a little while to live.

O look with pity upon those, the number of whose months is to be cut off in the midst for their sins;[374] O give them repentance unto salvation, as thou didst to the thief upon the cross,[375] that they may own the justice of God in all that is brought upon them, that he has done right, but they have done wickedly.[376] O turn them, and they shall be turned, that being instructed they may smite upon the thigh, and may be ashamed, yea, even confounded, because they do bear the reproach of their own iniquity.[377] O pluck them as brands out of the fire:[378] let them be delivered from the wrath to come.[379]

Enable them to give glory to God by making confession,[380] that they may find mercy,[381] and that others may hear and fear, and do no more presumptuously.[382]

Lord Jesus, remember them now, thou art in thy kingdom;[383] O let them not be hurt of the second death;[384] Deliver them from going down to the pit;[385] Though the flesh be destroyed, O let the spirit be saved in the day of the Lord Jesus.[386] The God of infinite mercy be merciful to these sinners,[387] these sinners against their own souls.[388]

22.12. When we pray with, or for those that are at sea.

Let those that go down to the sea in ships, that do business in great waters, observe the works of the Lord there and his wonders in the deep:[389] And acknowledge what a great God he is whom the winds and the seas obey;[390] who hath placed the sand for the bound of the sea, by a perpetual decree, that it cannot pass it; and though the waves thereof toss themselves, yet can they not prevail; though they roar, yet can they not pass over.[391]

O preserve them through the paths of the seas,[392] and in perils by waters, and perils by robbers.[393] If the stormy wind be raised which lifteth up the waves, so that they are at their wit's end, deliver them out of their distresses, make the storm a calm, and bring them to their desired haven: And, O that those who are delivered may praise the Lord for his goodness, and for his wonderful works to the children of men.[394]

References

[1] Phil. 4:6.
[2] Heb. 10:19.
[3] 2 Chron. 6:29.
[4] Prov. 3:6.
[5] Ps. 37:23.
[6] Ps. 5:3.
[7] Ps. 130:6.
[8] Ps. 59: 16.
[9] Job 38:12-14.
[10] Ps. 74:16.
[11] Luke 1:77-78.
[12] Mal. 4:2.
[13] Prov. 4:18.
[14] Lam. 3:22-23.
[15] Ps. 30:5.
[16] Ps. 3:5.
[17] Matt. 8:20.
[18] Heb. 11:38.
[19] Job 7:3-4, 13.
[20] Ps. 127:2.
[21] Ps. 13:3.
[22] Ps. 91:6.
[23] Eph. 6:12.
[24] 1 Pet. 5:8.
[25] Ps. 121:4.
[26] Ps. 39:18.
[27] Ps 119:148.
[28] Jer. 4:14.
[29] Ps. 143:8, 10.
[30] Ps. 121:7-8.
[31] Ps. 91:11-12.
[32] Ezra 3:4.
[33] Ps. 65:8.
[34] Ps. 104:23.
[35] Mark 6:31.
[36] Ps. 116:7.
[37] Jer. 31:26.
[38] Ps. 68:19, 121:8.
[39] Matt. 6:11-12.
[40] Ps. 4:8.
[41] Job 1:10.
[42] Ps. 34:7.
[43] Job 11:19.
[44] Ps. 31:5.
[45] Job 33:15-16.
[46] Ps. 16:7.
[47] Ps. 17:3.
[48] Ps. 4:4.
[49] Ps. 63:6.
[50] Ps. 149:5.
[51] Ps. 136:25.
[52] Ps. 145:15.
[53] Ps. 111:5.
[54] Deut 30:20.
[55] Gen. 48:15.
[56] 1 Tim. 6:17.
[57] Gen. 1:29.
[58] Gen. 9:3.
[59] Acts 10:15.
[60] Matt. 15:11.
[61] 1 Tim. 4:3-4.
[62] Matt. 15:27.
[63] Isa. 3:1.
[64] Ezek. 4:16.
[65] Deut. 32:15.
[66] Ps. 69:22.
[67] 1 Tim. 4:5.
[68] Matt. 4:4.
[69] Matt. 14:19.
[70] Ps. 132:15.
[71] Jude 12.
[72] Phil. 3:19.
[73] Luke 21:34.
[74] 1 Cor. 10:31.
[75] Deut. 8:10.
[76] Ps. 23:5.
[77] Ps. 16:5-6.
[78] John 6:27, 33-34.
[79] Ps. 146:7.
[80] Neh. 8:10.
[81] Luke 14:15.
[82] Rev. 2:17.
[83] Gen 28:20.
[84] Ps. 91:10.

85 Rom. 1:10.
86 Ps. 5:12.
87 Prov. 3:5.
88 Ps. 91:12.
89 1 Thess. 3:11.
90 Ps. 112:5.
91 Gen. 24:12.
92 Gen 31:49.
93 Gen. 24:27.
94 Ps. 35:10.
95 Ps. 18:32.
96 Exod. 16:23.
97 John 19:31.
98 Isa. 58:13.
99 Josh. 3:5.
100 Luke 23:54.
101 Gen. 1:31.
102 James 3:2.
103 John 13:9.
104 Ps. 26:6.
105 Heb. 4:10.
106 Gen. 22:5.
107 Ps. 118:27.
108 Luke 17:22.
109 Psalm 84:10.
110 Luke 10:21-24.
111 2 Tim. 1:10.
112 Rev. 1:10.
113 Isa. 58:13.
114 Mark 2:28.
115 Ps. 89:7.
116 Heb. 12:28-29.
117 Lev. 10:3.
118 Ezek. 20:12.
119 John 17:17.
120 Isa. 8:13.
121 Exod. 20:11.
122 Ps. 124:8.
123 2 Cor. 5:17.
124 Eph. 2:10.
125 2 Cor. 4:6.
126 Ps. 118:22-24.
127 Rev. 2:8.
128 Phil. 3:10.
129 Rom. 6:4-5.
130 Eph. 2:6.
131 Col. 3:1.
132 Acts 1:4, 8.
133 Eph 5:8, 9, 18.
134 1 Cor. 10:17, 8:6.
135 1 Cor. 12:11.
136 Gal 6:16.
137 Tit 2:13.
138 Prov. 9:5.
139 Matt. 5:6.
140 Rev 19:9.
141 Matt. 22:11.
142 Song. 4:16.
143 Song. 1:4, 12.
144 2 Chron. 30:18-20.
145 1 Cor. 10:16.
146 1 Cor. 11:26.
147 Jer. 50:5.
148 1 Cor. 6:17.
149 Heb. 3:14.
150 John 6:55-57.
151 1 Cor. 1:23-24.
152 Acts 2:38.
153 1 John 2:25.
154 Ps. 116:13.
155 Rev. 3:11.
156 1 Chron. 29:18.
157 Col. 2:6.
158 Phil. 1:27.
159 2 Cor. 4:10.
160 Phil. 1:21.
161 Ps. 56:12.
162 Ps. 61:8.
163 Ezek. 18:4.
164 Rom. 12:1.
165 Matt. 28:19.
166 Ps. 51:5.
167 Zech. 13:1.
168 Heb. 10:22.
169 Acts 3:25.
170 Ezek. 16:20.
171 Ps. 116:16.
172 Gen. 17:7.
173 Gal. 3:14.
174 Acts 2:39.
175 Mark 10:14, 16.
176 2 Tim. 2:21.
177 Mal. 3:17.
178 Isa. 44:4-5.
179 Eccles. 7:2.
180 Deut. 32:29.
181 Num. 27:13.
182 John 13:36.
183 1 Cor. 15:23.
184 Job 30:23.
185 Luke 2:26, 29.
186 2 Cor. 5:1.
187 Job 19:25-26.
188 1 Cor. 7:39.
189 John 2:1, 9.
190 Gen. 2:18.
191 1 Cor. 7:16.
192 1 John 4:16.
193 Ps. 128:3.
194 1 Pet. 3:7.
195 Luke 20:35.
196 2 Tim. 2:2.
197 John 5:35.
198 1 Tim 1:12.
199 1 Tim 5:22.
200 Col. 4:17.
201 2 Tim. 4:5.
202 Luke 24:47, 49.
203 1 Sam. 10:9.
204 1 Tim. 4:6.
205 Amos 4:7.
206 1 Kings 8:35.
207 Zech. 10:1.
208 Jer. 14:22.
209 Job 37:13.
210 Prov. 28:3.
211 Isa. 54:9.
212 Job 37:22.
213 Exod 23:25.
214 Ps. 91:3.
215 2 Sam. 24:16.
216 Amos 7:4.
217 Lev. 10:6.
218 Amos 7:5.
219 Num. 11:1-2.
220 Prov. 30:4.
221 Ps. 135:7.
222 Ps. 148:8.
223 Job 1:19.
224 Isa. 50:10.
225 Zech 14:7.
226 Isa. 35:3-4.
227 Zech. 1:13.
228 Matt. 9:2.

229 Mark 6:50.
230 Ps. 35:3.
231 Ps. 51:8.
232 Ps. 77:2.
233 Ps. 13:5.
234 Job 13:15.
235 Ps. 42:7-8, 11.
236 Ps. 51:10-12.
237 Ps. 71:15.
238 Ps. 40:2-3.
239 Ps. 90:15.
240 Isa. 54:7-8.
241 Rom. 8:16.
242 Heb. 10:22
243 Zech. 3:2.
244 Jer. 50:5.
245 1 Sam. 7:2.
246 Acts 2:37.
247 1 Sam. 12:23.
248 Matt. 19:16.
249 John 14:6.
250 Matt. 12:20.
251 Isa. 40:11.
252 Mark 9:24.
253 Rev. 12:4-5.
254 James 5:14-15.
255 Heb. 13:3.
256 Matt. 4:23-24.
257 Matt. 8:8-9.
258 Heb. 4:15.
259 Luke 5:18.
260 Heb. 12:5.
261 Mic. 6:9.
262 Lev. 26:41.
263 Job 5:6.
264 2 Chron. 16:12.
265 Ps. 68:20.
266 Job 10:2.
267 2 Chron. 33:12.
268 Jer. 18:11.
269 1 Cor. 11:32.
270 Eccles. 7:3.
271 Ps. 6:1-4.
272 1 Cor. 10:13.
273 Ps. 39:10-11, 13.
274 Job 33:19-20, 23-24.
275 Deut. 33:27.
276 Ps. 103:14.

277 Ps. 41:1-4.
278 Ps. 25:16 18.
279 Ps. 31:16.
280 2 Cor. 7:6.
281 Ps. 25:13.
282 Job 38:11.
283 Isa. 27:8-9.
284 James 1:4.
285 Lam. 3:26.
286 Rom. 5:3-5.
287 2 Cor. 4:17.
288 Job 23:10.
289 Ps. 119:17, 175.
290 Isa. 38:16-17.
291 Matt. 8:8.
292 Ezek 16:6, 8.
293 Matt. 26:39, 42.
294 Acts 21:14.
295 Ps. 138:8.
296 Rom. 14:8.
297 Ps. 73:26.
298 Ps. 23:4.
299 Heb.13:5.
300 Ps. 46:1.
301 Ps. 31:5.
302 1 Pet. 4:19.
303 Luke 16:22.
304 Eph. 5:27.
305 Acts 7:59.
306 Heb. 12:23.
307 2 Cor. 5:8.
308 Luke 23:43.
309 Luke 16:25.
310 Rom. 6:7.
311 Job 21:33.
312 1 Thess. 4:17.
313 Rev. 21:4.
314 Luke 21:19.
315 Job 27:2.
316 Job 7:15.
317 Luke 15:17.
318 Acts 16:28.
319 Rom. 5:14.
320 2 Tim. 1:10.
321 Mark 10:14.
322 Ps. 103:13.
323 Job 14:2, 6.
324 2 Sam.12:22.

325 Acts 21:14.
326 1 Cor. 5:5.
327 John 11:23, 25.
328 Matt. 9:24.
329 1 Thess. 4:13.
330 1 Tim. 6:17.
331 Jer. 2:13.
332 Ps. 68:5.
333 Hosea 14:3.
334 Jer. 49:11.
335 1 Tim. 5:5.
336 Ps. 27:10.
337 John 14:18.
338 1 Tim. 2:14.
339 Gen 3:16.
340 1 Tim. 2:15.
341 Ps. 55:22.
342 Ps. 56:3.
343 1 Sam. 30:6.
344 Job 18:16.
345 Ps. 71:3.
346 1 Thess. 5:3.
347 Ps. 40:13, 17.
348 John 16:21.
349 Ps. 30:1-3.
350 Ps. 116:6, 8-9, 17-18.
351 Isa. 38:18-19.
352 Luke 17:18.
353 2 Chron. 32:25.
354 Ps. 50:23.
355 Ps. 118:18, 21.
356 2 John 4.
357 Gal. 4:19.
358 1 Chron. 28:9.
359 Ps. 127:4-5.
360 Prov. 17:25, 30:17.
361 Philem. 11.
362 Mal. 4:6.
363 Luke 1:17.
364 Job 36:9-10.
365 Ps. 107:10-11, 13.
366 Eccles. 7:14.
367 1 Kings 8:47-48.
368 Ps. 142:7.
369 Rom. 8:21.
370 John 8:36.
371 Gen. 39:21.
372 Ps. 69:33.

373 Ps.79:11.
374 Job 21:21.
375 2 Cor. 7:10.
376 Neh. 9:33.
377 Jer. 31:18-19.
378 Jude 23.
379 1 Thess. 1:10.
380 Josh 7:19.

381 Prov. 3:4.
382 Deut. 17:13.
383 Luke 23:42.
384 Rev. 2:11.
385 Job 33:24.
386 1 Cor. 5:5.
387 Luke 18:13.
388 Numb. 16:38.

389 Ps. 107:23-24.
390 Matt. 8:27.
391 Jer. 5:22.
392 Ps. 8:8.
393 2 Cor. 11:26.
394 Ps. 107:25, 27-31.

CHAPTER 7

Of the Conclusion of our PRAYERS.

We are commanded to pray always, to pray without ceasing, to continue in prayer, because we must always have in us a disposition to the duty, must be constant to it, and never grow weary of it, or throw it up; and yet we cannot be always praying, we must come down from this mount: nor may we be over long, so as to make the duty a task or a toil to ourselves, or those that join with us. We have other work that calls for our attendance. Jacob wrestles with the angel; but he must go for the day breaks: We must therefore think of concluding. The prayers of David the son of Jesse must be ended. But how shall we conclude so as to have the impressions of the duty kept always in the imagination of the thought of our heart?

1. We may then sum up our requests in some comprehensive petitions, at the conclusion of the whole matter.

Now the God of peace that brought again from the dead our Lord Jesus, that great Shepherd of the sheep, through the blood of the everlasting covenant, make us perfect in every good work to do his will, working in us that which is well-pleasing in his sight, through Christ Jesus.[1]

Now the Lord direct our hearts into the love of God, and into a patient waiting for Christ.[2]

And the God of all grace, who hath called us to his eternal glory by Christ Jesus, after that we have suffered a while, make us perfect, stablish, strengthen, settle us.[3]

And now, Lord, what wait we for;[4] Truly our hope is even in thee, and on thee do we depend to be to us a God all-sufficient.[5]

Do for us exceeding abundantly above what we are able to ask or think, according to the power that worketh in us:[6] And supply all our needs according to thy riches in glory by Christ Jesus.[7]

2. We may then beg for the audience and acceptance of our poor weak prayers for Christ's sake.

Now the God of Israel grant us the things we have requested of him.[8]

Let the words of our mouths, and the meditations of our hearts be acceptable in thy sight, O Lord, our strength and our Redeemer.[9]

Let thine eyes be open unto the supplication of thy servants, and unto the supplication of thy people Israel, to hearken unto them in all that they call unto thee for; for they be thy people, and thine inheritance.[10]

O our God, let thine ears be attent unto the prayers that we have made; O turn not away the face of thine anointed; remember the mercies of David thy servant;[11] even Jesus, who is at thy right hand making intercession for us.

Lord, thou hast assured us, that whatever we ask the Father in Christ's name, he will give it us.[12] We ask all these things in that name, that powerful name which is above every name,[13] that precious name which is as ointment poured forth.[14] O make thy face to shine upon us for the Lord's sake,[15] who is the Son of thy love, and whom thou hearest always;[16] good Lord, give us to hear him, and be well pleased with us in him.[17]

3. We may then beg for the forgiveness of what has been amiss in our prayers.

Lord, we have not prayed as we ought;[18] who is there that does good, and sins not?[19] Even when we would do good, evil is present with us, and if to will be present, yet how to perform that which is good we know not; for the good that we would, we do not,[20] so that thou mightest justly refuse to hear, even when we make many prayers.[21] But we have a great High-Priest, who bears the iniquity of the holy things, which the children of Israel hallow in all their holy gifts:[22] for his sake take away all that iniquity from us, even all the iniquity of our holy things, and receive us graciously, and love us freely;[23] and deal not with us after our folly.[24]

4. We may then recommend ourselves to the conduct, protection, and government of the divine grace, in the further services that lie before us, and in the whole course of our conversation.

And now let us be enabled to go from strength to strength, until we appear before God in Zion; and while we pass through the valley of Baca, let it be made a well, and let the rain of the divine grace and blessing fill the pools.[25]

Now speak, Lord, for thy servants hear.[26] What saith our Lord unto his servants?[27] Grant that we may not turn away our ear from hearing the law; for then our prayers will be an abomination;[28] but may hearken unto God, that he may hearken unto us.[29]

And now, the Lord our God be with us, as he was with our fathers; let him not leave us, nor forsake us, that he may incline our hearts unto him, to walk in all his ways, and to keep his commandments, and his statutes, and his judgments: And let our hearts be perfect with the Lord our God all our days, and continue so till the end be,[30] and then we may rest, and may stand in our lot, and let it be a blessed lot in the end of the days.

5. We may conclude all with doxologies, or solemn praises of God, ascribing honour and glory to the Father, the Son, and the Holy Ghost, and sealing up all our praises and prayers with an affectionate Amen.

Now blessed be the Lord God of Israel, from everlasting to everlasting,[31] Amen and Amen.

For ever blessed be the Lord God, the God of Israel, who only doth wondrous things, and blessed be his glorious name for ever, and let the whole earth be filled with his glory, Amen and Amen.[32] Yea, let all the people say, Amen, hallelujah.[33]

To God only wise be glory, through Jesus Christ, for ever,[34] Amen.

Now to God the Father, and our Lord Jesus Christ, who gave himself for our sins, that he might deliver us from this present evil world, according to the will of God and our Father, be glory for ever and ever,[35] Amen.

To God be glory in the church by Christ Jesus, throughout all ages, world without end,[36] Amen.

Now to the King eternal, immortal, invisible, the only wise God, be honour and glory for ever and ever,[37] Amen: To him be honour and power everlasting,[38] to him be glory and dominion,[39] Amen.

Now unto him that is able to keep us from falling, and to present us faultless before the presence of his glory with exceeding joy, to the only wise God our Saviour, be glory and majesty, dominion and power, now and ever,[40] Amen.

Hallelujah, salvation, and glory, and honour, and power, unto the Lord our God, Amen, hallelujah.[41]

And now, we prostrate our souls before the throne and worship God, saying, Amen, blessing, and glory and wisdom, and thanksgiving, and honour and power, and might, be unto God, for ever and ever, Amen.[42]

Blessing, and honour, and glory, and power, be unto him that sitteth upon the throne, and unto the Lamb for ever and ever; and let the whole creation say, Amen, Amen.[43]

6. It is very proper to sum up our prayers in that form of prayer which Christ taught his disciples.

Our Father which art in Heaven; hallowed be thy name; thy kingdom come; thy will be done on earth as it is in heaven; give us this day our daily bread; and forgive us our trespasses, as we forgive them that trespass against us; and lead us not into temptation, but deliver us from evil; for thine is the kingdom, and the power, and the glory, for ever and ever, Amen.[44]

References

[1] Heb. 13:20-21.
[2] 2 Thess. 3:5.
[3] 1 Pet. 5:10.
[4] Ps. 39:7.
[5] Gen. 17:1.
[6] Eph. 3:20.
[7] Phil. 4:19.
[8] 1 Sam. 1:17.
[9] Ps. 19:14.
[10] 1 Kings 8:51-52.
[11] 2 Chron. 6:40, 42.
[12] John 16:23.
[13] Phil. 2:9.
[14] Song. 1:3.
[15] Dan. 9:17.
[16] John 11:42.
[17] Matt. 17:5.
[18] Rom. 8:26.
[19] Eccles. 7:20.
[20] Rom. 7:18-19.
[21] Isa 1:15.
[22] Exod. 28:38.
[23] Hosea 14:2, 4.
[24] Job 42:8.
[25] Ps. 84:6-7.
[26] 1 Sam. 3:9.
[27] Josh. 5:14.
[28] Prov. 28:9.
[29] Judg. 9:7.
[30] 1 Kings 8:57-58, 61.
[31] Ps. 41:13.
[32] Ps. 72:18-19.
[33] Ps. 106:48.
[34] Rom. 16:27.
[35] Gal. 1:3-5.
[36] Eph. 3:21.
[37] 1 Tim. 1:17.
[38] 1 Tim. 6:16.
[39] 1 Pet. 5:11.
[40] Jude 24, 25.
[41] Rev. 19:1, 4.
[42] Rev. 7:11-12.
[43] Rev 5:13.
[44] Matt. 6:9-13.

CHAPTER 8

A Paraphrase on the Lord's Prayer, in Scripture Expressions

The Lord's prayer being intended not only for a form of prayer itself, but a rule of direction, a plan or model in little, by which we may frame our prayers; and the expressions being remarkably concise and yet vastly comprehensive, it will be of good use sometimes to lay it before us, and observing the method and order of it, to dilate upon the several passages and petitions of it, that we may use it the more intelligently; of which we shall only here give a specimen, in the assistance we may have from some other scriptures.

1. Our Father which art in heaven.

O Lord our God, doubtless thou art our Father, though Abraham be ignorant of us, and Israel acknowledge us not; thou, O Lord, art our Father, our Redeemer, thy name is from everlasting;[1] and we will from this time cry unto thee, our Father, thou art the guide of our youth.[2]

Have we not all one Father? has not one God created us?[3] Thou art the Father of our spirits, to whom we ought to be in subjection and live.[4]

Thou art the Father of lights,[5] and the Father of mercies, and the God of all consolation:[6] The eternal Father,[7] of whom, and through whom, and to whom, are all things.[8]

Thou art the Father of our Lord Jesus Christ,[9] whose glory was that of the only begotten of the Father, who is in his bosom,[10] by him, as one brought up with him, daily his delight, and rejoicing always before him.[11]

Thou art in Christ, our Father, and the Father of all believers, whom thou hast predestinated to the adoption of children,[12] and into whose hearts thou hast sent the Spirit of the Son, teaching them to cry Abba, Father,[13] behold what manner of love the Father hath bestowed upon us, that we should be called the children of God.[14] That the Lord God Almighty should be to us a Father, and we should be to him for sons and daughters:[15] And that as many as receive Christ, to them thou shouldest give power to become the sons of God, even to them that believe on his name; which are born, not of the will of man, but of God, and his grace.[16]

O that we may receive the adoption of sons,[17] and that as obedient and genuine children we may fashion ourselves according to the example of him who hath called us, who is holy;[18] and may be followers of God as dear children,[19] and conformed to the image of his Son, who is the first-born among many brethren.[20]

Enable us to come to thee with humble boldness and confidence,[21] as to a Father, a tender Father, who spares us as a man spares his son who serves him;[22] and as having an advocate with the Father,[23] who yet has told us, that the Father himself loves us.[24]

Thou art a Father, but where is thine honour?[25] Lord, give us grace to serve thee as becomes children, with reverence and godly fear.[26]

Thou art a Father, and if earthly parents, being evil, yet know how to give good gifts unto their children, how much more shall our heavenly Father, give the Holy Spirit to them that ask him.[27] Lord, give us the Spirit of grace and supplication.[28]

We come to thee as prodigal children, that have gone from our Father's house into a far country; but we will arise and go to our Father, for in his house there is bread enough, and to spare; and if we continue at a distance from him, we perish with hunger. Father, we have sinned against heaven, and before thee, and are no more worthy to be called thy children, make us even as thy hired servants.[29]

Thou art our Father in heaven and therefore unto thee, O Lord, do we lift our souls.[30] Unto thee we lift up our eyes, O thou that dwellest in the heavens: As the eyes of a servant are to the hand of his master and the eyes of a maiden to the hand of her mistress, so do our eyes wait upon thee, O Lord our God;[31] a God whom the heaven of heavens cannot contain, and yet whom we may have access to,[32] having a High-Priest that is passed into the heavens as our forerunner.[33]

Thou, O God, dwellest in the high and holy place,[34] and holy and reverend is his name.[35] God is in heaven, and we are upon earth,[36] therefore should we choose our words to reason with him,[37] and yet through a Mediator we have boldness to enter into the holiest.[38]

Look down, we pray thee, from heaven, and behold, from the habitation of thy holiness, and of thy glory,[39] and have compassion upon us, and help us.[40] Heaven is the firmament of thy power:[41] O hear us from thy holy heaven, with the saving strength of thy right hand; send us help from thy sanctuary, and strengthen us out of Zion.[42]

And, O that, since heaven is our Father's house,[43] we may have our conversation there,[44] and may seek things that are above.[45]

2. Hallowed be thy Name.

And now, what is our petition, and what is our request?[46] What would we that thou shouldest do for us?[47] This is our heart's desire and prayer in the first place,[48] Father, in heaven, let thy name be sanctified. We pray that thou mayest be glorified as a holy God.[49]

We desire to exalt the Lord our God, to worship at his footstool, at his holy hill, and to praise his great and terrible name, for it is holy, for the Lord our God is holy.[50] Thou art holy, O thou that inhabitest the praises of Israel.[51]

We glory in thy holy name, and therefore shall our hearts rejoice,[52] because that we have trusted in that holy name of thine,[53] to which we will always give thanks, and triumph in thy praise.[54]

Lord enable us to glorify thy holy name for evermore, by praising thee with all our hearts,[55] and by bringing forth much fruit, for herein is our heavenly Father glorified.[56] O that we may be to our God for a name, and for a praise, and for a glory,[57] that being called out of darkness into his marvellous light, to be to him a peculiar people, we may show forth the praises of him that hath called us.[58]

O that we may be thy children, the work of thy hands, that we may sanctify thy name, and sanctify the Holy One of Jacob, and fear the God of Israel,[59] and may be to the praise of his glory.[60]

Enable us as we have received the gift, so to minister the same, as good stewards of the manifold grace of God, that God in all things may be glorified through Jesus Christ: And if we suffer, enable us to suffer as Christians, and to glorify God therein;[61] for this is our earnest expectation and hope, that always Jesus Christ may be magnified in our bodies, in life and death.[62]

Lord, enable others to glorify thee, even the strong people to glorify thee, and the city of the terrible nations fear thee;[63] but especially let the Lord be magnified from the border of Israel.[64] Let them glorify the Lord in the fires, even the Lord God of Israel in the isles of the sea.[65] O let all nations, whom thou hast made, come and worship before thee, O Lord, and glorify thy name: for thou art great and dost wondrous things, thou art God alone.[66]

O let the Gentiles glorify God for his mercy, let his name be known among the Gentiles, and let them rejoice with his people,[67] O let thy name be great among the Gentiles,[68] and let all the ends of the world remember and turn to the Lord, and all kindreds of the nations worship before thee; and let them declare thy righteousness to a people that shall be born.[69]

Lord, do thou thyself dispose of all things to thy own glory, both as King of nations, and King of saints:[70, 71] Do all according to the counsel of thy own will,[72] that thou mayest magnify thyself, and sanctify thyself, and mayest be known in the eyes of many nations, that thou art the Lord.[73] O sanctify thy great name, which has been profaned among the heathen, and let them know that thou art the Lord, when thou shalt be sanctified in them.[74]

Father, glorify thine own name: Thou hast glorified it, glorify it yet again:[75] Father, glorify thy Son, that thy Son also may glorify thee.[76] O Give him a name above every name,[77] and in all places, in all things let him have the pre-eminence.[78]

Lord, what wilt thou do for thy great name?[79] Do this for thy great name: Pour out of thy Spirit upon all flesh;[80] and let the word of Christ dwell richly in the hearts of all.[81] Be thou exalted, O Lord, among the heathen, be thou exalted in the earth:[82] Be thou exalted, O God, above the heavens, let thy glory be above all the earth:[83] Be thou exalted, O Lord, in thine own strength, so will we sing and praise thy power.[84] Do great things with thy glorious and everlasting arm, to make unto thyself a glorious and everlasting name.[85]

O let thy name be magnified for ever, saying, The Lord of hosts is the God of Israel, even a God to Israel.[86]

3. Thy kingdom come.

In order to the sanctifying and glorifying of thy holy name, Father in heaven, let thy kingdom come, for thine is the kingdom, O Lord, and thou art exalted as head above all: Both riches and honour come of thee; thou reignest over all, and in thine hand is power and might, and in thine hand it is to make great, and to give strength unto all.[87] And we desire to speak of the glorious majesty of thy kingdom, for it is an everlasting kingdom, and thy dominion endures throughout all generations.[88]

Thou rulest by thy power for ever, thine eyes be hold the nations. O let not the rebellious exalt themselves,[89] but through the greatness of thy power let thine enemies submit themselves unto thee.[90]

O make it to appear that the kingdom is thine, and that thou art the governor among the nations,[91] so evident, that they may say among the heathen, The Lord reigneth;[92] that all men may fear, and may declare the works of God,[93] and may say, Verily, he is a God that judgeth in the earth.[94] Make all the kings of the earth to know the heavens do rule, even that the Most High ruleth in the kingdom of men, and giveth it to whomsoever he will, and to praise, and to extol, and honour the King of heaven, all whose works are truth, and his ways judgment, and those that walk in pride he is able to abase.[95]

O let the kingdom of thy grace come more and more in the world, that kingdom of God which cometh not with observation, that kingdom of God, which is within men.[96] Let it be like leaven in the world, diffusing its relish, till the whole be leavened, and like a grain of mustard-seed, which, though it be the least of all seeds, yet, when it is grown, is the greatest among herbs.[97]

Let the kingdoms of the world become the kingdoms of the Lord, and of his Christ: Take unto thy-self thy great power, and reign, though the nations be angry.[98] Set up thy throne there where Satan's seat is,[99] let every thought be brought into obedience to thee,[100] and let the law of thy kingdom be magnified and honourable.[101]

Let that kingdom of God, which is not in word but in power, be set up in all the churches of Christ:[102] Send forth the rod of thy strength out of thy Zion, and rule by the beauty of holiness.[103]

Where the strong man armed hath long kept his palace, and his goods are in peace, let Christ, who is stronger than he, come upon him, and take from him all his armour, wherein he trusted, and divide the spoil.[104]

O give to the Son of man dominion and glory, and a kingdom, that all people, nations and languages may serve him, and the judgment may be given to the saints of the Most High.[105]

Let the kingdom of thy grace come more and more in our land, and the places where we live. There let the word of God have free course, and be glorified,[106] and let not the kingdom of God be taken from us, as we have deserved it should, and given to a nation bringing forth the fruits thereof.[107]

Let the kingdom of thy grace come into our hearts, that they may be the temples of the Holy Ghost.[108] Let no iniquity have dominion over us.[109] Overturn, overturn, overturn the power of corruption there, and let him come whose right our hearts are, and give them him;[110] make us willing, more and more willing in the day of thy power.[111] Rule in us by the power of truth, that being of the truth, we may always hear Christ's voice,[112] and may not only call him Lord, Lord, but do the things that he saith.[113] And let the love of Christ command us, and constrain us,[114] and his fear be before our eyes, that we sin not.[115]

O let the kingdom of thy glory be hastened; we believe it will come; we look for the Saviour, the Lord Jesus,[116] to come in the clouds of heaven with power and great glory;[117] we hope that he shall appear to our joy;[118] we love his appearing;[119] we are looking for, and hasting to the coming of the day of God;[120] make us ready for it,[121] that we may then lift up our heads with joy, knowing that our redemption draws nigh.[122] And, O that we may have such first-fruits of the Spirit, as that we ourselves may groan within ourselves, waiting for the adoption, even the redemption of our body;[123] and may have a desire to depart, and to be with Christ, which is best of all.[124]

Blessed Jesus, be with thy ministers and people (as thou hast said) always even unto the end of the world:[125] And then (as thou hast said) surely I come quickly; even so come, Lord Jesus, come quickly:[126] When the mystery of God shall be finished,[127] make haste our beloved, and be thou like to a roe, or to a young hart, upon the mountains of spices.[128]

4. Thy Will be done on Earth, as it is in Heaven.

And as an evidence that thy kingdom comes, and in order to the sanctifying of thy name, Father in heaven, let thy holy will be done.

We know, O Lord, that whatsoever thou pleaseth, that thou dost in heaven and in earth, in the sea, and in all deep places:[129] thy counsel shall stand, and thou wilt do all thy pleasure;[130] even so be it, holy Father, not our will, but thine be done.[131] As thou hast thought, so let it come to pass, and as thou hast purposed, let it stand.[132] Do all according to the counsel of thine own will.[133] Make even those to serve thy purposes that have not known thee, and that mean not so, neither doth their heart think so.[134]

Father, let thy will be done concerning us, and ours:[135] Behold, here we are: it is the Lord, let him do to us as seemeth good unto him:[136] The will of the Lord be done.[137] O give us to submit to thy will in conformity to the example of the Lord Jesus, who said, Not as I will, but as thou wilt,[138] and to say, The Lord gave and the Lord hath taken away, blessed be the name of the Lord.[139] Shall we receive good at the hand of the Lord, and shall we not receive evil also.[140]

Father, let the scriptures be fulfilled;[141] the scriptures of the prophets, which cannot be broken.[142] Though heaven and earth pass away, let not one jot or tittle of thy word pass away.[143] Do what is written in the scriptures of truth;[144] and let it appear that for ever, O Lord, thy word is settled in heaven.[145]

Father, give grace to each of us to know and do the will of our Father which is in heaven.[146] This is the will of God, even our sanctification. [147] Now the God of peace sanctify us wholly.[148] O let us be filled with the knowledge of thy will in all wisdom and spiritual understanding,[149] and make us perfect in every good work to do thy will.[150] O let the time past of our life suffice us to have wrought the will of the flesh,[151] and to have walked according to the course of this world.[152] And from henceforth grant that it may always be our meat and drink to do the will of our Father, and to finish his work;[153] not to do our own will, but his that sent us,[154] that we may be of those that shall enter into the kingdom[155] of heaven and not those that shall be beaten with many stripes.[156]

Lord, give grace to others also to know and do thy will; to prove what is the good, and acceptable and perfect will of God,[157] not to be unwise, but understanding what the will of the Lord is;[158] and then give them to stand perfect and complete in all the will of God:[159] And let us all serve our generations according to that will.[160]

And when we have done the will of God, let us inherit the promises;[161] and let that part of the will of God be done; Lord, let the word which thou hast spoken concerning thy servants be established for ever, and do as thou hast said.[162]

We rejoice that thy will is done in heaven: that the holy angels do thy commandments, and always hearken to the voice of thy word;[163] that they always behold the face of our Father.[164] And we lament it, that thy will is so little done on earth, so many of the children of men being led captive by Satan at his will.[165] O that this earth may be made more like to heaven! and saints more like to the holy angels! and that we who hope to be shortly as the angels of God in heaven,[166] may now, like them, not rest from praising him:[167] may now, like them, resist and withstand Satan;[168] may be as a flame of fire,[169] and fly swiftly, and may go straight forward whithersoever the Spirit goes,[170, 171] may minister for the good of others,[172] and thus may come into communion with the innumerable company of angels.[173]

5. Give us this day our daily bread.

Thou O God, who hath appointed us to seek first the kingdom of God and the righteousness thereof, hast promised that if we do so, other things shall be added unto us:[174] and therefore having prayed for the sanctifying of thy name, the coming of thy kingdom, and the doing of thy will, we next pray, Father in heaven, give us this day, and day by day our daily bread.[175]

Remove far from us vanity and lies; give us neither poverty nor riches; feed us with food convenient for us, lest we be full and deny thee, and say, Who is the Lord? or lest we be poor and steal, and take the name of our God in vain.[176]

Lord, we ask not for dainties, for they are deceitful meat;[177] nor do we pray that we may fare sumptuously every day, for we would not in our life time receive our good things;[178] but we pray for that bread which is necessary to strengthen man's heart.[179] We desire not to eat the bread of deceit,[180] nor to drink any stolen waters,[181] nor would we eat the bread of idleness,[182] but that if it be thy will we may eat the labour of our own hands,[183] that with quietness we may work, and eat our own bread;[184] and having food and raiment, give us to be therewith content,[185] and to say, we have all, and abound.[186]

Bless, Lord, our substance, and accept the work of our hands;[187] and give us wherewithal to provide for our own, even for those of our own house,[188] and to leave an inheritance, as far as is just, to our children's children.[189] Let the beauty of the Lord our God be upon us, prosper thou the work of our hands upon us, yea, the work of our hands establish thou it.[190] Bless, Lord, our land with the precious things of the earth, and the fulness thereof; but above all let us have the good-will of him that dwelt in the bush, even the blessing that was upon the head of Joseph, and upon the crown of the head of him that was separated from his brethren.[191]

But if the fig-tree should not blossom, and there should be no fruit in the vine; if the labour of the olive should fail, and the fields should yield no meat; if the flock should be cut off from the fold, and there should be no herd in the stall, yet let us have grace to rejoice in the Lord, and to joy in the God of our salvation.[192]

Father, we ask not for bread for a great while to come, but that we may have this day our daily bread; for we would learn, and the Lord teach us not to take thought for the morrow, what we shall eat, or what we shall drink, or wherewithal we shall be clothed, but we cast the care upon thee, our heavenly Father, who knowest that we have need of all these things; who feedest the fowls of the air, though they sow not, neither do they reap, and wilt much more feed us,[193] who are of more value that many sparrows.[194]

Not do we pray for daily bread for ourselves only but for others also. O satisfy thy poor with bread;[195] Let all that walk righteously and speak uprightly dwell on high: Let the place of their defence be the munition of rocks, let bread be given to them, and let their waters be sure.[196]

6. And forgive us our debts as we forgive our debtors.

And, Lord, as duly as we pray every day for our daily bread, we pray for the forgiveness of our sins: For we are all guilty before God, have all sinned, and have come short of the glory of God.[197] In many things we all offend every day:[198] Who can tell how oft he offends?[199] If thou shouldest mark iniquities, O Lord, who shall stand? But there is forgiveness with thee that thou mayest be feared.[200] God be merciful to us sinners.

We have wasted our Lord's goods,[201] we have buried the talents we were intrusted with,[202] nor have we rendered again according to the benefit done unto us, and thus we came to be in debt.[203] The scripture has concluded us all under sin;[204] we have done such things as are worthy of death;[205] things for which the wrath of God comes upon the children of disobedience.[206] Our debt is more than ten thousand talents. It is a great debt; and we have nothing to pay, so far are we from being able to say, Have patience with us, and we will pay thee all.[207] Justly therefore might our adversary deliver us to the judge, and the judge to the officer, to be cast into prison, the prison of hell, till we should pay the last farthing.[208]

But blessed be God, there is a way found out of agreeing with our adversary; for if any man sin, we have an advocate with the Father, even Jesus Christ the righteous, and he is the propitiation for our sins.[209]

For his sake, we pray thee, blot out all our transgressions,[210] and enter not into judgment with us.[211] He is our surety,[212] who restored that which he took not away,[213] that blessed days-man, who hath laid his hand upon us both,[214] through him let us be reconciled unto God,[215] and let the hand-writing which was against, which was contrary to us, be blotted out, and taken out of the way, being nailed to the cross of Christ, that we may be quickened together with Christ, having all our trespasses forgiven us.[216] Be thou merciful to our unrighteousness, and our sins and our iniquities do thou remember no more.[217]

And give us, we pray thee, to receive the atonement,[218] to know that our sins are forgiven us:[219] Speak peace to us,[220] and make us to hear joy and gladness.[221] Let the blood of Christ thy son cleanse us from all sin,[222] and purge our consciences from dead works, to serve the living God.[223]

And as an evidence that thou hast forgiven our sins, we pray thee, give us grace to forgive our enemies, to love them that hate us, and bless them that curse us;[224] for we acknowledge, that if we forgive not men their trespasses, neither will our Father forgive our trespasses:[225] And therefore we forgive, Lord, we desire heartily to forgive,[226] if we have a quarrel against any, even as Christ forgave us.[227] Far be it from us to say, that we will recompense evil,[228] or that we should avenge our-selves.[229] But we pray that all bitterness, and wrath, and anger, and clamour, and evil speaking may be put away from us, with all malice; and that we may be kind one to another, and tender-hearted, forgiving one another, even as God for

Christ's sake, we hope, hath forgiven us.[230] O make us merciful, as our Father who is in heaven is merciful,[231] who hath promised that with the merciful he will shew himself merciful.[232]

7. And lead us not into temptation, but deliver us from evil.

And, Lord, forasmuch as there is in us a bent to backslide from thee,[233] so that when our sins are forgiven, we are ready to return again to folly,[234] we pray that thou wilt not only forgive us our debts, but take care of us, that we may not offend any more.[235] Lord, lead us not into temptation. We know that no man can say when he is tempted, that he is tempted of God, for God tempteth not any man;[236] but we know that God is able to make all grace abound towards us,[237] and to keep us from falling, and present us faultless.[238] We therefore pray that thou wilt never give us up to our own heart's lust, to walk in our own counsels,[239] but restrain Satan, that roaring lion that goes about seeking whom he may devour;[240] and grant that we may not be ignorant of his devices.[241] O let not Satan have us to sift us as wheat: or however, let not our faith fail.[242] Let not the messengers of Satan be permitted to buffet us; but if they be, let thy grace be sufficient for us that where we are weak, there we may be strong,[243] and may be more than conquerors through him that loved us.[244] And, the God of peace tread Satan under our feet, and do it shortly.[245] And since we wrestle not against flesh and blood, but against principalities and powers, and the rulers of the darkness of this world, let us be strong in the Lord, and in the power of his might.[246]

Lord, grant that we may never enter into temptation,[247] but having prayed may set a watch,[248] and let thy wise and good providence so order all our affairs and all events that are concerning us, that no temptation may take us but such as is common to men, and that we may never be tempted above what we are able to discern, resist, and overcome through the grace of God.[249] Lord, do not lay any stumbling block before us, that we should fall upon them and perish.[250] Let nothing be an occasion of falling to us,[251] but give us that great peace which they have that love thy law, whom nothing shall offend.[252]

And lead us, we pray thee, into all truth;[253] lead us in thy truth, and teach us, for thou art the God of our salvation.[254] Show us thy ways, O God, and teach us thy paths, the paths of righteousness:

O lead us in those paths for thy name's sake, that so we may be led beside the still waters.[255]

And deliver us, we pray thee, from the evil one; keep us that the wicked one touch us not,[256] that he sow not his tares in the field of our hearts,[257] that we be not ensnared by his wiles, or wounded by his fiery darts,[258] let the word of God abide in us, that we may be strong, and may overcome the wicked one.[259]

Deliver us from every evil thing, we pray, that we may do no evil:[260] O deliver us from every evil work,[261] save us from our sins,[262] redeem us from all iniquity,[263] especially the sin that doth most easily beset us:[264]

Hide pride from us;[265] remove from us the way of lying;[266] let us not eat of sinners' dainties:[267] incline our hearts to thy testimonies, and not to covetousness;[268] and keep us that we never speak unadvisedly with our lips.[269] But especially keep back thy servant from presumptuous sins, let them not have dominion over us.[270]

Preserve us, we pray thee, that no evil thing may befall us,[271] and keep us from evil, that it may not hurt us.[272] O thou that savest by thy right hand them which put their trust in thee, from those that rise up against them, shew us thy marvellous loving-kindness, and keep us as the apple of thine eye, hide us under the shadow of thy wings.[273] Keep that which we commit unto thee.[274] Thou that hast delivered, dost deliver,[275] and we trust and pray, that thou wilt yet deliver, wilt deliver us from all our fears.[276] O make us to dwell safely, and grant that we may be quiet from the fear of evil.[277] And bring us safe at last to thy holy mountain, where there is no pricking briar, or grieving thorn, nothing to hurt or destroy.[278, 279]

8. *For thine is the Kingdom, the Power, and the Glory, for ever. Amen.*

Father, in heaven, let thy kingdom come, for thine is the kingdom, thou art God in heaven, and rulest over all the kingdoms of the heathen:[280] Let thy will be done, for thine is the power, and there is nothing too hard for thee:[281] Let thy name be sanctified, for thine is the glory, and thou hast set thy glory above the heavens.[282]

Father in heaven, supply our wants, pardon our sins, and preserve us from evil, for thine is the kingdom, the power , and the glory, and thou art Lord over all, who art rich to all that call upon thee;[283] None can forgive sins but thou only,[284] let thy power be great in pardoning our sins;[285] And since it is the glory of God to pardon sin, and to help the helpless,[286] help us, O God of our salvation: for the glory of thy name deliver us, and purge away our sins, for thy name's sake.[287]

We desire in all our prayers to praise thee, for thou art great and greatly to be praised.[288] We praise thy kingdom, for it is an everlasting kingdom, and endures throughout all generations,[288] and the sceptre of thy kingdom is a right sceptre:[289] Thou lovest righteousness, and hatest wickedness: To thee belongeth mercy, and thou renderest to every man according to his works.[290] We praise thy power, for thou hast a mighty arm, strong is thy hand and high is thy right hand, and yet judgment and justice are the habitation of thy throne, mercy and truth shall go before thy face.[291] We praise thy glory, for the glory of the Lord shall endure for ever.[292] Glory be to the Father, to the Son, and to the Holy Ghost: As it was in the beginning, is now, and ever shall be. O let God be praised in his sanctuary, and praised in the firmament of his power; let him be praised for his mighty acts, and praised according to his excellent greatness. Let every thing that hath breath praise the Lord.[293] Hallelujah.

And forasmuch as we know that he heareth us, and whatsoever we ask, according to his will, in faith, we have the petitions that we desired of him,[294] we will triumph in his praise.[295] Now know we that the Lord heareth his anointed,[296] and for his sake will hear us from his holy heaven, with the saving strength of his right hand; and therefore in token not only of our desire, but of our assurance to be heard in Christ's name, we say, *Amen, Amen.*

Our Father which art in heaven, hallowed be thy name, &c.

References

1 Isa. 63:16.
2 Jer. 3:4.
3 Mal. 2:10.
4 Heb. 12:9.
5 James 1:17.
6 2 Cor. 1:3.
7 Isa. 9:6.
8 Rom. 11:36.
9 Eph. 1:3.
10 John 1:14, 18.
11 Prov. 8:30.
12 Eph. 1:5.
13 Gal. 4:6.
14 1 John 3:1.
15 2 Cor. 6:18.
16 John 1:12-13.
17 Gal. 4:5.
18 1 Pet. 1:14-15.
19 Eph. 5:1.
20 Rom. 8:29.
21 Eph. 3:12.
22 Mal. 3:17.
23 1 John 2:1.
24 John 16:27.
25 Mal. 1:6.
26 Heb. 12:28.
27 Luke 11:13.
28 Zech 12:10.
29 Luke 15:13, 17-19.
30 Ps. 86:4, 16.

[31] Ps. 123:1-2.
[32] 1 Kings 8:27.
[33] Heb. 4:14.
[33] Isa. 57:15.
[34] Ps. 111:9.
[35] Eccles. 5:2.
[36] Job 9:14.
[37] Heb 10:19.
[38] Isa. 63:15.
[39] Mark 9:22.
[40] Ps. 150:1.
[41] Ps. 20:2, 6.
[42] John 14:2.
[43] Phil. 3:20.
[44] Col. 3:1.
[45] Esth. 5:6.
[46] Matt. 20:32.
[47] Rom. 10:1.
[48] Lev. 10:3.
[49] Ps. 99:3, 5, 9.
[50] Ps. 22:3.
[51] Ps. 105:3.
[52] Ps. 33:21.
[53] Ps. 106:47.
[54] Ps. 86:12.
[55] John 15:8.
[56] Jer. 13:11.
[57] 1 Pet. 2:9.
[58] Isa. 29:23.
[59] Eph. 1:12.
[60] 1 Pet. 4:10-11, 16.
[61] Phil. 1:20.
[62] Isa. 25:3.
[63] Mal. 1:5.
[64] Isa. 24:15.
[65] Ps. 86:9-10.
[66] Rom. 15:9-10.
[67] Mal. 1:11.
[68] Ps. 22:27, 31.
[69] Jer. 10:7.
[70] Rev:15:3.
[71] Eph. 1:11.
[72] Ezek. 38:23.
[73] Ezek. 36:23.
[74] John 12:28.
[75] John 17:1.
[76] Phil. 2:9.
[77] Col. 1:18.

[78] Josh. 7:9.
[79] Joel 2:28.
[80] Col. 3:16.
[81] Ps. 46:10.
[82] Ps. 57:11.
[83] Ps. 21:13.
[84] Isa. 63:12, 14.
[85] 1 Chron. 17:24.
[86] 1 Chron. 29:11-12.
[87] Ps. 145:11, 13.
[88] Ps. 66:7.
[89] Ps. 66:3.
[90] Ps. 22:28.
[91] Ps. 96:10.
[92] Ps. 64:9.
[93] Ps. 58:11.
[94] Dan. 4:25-26, 37.
[95] Luke 17:20-21.
[96] Matt. 13:31-33.
[97] Rev. 11:15, 17.
[98] Rev. 2:13.
[99] 2 Cor. 10:5.
[100] Isa. 42:21.
[101] 1 Cor. 4:20.
[102] Ps. 110:2-3.
[103] Luke 11:21-22.
[104] Dan. 7:14, 22.
[105] 2 Thess. 3:1.
[106] Matt. 21:43.
[107] 1 Cor. 3:16.
[108] Ps. 119:133.
[109] Ezek. 21:27.
[110] Ps. 110:3.
[111] John 18:37.
[112] Luke 6:46.
[113] 2 Cor. 5:14.
[114] Exod 20:20.
[115] Phil. 3:20.
[116] Matt. 24:30.
[117] Isa. 66:5.
[118] 2 Tim. 4:8.
[119] 2 Pet. 3:12.
[120] Matt. 24:44.
[121] Luke 21:28.
[122] Rom. 8:23.
[123] Phil. 1:23.
[124] Matt. 28:20.
[125] Rev. 22:20.

[126] Rev. 10:7.
[127] Dan. 8:14.
[128] Ps. 135. 6.
[129] Isa. 46:10.
[130] Luke 22:42.
[131] Isa. 46:11.
[132] Eph 1:11.
[133] Isa. 10:7.
[134] 1 Sam. 3:18.
[135] 2 Sam. 15:26.
[136] Acts 21:14.
[137] Matt. 26:39.
[138] Job 1:21.
[139] Job 2:10.
[140] Matt. 26:56.
[141] John 10:35.
[142] Matt. 5:17-18.
[143] Dan. 10:21.
[144] Ps. 119:89.
[145] Matt. 12:50.
[146] 1 Thess. 4:3.
[147] 1 Thess. 5:23.
[148] Col. 1:9
[149] Heb. 13:21.
[150] 1 Pet. 4:3.
[151] Eph. 2:2.
[152] John 4:34.
[153] John 6:38.
[154] Matt. 7:21.
[155] Luke 12:47.
[156] Rom. 12:2.
[157] Eph. 5:17.
[158] Col. 4:12.
[159] Acts 13:36.
[160] Heb. 10:36.
[161] 1 Chron. 17:23.
[162] Ps. 103:20.
[163] Matt. 18:10.
[164] 2 Tim. 2:26.
[165] Matt. 22:30.
[166] Rev. 4:8.
[167] Dan. 10:13.
[168] Ps. 104:4.
[169] Dan. 9:21.
[170] Ezek. 1:9, 12.
[171] Heb. 1:14.
[172] Heb. 12:22.
[173] Matt. 6:33.

[174] Luke 11:3.
[175] Prov. 30:8-9.
[176] Prov. 23:3.
[177] Luke 16:19, 25.
[178] Ps. 104:15.
[179] Prov. 20:17.
[180] Prov. 9:17.
[181] Prov. 31:27.
[182] Ps. 128:2.
[183] 2 Thess. 3:12.
[184] 1 Tim. 6:8.
[185] Phil. 4:18.
[186] Deut. 33:11.
[187] 1 Tim. 5:8.
[188] Prov. 13:22.
[189] Ps. 90:17.
[190] Deut. 33:13, 16.
[191] Hab. 3:17-18.
[192] Matt. 6:31-32.
[193] Matt. 10:31.
[194] Ps. 132:15.
[195] Isa. 33:15-16.
[196] Rom. 3:19, 23.
[197] James 3:2.
[198] Ps. 40:12.
[199] Ps. 130:3-4.
[200] Luke 16:1.
[201] Matt. 25:18.
[202] 2 Chron. 32:25.
[203] Gal. 3:22.
[204] Rom. 1:32.
[205] Eph. 5:6.
[206] Matt. 18:24-26, 32.
[207] Matt. 5:25-26, 29.
[208] 1 John 2:1-2.
[209] Ps. 51:1.
[210] Ps. 143:2.
[211] Heb. 7:22.
[212] Ps. 69:4.
[213] Job 9:33.
[214] 2 Cor. 5:20.
[215] Col. 2:13-14.
[216] Heb. 8:12.
[217] Rom. 5:11.
[218] 1 John 2:12.
[219] Ps. 85:8.
[220] Ps. 51:8.
[221] 1 John 1:7.
[222] Heb. 9:14.
[223] Matt. 5:44.
[224] Matt 6:15.
[225] Matt. 18:35.
[226] Col. 3:13.
[227] Prov. 20:22.
[228] Rom. 12:19.
[229] Eph. 4:31-32.
[230] Matt. 5:7.
[231] Ps. 18:25.
[232] Hosea 11:7.
[233] Ps. 85:8.
[234] Job 34:32.
[235] James 1:13.
[236] 2 Cor. 9:8.
[237] Jude 24.
[238] Ps. 81:12.
[239] 1 Pet. 5:8.
[240] 2 Cor. 2:11.
[241] Luke 22:31-32.
[242] 2 Cor. 12:7, 9-10.
[243] Rom. 8:37.
[244] Rom. 16:20.
[245] Eph. 6:10, 12.
[246] Matt. 26:41.
[247] Neh. 4:9.
[248] 1 Cor. 10:13.
[249] Jer. 6:21.
[250] Rom. 14:13.
[251] Ps. 119:165.
[252] John 16:13.
[253] Ps. 25:5.
[254] Ps. 23:2-3.
[255] 1 John 5:18.
[256] Matt. 13:25.
[257] Eph. 6:11, 16.
[258] 1 John 2:14.
[259] 2 Cor. 13:7.
[260] 2 Tim. 4:18.
[261] Matt. 1:21.
[262] Titus 2:14.
[263] Heb 12:1.
[264] Job 33:17.
[265] Ps. 119:29.
[266] Ps. 141:4.
[267] Ps. 119:36.
[268] Ps. 106:33.
[269] Ps. 19:13.
[270] Ps. 91:10.
[271] Ps. 121:7.
[272] Ps. 17:7-8.
[273] 2 Tim. 1:12.
[274] 2 Cor. 1:10.
[275] Ps. 34:4.
[276] Prov. 1:33.
[277] Ezek. 28:24.
[278] Isa. 11:9.
[279] 2 Chron. 20:6.
[280] Jer. 32:17.
[281] Ps. 8:1.
[282] Rom. 10:12.
[283] Mark 2:7.
[284] Num. 14:17.
[285] Prov. 25:2.
[286] Ps. 79:9.
[287] Ps. 145:3.
[288] Ps. 145:13.
[289] Ps. 45:6-7.
[290] Ps. 62:12.
[291] Ps. 89:13-14.
[292] Ps. 104:31.
[293] Ps. 150:1-2, 6.
[294] 1 John 5:15.
[295] Ps. 106:47.
[296] Ps. 20:6.

CHAPTER 9

**Some short Forms of Prayer,
for the use of those who may not be able to collect for
themselves out of the foregoing Materials.**

1. A Prayer to be used by Children.
O God, thou art my God, early will I seek thee. Thou art my God, and I will praise thee; my father's God, and I will extol thee.

Who is a God like unto thee, glorious in holiness, fearful in praises, doing wonders?

Whom have I in heaven but thee; and there is none upon earth that I desire besides thee. When my flesh and my heart fail, thou art the strength of my heart and portion for ever.

Thou madest me for thyself, to show forth thy praise.

But I am a sinner; I was shapen in iniquity, and in sin did my mother conceive me.

God be merciful to me a sinner.

O deliver me from the wrath to come, through Jesus, who died for me, and rose again.

Lord, give me a new nature. Let Jesus Christ be formed in my soul, that to me to live may be Christ, and to die may be gain.

Lord, I was in my baptism given up to thee; receive me graciously, and love me freely.

Lord Jesus, thou hast encouraged little children to come to thee, and hast said, that of such is the kingdom of God; I come to thee: O make me a faithful subject of thy kingdom, take me up in thy arms, put thy hands upon me, and bless me.

O give me grace to redeem me from all iniquity, and particularly from the vanity which childhood and youth is subject to.

Lord, give me a wise and an understanding heart, that I may know and do thy will in everything, and may in nothing sin against thee.

Lord, grant that from my childhood I may know the holy scriptures, and may continue in the good things that I have learned.

Remove from me the way of lying, and grant me thy law graciously.

Lord, be thou a Father to me; teach me and guide me; provide for me, and protect me, and bless me, even me, O my Father.

Bless all my relations, (father, mother, brothers, sisters,) and give me grace to do my duty to them in every thing.

Lord, prepare me for death, and give me wisely to consider my latter end.

O Lord, I thank thee for all thy mercies to me; for life and health, food and raiment, and for my education; for my creation, preservation, and all the blessings of this life; but above all for thine inestimable love in the means of grace, and the hopes of glory.

Thanks be to God for his unspeakable gift; blessed be God for JESUS CHRIST. None but Christ, none but Christ for me.

Now to God the Father, the Son, and the Holy Ghost, that great name into which I was baptized, be honour and glory, dominion and praise, for ever and ever. *Amen.*

Our Father, which art in heaven, &c.

2. Another Paraphrase on the Lord's Prayer, in the Words of the Assembly's Shorter Catechism.

Our Father in heaven, we come to thee as children to a Father able and ready to help us.

We beseech thee, let thy name be sanctified; enable us and others to glorify thee in all that whereby thou hast made thyself known, and dispose of all things to thine own glory.

Let thy kingdom come; Let Satan's kingdom be destroyed, and let the kingdom of thy grace be advanced; let us and others be brought into it, and kept in it, and let the kingdom of thy glory be hastened.

Let thy will be done on earth as it is done in heaven; make us by thy grace able and willing to know, obey, and submit to thy will in all things as the angels do in heaven.

Give us this day our daily bread; of thy free gift let us receive a competent portion of the good things of this life, and let us enjoy thy blessing with them.

And forgive us our trespasses as we forgive them that trespass against us. We pray that for Christ's sake thou wouldst freely pardon all our sins, and that by thy grace thou wouldst enable us from the heart to forgive others.

And lead us not into temptation, but deliver us from evil. Either keep us, O Lord, from being tempted to sin, or support and deliver us when we are tempted.

For thine is the kingdom, the power, and the glory, for ever. Lord, we take our encouragement in prayer from thyself only, and desire in our prayers to praise thee, ascribing kingdom, power, and glory to thee: And in testimony of our desires and assurance to be heard through Jesus Christ, we say Am*en*.

3. Another Prayer drawn out of my plain Catechism for Children, (which was first published in the Year 1703) which will be easy to those children who have learned that Catechism.

O Lord, thou art an infinite and eternal Spirit, most wise and powerful, holy, just, and good.

Thou art the great God that madest the world, and art my Creator; and thou that madest me dost preserve and maintain me, and in thee I live and move and have my being. O that I may remember thee as my Creator in the days of my youth, and never forget thee.

Lord, give me grace to serve and honour thee, to worship and obey thee, and in all my ways to trust in thee, and to please thee.

Lord, I thank thee for thy holy word, which thou hast given me to be the rule of my faith and obedience, and which is able to make me wise unto salvation.

I confess, O Lord, that the condition which I was born in is sinful and miserable. I am naturally prone to that which is evil, and backward to that which is good, and foolishness is bound up in my heart; and I am by nature a child of wrath; so that if thou hadst not raised up a Saviour for me, I had been certainly lost and undone for ever. I have been disobedient to the command of God, and have eaten forbidden fruit.

But, blessed, and for ever blessed be God for the Saviour Jesus Christ, the eternal Son of God, and the only Mediator between God and man, who took our nature upon him, and became man, that he might redeem and save us.

Lord, I bless thee, for his holy life, give me to follow his steps; I bless thee for the true and excellent doctrine which he preached, give me to mix faith with it, I bless thee for the miracles which he wrought to confirm his doctrine: And especially that he died the cursed death of the cross to satisfy our sin, and to reconcile us to God; and that he rose again from the dead on the third day, and ascended up into heaven, where he ever lives, making intercession for us, and hath all power both in heaven and in earth: and that we are assured he will come again in glory to judge the world at the last day.

Lord, I thank thee that I am one of his disciples; for I am a baptized Christian; and I give glory to Father, Son, and Holy Ghost, in whose name I was baptized.

Lord, be thou in Christ to me a God, and make me one of thy people.

Be thou my chief good, and highest end; let Jesus Christ be my prince and Saviour; and let the Holy Ghost be my sanctifier, teacher, guide, and comforter.

Lord, enable me to deny all ungodliness, and worldly fleshly lusts, and live soberly, righteously, and godly, in this present world, always looking for the blessed hope.

Work in me repentance towards God, and faith towards our Lord Jesus Christ; and give me to live a life of faith and repentance.

Lord, make me truly sorry that I have offended thee in what I have thought, and spoken, and done amiss, and give me grace to sin no more.

And enable me to receive Jesus Christ, and to rely upon him as my prophet, priest, and king, and to give up myself to be ruled and taught, and saved by him.

Lord, grant unto me the pardon of my sins, the gift of the Holy Ghost, and eternal life.

And give me grace to manifest the sincerity of my faith and repentance, by a diligent and conscientious obedience to all thy commandments.

Enable me to love thee with all my heart, and to love my neighbor as myself.

Give me grace always to make mention of thy name with reverence and seriousness, to read and hear thy word with diligence and attention, to meditate upon it, to believe it, and to frame my life according to it.

Lord, grant that I may receive all thy mercies with thankfulness, and bear all afflictions with patience and submission to thy holy will.

Lord, grant that my heart may never be lifted up with pride, disturbed with anger, or any sinful passion; and that my body may be never defiled with intemperance, uncleanness, or any fleshly lusts; and keep me from ever speaking any sinful words.

Lord, give me grace to reverence and obey my parents and governors; I thank thee for their instructions and reproofs: I pray thee bless them to me, and make me in every thing a comfort to them.

Lord, pity, help, and succour the poor, and those in affliction and distress.

Lord, bless my friends, forgive my enemies, and enable me to do my duty to all men.

Wherein I have in any thing offended thee, I humbly pray for pardon in the blood of Christ, and grace to do my duty better for the time to come, and so to live in fear of God, as that I may be happy in this world, and that to come.

Lord, prepare me to die, and leave this world: O save me from that state of everlasting misery and torment, which will certainly be the portion of all the wicked and ungodly, and bring me safe to the world of everlasting rest and joy with thee and Jesus Christ.

And give me wisdom and grace to live a holy, godly life, and to make it my great care and business to serve thee, and to save my own soul.

All this I humbly beg in the name, and for the sake of Jesus Christ, my blessed Saviour and Redeemer, to whom with thee, O Father, and the eternal Spirit, be honour, glory, and praise, henceforth and for evermore. Amen.

4. A Morning Prayer for a Family.

O Lord our God, we desire with all humility and reverence to adore thee, as a being infinitely bright, and blessed, and glorious; thou hast all perfection in thyself, and art the fountain of all being, power, life, motion, and perfection.

Thou art good to all, and thy tender mercies are over all thy works; and thou art continually doing us good, though we are evil and unthankful.

We reckon it an unspeakable privilege, that we have liberty of access to thee through Jesus Christ, and leave to call thee our Father in him. O look upon us now, and be merciful to us, as thou usest to do unto those that love thy name.

O give us all to account our daily worship of thee in our family, the most needful part of our daily business, and the most pleasant part of our daily comforts.

Thou art the God of all the families of Israel, be thou the God of our family, and grant whatever others do, we and ours may always serve the Lord; that thou mayest cause thy blessing to rest on our house, from the beginning of the year to the end of it, Lord, bless us, and we are blessed indeed.

We humbly thank thee for all the mercies of this night past, and this morning, that we have laid us down and slept, and waked again, because thou hast sustained us; that no plague has come nigh our dwelling; but that we are brought in safety to the light and comforts of another day.

It is of thy mercies, O Lord, that we are not consumed, even because thy compassions fail not; they are new every morning, great is thy faithfulness.

We have rested and are refreshed, when many have been full of tossings to and fro till the dawning of the day: we have a safe and quiet habitation, when many are forced to wander and lie exposed.

We own thy goodness to us, and ourselves we acknowledge less than worthy of the least of all the mercy, and of all the truth thou hast shewed unto us.

We confess we have sinned against thee, we are guilty before thee, we have sinned, and have come short of the glory of God: we have corrupt and sinful natures, and are bent to backslide from thee; backward to good, and prone to evil continually.

Vain thoughts come into us, and lodge within us, lying down or rising up, and they defile or disquiet our minds, and keep out good thoughts. We are too apt to burden ourselves with that care which thou hast encouraged us to cast upon thee.

We are very much wanting in the duties of our particular relations, and provoke one another more to folly and passion, than to love and to good works. We are very cold and defective in our love to God, weak in our desires towards him, and unsteady and uneven in our walking with him; and are at this time much out of frame for his service.

We pray thee forgive all our sins, for Christ's sake, and be at peace with us in him who died to make peace, and ever lives, making intercession.

There be many that say, Who will show us any good? but, Lord, let us not be put off with the good of this world for a portion: For this is our hearts desire and prayer, Lord, lift up the light of thy countenance upon us, and that shall put gladness into our hearts, more than they have, whose corn, and wine, and oil increaseth.

Lord, let thy peace rule in our hearts, and give thy law to us, and let thy peace keep our hearts and minds, and give comfort to us; and let the consolations of God, which are neither few nor small, be our strength and our song in the house of our pilgrimage.

Lord, we commit ourselves to thy care and keeping this day: Watch over us for good; compass us about with thy favour as with a shield; preserve us from all evil, yea, the Lord preserve and keep our souls; preserve our going out and coming in.

Our bodies and all our worldly affairs we commit to the conduct of thy wise and gracious providence, and submit to its disposals. Let no hurt or harm happen to us; keep us in health and safety; bless our employments, prosper us in all our lawful undertakings, and give us comfort and success in them. Let us eat the labour of our hands, and let it be well with us.

Our precious souls and all their concerns we commit to the government of thy Spirit and grace. O let thy grace be mighty in us, and sufficient for us, and let it work in us both to will and to do that which is good, of thine own good pleasure.

O give us grace to do the work of this day in its day, according as the duty of the day requires; and to do even common actions after a godly sort, acknowledging thee in all our ways, and having our eyes ever up to thee, and be thou pleased to direct our steps.

Lord, keep us from sin; give us rule over our own spirits, and grant that we may not this day break out into passion upon provocation, or speak unadvisedly with our lips: Give us grace to live together in peace and holy love, that the Lord may command the blessing upon us, even life evermore. Make us conscientious in all our dealings, and always watchful against sin, as becomes those who see thine eye ever upon us: Arm us against every temptation, uphold us in our integrity, keep us in the way of our duty; and grant that we may be in thy fear every day, and all the day long.

In every doubtful case, let our way be made plain before us; and give us that wisdom of the prudent, which is at all times profitable to direct; and let integrity and uprightness preserve us, for we wait on thee.

Sanctify to us all our losses, crosses, afflictions, and disappointments, and give us grace to submit to thy holy will in them, and let us find it good for us to be afflicted, that we may be partakers of thy holiness.

Prepare us for all the events of this day, for we know not what a day may bring forth; Give us to stand complete in thy whole will; to deny ourselves, to take up our cross daily, and to follow Jesus Christ.

Lord, fit us for death, and judgment, and eternity, and give us grace to live every day as those that do not know but it may be our last day.

Lord, plead thy cause in the world; build up thy church into perfect beauty; set up the throne of the exalted Redeemer in all places upon the ruins of the devil's kingdom. Let the reformed churches be more and more reformed, and let everything that is amiss be amended; and let those that suffer for righteousness' sake be supported and delivered.

Do us good in these nations; bless the king, and all in authority; guide public counsels and affairs; overrule all to thine own glory; let peace and truth be in our days, and be preserved to those that shall come after us.

Be gracious to all our relations, friends, neighbors, and acquaintances, and do them good according as their necessities are. Supply the wants of all thy people. Dwell in the families that fear thee, and call upon thy name. Forgive our enemies, and those that hate us; give us a right and charitable frame of spirit towards all men, and all that is theirs.

Visit those that are in affliction, and comfort them, and be unto them a very present help. Recover the sick, ease the pained, succour the tempted, relieve the oppressed, and give joy to those that mourn in Zion.

Deal with us and our family according to the tenure of the everlasting covenant, which is well ordered in all things and sure, and which is all our salvation, and all our desire; however it pleaseth God to deal with us and with our house.

Now blessed be God for all his gifts both of nature and grace, for those that concern this life and that to come; especially for Jesus Christ the fountain and foundation of all; thanks be to God for his unspeakable gift.

We humbly beseech thee, for Christ Jesus' sake, to pardon our sins, accept our services, and grant an answer of peace to our prayers, even for his sake who died for us, and rose again, who hath taught us to pray, *Our Father which art in heaven, &c.*

5. An Evening Prayer for a Family.

Most holy, and blessed, and glorious Lord God, whose we are, and whom we are bound to serve; for, because thou madest us, and not we ourselves, therefore we are not our own, but thine, and unto thee, O Lord, do we lift up our souls; thy face, O Lord, do we seek; whither shall we go for happiness, but to thee, from whom we derive our being.

Thou art the great Benefactor of the whole creation, thou givest to all life and breath and all things: thou art our Benefactor, the God that hast fed us, and kept us all our life long unto this day. Having obtained help of God, we continue hitherto monuments of sparing mercy, and witnesses for thee that thou art gracious, that thou art God, and not man; for therefore it is that we are not cut off.

One day tells another, and one night certifies to another, that thou art good, and doest good, and never failest those that seek thee, and trust in thee. Thou makest the outgoings of the morning and of the evening to praise thee.

It is through the good hand of our God upon us, that we are brought in safety to the close of another day, and that after the various employments of the day, we come together at night to mention the loving-kindness of the Lord, and the praises of our God, who is good, and whose mercy endureth for ever.

Blessed be the Lord, who daily loads us with his benefits, even the God of our salvation; for he that is our God is the God of salvation. We have from thee the mercies of the day in its day, according as the necessity of the day requires, though we come far short of doing the work of the day in its day, according as the duty of the day requires.

We bless thee for the ministration of the good angels about us, the serviceableness of the inferior creatures to us, for our bodily health and ease, comfort in our relations, and a comfortable place of abode, that thou hast not made the wilderness our habitation, and the barren land our dwelling; and especially that thou continuest to us the use of our reason, and the quiet and peace of our consciences.

We bless thee for our share in the public tranquility, that thou hast given us a good land, in which we dwell safely under our own vines and fig-trees.

Above all, we bless thee for Jesus Christ, and his mediation between God and man, for the covenant of grace made with us in him, and all the exceeding great and precious promises and privileges of that covenant, for the throne of grace erected for us, to which we may in his name come with humble boldness, and for the hope of eternal life through him.

We confess we have sinned against thee; this day we have sinned and done foolishly: O God, thou knowest our foolishness, and our sins are not hid from thee; we misspend our time, we neglect our duty, we follow after lying vanities, and forsake our own mercies. We offend with our tongues: are we not carnal and walk as men, below Christians? Who can understand his errors? Cleanse us from our secret faults.

We pray thee give us repentance for our sins of daily infirmity, and make us duly sensible of the evil of them, and of our danger by them, and let the blood of Christ, thy Son, which cleanseth from all sin, cleanse us from it, that we may lie down to night at peace with God, and our souls may comfortably return to him, and repose in him as our rest.

And give us grace to repent every day for the sins of every day, so that when we come to die, we may have the sins but of one day to repent of, and so we may be continually easy.

Do us good by all the providences we are under, merciful or afflictive: give us grace to accommodate ourselves to them, and by all bring us nearer to thee, and make us fitter for thee.

We commit ourselves to thee this night, and desire to dwell in the secret place of the Most High, and to abide under the shadow of the Almighty. Let the Lord be our habitation, and let our souls be at home in him.

Make a hedge of protection (we pray thee) about us, and about our house, and about all that we have round about, that no evil may befall us, nor any plague come nigh our dwelling. The Lord be our keeper, who neither slumbers nor sleeps: Lord, be thou a sun and a shield to us.

Refresh our bodies (we pray thee) with quiet and comfortable rest, not to be disturbed with any distrustful disquieting cares and fears; but especially let our souls be refreshed with thy love, and the light of thy countenance, and thy benignity, which is better than life.

When we awake, grant that we may be still with thee, and may remember thee upon our beds, and meditate upon thee in the night-watches, and may improve the silence and solitude of our retirements for communion with God and our own hearts: that when we are alone, we may not be alone, but God may be with us, and we with him.

Restore us to another day in safety, and prepare us for the duties and events of it; and by all supports and comforts of this life, let our bodies be fitted to serve our souls in thy service, and enable us to glorify thee with both, remembering that we are not our own, we are bought with a price.

And forasmuch as we are now brought one day nearer our end, Lord, enable us so to number our days, as that we may apply our hearts unto wisdom: Let us be minded by our putting off our clothes, and going to sleep in our beds, of putting off the body, sleeping the sleep of death, and making our bed in the darkness shortly, that we may be daily dying in expectation of it, and preparing for our change, that when we come to die indeed, it may be no surprise or terror to us, but we may with comfort put off the body, and resign the spirit, knowing whom we have trusted.

Lord, let our family be blessed in him, in whom all the families of the earth are blessed, blessed with all spiritual blessings in heavenly things, by Christ Jesus, and with temporal blessings as far as thou seest good for us: Give us health and prosperity, but especially let our souls prosper and be in health, and let all that belong to us belong to Christ, that we who live in a house together on earth, may be together for ever with the Lord.

Look with pity upon a lost world, we beseech thee, and set up Christ's throne there where Satan's seat is; send the gospel where it is not, make it successful where it is; let it be mighty through God to the pulling down of the strong holds of sin.

Let the Church of Christ greatly flourish in all places, and make it to appear that it is built upon a rock, and that the gates of hell cannot prevail against it: and suffer not the rod of the wicked any where to rest upon the lot of the righteous.

Let the land of our nativity be still the particular care of thy good providence, that in the peace thereof we may have peace. Let glory dwell in our land, and upon all the glory let there be a defence.

Rule in the hearts of our rulers. We pray thee continue the king's life and government long a public blessing; make all that are in places of public trust faithful to the public interest; and all that bear the sword, a terror to evil doers, and a protection and praise to them that do well. Own thy ministers in their work, and give them skill and will to help souls to heaven.

Be gracious to all that are dear to us: Let the rising generation be such as thou wilt own, and do thee more and better service in their day than this has done.

Comfort and relieve all that are in sorrow or affliction, lay no more upon them than thou wilt enable them to bear, and enable them to bear what thou dost lay upon them.

Do for us, we pray thee, abundantly above what we are able to ask or think, for the sake of our blessed Saviour Jesus Christ, who is the Lord our Righteousness. To him with the Father and the eternal Spirit, be glory and praise, now and for ever. *Amen.*

6. A Family Prayer for the Lord's Day Morning.

Most gracious God, and our Father in our Lord Jesus Christ; it is good for us to draw near to thee; the nearer the better; and it will be best of all, when we come to be nearest of all in the kingdom of glory.

Thou hast thy being of thyself, and thy happiness in thyself; We therefore adore thee, as the great Jehovah: We have our being from thee, and our happiness is in thee, and therefore it is both our duty and our interest to seek thee, to implore thy favour, and to give unto thee the glory due unto thy name.

We bless thee for the return of the morning light, and that thou causest the day-spring to know its place and time. O let the day-spring from on high visit our dark souls, and the Sun of Righteousness arise with healing under his wings.

We bless thee that the light we see is the Lord's: That this is the day which the Lord hath made, hath made for man, hath made for himself, we will rejoice and be glad in it: That thou hast revealed unto us thy holy sabbaths, and that we were betimes taught to put a difference between this day and other days, and that we live in a land, in all parts of which God is publicly and solemnly worshipped on this day.

We bless thee that sabbath liberties and opportunities are continued to us; and that we are not wishing in vain for these days of the Son of man; that our candlestick is not removed out of its place, as justly it might have been, because we have left our first love.

Now we bid this sabbath welcome: Hosanna to the Son of David, blessed is he that cometh in the name of the Lord, Hosanna in the highest. O that we may be in the Spirit on this Lord's day; that this may be the sabbath of the Lord in our dwelling; in our hearts, a sabbath of rest from sin, and a sabbath of rest in God. Enable us, we pray thee, so to sanctify this sabbath, as that it may be sanctified to us, and be a means of our sanctification; that by resting to-day from our worldly employments, our hearts may be more and more taken off from present things, and prepared to leave them; and that by our employing our time to-day in the worship of God, we may be led into a more experimental acquaintance with the work of heaven, and be made more meet for that blessed world.

We confess we are utterly unworthy of the honour, and unable for the work of communion with thee, but we come to thee in the name of the Lord Jesus Christ, who is worthy, and depend upon the assistance of thy blessed Spirit to work all our work in us, and so to ordain peace for us.

We keep this day holy, to the honour of God the Father Almighty, the Maker of heaven and earth, in remembrance of the work of creation, that work of wonder, in which thou madest all things out of nothing by the word of thy power, and all very good: and they continue to this day according to thine ordinance, for all are thy servants. Thou art worthy to receive blessing, and honour, and glory, and power: for thou hast created all things, and for thy pleasure they are and were created. O thou who at first didst command the light to shine out of darkness, who saidst on the first day of the first week, Let there be light, and there was light; we pray thee shine this day into our hearts, and give us more and more of the light of the knowledge of the glory of God in the face of Jesus Christ; and let us be thy workmanship created in Christ Jesus unto good works, a kind of first fruits of thy creatures.

We likewise sanctify this day to the honour of our Lord Jesus Christ, the eternal Son of God, and our exalted Redeemer, in remembrance of his resurrection from the dead on the first day of the week, by which he was declared to be the Son of God with power. We bless thee, that having laid down his life to make atonement for sin, he rose again for our justification, that he might bring in an everlasting righteousness. That the stone which the builders refused, the same is become the head stone of the corner: this is the Lord's doing, and it is marvellous in our eyes. We bless thee, that he is risen from the dead, as the first fruits of them that slept, that he might be the resurrection and the life to us. Now we pray, that while we are celebrating the memorial of his resurrection with joy and triumph, we may experience in our souls the power and virtue of his resurrection, that we may rise with him, may rise from the death of sin to the life of righteousness, from the dust of this world to a holy, heavenly, spiritual, and divine life. O that we may be planted together in the likeness of Christ's resurrection, that as Christ was raised from the dead by the glory of the Father, so we also may walk in newness of life.

We sanctify this day also to the honour of the eternal Spirit, that blessed Spirit of grace, the Comforter, rejoicing at the remembrance of the descent of the Spirit upon the apostles on the day of Pentecost, the first day of the week likewise. We bless thee, that when Jesus was glorified, the Holy Ghost was given to make up the want of his bodily presence, to carry on his undertakings, and to ripen things for his second coming; and that we have a promise that he shall abide with us for ever. And now we pray that the Spirit of him that raised up Jesus from the dead, may dwell and rule in every one of us to make us partakers of a new and divine nature. Come, O blessed spirit of grace, and breathe upon these dry bones, these dead hearts of ours, that they may live and be in us a spirit of faith and love and holiness, a spirit of power and of a sound mind.

O Lord, we bless thee for thy holy word, which is a light to our feet, and a lamp to our paths, and which was written for our learning, that we through patience and comfort of the scriptures might have hope; that the Scriptures are preserved pure and entire to us, and that we have them in a language that we understand. We beg that we may not receive the grace of God herein in vain. We bless thee that our eyes see the joyful light, and our ears hear the joyful sound of a Redeemer and a Saviour, and of redemption and salvation by him: that life and immortality are brought to light by the gospel. Glory be to God in the highest, for in and through Jesus Christ, there is on earth peace, and good will towards men.

We bless thee for the great gospel-record, that God hath given to us eternal life, and this life is in his Son. Lord, we receive it as a faithful saying, and well worthy of all acceptation: we will venture our immortal souls upon it; and we are encouraged by it to come to thee, to beg for an interest in the mediation of thy Son. O let him be made of God to us wisdom, righteousness, sanctification, and redemption, let us be effectually called into fellowship with him, and by faith be united to him, so that Christ may live in us, and we may grow up into him in all things, who is the head; that we may bring forth fruit in him, and whatever we do in word or deed, we may do all in his name. O let us have the Spirit of Christ, that thereby we may make it appear we are his. And through him, we pray that we may have eternal life, that we may none of us come short of it, but may all of us have the first fruits and earnests of it abiding in us.

We bless thee for the new covenant made with us, in Jesus Christ; that when the covenant of innocency was irreparably broken, so that it was become impossible for us to get to heaven by that covenant, thou wast then pleased to deal with us upon new terms; that we are under grace, and not under the law; that this covenant is established upon better promises in the hand of a mediator. Lord, we fly for refuge to it, we take hold of it as the hope set before us. O receive us graciously into the bond of this covenant, and make us accepted in the beloved, according to the tenor of the covenant. Thou hast declared concerning the Lord Jesus, that he is thy beloved Son, in whom thou art well pleased, and we humbly profess that he is our beloved Saviour in whom we are well pleased; Lord, be well pleased with us in him.

O that our hearts may be filled this day with pleasing thoughts of Christ and his love to us, that great love wherewith he loved us. O the admirable dimensions of that love; the height, the depth, and length, and breadth of the love of Christ, which passeth knowledge! Let this love constrain us to love him, and to live to him, who died for us, and rose again. O that it may be a pleasure and mighty satisfaction to us to think that while we are here praying at the footstool of the throne of grace, our blessed Saviour is sitting at the right hand of the throne of glory, interceding for us. We earnestly beg that through him we may find favour with thee our God, and may be taken into covenant and communion with thee.

We humbly pray thee, for his sake, forgive all our sins, known and unknown, in thought, word, and deed: Through him let us be acquitted of guilt, and accepted as righteous in thy sight: Let us not come into condemnation, as we have deserved: let our iniquity be taken away, and our sin covered; and let us be clothed with the spotless robe of Christ's righteousness, that the shame of our nakedness may not appear. O let there be no cloud of guilt to interpose between us and our God this day, and to intercept our comfortable communion with him. And let our lusts be mortified and subdued, that our corruptions may not be as a clog to us, to hinder the ascent of our souls heaven-wards.

We pray thee assist us in all the religious services of this thine own holy day; Go along with us to the solemn assembly, for if thy presence go not up with us, wherefore should we go up? Give us to draw nigh to thee with a true heart, with a free heart, with a fixed heart, and in full assurance of faith. Meet us with a blessing: Grace thine own ordinances with thy presence, that special presence of thine which thou hast promised there, where two or three are gathered together in thy name. Help us against our manifold infirmities, and the sins that do most easily beset us in our attendance upon thee: Let thy word come with life and power to our souls, and be as good seed sown in good soil, taking root, and bringing forth fruit to thy praise; and let our prayers and praises be spiritual sacrifices, acceptable in thy sight, through Christ Jesus; and let those that tarry at home divide the spoil.

Let thy presence be in all assemblies of good Christians this day: Grace be with all them that love the Lord Jesus Christ in sincerity; let grace be upon them all. In the chariot of the everlasting gospel, let the great REDEEMER ride forth triumphantly, conquering and to conquer, and let every thought be brought into obedience to him; Let many be brought to believe the report of the gospel, and to many let the arm of the Lord be revealed: Let sinners be converted unto thee, and thy saints edified and built up in faith, holiness, and comfort, unto salvation: Complete the number of thine elect, and hasten thy kingdom.

Now the Lord of peace himself give us peace always by all means. The God of hope fill us with joy and peace in believing, for Christ Jesus' sake, our blessed Saviour and Redeemer, who hath taught us to pray, *Our Father which art in heaven, &c.*

7. A Family Prayer for the Lord's Day Evening.

O Eternal, and for ever blessed and glorious, Lord God! Thou art God over all, and rich in mercy to all that call upon thee, most wise and powerful, holy, just, and good; the King of kings, and Lord of lords; our Lord and our God.

Thou art happy without us, and hast no need of our services, neither can our goodness extend unto thee, but we are miserable without thee; we have need of thy favours, and are undone, for ever undone, if thy goodness extend not unto us, and therefore, Lord, we entreat thy favour with our whole hearts; O let thy favour be towards us in Jesus Christ, for our happiness is bound up in it, and it is to us better than life. We confess we have forfeited thy favour, we have rendered ourselves utterly unworthy of it; yet we are humbly bold to pray for it in the name of Jesus Christ, who loved us, and gave himself for us.

We bewail it before thee, that by the corruption of our natures we are become odious to thine holiness, and utterly unfit to inherit the kingdom of God and that by our many actual transgressions we are become obnoxious to thy justice, and liable to thy wrath and curse. Being by nature children of disobedience, we are children of wrath, and have reason both to blush and tremble in all our approaches to the holy and righteous God. Even the iniquity of our holy things would be our ruin, if God should deal with us according to the desert of them.

But with thee, O God, there is mercy and plenteous redemption: Thou hast graciously provided for all those that repent and believe the gospel, that the guilt of their sin shall be removed through the merit of Christ's death, and the power of their sins broken by his Spirit and grace; and he is both ways able to save to the uttermost all those that come unto God by him, seeing he ever lives making intercession for us.

Lord, we come to thee as a Father, by Jesus Christ, the Mediator, and earnestly desire, by repentance and faith to turn from the world, and the flesh, to God in Jesus Christ, as our ruler and portion. We are sorry that we have offended thee, we are ashamed to think of our treacherous and ungrateful carriage towards thee. We desire that we may have no more to do with sin, and pray as earnestly that the power of sin may be broken in us, as that the guilt of sin may be removed from us: and we rely only upon the righteousness of Jesus Christ, and upon the merit of his death for the procuring of thy favour. O look upon us in him, and for his sake receive us graciously: heal our backslidings, and love us freely; and let not our iniquity be our ruin.

We beg that being justified by faith, we may have peace with God through our Lord Jesus Christ, whom God hath set forth to be a propitiation for sin, that he may be just, and the justifier of them which believe in Jesus. Through him who was made sin for us, though he knew no sin, let us who know no righteousness of our own, be accepted as righteous.

And the God of peace sanctify us wholly, begin and carry on that good work in our souls, renew us in the spirit of our minds, and make us in every thing such as thou wouldest have us to be. Set up thy throne in our hearts, write thy law there, plant thy fear there, and fill us with all the graces of thy Spirit that we may be fruitful in the fruits of righteousness, to the glory and the praise of God,

Mortify our pride, and clothe us with humility; mortify our passions, and put upon us the ornament of a meek and quiet spirit, which is in the sight of God a great price. Save us from the power of a vain mind, and let thy grace be mighty in us to make us serious and sober-minded. Let the flesh be crucified in us, with all its affections and lusts, and give us grace to keep under our body, and to bring it into subjection to the laws of religion and right reason, and always to possess our vessel in sanctification and honour.

Let the love of the world be rooted out of us, and that covetousness which is idolatry; and let the love of God in Christ be rooted in us. Shed abroad that love in our hearts by the Holy Ghost, and give us to love thee the Lord our God with all our heart, and soul, and mind, and might; and to do all we do in religion from a principle of love to thee.

Mortify in us all envy, hatred, malice, and uncharitableness; pluck up these roots of bitterness out of our minds, and give us grace to love one another with a pure heart fervently, as becomes the followers of the Lord Jesus, who has given us this as his new commandment. O that brotherly love may continue among us, love without dissimulation.

We pray thee, rectify all our mistakes; if in any thing we be in an error, discover it to us, and let the Spirit of truth lead us into all truth, the truth as it is in Jesus, the truth which is according to godliness; and give us that good understanding which they have that do thy commandments; and our love and all good affections abound in us yet more and more, in knowledge, and in all judgment.

Convince us, we pray thee, of the vanity of this world and its utter insufficiency to make us happy, that we may never set our hearts upon it, nor raise our expectation from it: And convince us of the vileness of sin, and its certain tendency, to make us miserable, that we may hate it, and dread it, and every thing that looks like it, or leads to it.

Convince us, we pray thee, of the worth of our own souls and the weight of eternity, and the awfulness of that everlasting state which we are standing upon the brink of, and make us diligent and serious in our preparation for it, labouring less for the meat that perisheth, and more for that which endures to eternal life, as those who have set their affections on things above, and not on things that are on earth, which are trifling and transitory.

O that time and the things of time may be as nothing to us in comparison with eternity, and the things of eternity; that eternity may be much upon our heart, and ever in our eye; that we may be governed by that faith which is the substance of things hoped for, and the evidence of things not seen; looking continually at the things that are not seen, that are eternal.

Give us grace, we pray thee, to look up to the other world with such a holy concern, as that we may look down upon this world with a holy contempt and indifferency, as those that must be here but a very little while, and must be some-where for ever; that we may rejoice as though we rejoiced not, and weep as though we wept not, and buy as though we possessed not, and may use this world as not abusing it, because the fashion of this world passeth away, and we are passing away with it.

O let thy grace be mighty in us and sufficient for us, to prepare us for the great change which will come certainly and shortly, and may come very suddenly, which will remove us from a world of sense to a world of spirits; from our state of trial and probation to that of recompense and retribution; and to make us meet for the inheritance of the saints in light; that when we fail, we may be received into everlasting habitations.

Prepare us, we beseech thee, for whatever we may meet with betwixt us and the grave: We know not what is before us, and therefore know not what particular provision to make; but thou dost, and therefore we beg of thee to fit us by thy grace for all the services and all the sufferings which thou shalt at any time call us out to: and arm us against every temptation which we may at any time be assaulted with, that we may at all times and in all conditions glorify God, keep a good conscience, and be found in the way of our duty, and may keep up our hope and joy in Christ, and a believing prospect of eternal life, and then welcome the holy will of God.

Give us grace, we pray thee, to live a life of communion with thee both in ordinances and providences, to set thee always before us, and to have our eyes ever upon thee, and to live a life of dependance upon thee, upon thy power, providence and promise, trusting in thee at all times, and pouring out our hearts before thee; and to live a life of devotedness to thee, and to thine honour and glory, as our highest end. And that we may make our religion not only our business, but our pleasure, we beseech thee, enable us to live a life of complacency in thee, to rejoice in thee always; making God our heart's delight, so that we may have our heart's desire; and this is our heart's desire, to know, and love, and live to God; to please him and to be pleased in him.

We beseech thee, preserve us in our integrity to our dying day, and grant that we may never forsake thee, or turn from following after thee, but that with purpose of heart we may cleave unto the Lord, and may not count life itself so dear to us, so we may but finish our course with joy and true honour.

Let thy good providence order all the circumstances of our dying, so as may best befriend our comfortable removal to a better world; and let thy grace be sufficient for us then to enable us to finish well; and let us then have an abundant entrance ministered to us into the everlasting kingdom of our Lord and Saviour Jesus Christ.

And while we are here, make us wiser and better every day than others, more weaned from the world; and more willing to leave it; more holy, heavenly, and spiritual; that the longer we live in this world, the fitter we may be for another, and our last days may be our best days, our last works our best works, and our last comforts our sweetest comforts.

We humbly pray thee, accomplish all that which thou hast promised concerning thy church in the latter days; let the earth be filled with thy glory. Let the fulness of the Gentiles be brought in, and let all Israel be saved. Let the mountain of the Lord's house be established upon the top of the mountains, and exalted above the hills, and let all nations flow unto it.

Propagate the gospel in the plantations, and let the enlargement of trade and commerce contribute to the enlargement of thy church. Let the kingdom of Christ be set up in all places upon the ruins of the devil's kingdom.

Hasten the downfall of the man of sin, and let primitive Christianity, even pure religion and undefiled before God and the Father, be revived, and be made to flourish in all places; and let the power of godliness prevail and get ground among all that have the form of it.

Let the wars of the nations end in the peace of the church, the shakings of the nations end in the establishment of the church, and the convulsions and revolutions of states and kingdoms in the settlement and advancement of the kingdom of God among men, that kingdom which cannot be moved.

Let Great Britain and Ireland flourish in all their public interests; let thine everlasting gospel be always the glory in the midst of us, and let thy providence be a wall of fire round about us; destroy us not, but let a blessing be among us, even a meat-offering and a drink-offering to the Lord our God.

Be very gracious to our sovereign lord the king, protect his person, preserve his health, prolong his days, guide his councils, let his reign be prosperous, and crown all his undertakings for the public good.

Bless the privy counsellors, the nobility, the judges and magistrates in our several counties and corporations, and make them in all their places faithful and serviceable to the interest of the nation, and every way public blessings.

Bless all the ministers of thy holy word and sacraments; make them burning and shining lights, and faithful to Christ, and to the souls of men; unite all thy ministers and people together in the truth, and in true love one to another; pour out a healing spirit upon them, a spirit of love and charity, mutual forbearance and condescension, that with one shoulder and with one consent all may study to promote the common interests of our great Master, and the common salvation of precious souls.

We pray thee, prosper the trade of the nation, and our coasts, disappoint the devices of our enemies against us, preserve the public peace, and keep all the people of these lands in quietness among themselves, and due subjection to the authority God hath set over us: and let the Lord delight to dwell among us, and to do us good.

Bless the fruits of the earth, continue our plenty, abundantly bless our provision, and satisfy even our poor with bread.

We bless thee for all the mercies of this thine own holy day; we have reason to say that a day in thy courts is better than a thousand. How amiable are thy tabernacles, O Lord of hosts, Bless the word we have heard this day to us, and to all that heard it; hear our prayers, accept our praises, and forgive what thy pure eye hath seen amiss in us and our performances.

Take us under thy protection this night, and enable us to close the day with thee, that we may lie down, and our sleep may be sweet. Be with us the week following in all our ways; forgive us that we brought so much of the week with us into the sabbath, and enable us to bring a great deal of the sabbath with us into the week, that we may be the fitter for the next sabbath, if we should live to see it.

Make us meet for the everlasting sabbath, which we hope to keep within the veil, when time and days shall be no more: And let this day bring us a sabbath-day's journey nearer heaven, and make us a sabbath-day's work fitter for it.

As we began this Lord's day with the joyful memorials of Christ's resurrection, so we desire to conclude it with the joyful expectations of Christ's second coming, and of our own resurrection, then to a blessed immortality, triumphing in hope of the glory of God.

Bless the Lord, love the Lord, O our souls, and let all that is within us love and bless his holy name, for he is good and his mercy endures for ever. In praising God, we desire to spend as much of our time as may be, that we may begin our heaven now; for in this good work we hope to be spending a happy eternity.

Now unto the King eternal, immortal, invisible, the only wise God, and our God, in three persons, Father, Son, and Holy Ghost, be honour and glory, dominion and praise, henceforth and for ever. *Amen.*

8. *A Prayer proper to be put up by Parents for their Children*

O Lord our God, the God of the spirits of all flesh! all souls are thine, the souls of the parents and the souls of the children are thine, and thou hast grace sufficient for both.

Thou wast our father's God, and as such we will exalt thee; thou art our children's God, and also we will plead with thee, for the promises to us and our children, and thou art a God in covenant with believers, and their seed.

Lord, it is thy good providence that hath built us up into a family; we thank thee for the children thou hast graciously given thy servants; the Lord that hath blessed us with them, make them blessings indeed to us, that we may never be tempted to wish we had been written childless.

We lament the iniquity which our children are conceived and born in; and that corrupt nature which they derive through our loins.

But we bless thee there is a fountain opened for their cleansing from that original pollution, and that they were betimes by baptism dedicated to thee, and admitted into the bonds, and under the blessings of thy covenant: that they are born in thy house, and taken in as members of thy family upon earth.

It is a comfort to us to think, that they are baptized, and we desire humbly to plead it with thee: they are thine, save them: enable them, as they become capable, to make it their own act and deed to join themselves unto the Lord, that they may be owned as thine in that day when thou makest up thy jewels.

Give them a good capacity of mind, and a good disposition, make them towardly and tractable, and willing to receive instruction; incline them betimes to religion and virtue: Lord give them wisdom and understanding, and drive out the foolishness that is bound up in their hearts.

Save them from the vanity which childhood and youth is subject to, and fit them every way to live comfortably and usefully in this world. We ask not for great things in this world for them: Give them, if it please thee, a strong and healthful constitution of body, preserve them from all ill accidents, and feed them with food convenient for them, according to their rank.

But the chief thing we ask of God for them is, that thou wilt pour thy Spirit upon our seed, even thy blessing, that blessing of blessings, upon our offspring, that they may be a seed to serve thee, which shall be accounted unto the Lord for a generation; Give them that good part which never shall be taken away from them.

Give us wisdom and grace to bring them up in thy fear, in the nurture and admonition of the Lord, with meekness and tenderness, and having them in subjection with all gravity. Teach us how to teach them the things of God as they are able to bear them, and how to reprove and admonish, and when there is need to correct them in a right manner: and how to set them good examples of every thing that is virtuous and praise-worthy, that we may recommend religion to them, and so train them up in the way wherein they should go, that if they live to be old, they may not depart from it.

Keep them from the snare of evil company, and all the temptations to which they are exposed, and make them betimes sensible how much it is their interest as well as their duty to be religious; And, Lord grant that none that come of us, may come short of eternal life, or be found on the left hand of Christ in the great day.

We earnestly pray that Christ may be formed in their souls betimes, and that the seeds of grace may be sown in their hearts while they are young; and may have the satisfaction of seeing them walking in the truth and setting their faces heaven-wards. Give them now to hear counsel and receive instruction, that they may be wise in their latter end: and if they be wise, our hearts shall rejoice, even ours.

Prosper the means of their education; let our children be taught of the Lord, that great may be their peace; and give them so to know thee the only true God, and Jesus Christ whom thou hast sent, as may be life eternal to them.

O that they may betimes get wisdom, and get understanding, and never forget it: As far as they are taught the truth as it is in Jesus, give them to continue in the things which they have learned.

It is our heart's desire and prayer that our children may be praising God on earth when we are gone to praise him in heaven, and that we and they may be together for ever, serving him day and night in his temple.

If it should please God to remove any of them from us while they are young, let us have grace submissively to resign them to thee, and let us have hope in their death.

If thou remove us from them while they are young, be thou thyself a Father to them, to teach them and provide for them, for with thee the fatherless findeth mercy.

Thou knowest our care concerning them, we cast it upon thee; ourselves and ours we commit to thee.

Let not the light of our family-religion be put out with us, nor that treasure be buried in our graves, but let those that come after us do thee more and better service in their day than we have done in ours, and be unto thee for a name and a praise.

In these prayers we aim at thy glory: Father, let thy name be sanctified in our family, there let thy kingdom come, and let thy will be done by us and ours, as it is done by the angels in heaven; for Christ Jesus' sake, our blessed Saviour and Redeemer, whose seed shall endure for ever, and his throne as the days of heaven. Now to the Father, Son, and Holy Ghost, that great and sacred name, into which we and our children were baptized, be honour and glory, dominion and praise, henceforth and for ever. *Amen.*

9. *A Prayer for the use of a particular Person, before the receiving of the sacrament of the Lord's Supper.*

Most holy, and blessed, and gracious Lord God, with all humility and reverence, I here present myself before thee, to seek thy face and entreat thy favour, and, as an evidence of thy good-will towards me, to beg that I may experience thy good work in me.

I acknowledge myself unworthy, utterly unworthy of the honour; unfit, utterly unfit for the service to which I am now called. It is an inestimable privilege, that I am permitted so often to hear from thee in thy word, and to speak to thee in prayer: and yet, as if this had been a small matter, I am now invited into communion with thee at thy holy table, there to celebrate the memorial of my Saviour's death, and to partake by faith of the precious benefits which flow from it. I who deserve not the crumbs, am called to eat the children's bread.

O Lord, I thank thee for the institution of this blessed ordinance, this precious legacy and token of love, which the Lord Jesus left to his church, that it is preserved to this age; that it is administered in this land; that I am admitted to it, and have now before me an opportunity to partake of it: Lord, grant that I may not receive thy grace herein in vain.

O thou who hast called me to the marriage-supper of the Lamb, give me a wedding garment; work in me a disposition of soul, and all those pious and devout affections which are suited to the solemnities of this ordinance, and requisite to qualify me for an acceptable and advantageous participation of it. Behold the fire and the wood, all things are now ready; but where is the lamb, for the burnt-offering? Lord, provide thyself a lamb, by working in me all that thou requirest of me upon this occasion. The preparation of the heart, and the answer of the tongue are both from thee; Lord prepare my unprepared heart for communion with thee.

Lord, I confess I have sinned against thee, I have done foolishly, very foolishly, for foolishness is bound up in my heart, I have sinned, and have come short of being glorified with thee. The imagination of my heart is evil continually, and the bias of my corrupt nature is very strong toward the world, and the flesh, and the gratifications of sense; but towards God, and Christ, and heaven, I move slowly, and with a great many stops and pauses. Nay, there is in my carnal mind a wretched aversion to divine and spiritual things. I have misspent my time, trifled away my opportunities, have followed after lying vanities, and forsaken my own mercies. God be merciful to me a sinner! for how little have I done, since I came into the world, of the great work that I was sent into the world about?

Thou hast taken me into covenant with thee, for I am a baptized Christian, set apart for thee, and sealed to be thine; thou hast laid me, and I also have laid myself under all possible obligations to love thee, and serve thee, and live to thee. But I have started aside from thee like a deceitful bow, I have not made good my covenant with thee, nor hath the temper of my mind, and the tenor of my conversation been agreeable to that holy religion which I make profession of, to my expectations from thee, and engagements to thee. I am bent to backslide from the living God; and if I were under the law I were undone; but I am under grace, a covenant of grace which leaves room for repentance, and promiseth pardon upon repentance, which invites even backsliding children to return, and promises that their backslidings shall be healed. Lord, I take hold of this covenant, seal it to me at thy table. There let me find my heart truly humbled for sin, and sorrowing for it after a godly sort: O that I may there look on him whom I have pierced, and mourn, and be in bitterness for him; that there I may sow in tears, and receive a broken Christ into a broken heart: and there let the blood of Christ, which speaks better things than that of Abel, be sprinkled upon my conscience, to purify and pacify that; There let me be assured that thou art reconciled to me, that my iniquities are pardoned, and that I shall not come into condemnation. There say unto me, be of good cheer, thy sins are forgiven thee.

Chapter 9

And that I may not come unworthily to this blessed ordinance, I beseech thee lead me into a more intimate and experimental acquaintance with Jesus Christ and him crucified; with Jesus Christ and him glorified; that knowing him, and the power of his resurrection, and the fellowship of his sufferings, and being by his grace planted in the likeness of both, I may both discern the Lord's body, and shew forth the Lord's death.

Lord, I desire by a true and lively faith to close with Jesus Christ, and consent to him as my Lord, and my God; I here give up myself to him as my Prophet, Priest, and King, to be ruled, and taught, and saved by him; this is my beloved, and this is my friend. None but Christ, none but Christ. Lord, increase this faith in me, perfect what is lacking in it; and enable me, in receiving the bread and wine at thy table, by a lively faith to receive Christ Jesus the Lord. O let the great gospel doctrine of Christ's dying to save sinners, which is represented in that ordinance, be meat and drink to my soul, meat indeed, and drink indeed. Let it be both nourishing and refreshing to me, let it be both my strength and my song, and be the spring both of my holiness and my comfort. And let such deep impressions be made upon my soul, by actual commemoration of it, as may abide always upon me, and have a powerful influence upon me in my whole conversation, that the life I now live in the flesh, I may live by the faith of the Son of God, who loved me, and gave himself for me.

Lord, I beseech thee fix my thoughts; let my heart be engaged to approach unto thee, that I may attend upon thee without distraction. Draw out my desires towards thee: give me to hunger and thirst after righteousness, that I may be filled; and to draw near to thee with a true heart, and in full assurance of faith; and since I am not straitened in thee, O let me not be straitened in my own bosom.

Draw me, Lord, and I will run after thee: O send out thy light and thy truth, let them lead and guide me; pour thy Spirit upon me, put thy Spirit within me, to work in me both to will and to do that which is good, and leave me not to myself. Awake, O north wind, and come thou south, and blow upon my garden; come, O blessed Spirit of grace, and enlighten my mind with the knowledge of Christ, bow my will to the will of Christ, fill my heart with the love of Christ, and confirm my resolutions to live and die with him.

Work in me (I pray thee) a principle of holy love and charity towards all men, that I may forgive my enemies (which by grace I heartily do) and may keep up a spiritual communion in faith, hope, and holy love, with all that in every place call on the name of Jesus Christ our Lord. Lord, bless them all, and particularly that congregation with which

I am to join in this solemn ordinance. Good Lord, pardon every one
that engageth his heart to seek God, the Lord God of their fathers,
though not cleansed according to the purification of the sanctuary.
Hear my prayers, and heal the people.

Lord, meet me with a blessing, a Father's blessing at thy table;
grace thine own institution with thy presence; and fulfil in me all the
good pleasure of thy goodness, and the work of faith with power, for
the sake of Jesus Christ my blessed Saviour and Redeemer. To him,
with the Father, and the eternal Spirit, be everlasting praises. *Amen.*

10. Another after the receiving of the Lord's Supper.
O Lord, my God and my Father in Jesus Christ, I can never sufficiently
admire the condescension of thy grace to me; what is man that thou
dost thus magnify him, and the son of man that thou thus visitest him!
Who am I? and what is my house, that thou hast brought me hitherto;
hast brought me into the banqueting-house, and thy banner over me
hath been love? I have reason to say, That a day in thy courts, an hour
at thy table, is better, far better, than a thousand days, than ten thousand
hours elsewhere; it is good for me to draw near to God: Blessed be
God for the privileges of his house, and those comforts with which he
makes his people joyful in his house of prayer.

But I have reason to blush and be ashamed of myself that I have not
been more affected with the great things which have been set before
me, and offered to me at the Lord's table. O what a vain, foolish, and
trifling heart have I! When I would do good, even evil is present with
me; Good Lord, be merciful to me, and pardon the iniquity of my holy
things, and let not my many defects in my attendance upon thee be laid
to my charge, or hinder my profiting by the ordinance.

I have now been commemorating the death of Christ; Lord, grant
that by the power of that, sin may be crucified in me, the world
crucified to me, and I to the world: and enable me so to bear about
with me continually the dying of the Lord Jesus, as that the life also of
Jesus may be manifested in my mortal body.

I have now been receiving the precious benefits which flow from
Christ's death; Lord, grant that I may never lose, may never forfeit those
benefits, but as I have received Christ Jesus the Lord, give me grace so
to walk in him, and to live as one that am not my own, but am bought
with a price, glorifying God, with my body and spirit, which are his.

I have now been renewing my covenant with thee, and engaging
myself afresh to thee to be thine; now, Lord, give me grace to perform
my vow. Keep it always in the imagination of the thought of my heart,

and establish my way before thee. Lord, preserve me by thy grace, that I may never return again to folly; after God hath spoken peace, may I never by my loose and careless walking undo what I have been doing to day: But having my heart enlarged with the consolation of God, give me to run the way of thy commandments with cheerfulness, and constancy, and still to hold fast in my integrity.

This precious soul of mine, which is the work of thine own hands, and the purchase of thy Son's blood, I commit into thy hands, to be sanctified by thy Spirit and grace, and wrought up into conformity to thy holy will in every thing: Lord, set up thy throne in my heart, write thy law there, shed abroad thy love there, and bring every thought within into obedience to thee, to the commanding power of thy law, and the constraining power of thy love. Keep through thine own name that which I commit unto thee, keep it against that day, when it shall be called for; let me be preserved blameless to the coming of thy glory, that I then may be presented faultless with exceeding joy.

All my outward affairs I submit to the disposal of thy wise and gracious providence; Lord, save my soul, and then as to other things do as thou pleasest with me; only make all providences work together for my spiritual and eternal advantage. Let all things be pure to me, and give me to taste covenant love, in common mercies; and by thy grace let me be taught, both how to want, and how to abound, how to enjoy prosperity, and how to bear adversity as becomes a Christian: and at all times let thy grace be sufficient for me, and mighty in me, to work in me both to will and to do that which is good of thine own good pleasure.

And that in every thing I may do my duty, and stand complete in it, let my heart be enlarged in love to Jesus Christ, and affected with the height and depth, the length and breadth of that love of his to me, which passeth all conception and expression.

And as an evidence of that love, let my mouth be filled with his praises. Worthy is the Lamb that was slain to receive blessing, and honour, and glory and power; for he was slain, and hath redeemed a chosen remnant unto God by his blood, and made them to him kings and priests. Bless the Lord, O my soul, and let all that is within me bless his holy name, who forgiveth all mine iniquities, and healeth all my diseases; who redeemeth my life from destruction, and crowneth me with thy loving-kindness and tender mercy; who hath begun a good work, will perform it unto the day of Christ. As long as I live will I bless the Lord; I will praise my God while I have any being; and when I have no being upon earth, I hope to have a being in heaven to be doing it better. O let me be borne up in everlasting arms, and carried from strength to strength, till I appear before God in Zion, for Jesus' sake, who died for me, and rose again, in whom I desire to be found living and dying. Now to God the Father, Son, and Spirit be ascribed kingdom, power and glory, henceforth and for ever. *Amen.*

11. An Address to God before Meat.

O Lord our God, in thee we live and move, and have our being, and from thee receive all supports and comforts of our being: Thou spreadest our table, and fillest our cup, and comfortest us with the gifts of thy bounty from day to day. We own our dependence upon thee, and our obligations to thee, pardon our sins we pray thee; sanctify thy good creatures to our use, and give us grace to receive them soberly and thankfully, and to eat and drink not to ourselves, but to thy glory, through Jesus Christ our blessed Lord and Saviour. *Amen.*

12. Another.

Gracious God, thou art the protector and preserver of the whole creation, thou hast fed us all our lives, unto this day, with food convenient for us, though we are evil and unthankful. We pray thee forgive all our sins, by which we have forfeited all thy mercies, and let us see our forfeited right restored in Christ Jesus: Give us to taste covenant-love in common mercies, and to use these and all our creature-comforts to the glory of our great Benefactor, through the grace of our great Redeemer. *Amen.*

13. An Address to God after Meat.

Blessed be the Lord, who daily loads us with his benefits, and gives us all things richly to enjoy, though we serve him but poorly. O Lord, we thank thee for present refreshments in the use of thy good creatures, and for thy love to our souls in Jesus Christ, which sweetens all: We pray thee pardon our sins, go on to do us good, provide for the poor that are destitute of daily food, fit us for thy whole will, and be our God, and guide, and portion for ever, through Jesus Christ our Lord and Saviour. *Amen.*

14. Another.

We thank thee, Father, Lord of heaven and earth, for all the gifts both of thy providence and of thy grace; for those blessings which relate to the life that now is, and that to come; for the use of thy good creatures at this time: Perfect, O God, that which concerns us, nourish our souls with the bread of life to life eternal, and let us be of those that shall eat bread in the kingdom of our Father, for Christ Jesus' sake, our Lord and Saviour. *Amen.*

TO THE
READER

The two first of these Discourses was preached (that is, the substance of them) at the Morning Lecture at Bednal Green, the former, August 13, the other, August 21, 1712. The latter of them I was much importuned to publish by divers that heard it; which yet I then had no thoughts at all of doing, because in divers practical treatises, we have excellent directions given of the same nature and tendency, by better hands than mine. But upon second thoughts I considered, that both those sermons of beginning and spending the day with God, put together, might perhaps be of some use to those into whose hands those larger treatises do not fall. And the truth is, the subject of them is of such a nature, that if they may be of any use, they may be of general and lasting use; whereupon I entertained the thought of writing them over, with very large additions throughout, as God should enable me, for the Press. Communicating this thought to some of my friends, they very much encouraged me to proceed in it, but advised me to add a third discourse of closing the day with God, which I thereupon took for my subject at an evening Lecture, Sept. 3. and have likewise much enlarged and altered that. And so this came to be what it is.

I am not without hopes, that something may hereby be contributed among plain people, by the blessing of God upon the endeavour, and the working of his grace with it, to the promoting of serious godliness, which is the thing I aim at. And yet I confess I had not published it, but designing it for a present to my dearly beloved friends in the country, whom I have lately been rent from.

And to them with the most tender affection, and most sincere respects I dedicate it, as a testimony of my abiding concern for their spiritual welfare; hoping and praying, that their conversation may be in every thing as becomes the gospel of Christ, that whether I come and see them, or else be absent, I may hear comfortably of their affairs, that they stand fast in one spirit with one mind, striving together for the Faith of the gospel.

I am,

Their Cordial and Affectionate Well wisher,

MATTHEW HENRY, Sept. 8, 1712

THE FIRST DISCOURSE SHEWING HOW TO BEGIN EVERY DAY WITH GOD

PSALM 5:3
My voice shalt thou hear in the morning, O Lord, in the morning will I direct my Prayer unto thee, and will look up.

You would think it a rude question, if I should ask you, and yet I must entreat you seriously to ask yourselves, What brings you hither so early this morning? And what is your business here? Whenever we are attending on God in holy ordinances (nay, wherever we are) we should be able to give a good answer to the question which God put to the prophet, *What dost thou here, Elijah?* As when we return from holy ordinances, we should be able to give a good answer to the question which Christ put to those that attended on John the Baptist's ministry, *What went ye out into the wilderness to see?*

It is surprising to see so many got together here: surely the fields are white unto the harvest; and I am willing to hope, it is not merely for a walk this pleasant morning, that you are come hither; or for curiosity, because the morning lecture was never here before; that it is not for company, or to meet your friends here, but that you are come with a pious design to give glory to God, and to receive grace from him, and in both to keep up your communion with him. And if you ask us that are ministers, what our business is, we hope we can truly say, it is (as God shall enable us) to assist and further you herein. Comest thou peaceably? said the elders of Bethlehem to Samuel; and so perhaps you will say to us; to which we answer, as the Prophet did, peaceably we come to sacrifice unto the Lord, and invite you to the sacrifice.

While the lecture continues with you, you have an opportunity of more than doubling your morning devotions; besides your worshipping of God in secret, and in your families, which this must not supersede, or justle out, you here call upon God's name in the solemn assembly; and it is as much your business in all such exercises to pray a prayer together, as it is to hear a sermon; and it is said, the original of the morning exercise was a meeting for prayer, at the time when the nation was groaning under the dreadful desolating judgment of a civil war. You have also an opportunity of conversing with the word of God; you have precept upon precept, and line upon line. O that as the opportunity wakens you morning by morning, so (as the prophet speaks) your ears may be wakened to hear as the learned, Isa. 50:4.

But this is not all; we desire that such impressions may be made upon you by this cluster of opportunities, as you may always abide under the influence of; that this morning lecture may leave you better disposed to morning worship ever after; that these frequent acts of devotion may so confirm the habit of it, as that from henceforward your daily worship may become more easy, and if I may say so, in a manner natural to you.

For your help herein I would recommend to you holy David's example in the text, who having resolved in general (verse 2) that he would abound in the duty of prayer, and abide by it, unto thee will I pray, here fixeth one proper time for it, and that is the morning; My voice shalt thou hear in the morning; not in the morning only. David solemnly addressed himself to the duty of prayer three times a day, as Daniel did; Morning and evening, and at noon will I pray, and cry aloud (Ps. 55:17). Nay, he doth not think that enough, but seven times a day will I praise thee (Ps. 119:164). But particularly in the morning.

Doct. It is our wisdom and duty, to begin every day with God.

Let us observe in the text,

1. The good work itself that we are to do. God must hear our voice, we must direct our prayer to him, and we must look up.

2. The special time appointed, and observed for the doing of this good work; and that is in the morning, and again in the morning, that is, every morning, as duly as the morning comes.

1. *For the first*, The good work which by the example of David we are here taught to do, is in one word to pray; a duty dictated by the light and law of nature, which plainly and loudly speaks, Should not a people seek unto their God? But which the gospel of Christ gives

us much better instructions in, and encouragement to, than any that nature furnisheth us with, for it tells us what we must pray for, in whose name we must pray, and by whose assistance, and invites us to come boldly to the throne of grace, and to enter into the holiest by the blood of Jesus. This work we are to do not on the morning only, but at other times, at all times; we read of preaching the word out of season, but we do not read of praying out of season, for that is never out of season; the throne of grace is always open, and humble supplicants are always welcome, and cannot come unseasonably.

But let us see how David here expresseth his pious resolution to abide by this duty.

1.1. *My voice shalt thou hear*. Two ways David may here be understood. Either,

1.1.1. *As promising himself a gracious acceptance with God.* Thou shalt, *i.e.* thou wilt hear my voice, when in the morning I direct my prayer to thee; so it is the language of his faith, grounded upon God's promise, that his ear shall be always open to his people's cry. He had prayed, Give ear to my words, O Lord (*verse* 1); and *verse* 2, Hearken unto the voice of my cry; and here he receives an answer to that prayer, thou wilt hear, I doubt not but thou wilt; and though I have not presently a grant of the thing I prayed for, yet I am sure my prayer is heard, is accepted, and comes up for a memorial, as the prayer of Cornelius did; it is put upon the file, and shall not be forgotten. If we look inward, and can say by experience that God has prepared our heart; we may look forward, and say with confidence that he will cause his ear to hear.

We may be sure of this, and we must pray in the assurance of it, in a full assurance of his faith, that wherever God finds a praying heart, he will be found a prayer-hearing God; though the voice of prayer be a low voice, a weak voice, yet if it come from an upright heart, it is a voice that God will hear, that he will hear with pleasure, it is his delight, and that he will return a gracious answer to; he hath heard thy prayers, he hath seen thy tears. When therefore we stand praying, this ground we must stand upon, this principle we must stand to, nothing doubting, nothing wavering, that whatever we ask of God as a father, in the name of Jesus Christ the Mediator, according to the will of God revealed in the scripture, it shall be granted us either in kind or kindness; so the promise is, John 16:23, and the truth of it is sealed to by the concurring experience of the saints in all ages, ever since men began to call upon the name of the Lord, that Jacob's God never yet said to Jacob's seed, seek ye me in vain, and he will not begin now. When we come to God by prayer, if we come aright we may be confident of this, that notwithstanding the distance between heaven and earth, and our great unworthiness to have any notice taken of us, or any favour shewed us; yet God doth hear our voice, and will not turn away our prayer, or his mercy. Or,

1.1.2. It is rather to be taken, as David's promising God a constant attendance on him, in the way he has appointed. My voice shalt thou hear, *i. e.* I will speak to thee; because thou hast inclined thine ear unto me many a time, therefore I have taken up a resolution to call upon thee at all times, even to the end of my time. Not a day shall pass, but thou shalt be sure to hear from me. Not that the voice is the thing that God regards, as they seemed to think, who in prayer made their voice to be heard on high (Isa. 58:4). Hannah prayed and prevailed, when her voice was not heard; but it is the voice of the heart that is here meant; God saith to Moses, wherefore criest thou unto me, when we do not find that he said one word (Exod. 14:15). Praying is lifting up the soul to God, and pouring out the heart before him; yet as far as the expressing of the devout affections of the heart by words may be of use to fix the thoughts, and to excite and quicken the desires, it is good to draw near to God, not only with a pure heart, but with a humble voice; so must we render the calves of our lips.

However, God understands the language of the heart, and that is the language in which we must speak to God; David prays here, *ver*se 1, not only give ear to my words, but consider my meditation, and Psalm 19:14, Let the words of my mouth, proceeding from the meditation of my heart, be acceptable in thy sight.

This therefore we have to do in every prayer, we must speak to God; we must write to him; we say we hear from a friend whom we receive a letter from; we must see to it that God hears from us daily.

1.1.2.1. He expects and requires it. Though he has no need of us or our services, nor can be benefited by them, yet he has obliged us to offer the sacrifice of prayer and praise to him continually.

1.1.2.1.1. Thus he will keep up his authority over us, and keep us continually in mind of our subjection to him, which we are apt to forget. He requires that by prayer we solemnly pay our homage to him, and give honour to his name, that by this act and deed of our own, thus frequently repeated, we may strengthen the obligations we lie under to observe his statutes and keep his laws, and be more and more sensible of the weight of them. He is thy Lord, and worship thou him, that by frequent humble adorations of his perfections, thou mayest make a constant humble compliance with his will the more easy to thee. By doing obeisance we are learning obedience.

1.1.2.1.2. Thus he will testify his love and compassion towards us. It would have been an abundant evidence of his concern for us, and his goodness to us, if he had only said, let me hear from you as often as there is occasion; call upon me in the time of trouble or want, and that is enough; but to shew his complacency to us, as a father doth his affection to his child when he is sending him abroad, he gives us this charge, let me hear from you every day, by every post, though you have no particular business; which shews, that the prayer of the upright is his delight; it is music in his ears; Christ saith to his dove, let me see thy countenance, let me hear thy voice, for sweet is thy voice, and thy countenance is comely (Dan. 2:14). And it is to the spouse the church that Christ speaks in the close of that Song of Songs, O thou that dwellest in the gardens, (in the original it is feminine) the companions hearken to thy voice, cause me to hear it. What a shame is this to us, that God is more willing to be prayed to, and more ready to hear prayer, than we are to pray.

1.1.2.2. We have something to say to God every day. Many are not sensible of this, and it is their sin and misery; they live without God in the world, they think they can live without him, are not sensible of their dependence upon him, and their obligations to him, and therefore for their parts they have nothing to say to him, he never hears from them, no more than the father did from his prodigal son, when he was upon the ramble, from one week's end to another. They ask scornfully, what can the Almighty do for them? and then no marvel if they ask next, what profit shall we have if we pray unto him? And the result is, they say to the Almighty, depart from us, and so shall their doom be. But I hope better things of you my brethren, and that you are not of those who cast off fear, and restrain prayer before God, you are all ready to own that there is a great deal that the Almighty can do for you, and that there is profit in praying to him, and therefore resolve to draw nigh to God, that he may draw nigh to you.

We have something to say to God daily.

1.1.2.2.1. As to a friend we love and have freedom with; such a friend we cannot go by without calling on, and never want something to say to, though we have no particular business with him; to such a friend we unbosom ourselves, we profess our love and esteem, and with pleasure communicate our thoughts; Abraham is called the friend of God, and this honour have all the saints, I have not called you servants, (saith Christ) but friends; his secret is with the righteous; we are invited to acquaint ourselves with him, and to walk with him as one friend walks with another; the fellowship of believers is said to be with the Father, and with his Son Jesus Christ; and have we nothing to say to him then?

Is it not errand enough to the throne of his grace to admire his infinite perfections, which we can never fully comprehend, and yet never sufficiently contemplate, and take complacency in? To please ourselves in beholding the beauty of the Lord, and giving him the glory due to his name? Have we not a great deal to say to him in acknowledgment of his condescending grace and favour to us, in manifesting himself to us and not to the world: and in profession of our affection and submission to him; Lord, thou knowest all things, thou knowest that I love thee.

God hath something to say to us as a friend every day, by the written word, in which we must hear his voice, by his providences, and by our own consciences, and he hearkens and hears whether we have any thing to say to him by way of reply, and we are very unfriendly if we have not. When he saith to us, Seek ye my face, should not our hearts answer as to one we love, Thy face, Lord, we will seek. When he saith to us, Return ye backsliding children, should not we readily reply, Behold we come unto thee, for thou art the Lord our God. If he speak to us by way of conviction and reproof, ought not we to return an answer by way of confession and submission. If he speak to us by way of comfort, ought not we to reply in praise? If you love God, you cannot be to seek for something to say to him, something for your hearts to pour out before him, which his grace has already put there.

1.1.2.2.2. As to a master we serve, and have business with. Think how numerous and important the concerns are that lie between us and God, and you will readily acknowledge that you have a great deal to say to him. We have a constant dependence upon him, all our expectation is from him; we have constant dealings with him; he is God with whom we have to do (Heb. 4:13).

Do we not know that our happiness is bound up in his favour; it is life, the life of our souls, it is better than life, than the life of our bodies? And have we not business with God to seek his favour, to entreat it with our whole hearts, to beg as for our lives that he would lift up the light of his countenance upon us, and to plead Christ's righteousness, as that only through which we can hope to obtain God's loving kindness?

Do we not know that we have offended God, that by sin we have made ourselves obnoxious to his wrath and curse, and that we are daily contracting guilt? And have we not then business enough with him to confess our fault and folly, to ask for pardon in the blood of Christ, and in him who is our peace to make our peace with God, and renew our covenants with him in his own strength to go and sin no more?

Do we not know that we have daily work to do for God, and our own souls, the work of the day that is to be done in its day? And have we not then business with God to beg of him to shew us what he would have us do, to direct us in it, and strengthen us for it? To seek to him for assistance and acceptance, that he will work in us both to will and to do that which is good, and then countenance and own his own work? Such business as this the servant has with his master.

Do we not know that we are continually in danger? Our bodies are so, and their lives and comforts, we are continually surrounded with diseases and deaths, whose arrows fly at mid-night and at noon-day; and have we not then business with God going out and coming in, lying down and rising up, to put ourselves under the protections of his providence, to be the charge of his holy angels? Our souls much more are so, and their lives and comforts; it is those our adversary the devil, a strong and subtle adversary, wars against, and seeks to devour; and have we not then business with God to put ourselves under the protection of his grace, and clad ourselves with his armour, that we may be able to stand against the wiles and violences of Satan; so as we may neither be surprised into sin by a sudden temptation, nor over-powered by a strong one.

Do we not know that we are dying daily, that death is working in us, and hastening towards us, and that death fetches us to judgment, and judgment fixeth us in our everlasting state? And have we not then something to say to God in preparation for what is before us. Shall we not say, Lord make us to know our end! Lord teach us to number our days! Have we not business with God to judge ourselves that we may not be judged, and to see that our matters be right and good?

Do we not know that we are members of that body whereof Christ is the head, and are we not concerned to approve ourselves living members? Have we not then business with God upon the public account to make intercession for his church? Have we nothing to say for Zion? Nothing in behalf of Jerusalem's ruined walls? Nothing for the peace and welfare of the land of our nativity? Are we not of the family, or but babes in it, that we concern not ourselves in the concerns of it?

Have we no relations, no friends, that are dear to us, whose joys and griefs we share in? And have we nothing to say to God for them? No complaints to make, no requests to make known? Are none of them sick or in distress? None of them tempted or disconsolate? And have we not errands at the throne of grace, to beg relief and succour for them?

Now lay all this together, and then consider whether you have not something to say to God every day; and particularly in days of trouble, when it is meet to be said unto God. I have bourne chastisement; and when if you have any sense of things, you will say unto God, do not condemn me.

1.1.2.3. If you have all this to say to God, what should hinder you from saying it? From saying it every day? Why should not he hear your voice, when you have so many errands to him?

1.1.2.3.1. Let not distance hinder you from saying it. You have occasion to speak with a friend, but he is a great way off, you cannot reach him, you know not where to find him, nor how to get a letter to him, and therefore your business with him is undone; but this needs not keep you from speaking to God, for though it is true God is in heaven, and we are upon earth, yet he is nigh to his praying people in all that they call upon him for, he hears their voice wherever they are. Out of the depths I have cried unto thee, saith David (Ps 130:1). From the ends of the earth I will cry unto thee (Ps 61:2). Nay, Jonah saith, Out of the belly of hell cried I, and thou heardest my voice. In all places we may find a way open heavenward. Thanks to him who by his own blood has consecrated for us a new and living way into the holiest, and settled a correspondence between heaven and earth.

1.1.2.3.2. Let not fear hinder you from saying what you have to say to God. You have business with a great man it may be, but he is far above you, or so stern and severe towards all his inferiors, that you are afraid to speak to him, and you have none to introduce you, or speak a good word for you, and therefore you choose rather to drop your cause; but there is no occasion for your being thus discouraged in speaking to God; you may come boldly to the throne of his grace, you have there *a liberty of speech*, leave to pour out your whole souls. And such are his compassions to humble supplicants, that even his terror need not make them afraid. It is against the mind of God that you should frighten yourselves, he would have you encourage yourselves, for you have not received the spirit of bondage again to fear, but the spirit of adoption, by which you are brought into this among other the glorious liberties of the children of God. Nor is this all, we have one advocate with the Father. Did ever children need an advocate with a father? But that by those two immutable things in which it is impossible for God to lie, we might have strong consolation, we have not only the relation of a father to depend upon, but the interest and intercession of an advocate; a High Priest over the house of God, in whose name we have access with confidence.

1.1.2.3.3. Let not his knowing what your business is, and what you have to say to him hinder you, you have business with such a friend, but you think you need not put yourselves to any trouble about it, for he is already apprized of it; he knows what you want and what you desire, and therefore it is no matter for speaking to him, it is true all your desire is before God, he knows your wants and burdens, but he will know them from you; he hath promised your relief; but his promise must be put in suit, and he will for this be inquired of by the house of Israel to do it for them (Ezek. 36:37). Though we cannot by our prayers give him any information, yet we must by our prayers give him honour. It is true, nothing we can say can have any influence upon him, or move him to shew us mercy, but it may have an influence upon ourselves, and help to put us into a frame fit to receive mercy. It is a very easy and reasonable condition of his favours, Ask, and it shall be given you. It was to teach us the necessity of praying, in order to our receiving favour, that Christ put that strange question to the blind men, what would ye that I should do unto you? He knew what they would have, but those that touch the top of the golden sceptre must be ready to tell, what is their petition and what is their request?

1.1.2.3.4. Let not any other business hinder our saying what we have to say to God. We have business with a friend perhaps, but we cannot do it, because we have not leisure; we have something else to do, which we think more needful; but we cannot say so concerning the business we have to do with God; for that is without doubt the one thing needful, to which everything else must be made to truckle and give way. It is not at all necessary to our happiness that we be great in the world, or raise estates to such a pitch. But it is absolutely necessary that we make our peace with God, that we obtain his favour, and keep ourselves with his love. Therefore no business for the world will serve to excuse our attendance upon God, but on the contrary, the more important our worldly business is, the more need we have to apply ourselves to God by prayer for his blessing upon it, and so take him along with us in it. The closer we keep to prayer, and to God in prayer, the more will all our affairs prosper.

Shall I prevail with you now to let God frequently hear from you; let him hear your voice, though it be but a voice of your breathing, (Lam. 3:56.) that is a sign of life; though it be the voice of your groanings, and those so weak that they cannot be uttered (Rom. 8:26). Speak to him, though it be in broken language, as Hezekiah did; *Like a crane or a swallow, so did I chatter* (Isa. 38:14). Speak often to him, he is always within hearing. Hear him speaking to you, and have an eye to that in every thing you say to him: as when you write an answer to a letter of business, you lay it before you; God's word must be the guide of your desires, and the ground of your expectations in prayer, nor can you expect he should give a gracious ear to what you say to him, if you turn a deaf ear to what he saith to you.

You see you have frequent occasion to speak with God, and therefore are concerned to grow in your acquaintance with him, to take heed of doing any thing to displease him; and to strengthen your interest in the Lord Jesus, through whom alone it is that you have access with boldness to him. Keep your voice in tune for prayer, and let all your language be a pure language, that you may be fit to call on the name of the Lord (Zeph. 3:9). And in every prayer remember you are speaking to God, and make it to appear you have an awe of him upon your spirits; let us not be rash with our mouth, nor hasty to utter any thing before God, but let every word be well weighed because God is in heaven, and we upon earth (Eccles. 5:2). And if he had not invited and encouraged us to do it, it had been unpardonable presumption for such sinful worms as we are to speak to the Lord of glory (Gen. 18:27). And we are concerned to speak from the heart heartily, for it is for our lives and for the lives of our souls that we are speaking to him.

1.2. We must direct our prayer unto God. He must not only hear our voice, but we must with deliberation and design address ourselves to him. In the original it is no more but I will direct unto thee; it might be supplied, I will direct my soul unto thee, agreeing with Psalm 25:1, Unto thee, O Lord, do I lift up my soul. Or, I will direct my affections to thee; having set my love upon thee, I will let out my love to thee. Our translation supplies it very well, I will direct my prayer unto thee. That is,

1.2.1 When I pray to thee I will direct my prayers; and then it notes a fixedness of thoughts, and a close application of mind, to the duty of prayer. We must go about it solemnly, as those that have something of moment much at heart, and much in view therein, and therefore dare not trifle in it. When we go to pray, we must not give the sacrifice of fools, that think not either what is to be done, or what is to be gained, but speak the words of the wise, who aim at some good end in what they say, and suit it to that end, we must have in our eye God's glory and our own true happiness; and so well ordered is the covenant of grace, that God has been pleased therein to twist interests with us, so that in seeking his glory, we really and effectually seek our own true interests. This is directing the prayer, as he that shoots an arrow at a mark directs it, and with a fixed eye and steady hand takes aim aright. This is engaging the heart to approach to God, and in order to that disengaging it from everything else. He that takes aim with one eye shuts the other; if we would direct a prayer to God, we must look off all other things, must gather in our wandering thoughts, must summon them all to draw near and give their attendance, for here is work to be done that needs them all, and is well worthy of them all; thus we must be able to say with the psalmist, O God, my heart is fixed, my heart is fixed.

1.2.2. When I direct my prayer, I will direct it to thee. And so it speaks,

1.2.2.1. The sincerity of our habitual intention in prayer. We must not direct our prayer to men, that we may gain praise and applause with them, as the Pharisees did, who proclaimed their devotions as they did their alms, that they might gain a reputation, which they knew how to make a hand of; verily they have their reward, men commend them, but God abhors their pride and hypocrisy. We must not let our prayers run at large, as they did that said, Who will shew us any good? Nor direct them to the world, courting its smiles, and pursuing its wealth, as those that are therefore said not to cry unto God with their hearts, because they assembled themselves for corn and wine (Hosea 7:14). Let not self, carnal self, be the spring and centre of your prayers, but God; let the eye of the soul be fixed upon him as your highest end in your applications to him; let this be the habitual disposition of your souls, to be to your God for a name and a praise; and let this be your design in all your desires, that God may be glorified, and by this let them all be directed, determined, sanctified, and when need is, over-ruled. Our Saviour hath plainly taught us this, in the first petition of the Lord's prayer; which is, hallowed be thy name: in that we fix our end, and other things are desired in order to that; in that the prayer is directed to the glory of God, in all that whereby he has made himself known, the glory of his holiness, and it is with an eye to the sanctifying of his name, that we desire his kingdom may come, and his will be done, and that we may be fed, and kept, and pardoned. An habitual aim at God's glory is that sincerity which is our gospel-perfection.

That single eye, which, where it is, the whole body, the whole soul is full of light. Thus the prayer is directed to God.

1.2.2.2. It speaks the steadiness of our actual regard to God in prayer. We must direct our prayer to God, that is, we must continually think of him, as one with whom we have to do in prayer. We must direct our prayer, as we direct our speech to the person we have business with. The Bible is a letter God hath sent to us, prayer is a letter we send to him; now you know it is essential to a letter that it be directed, and material that it be directed right; if it be not, it is in danger of miscarrying: which may be of ill consequence; you pray daily, and therein send letters to God; you know not what you lose, if your letters miscarry; will you therefore take instructions how to direct to him?

1.2.2.2.1. Give him his titles as you do when you direct to a person of honour; address yourselves to him as the great Jehovah, God over all, blessed for evermore; the King of kings, and Lord of lords: as the Lord God gracious and merciful; let your hearts and mouths be filled with holy adorings and admirings of him, and fasten upon those titles of his, which are proper to strike a holy awe of him upon your minds, that you may worship him with reverence and godly fear. Direct your prayer to him as the God of glory, with whom is terrible majesty, and whose greatness is unsearchable, that you may not dare to trifle with him, or to mock him in what you say to him.

1.2.2.2.2. Take notice of your relation to him, as his children, and let not that be overlooked and lost in your awful adorations of his glories. I have been told of a good man, among whose experiences, which he kept a record of, after his death, this among other things was found: that such a time in secret prayer, his heart at the beginning of the duty was much enlarged in giving to God those titles which are awful and tremendous, in calling him the Great, the Mighty, and the Terrible God, but going on thus, he checked himself with this thought, and why not my Father? Christ hath both by his precept and by his pattern, taught us to address ourselves to God as our Father: and the spirit of adoption teacheth us to cry, Abba, Father; a son, though a prodigal, when he returns and repents, may go to his father, and say unto him, Father, I have sinned; and though no more worthy to be called a son, yet humbly bold to call him father. When Ephraim bemoans himself as a bullock unaccustomed to the yoke, God bemoans him as a dear son, as a pleasant child (Jer. 31:18, 20). And if God is not ashamed, let us not be afraid to own the relation.

1.2.2.2.3. Direct your prayer to him in heaven; this our Saviour has taught us in the preface to the Lord's prayer, Our Father which art in heaven. Not that he is confined to the heavens, or as if the heaven, or heaven of heavens could contain him, but there he is said to have prepared his throne, not only his throne of government by which his kingdom ruleth over all, but his throne of grace to which we must by faith draw near. We must eye him as God in heaven, in opposition to the God of the heathen, which dwelt in temples made with hands. Heaven is a high place, and we must address ourselves to him as a God infinitely above us; it is the fountain of light, and to him we must address ourselves as the Father of lights; it is a place of prospect, and we must see his eye upon us, from thence beholding all the children of men; it is a place of purity, and we must in prayer eye him as an holy God, and give thanks as the remembrance of his holiness, it is the firmament of his power, and we must depend upon him as one to whom power belongs. When our Lord Jesus prayed, he lifted up his eyes to heaven, to direct us whence to expect the blessings we need.

1.2.2.2.4 Direct this letter to be left with the Lord Jesus, the only Mediator between God and man; it will certainly miscarry if it be not put into his hand, who is that other angel that puts much incense to the prayers of the saints, and so perfumed presents them to the Father (Rev. 8:3). What we ask of the Father must be in his name; what we expect from the Father must be by his hand, for he is the High Priest of our profession, that is ordained for men to offer their gifts (Heb. 5:1). Direct the letter to be left with him, and he will deliver it with care and speed, and will make our service acceptable. Mr. George Herbert, in his poem called the Bag, having pathetically described the wound in Christ's side as he was hanging on the cross, makes him speak thus to all believers as he was going to heaven.

If you have any thing to send or write,
    I have no bag, but here is room,
Unto my Father's hands and sight,
    Believe me it shall safely come;
That I shall mind what you impart,
    Look, you may put it very near my heart;
Or, if hereafter any of my friends
    Will use me in this kind, the door
Shall still be open, what he sends
    I will present, and something more,

Not to his hurt; sighs will convey
>   Any thing to me; hark, despair, away.

1.3. We must look up, that is.

1.3.1. We must look up in our prayers, as those that speak to one above us, infinitely above us, the high and holy one that inhabiteth eternity, as those that expect every good and perfect gift to come from above, from the Father of lights; as those that desire in prayer to enter into the holiest, and to draw near with a true heart. With an eye of faith we must look above the world and every thing in it, must look beyond the things of time; what is this world, and all things here below, to one that knows how to put a due estimate upon spiritual blessings in heavenly things by Jesus Christ? The spirit of a man at death goes upward (Eccles. 3:21); for it returns to God who gave it, and therefore as mindful of its original, it must in every prayer look upwards, towards its God, towards its home, as having set its affections on things above, wherein it has laid up its treasure. Let us therefore in prayer lift up our hearts with our hands unto God in the heavens (Lam. 3:41). It was anciently usual in some churches for the minister to stir up the people to pray with this word, *Sursum Corda,* up with your hearts; unto thee, O Lord, do we lift up our souls.

1.3.2. We must look up after our prayers.

1.3.2.1. With an eye of satisfaction and pleasure; looking up is a sign of cheerfulness; as a down look is a melancholy one. We must look up as those that having by prayer referred ourselves to God, are easy and well pleased, and with an entire confidence in his wisdom and goodness patiently expect the issue. Hannah, when she had prayed, looked up, looked pleasant; she went her way, and did eat, and her countenance was no more sad (I Sam. 1:18). Prayer is heart's ease to a good Christian; and when we have prayed, we should look up as those that through grace have found it so.

1.3.2.2. With an eye of observation, what returns God makes to our prayers. We must look up as one that has shot an arrow looks after it to see how near it comes to the mark; we must look within us, and observe what the frame of our spirit is after we have been at prayer, how well satisfied they are in the will of God, and how well disposed to accommodate themselves to it; we must look about us, and observe how providence works concerning us, that if our prayers be answered, we may return to give thanks; if not, we may remove what hinders, and may continue waiting. Thus we must set ourselves upon our watchtower to see what God will say unto us (Heb. 2:1). and must be ready to hear it (Ps. 85:8), expecting that God will give us an answer of peace, and resolving that we will return no more to folly. Thus must we keep up our communion with God; hoping that whenever we lift up our hearts to him, he will lift up the light of his countenance upon us. Sometimes the answer is quick, while they are yet speaking I will hear; quicker than the return of any of your posts, but if it be not, when we have prayed we must wait.

Let us learn thus to direct our prayers, and thus to look up; and be inward with God in every duty, to make heart-work of it, or we make nothing of it. Let us not worship in the outward court, when we are commanded and encouraged to enter within the veil.

2. *For the Second.* The particular time fixed in the text for this good work, is the morning; and the Psalmist seems to lay an emphasis upon this, in the morning, and again, in the morning; not then only, but then to begin with: Let that be one of the hours of prayer. Under the law, we find that every morning there was a lamb offered in sacrifice (Exod. 29:39), and every morning the priest burned incense (Exod. 30:7), and the singers stood every morning to thank the Lord (I Chron. 23:30). And so it was appointed in Ezekiel's temple (Ezek. 46:13, 14, 15). By which an intimation was plainly given, that the spiritual sacrifices should be offered by the spiritual priests every morning, as duly as the morning comes. Every Christian should pray in secret, and every master of a family with his family morning by morning; and there is good reason for it.

2.1. The morning is the first part of the day, and it is fit that he that is the first should have the first, and be first served. The heathen could say, *A Jove Principium*, whatever you do begin with God. The world had its beginning from him, we had ours, and therefore whatever we begin, it concerns us to take him along with us in it. The days of our life, as soon as ever the sun of reason riseth in the soul, should be devoted to God, and employed in his service; from the womb of the morning, let Christ have the dew of the youth (Ps. 110:3). The first-fruits were always to be the Lord's, and the firstlings of the flock. By morning and evening prayer we give glory to him who is the Alpha and the Omega, the first and the last; with him we must begin and end the day, begin and end the night, who is the beginning and the end, the first cause, and the last end.

Wisdom hath said, Those that seek me early shall find me; early in their lives, early in the day; for hereby we give to God that which he ought to have, the preference above other things. Hereby we shew that we are in care to please him, and to approve ourselves to him, and that we seek him diligently. What we do earnestly, we are said in scripture to do early, (as Ps. 101:8.) Industrious men rise betimes; David expresseth the strength and warmth of his devotion, when he saith, O God thou art my God, early will I seek thee (Ps. 63:1).

2.2. In the morning we are fresh and living, and in the best frame. When our spirits are revived with the rest and sleep of the night, and we live a kind of new life; and the fatigues of the day before are forgotten; the God of Israel neither slumbers or sleeps, yet when he exerts himself more than ordinary on his people's behalf, he is said to awake as one out of sleep (Ps. 78:65). If ever we be good for any thing, it is in the morning, it is therefore become a Proverb, *Aurora Musis Amica*[1]; and if the morning be a friend to the muses, I am sure it is no less so to the graces. As he that is the first should have the first; so he that is the best should have the best; and then when we are fittest for business, we should apply ourselves to that which is the most needful business.

Worshipping God is work that requires the best powers of the soul, when they are at the best; and it well deserves them; how can they be better bestowed, or so as to turn to a better account? Let all that is within me bless his holy name, saith David, and all little enough. If there be any gift in us by which God may be honoured, the morning is the most proper time to stir it us, (2 Tim. 1:6.) when our spirits are refreshed, and have gained new vigour; then awake my Glory, awake psaltery and harp, for I myself will awake early (Ps. 57:8). Then let us stir up ourselves to take hold on God.

2.3. In the morning we are most free from company and business, and ordinarily have the best opportunity for solitude and retirement; unless we be of those sluggards that lie in bed with yet a little sleep, a little slumber, till the work of their calling calls them up, with how long wilt thou sleep, O sluggard? It is the wisdom of those that have much to do in the world, that have scarce a minute to themselves of all day, to take time in the morning before business crowds in upon them, for the business of their religion: that they may be entire for it, and therefore the more intent upon it.

As we are concerned to worship God, then when we are least burdened with deadness and dulness within, so also when we are

---

1. Literally, 'Aurora [the goddess of the morning] is a friend of the Muses.' Hence: 'morning is a friend to the muses.' In other words, if morning is a time for creative inspiration (poetry), so also for spiritual exercises (devotions).

least exposed to distraction and diversion from without; the apostle intimates how much it should be our care to attend upon the Lord without distraction (I Cor. 7:35). And therefore that one day in seven, (and it is the first day too, the morning of the week) which is appointed for holy work, is appointed to be a day of rest from other work. Abraham leaves all at the bottom of the hill, when he goes up into the mount to worship God. In the morning therefore let us converse with God, and apply ourselves to the concerns of the other life, before we are entangled in the affairs of this life. Our Lord Jesus has set us an example of this, who because his day was wholly filled up with public business for God and the souls of men, rose up in the morning a great while before day, and before company came in, and went out into a solitary place, and there prayed (Mark 1:35).

2.4. In the morning we have received fresh mercies from God, which we are concerned to acknowledge with thankfulness to his praise. He is continually doing us good, and loading us with his benefits. Every day we have reason to bless him, for every day he is blessing us; in the morning particularly; and therefore as he is giving out to us the fruits of his favour, which are said to be new every morning (Lam. 3:23), because though the same that we had the morning before, they are still forfeited, and still needed, and upon that account may be called still new; so we should be still returning the expressions of our gratitude to him, and of other pious and devout affections, which like the fire on the altar, must be new every morning (Lev. 6:12).

Have we had a good night, and have we not an errand to the throne of grace to return thanks for it? How many mercies concurred to make it a good night! Distinguishing mercies granted to us, but denied to others; many have not where to lay their heads; our master himself had not; the foxes have holes, and the birds of the air have nests, but the Son of man hath not where to lay his head; but we have houses to dwell in, quiet and peaceable habitations, perhaps stately ones: we have beds to lie in, warm and easy ones, perhaps beds of ivory, fine ones, such as they stretched themselves upon that were at ease in Zion; and are not put to wander in deserts and mountains, in dens and caves of the earth, as some of the best of God's saints have been forced to do, of whom the world was not worthy. Many have beds to lie on, yet dare not, or cannot lie down in them, being kept up either by the sickness of their friends, or the fear of their enemies. But we have laid us down, and there has been none to make us afraid: no alarms of the sword, either of war or persecution. Many lay them down and cannot sleep, but are full of tossings to and fro until the dawning of the day, through pain of body, or anguish of mind. Wearisome nights are appointed to them, and their eyes are held waking: but we have laid us down and slept without any disturbance, and our sleep was sweet and refreshing, the pleasant parenthesis of our cares and toils; it is God that has given us sleep, has given it us as he gives it to his beloved. Many lay them down and sleep, and never rise again, they sleep the sleep of death, and their beds are their graves; but we have slept and waked again, have rested, and are refreshed; we shake ourselves, and it is with us as at other times; because the Lord hath sustained us; and if he had not upheld us, we had sunk with our own weight when we fell asleep (Ps. 3:5).

Have we a pleasant morning? Is the light sweet to us, the light of the sun, the light of the eyes, do these rejoice the heart? And ought not we to own our obligations to him who opens our eyes, and opens the eye-lids of the morning upon us. Have we clothes to put on in the morning, garments that are warm upon us (Job 37:17). Change of raiment, not for necessity only, but for ornament? We have them from God, it is his wool and his flax, that is given to cover our nakedness, and the morning when we dress ourselves, is the proper time of returning him thanks for it; yet, I doubt we do it not so constantly as we do for our food when we sit down to our tables, though we have as much reason to do it. Are we in health and at ease? Have we been long so? We ought to be thankful for a constant series of mercies, as for particular instances of it, especially considering how many are sick and in pain, and how much we have deserved to be so.

Perhaps we have experienced some special mercy to ourselves or our families, in preservation from fire or thieves, from dangers we have been aware of, and many more unseen; weeping perhaps endured for a night, and joy came in the morning, and that calls aloud upon us to own the goodness of God. The destroying angel perhaps has been abroad, and the arrow that flies at midnight, and wasteth in darkness, has been shot in at others' windows, but our houses have been passed over, thanks be to God for the blood of the covenant sprinkled upon our door posts; and for the ministration of the good angels about us, to which we owe it, that we have been preserved from the malice of the evil angels against us, those rulers of the darkness of this world, who perhaps creep forth like the beasts of prey, when he maketh darkness and it is dark. All the glory be to the God of the angels.

2.5. In the morning we have fresh matter ministered to us for adoration of the greatness and glory of God. We ought to take notice not only of the gifts of God's bounty to us, which we have the comfort and benefit of, they are little narrow souls that confine their regards to them; but we ought to observe the more general instances of his wisdom and power in the kingdom of providence which redound to his honour, and the common good of the universe. The 19th psalm seems to have been a *Morning Meditation*, in which we are directed to observe how the heavens declare the glory of God, and the firmament sheweth his handy-work; and to own not only the advantage we receive from their light and influence, but the honour they do to him who stretched out the heavens like a curtain, fixed their pillars, and established their ordinances, according to which, they continue to this day, for they are all his servants. Day by day utters this speech, and night unto night, sheweth this knowledge, even the eternal power and Godhead of the great Creator of the world, and its great ruler. The regular and constant succession and revolution of light and darkness, according to the original contract made between them, that they should reign alternately, may serve to confirm our faith, in that part of divine Revelation which gives us the history of the creation, and the promise of God to Noah and his sons (Gen. 8:22). His covenant with the day and with the night (Jer. 33:20).

Look up in the morning, and see how exactly the day-spring knows its place, knows its time, and keeps them, how the morning light takes hold of the ends of the earth, and of the air, which is turned to it as clay to the seal, instantly receiving the impressions of it (Job 38:12, 13, 14). I was pleased with an expression of a worthy good minister I heard lately, in his thanksgivings to God for the mercies of the morning; How many thousand miles, (said he) has the sun travelled this last night to bring the light of the morning to us poor sinful wretches, that justly might have been buried in the darkness of the night. Look up and see the sun as a bridegroom richly dressed, and hugely pleased, coming out of his chamber, and rejoicing as a strong man to run a race; observe how bright his beams are, how sweet his smiles, how strong his influences: and if there be no speech or language where their voice is not heard, the voice of these natural immortal preachers, proclaiming the glory of God, it is pity there should be any speech or language where the voice of his worshippers should not be heard, echoing to the voice of those preachers, and ascribing glory to him who thus makes the morning and evening to rejoice: But whatever others do, let him hear our voice to this purpose in the morning, and in the morning let us direct our praise unto him.

2.6. In the morning we have, or should have had fresh thoughts of God, and sweet meditations on his name, and those we ought to offer up to him in prayer. Have we been, according to David's example, remembering God upon our beds, and meditating upon him in the night watches? When we awake, can we say, as he did, we are still with God? If so, we have a good errand to the throne of grace by the words of our mouths, to offer up to God the meditations of our hearts, and it will be to him a sacrifice of a sweet smelling savour. If the heart has been inditing a good matter, let the tongue be as the pen of a ready writer, to pour it out before God (Ps. 45:1).

We have the word of God to converse with, and we ought to read a portion of it every morning: By it God speaks to us, and in it we ought to meditate day and night, which if we do, that will send us to the throne of grace, and furnish us with many a good errand there. If God in the morning by his grace direct his word to us, so as to make it reach our hearts, that will engage us to direct our prayer to him.

2.7. In the morning, it is to be feared, we find cause to reflect upon many vain and sinful thoughts that have been in our minds in the night season; and upon that account it is necessary we address ourselves to God by prayer in the morning, for the pardon of them. The Lord's prayer seems to be calculated primarily in the letter of it for the morning; for we are taught to pray for our daily bread this day: And yet we are then to pray, Father, forgive us our trespasses; for as in the hurry of the day we contract guilt by our irregular words and actions, so we do in the solitude of the night, by our corrupt imaginations, and the wanderings of an unsanctified ungoverned fancy. It is certain, the thought of foolishness is sin (Prov. 24:9). Foolish thoughts are sinful thoughts; the first-born of the old man, the first beginnings of all sin; and how many of these vain thoughts lodge within us wherever we lodge; their name is legion, for they are many: Who can understand these errors! They are more than the hairs of our head. We read of those that work evil upon their beds, because there they devise it; and when the morning is light they practise it (Micah 2:1). How often in the night season is the mind disquieted and distracted with distrustful careful thoughts; polluted with unchaste and wanton thoughts; intoxicated with proud aspiring thoughts; sowered and leavened with malicious revengeful thoughts; or at the best diverted from devout and pious thoughts by a thousand impertinences: out of the heart proceed evil thoughts which lie down with us, and rise up with us, for out of that corrupt fountain, which wherever we go, we carry about with us, these streams naturally flow. Yea, and in the multitude of dreams, as well as many words, there are also divers vanities (Eccles. 5:2).

And dare we go abroad till we have renewed our repentance, which we are every night as well as every day thus making work for? Are we not concerned to confess to him that knows our hearts, their wanderings from him, to complain of them to him as revolting and rebellious hearts, and bent to backslide; to make our peace in the blood of Christ, and to pray, that the thoughts of our heart may be forgiven us? We cannot with safety go into the business of the day under the guilt of any sin unrepented of, or unpardoned.

2.8. In the morning we are addressing ourselves to the work of the day, and therefore are concerned by prayer to seek unto God for his presence and blessing, we come, and are encouraged to come boldly to the throne of grace, not only for mercy to pardon what has been amiss, but for grace to help in every time of need: And what time is it that is not a time of need with us? And therefore what morning should pass without morning prayer? We read of that which the duty of every day requires (Ezra 3:4); and in reference to that we must go to God every morning to pray for the gracious disposals of his providence concerning us, and the gracious operations of his Spirit upon us.

We have families to look after it may be, and to provide for, and are in care to do well for them; let us then every morning by prayer commit them to God, put them under the conduct and government of his grace, and then we effectually put them under the care and protection of his providence. Holy Job rose up early in the morning to offer burnt-offerings for his children, and we should do so to offer up prayers and supplications for them, according to the number of them all (Job 1:5). Thus we cause the blessing to rest on our houses.

We are going about the business of our callings, perhaps, let us look up to God in the first place, for wisdom and grace to manage them well, in the fear of God, and to abide with him in them; and then we may in faith beg of him to prosper and succeed us in them, to strengthen us for the services of them, to support us under the fatigues of them, to direct the designs of them, and to give us comfort in the gains of them. We have journeys to go, it may be, let us look up to God for his presence with us, and go not whither, where we cannot in faith beg of God to go with us.

We have a prospect perhaps of opportunities of doing or getting good, let us look up to God for a heart to every price in our hands, for skill, and will, and courage, to improve it, that it may not be as a price in the hand of a fool. Every day has its temptations too, some perhaps we foresee, but there may be many more that we think not of, and are therefore concerned to be earnest with God; that we may not be led into any temptation, but guarded against every one; that whatever company we come into, we may have wisdom to do good, and no hurt to them; and to get good, and no hurt by them.

We know not what a day may bring forth; little think in the morning what tidings we may hear, and what events may befall us before night, and should therefore beg of God, grace to carry us through the duties and difficulties which we do not foresee, as well as those which we do: that in order to our standing complete in all the will of God, as the day is, so the strength shall be. We shall find that sufficient unto the day is the evil thereof, and that therefore, as it is folly to take thought for tomorrow's event, so it is wisdom to take thought for today's duty, that sufficient unto this day, and the duty of it, may be the supplies of the divine grace thoroughly to furnish us for every good word and work, and thoroughly to fortify us against every evil word or work; that we may not think of, or speak, or do any thing all day, which we may have cause upon any account to wish unthought, unspoke, and undone again at night.

For Application.
First, Let this word put us in the mind of our omissions; for omissions are sins, and must come into judgment; how often has our morning worship been either neglected or negligently performed. The work has been either not done at all, or done deceitfully; either no sacrifice at all brought, or it has been the torn and the lame, and the sick; either no prayer, or the prayer not directed aright, nor lifted up. We have had the morning's mercies, God has not been wanting in the compassion and care of a father for us, yet we have not done the morning's service, but have been shamefully wanting in the duty of children to him.

Let us be truly humbled before God this morning for our sin and folly herein, that we have so often robbed God of the honour, and ourselves of the benefit of our morning worship. God hath come into our closets, seeking this fruit, but has found none, or next to none, hath harkened and heard, but either we spake not to him at all, or spake not aright. Some trifling thing or other has served for an excuse to put it by once, and when once the good usage has been broken in upon, conscience has been wounded, and its bones weakened, and we have grown more and more cool to it, and perhaps by degrees it has been quite left off.

Secondly, I beseech you, suffer a word of exhortation concerning this. I know what an influence it would have upon the prosperity of your souls to be constant and sincere in your secret worship, and therefore give me leave to press it upon you with all earnestness; let God hear from you every morning, every morning let your prayer be directed to him, and look up.

1. Make conscience of your secret worship; keep it up, not only because it has been a custom you have received by tradition from your fathers, but because it is a duty, concerning which you have received commandments from the Lord. Keep up stated times for it, and be true to them. Let those that have hitherto lived in the total neglect, or in the frequent omission of secret prayer, be persuaded from henceforward to look upon it, as the most needful part of their daily business, and the most delightful part of their daily comfort, and do it accordingly with a constant care, and yet with a constant pleasure.

No persons that have the use of their reason, can pretend an exemption from this duty; what is said to some is said to all, Pray, pray, continue in prayer, and watch in the same. Rich people are not so much bound to labour with their hands as the poor. Poor people are not so much bound to give alms as the rich, but both are equally bound to pray. The rich are not above the necessity of the duty, nor the poor below acceptance with God in it. It is not too soon for the youngest to begin to pray; and those whom the multitude of years has taught wisdom, yet at their end will be fools, if they think they have now no further occasion for prayer.

Let none plead they cannot pray; if you were ready to perish with hunger, you could beg and pray for food, and if you see yourselves undone by reason of sin, can you not beg and pray for mercy and grace? Art thou a Christian? Never for shame say, Thou canst not pray, for that is as absurd as for a soldier to say, he knows not how to handle a sword, or a carpenter an ax. What are you called for into the fellowship of Christ, but that by him you may have fellowship with God. You cannot pray so well as others, pray as well as you can, and God will accept of you.

Let none plead they have no time in a morning for prayer; I dare say, you can find time for other things that are less needful; you had better take time from sleep, than want time for prayer; and how can you spend time better, and more to your satisfaction and advantage? All the business of the day will prosper the better, for your beginning it thus with God.

Let none plead, that they have not a convenient place to be private in for this work; Isaac retired into the field to pray; and the Psalmist could be alone with God in a corner of the house-top. If you cannot perform it with so much secrecy as you would, yet perform it; it is doing it with ostentation that is the fault, not doing it under observation, when it cannot be avoided. I remember when I was a young man, coming up hither to London in the stage coach, in King James' time, there happened to be a gentleman in the company, that then was not afraid to own himself a Jesuit; many encounters he and I had upon the road, and this was one; he was praising the custom in popish countries of keeping the church doors always open, for people to go into at any time to say their prayers: I told him it looked too like the practice of the pharisees, that prayed in the synagogues; and did not agree with Christ's command, thou when thou prayest thyself, enter not into the church with the doors open, but into thy closet and shut thy doors; when he was pressed with that argument he replied with some vehemence, I believe, you protestants say your prayers no where; for (said he) I have travelled a great deal in the coach in company with protestants, have often lain in inns in the same room with them, and have carefully watched them, and could never perceive that any of them said his prayers night or morning but one, and he was a presbyterian. I hope there was more malice than truth in what he said; but I mention it as an intimation, that though we cannot be so private as we would be in our devotions, yet we must not omit them, lest the omission should prove not a sin only, but a scandal.

2. Make a business of your secret worship, and be not slothful in this business, but fervent in spirit, serving the Lord. Take heed lest it degenerate into a formality, and you grow customary in your accustomed services. Go about the duty solemnly. Be inward with God in it; it is not enough to say your prayers, but you must pray your prayers, must pray in praying, as Elijah did (James 5:17). Let us learn to labour frequently in prayer, as Epaphras did (Col. 4:12). and we shall find it is the hand of the diligent in this duty that maketh rich. God looks not at the length of your prayers, nor shall you be heard for your much speaking, or fine speaking; but God requires truth in the inward part, and it is the prayer of the upright that is his delight. When you have prayed look upon yourselves as thereby engaged and encouraged, both to serve God and to trust in him; that the comfort and benefit of your morning devotions may not be as the morning cloud which passeth away, but as the morning light which shines more and more.

THE SECOND DISCOURSE SHEWING HOW TO SPEND THE DAY WITH GOD.

On thee do I wait all the day.

Which of us is there that can truly say thus! That lives this life of communion with God, which is so much our business, and so much our blessedness? How far short do we come of the spirit of holy David, though we have much better assistances for our acquaintance with God, than the saints then had by the clearer discoveries of the mediation of Christ. Yet that weak Christians who are sincere may not therefore despair, be it remembered, that David himself was not always in such a frame as that he could say so; he had his infirmities, and yet was a man after God's own heart: We have ours, which if they be sincerely lamented and striven against, and the habitual bent of our souls be towards God, and heaven, we shall be accepted through Christ, for we are not under the law, but under grace.

However David's profession in the text, shews us what should be our practice, on God we must wait all the day. That notes two things, a patient expectation, and a constant attendance.

1. It speaks a patient expectation of his coming to us in a way of mercy; and then, all the day must be taken figuratively, for all the time that the wanted and desired mercy is delayed. David, in the former part of the verse, prayed for divine conduct and instruction, Lead me in thy truth and teach me; he was at a loss, and very desirous to know what God would have him to do, and was ready to do it; but God kept him in suspense, he was not yet clear what was the mind and will

of God, what course he should steer, and how he should dispose of himself; will he therefore proceed without divine direction? No, on thee will I wait all the day, as Abraham attended on his sacrifice from morning till the sun went down, before God gave him an answer to his inquiries concerning his seed (Gen. 15:5, 12); and as Habakkuk stood upon his watch tower, to see what answer God would give him, when he consulted his oracle; and though it do not come presently, yet at the end it shall speak, and not lie.

David in the words next before the text, had called God the God of his salvation, the God on whom he depended for salvation, temporal and eternal salvation, from whom he expected deliverance out of his present distresses, those troubles of his heart that were enlarged, verse 17, and out of the hands of those enemies that were ready to triumph over him, *verse* 2, and that hated him with cruel hatred, verse 19. Hoping that God will be his Saviour, he resolves to wait on him all the day, like a genuine son of Jacob, whose dying profession was (Gen. 49:18). I have waited for thy salvation, O Lord. Sometimes God prevents his people with the blessings of his goodness, before they call he answers them, is in the midst of his church, to help her, and that right early (Ps. 46:5). But at other times he seems to stand afar off, he delays the deliverance, and keeps them long in expectation of it, nay, and in suspense about it: the light is neither clear nor dark, it is day, and that is all, it is a cloudy and dark day, and it is not till evening time, that it is light, that the comfort comes which they have been kept all the day waiting for; nay, perhaps it comes not till far in the night, it is at midnight that the cry is made, Behold the bridegroom comes; the deliverance of the church out of her troubles, the success of her struggles, and rest from them, a rescue from under the rod of the wicked, and the accomplishment of all that which God hath promised concerning it, is what we must continue humbly waiting upon God for without distrust or impatience; we must wait all the day.

1.1. Though it be a long day; though we be kept waiting a great while, quite beyond our own reckoning. Though when we have waited long, we are still put to wait longer, and are bid with the prophet's servant to go yet seven times (I Kings 18:43.) before we perceive the least sign of mercy coming. We looked that this and the other had been he that should have delivered Israel, but are disappointed; the harvest is past, the summer is ended, and we are not saved (Jer. 8:20). The time is prolonged, nay, the opportunities are let slip, the summer time and harvest time, when we thought to have reaped the fruit of all our prayers and pains, and patience is past and ended, and we are as far as ever from salvation; the time that the ark abode in Kirjath-jearim, was long, much longer than it was thought it would have been, when it was first lodged there; it was twenty years; so that the whole house of Israel lamented after the Lord, and began to fear it would abide forever in that obscurity (I Sam. 7:2).

But though it be a long day, it is but a day, but one day, and it is known to the Lord (Zech. 14:7). It seems long while we are kept waiting, but the happy issue will enable us to reflect upon it as short, and but for a moment. It is no longer than God hath appointed, and we are sure his time is the best time; and his favours are worth waiting for. The time is long, but is nothing to the days of eternity, when those that had long patience shall be recompensed for it with an everlasting salvation.

1.2. Though it be a dark day, yet let us wait upon God all the day. Though while we are kept waiting for what God will do, we are kept in the dark concerning what he is doing, and what is best for us to do, yet let us be content to wait in the dark. Though we see not our signs, though there is none to tell us how long, yet let us resolve to wait, how long soever it be; for though what God doth, we know not now, yet we shall know hereafter, when the mystery of God shall be finished.

Never was man more at a plunge concerning God's dealings with him than poor Job was; I go forward, but he is not there; backward, but I cannot perceive him, on the left hand, on the right hand, but I cannot see him (Job 23:8, 9), yet he sits down, verse 10, resolving to wait on God all the day with a satisfaction in this, that though I know not the way that he takes, he knows the way that I take, and when he has tried me, I shall come forth as gold, approved, and improved. He sits by as a refiner, and will take care that the gold be in the furnace, no longer than is needful for the refining of it. When God's way is in the sea, so that he cannot be traced, yet we are sure his way is in the sanctuary, so that he may be trusted, see Psalm 77:13, 19. And when the clouds and darkness are round about him, yet even then justice and judgment are the habitation of his throne.

1.3. Though it be a stormy day, yet we must wait upon God all the day. Though we are not only be calmed, and do not get forward, but though the wind be contrary, and drives us back, nay, though it be boisterous, and the church be tossed with tempests, and ready to sink, yet we must hope the best; yet we must wait and weather the storm by patience. It is some comfort, that Christ is in the ship, the church's cause is Christ's own cause, he has espoused it; and he will own it; he is embarked in the same bottom with his people, and therefore, why are ye fearful; doubt not but the ship will come safe to land; though Christ seem for the present to be asleep, the prayers of his disciples will awake him, and he will rebuke the winds and the waves; though the bush burn, if God be in it, it shall not be consumed. Yet this is not all, Christ is not only in the ship, but at the helm; whatever threatens the church, is ordered by the Lord Jesus, and shall be made to work for its good. It is excellently expressed by Mr. George Herbert,

> Away despair, my gracious God doth hear,
>> When winds and waves assault my keel,
> He doth preserve it, he doth steer,
>> Even when the boat seems most to reel.
> Storms are the triumph of his art,
>> Well may he close his eyes, but not his heart.

It is a seasonable word at this day; what God will do with us we cannot tell; but this we are sure, he is a God of judgment, infinitely wise and just, and therefore blessed are all they that wait for him (Isa. 30:18). He will do his own work in his own way and time; and though we be hurried back into the wilderness, when we thought we had been upon the borders of Canaan, we suffer justly for our unbelief and murmurings, but God acts wisely, and will be found faithful to his promise; his time to judge for his people, and to repent himself concerning his servants, is, when he sees that their strength is gone. This was seen of old in the mount of the Lord, and shall be again. And therefore let us continue in a waiting frame. Hold out faith and patience, for it is good that a man should both hope and quietly wait for the salvation of the Lord.

2. It speaks a constant attendance upon him in a way of duty. And so we understand the day literally; it was David's practice to wait upon God "all the day." It signifies both every day, and all the day long; it is the same with that command (Prov. 23:17). Be thou in the fear of the Lord all the day long.

Doct. It is not enough for us to begin every day with God, but on him we must wait every day, and all the day long.

For the opening of this I must shew, (I.) What it is to wait upon God; And, (II.) That we must do this every day, and all the day long.

1. F*or the first*, Let us inquire, what it is to wait on God. You have heard how much it is our duty in the morning to speak to him, in solemn prayer. But have we then done with him for all day? No, we must still be waiting on him; as one to whom we stand very nearly related, and very strongly obliged. To wait on God is to live a life of desire towards him, delight in him, dependence on him, and devotedness to him.

1.1. It is to live a life of desire towards God; to wait on him, as the beggar waits on his benefactor, with earnest desire to receive supplies from him; as the sick and sore in Bethesda's pool, waited for the stirring of the water, and attended in the porches with desire to be helped in and healed. When the prophet had said, Lord, in the way of thy judgments we have waited for thee, he explained himself thus in the next words, the desire of our soul is to thy name, and to the remembrance of thee; and with my soul have I desired thee (Isa. 26:8, 9). Our desire must be not only towards the good things that God gives, but towards God himself, his favour and love, the manifestation of his name to us, and the influences of his grace upon us. Then we wait on God, when our souls pant after him, and his favour, when we thirst for God, for the living God: O that I may behold the beauty of the Lord! O that I may taste his goodness! O that I may bear his image, and be entirely conformed to his will! For there is none in heaven or earth, that I can desire in comparison of him. O that I may know him more, and love him better, and be brought nearer to him, and made fitter for him. Thus upon the wings of holy desire should our souls be still soaring upwards towards God, still pressing forwards, forwards towards heaven.

We must not only pray solemnly in the morning, but that desire which is the life and soul of prayer, like the fire upon the altar, must be kept continually burning, ready for the sacrifices that are to be offered upon it. The bent and bias of the soul in all its motions must be towards God, the serving of him in all we do, and the enjoying of him in all we have. And this is principally intended in the commands given to us to pray always, to pray without ceasing, to continue in prayer. Even when we are not making actual addresses to God, yet we must have habitual inclinations towards him; as a man in health, though he is not always eating, yet has always a disposition in him towards the nourishments and delights of the body. Thus must we be always waiting on God, as our chief good, and moving towards him.

1.2. It is to live a life of delight in God, as the lover waits on his beloved. Desire is love in motion, as a bird upon the wing; delight is love at rest, as a bird upon the nest; now though our desire must still be so towards God, as that we must be wishing for more of God, yet our delight must be so in God, as that we must never wish for more than God. Believing him to be a God all-sufficient, in him we must be entirely satisfied; let him be mine, and I have enough. Do we love to love God? It is a pleasure to us to think that there is a God, that he is such a one as he has revealed himself to be, that he is our God by creation to dispose of us as he pleaseth, our God in covenant to dispose of all for the best to us; this is waiting on our God, always looking up to him with pleasure.

Something or other the soul has that it values itself by, something or other that it reposes itself in, and what is it? God or the world? What is it that we pride ourselves in? Which we make the matter of our boasting? It is the character of worldly people, that they boast themselves in the multitude of their riches (Ps. 49:6). and of their own might, and the power of their own hands, which they think has gotten them this wealth; it is the character of godly people, that in God they boast all the day long (Ps. 44:8). That is waiting on God; having our eye always upon him with a secret complacency, as men have upon that which is their glory, and which they glory in.

What is it that we please ourselves with, which we embrace with the greatest satisfaction, in the bosom of which we lay our heads, and in having which we hug ourselves, as having all we would have: the worldly man when his barns are full of corn, saith, soul, take thine ease, eat, drink, and be merry; the godly man can never say so till he finds his heart full of God, and Christ, and grace; and then, return unto thy rest, O my soul, here repose thyself; the gracious soul dwells in God, is at home in him, and there dwells at ease, is in him perpetually pleased; and whatever he meets with in the world to make him uneasy, he finds enough in God to balance it.

1.3. It is to live a life of dependence on God, as the child waits on his father, whom he has a confidence in, and on whom he casts all his care. To wait on God is to expect all good to come to us from him, as the worker of all good for us, and in us, the giver of all good to us, and the protector of us from all evil. Thus David explains himself (Ps. 62:5). My soul wait thou only upon God, and continue still to do so, for my expectation is from him, I look not to any other for the good I need; for I know that every creature is that to me, and no more than he makes it to be, and from him every man's judgment proceeds. Shall we lift up our eyes to the hills? Doth our help come from thence? Doth the dew that waters the valleys come no further, than from the tops of the hills? Shall we go higher, and lift up our eyes to the heavens, to the clouds? Can they of themselves give rain? No, if God hear not the heavens, they hear not the earth; we must therefore look above the hills, above the heavens, for all our help cometh from the Lord; it was the acknowledgment of a king, and no good one neither, if the Lord do not help thee, whence shall I help thee out of the barn-floor, or out of the wine-press?

And our expectations from God as far as they are guided by, and grounded upon the word which he hath spoken, ought to be humbly confident and with a full assurance of faith. We must know and be sure, that no word of God shall fall to the ground, that the expectation of the poor shall not perish. Worldly people say to their gold, thou art my hope; and to the fine gold, thou art my confidence, and the rich man's wealth is his strong city; but God is the only refuge and portion of the godly man here in the land of the living; it is to him only that he saith, and he saith it with a holy boldness, thou art my hope, and my confidence. The eyes of all things wait on him, for he is good to all; but the eyes of his saints especially, for he is in a peculiar manner good to Israel, good to them. They know his name and therefore will trust, and triumph in him, as those that know they shall not be made ashamed of their hope.

1.4. It is to live a life of devotedness to God, as the servant waits on his master, ready to observe his will, and to do his work, and in every thing to consult his honour and interest. To wait on God, is entirely and unreservedly to refer ourselves to his wise and holy directions, and disposals, and cheerfully to acquiesce in them, and comply with them. The servant that waits on his master, chooseth not his own way, but follows his master step by step: thus must we wait on God, as those that have no will of our own, but what is wholly reserved into his; and must therefore study to accommodate ourselves to his. It is the character of the redeemed of the Lord, that they follow the Lamb wheresoever he goes, with an implicit faith and obedience. As the eyes of a servant are to the hand of his master, and the eyes of a maiden to the hand of her mistress, so must our eyes wait on the Lord, to do what he appoints us, to take what he allots us; Father, thy will be done; Master, thy will be done.

The servant waits on his master, not only to do him service, but to do him honour; and thus must we wait on God that we may be to him for a name, and for a praise. His glory must be our ultimate end, to which we, and all we are, have, and can do, must be dedicated; we must wear his livery, attend in his courts, and follow his motions as his servant, for this end, that he may in all things be glorified

To wait on God, is to make his will our rule.

1.4.1 To make the will of his precept, the rule of our practice, and to do every duty with an eye to that. We must wait on him to receive his commands, with a resolution to comply with them, how much soever they may contradict our corrupt inclinations, or secular interests. We must wait on him, as the holy angels do, that always behold the face of their Father, as those that are at his beck, and are ready to go upon the least intimation of his will, though but by a wink of his eye, wherever he sends them. Thus must we do the will of God, as the angels do it that are in heaven, those ministers of his that do his pleasure, and are always about his throne in order to it; never out of the way.

David here prays, that God would shew him his way, and lead him, and teach him, and keep him, and forward him in the way of his duty; and so the text comes in as a plea to enforce that petition, for on thee do I wait all the day; ready to receive the law from thy mouth, and in every thing to observe thine orders. And then it intimates this, that those and those only can expect to be taught of God, who are ready and willing to do as they are taught. If any man will do his will, be stedfastly resolved in the strength of his grace to comply with it, he shall know what his will is. David prays, Lord, give me understanding, and then promiseth himself, I shall keep thy law, yea I shall observe it; as the servant that waits on his master. They that go up to the house of the Lord, with an expectation that he will teach them his ways, it must be with a humble resolution, that they will walk in his paths (Isa. 2:3). Lord, let the pillar of cloud and fire go before me, for I am determined with full purpose of heart to follow it, and thus to wait on my God all the day.

1.4.2. To make the will of his providence, the rule of our patience, and to bear every affliction with an eye to that. We are sure, it is God that performeth all things for us, and he performeth the thing that is appointed for us; we are sure, that all is well that God doth, and shall be made to work for good to all that love him: and in order to that, we ought to acquiesce in, and accommodate ourselves, to the whole will of God. To wait on the Lord, is to say, it is the Lord, let him do with me as seemeth good to him, because nothing seemeth good to him, but what is really good; and so we shall see, when God's work appears in a full light; it is to say, Not as I will, but as thou wilt, for should it be according to my mind? It is to bring our mind to our condition in every thing, so as to keep that calm and easy, whatever happens to make us uneasy.

And we must therefore bear the affliction, whatever it is, because it is the will of God; it is what he has allotted us, who doth all according to the counsel of his own will. This is Christian patience; I was dumb, I opened not my mouth, not because it was to no purpose to complain, but because thou didst it, and therefore I had no reason to complain. And this will reconcile us to every affliction, one as well as another, because whatever it is, it is the will of God; and in compliance with that we must not only be silent, because of the sovereignty of his will, Woe unto him that strives with his Maker; but we must be satisfied, because of the wisdom and goodness of it. Whatever the disposals of God's providence may be concerning those that wait on him, we may be sure that as he doth them no wrong, so he means them no hurt: Nay, they may say as the Psalmist did, even then when he was plagued all the day long, and chastened every morning, however it be, yet God is good; and therefore, Though he slay me, yet will I trust in him, yet will I wait on him.

I might open this duty of waiting on God by other scripture expressions which speak the same thing, and are, as this, comprehensive of a great part of that homage, which we are bound to pay to him, and that communion which it is our interest to keep up with him. Truly thus our fellowship is with the Father, and with the Son Jesus Christ.

It is to set God always before us (Ps. 16:8). To look upon him as one always near us, always at our right hand, and that has his eye upon us, wherever we are and whatever we are doing; nay, as one in whom we live, and move, and have our being, with whom we have to do, and to whom we are accountable. This is pressed upon us, as the great principle of gospel obedience; walk before me, and be thou upright; herein consists that uprightness which is our evangelical perfection, in walking at all time as before God, and studying to approve ourselves to him.

It is to have our eyes ever towards the Lord, as it follows here (Ps. 25:15). Though we cannot see him by reason of our present distance and darkness, yet we must look towards him, towards the place where his honour dwells; as those that desire the knowledge of him and his will, and direct all to his honour as the mark we aim at, labouring in this, that whether present or absent we may be accepted of him. To wait on him, is to follow him with our eye in all those things wherein he is pleased to manifest himself, and to admit the discoveries of his being and perfections.

It is to acknowledge God in all our ways (Prov. 3:6), in all the actions of life, and in all the affairs of life, we must walk in his hand, and set ourselves in the way of his steps. In all our undertakings, we must wait upon him for direction and success, and by faith and prayer commit our way to him to undertake for us; and him we must take with us wherever we go; If thy presence go not up with us, carry us not up hence. In all our comforts we must see his hand giving them out to us, and in all our crosses we must see the same hand laying them upon us, that we may learn to receive both good and evil, and to bless the name of the Lord both when he gives and when he takes.

It is to follow the Lord fully, as Caleb did (Num. 14:24). It is to fulfil after the Lord, so the word is; to have respect to all his commandments, and to study to stand complete in his whole will. Wherever God leads us and goes before us, we must be followers of him as dear children, must follow the Lamb whithersoever he goes, and take him for our guide whithersoever we go.

This is to wait on God, and those that do so may cheerfully wait for him, for he will without fail appear in due time to their joy, and that word of Solomon shall be made good to them; he that waits on his master shall be honoured, for Christ has said where I am, there shall also my servant be (John 12:26).

2. *For the second thing.* Having shewed you what it is to wait on God, I come next to shew, that this we must do every day; and all the day long.

2.1. We must wait on our God every day. This is the work of every day, which is to be done in its day, for the duty of every day requires it. Servants in the courts of princes have their weeks, or months of waiting appointed them, and are tied to attend only at certain times. But God's servants must never be out of waiting: all the days of our appointed time, the time of our work and warfare here on earth we must be waiting (Job 14:14), and not desire or expect to be discharged from this attendance, till we come to heaven, where we shall wait on God, as angels do, more nearly and constantly.

We must wait on God every day.

2.1.1. Both on sabbath days, and on week days. The Lord's day is instituted and appointed on purpose for our attendance on God in the courts of his house, there we must wait on him, to give glory to him, and to receive both commands, and favours from him, ministers must then wait on their ministry (Rom. 12:7); and people must wait on it too, saying as Cornelius for himself and his friends, now we are all here ready before God, to hear all things that are commanded thee of God (Acts 10:33). It is for the honour of God to help to fill up the assemblies of those that attend at the footstool of his throne, and to add to their number. The whole sabbath time except what is taken up in works of necessity and mercy, must be employed in waiting on our God. Christians are spiritual priests, and as such it is their business to wait in God's house at the time appointed.

But that is not enough; we must wait upon our God on week days, too, for every day of the week we want mercy from him, and have work to do for him. Our waiting upon him in public ordinances on the first day of the week, is designed to fix us to, and fit us for communion with him all the week after; so that we answer not the intentions of the sabbath, unless the impressions of it abide upon us, and go with us into the business of the week, and be kept always in the imagination of the thoughts of our heart. Thus from one sabbath to another, and from one new moon to another, we must keep in a holy gracious frame; must be so in the Spirit on the Lord's day, as to walk in the Spirit all the week.

2.1.2. Both on idle days, and busy days, we must be found waiting on God. Some days of our lives are days of labour and hurry, when our particular calling calls for our close and diligent application; but we must not think that will excuse us from our constant attendance on God. Even then when our hands are working about the world, our hearts may be waiting on our God, by an habitual regard to him, to his providence as our guide, and his glory as our end, in our worldly business; and thus we must abide with him in them. Those that rise up early, and sit up late, and eat the bread of carefulness in pursuit of the world, yet are concerned to wait on God, because otherwise all their care and pains will signify nothing; it is labour in vain (Ps. 127:1, 2), nay, it is labour in the fire.

Some days of our lives we relax from business, and take our ease. Many of you have your time for diversion, but then when you lay aside other business, this of waiting upon God must not be laid aside. When you prove yourselves with mirth, as Solomon did, and say, you will enjoy pleasure a little, yet let this wisdom remain with you (Eccles. 2:1, 3), let your eye be then up to God, and take heed of dropping your communion with him, in that which you call an agreeable conversation with your friends. Whether it be a day of work, or a day of rest, we shall find nothing like waiting upon God both to enlighten the toil of our work, and to sweeten the comfort of our repose. So that whether we have much to do, or little to do in the world, still we must wait upon God, that we may be kept from the temptation that attends both the one and the other.

2.1.3. Both in days of prosperity, and in days of adversity, we must be found waiting upon God. Doth the world smile upon us, and court us? Yet let us not turn from attending on God, to make our court to it: If we have never so much of the wealth of the world, yet we cannot say we have no need of God, no further occasion to make use of him, as David was ready to say, when in his prosperity he said he should never be moved; but soon saw his error, when God hid his face, and he was troubled (Ps. 30:6). When our affairs prosper, and into our hands God bringeth plentifully, we must wait upon God as our great landlord, and own our obligations to him; must beg his blessing on what we have, and his favour with it, and depend upon him both for the continuance, and for the comfort of it. We must wait upon God for wisdom and grace, to use what we have in the world for the ends for which we are intrusted with it, as those that must give account, and know not how soon. And how much soever we have of this world, and how richly soever it is given us to enjoy it, still we must wait upon God for better things, not only than the world gives, but than he himself gives in this world. Lord put me not off with this for a portion.

And when the world frowns upon us, and things go very cross, we must not so fret ourselves at its frowns, or so frighten ourselves with them, as thereby to be driven off from waiting on God, but rather let us thereby be driven to it. Afflictions are sent for this end, to bring us to the throne of grace, to teach us to pray, and to make the word of God's grace precious to us. In the days of our sorrow, we must wait upon God for those comforts which are sufficient to balance our grief; Job, when in tears, fell down and worshipped God, taking away, as well as giving. In the day of our fear we must wait upon God for those encouragements that are sufficient to silence our fears; Jehoshaphat, in his distress waited on God, and was not in vain, his heart was established by it; and so was David's often, which brought him to this resolution, which was an anchor to his soul, what time I am afraid, I will trust in thee.

2.1.4. Both in the days of youth, and in the days of old age, we must be found waiting on God. Those that are young cannot begin their attendance on God too soon: The child Samuel ministered to the Lord, and the scripture story puts a particular mark of honour upon it; and Christ was wonderfully pleased with the hosannas of the children that waited on him, when he rode in triumph into Jerusalem: when Solomon in his youth, upon his accession to the throne, waited upon God for wisdom, it is said, the saying pleased the Lord. I remember thee (saith God to Israel) even the kindness of thy youth, when thou wentest after me, and didst wait upon me in a wilderness (Jer. 2:2). To wait upon God, is to be mindful of our Creator, and the proper time for that is in the days of our youth (Eccles. 12:1). Those that would wait upon God aright, must learn betimes to do it; the most accomplished courtiers are those that are bred at court.

And may the old servants of Jesus be dismissed from waiting on him? No, their attendance is still required, and shall be still accepted: they shall not be cast off by their Master in the time of old age, and therefore let not them then desert his service. When through the infirmities of age they can no longer be working servants in God's family, yet they may be waiting servants. Those that like Barzillai are unfit for the entertainments of the courts of earthly princes, yet may relish the pleasures of God's courts as well as ever. The Levites when they were past the age of fifty, and were discharged from the toilsome part of their ministration, yet still must wait on God, must be quietly waiting, to give honour to him, and to receive comfort from him. Those that have done the will of God, and their doing work is at an end, have need of patience to enable them to wait till they inherit the promise: and the nearer the happiness is which they are waiting for, the dearer should the God be they are waiting on, and hope shortly to be with, to be with eternally.

2.2. We must wait on our God all the day. Every day from morning to night we must continue waiting on God; whatever change there may be of our employment, this must be the constant disposition of our souls, we must attend upon God, and have our eyes ever towards him; we must not at any time allow ourselves to wander from God or to attend on any thing beside him, but what we attend on for him; in subordination to his will, and in subserviency to his glory.

2.2.1. We must cast our daily cares upon him. Every day brings with it its fresh cares, more or less, these wake with us every morning, and we need not go so far forward as tomorrow to fetch care, sufficient unto the day is the evil thereof: you that are great dealers in the world, have your cares attending you all the day; though you keep them to yourselves, yet they sit down with you, and rise up with you; they go out and come in with you, and are more a load upon you than those you converse with are aware of. Some, through the weakness of their spirits, can scarce determine any thing but with fear and trembling.

Let this burden be cast upon the Lord, believing that his providence extends itself to all your affairs, to all events concerning you, and to all the circumstances of them, even the most minute, and seemingly accidental; that your times are in his hand; and all your ways at his disposal; believe his promise that all things shall be made to work for good to those that love him, and then refer it to him in every thing, to do with you and yours as seemeth good in his eyes, and rest satisfied in having done so, and resolve to be easy. Bring your cares to God by prayer in the morning, spread them before him, and then make it to appear all the day, by the composedness and cheerfulness of your spirits, that you left them with him as Hannah did, who, when she had prayed, went her way and did eat, and her countenance was no more sad (I Sam. 1:18). Commit your way to the Lord, and then submit to his disposal of it, though it may cross your expectations; and bear up yourselves upon the assurance God has given you, that he will care for you as the tender father for the child.

2.2.2. We must manage our daily business for him, with an eye to his providence, putting us into the calling and employment wherein we are; and to his precept, making diligence in it our duty; with an eye to his blessing, as that which is necessary to make it comfortable and successful; and to his glory, as our highest end in all. This sanctifies our common actions to God, and sweetens them, and makes them pleasant to ourselves. If Gaius brings his friends that he is parting with, a little way on their journey, it is but a piece of common civility, but let him do it after a godly sort; let him in it pay respect to them, because they belong to Christ, and for his sake; let him do it that he may have an opportunity of do much more profitable communication with them, and then it becomes an act of Christian piety (3 John 6). It is a general rule by which we must govern ourselves in the business of every day, Whatever we do in word or deed, to do all in the name of the Lord Jesus (Col. 3:17). and thus in and by the Mediator we wait on our God.

This is particularly recommended to servants, though their employments are but mean, and they are under the command of their masters according to the flesh, yet let them do their servile works as the servants of Christ, as unto the Lord, and not unto men; let them do it with singleness of heart as unto Christ, and they shall be accepted of him, and from him shall receive the reward of the inheritance (Eph. 6:5, 6, 7, 8, Col. 3:22, 24). Let them wait on God all the day, when they are doing their day's work, by doing it faithfully and conscientiously, that they may adorn the doctrine of God our Saviour, by aiming at his glory even in common business: they work that they may get bread, they would get bread that they may live, they would live not that they may live to themselves, and please themselves, but that they may live to God, and please him. They work that they may fill up time, and fill up a place in the world, and because that God who made and maintains us, has appointed us with quietness to work and mind our own business.

2.2.3. We must receive our daily comforts from him; we must wait on him as our benefactor, as the eyes of all things wait upon him, to give them their food in due season, and what he giveth them, that they gather. To him we must look as to our Father for our daily bread, and from him we are appointed to ask it, yea though we have it in the house, though we have it upon the table. We must wait upon him for a covenant right to it, for leave to make use of it, for a blessing upon it, for nourishment by it, and for comfort in it. It is in the word and prayer that we wait on God, and keep up communion with him, and by these every creature of God is sanctified to us (1 Tim. 4:4, 5). and the property of it is altered; to the pure all things are pure; they have them from the covenant, and not from common providence, which makes a little that the righteous man has, better than the riches of many wicked, and much more valuable and comfortable.

No inducement can be more powerful to make us see to it, that what we have we get it honestly, and use it soberly, and give God his due out of it, than this consideration, that we have our all from the hand of God, and are intrusted with it as stewards, and consequently are accountable. If we have this thought as a golden thread running through all the comforts of every day, these are God's gifts, every bite we eat, and every drop we drink is his mercy, every breath we draw, and every step we take, is his mercy, this will keep us continually waiting upon him, as the ass on his master's crib, and will put a double sweetness into all our enjoyments. God will have his mercies taken fresh from his compassions, which for this reason are said to be new every morning; and therefore it is not once a week that we are to wait upon him, as people go to market to buy provisions for the whole week, but we must wait on him every day, and all the day, as those that live from hand to mouth, and yet live very easy.

2.2.4. We must resist our daily temptations, and do our daily duties in the strength of his grace. Every day brings its temptations with it; our Master knew that when he taught us, as duly as we pray for our daily bread, to pray that we might not be led into temptation. There is no business we engage in, no enjoyment we partake of, but it has its snares attending it; Satan by it assaults us, and endeavors to draw us into sin: Now sin is the great evil we should be continually upon our guard against, as Nehemiah was *(ch.* 6:13). That I should be afraid, and do so, and sin. And we have no way to secure ourselves but by the waiting on God all the day, we must not only in the morning put ourselves under the protection of his grace, but we must all day keep ourselves under the shelter of it; must not only go forth, but go on in dependence upon that grace which he hath said shall be sufficient for us, that care which will not suffer us to be tempted above what we are able. Our waiting upon God will furnish us with the best arguments to make use of in resisting temptations, and with strength according to the day; be strong in the Lord, and in the power of his might, and then we wait on the Lord all the day.

We have duty to do, many an opportunity of speaking good words, and doing good works, and we must see and own that we are not sufficient of ourselves for any thing that is food, not so much as to think a good thought: we must therefore wait upon God, must seek to him, and depend on him, for that light and fire, that wisdom and zeal, which is necessary to the due discharge of our duty; that by his grace we may not only be fortified against every evil word and work, but furnished for every good word and work. From the fulness that is in Jesus Christ, we must by faith be continually drawing grace for grace, grace for all gracious exercises; grace to help in every time of need: We must wait on this grace, must follow the conduct of it, comply with the operations of it, and must be turned to it as wax to the seal.

2.2.5. We must bear our daily afflictions with submission to his will; We are bid to expect trouble in the flesh, something or other happens every day that grieves us, something in our relations, something in our callings, events concerning ourselves, our families, or friends, that are matter of sorrow: perhaps we have every day some bodily pain or sickness: or, some cross and disappointment in our affairs; now in these we must wait upon God. Christ requires it of all his disciples, that they take up their cross daily (Matt. 16:24). We must not willfully pluck the cross down upon us, but must take it up when God lays it in our way, and not go a step out of the way of duty either to it, or to miss it. It is not enough to bear the cross, but we must take it up, we must accommodate ourselves to it, and acquiesce in the will of God in it. Not, this is an evil, and I must bear it, because I cannot help it; but this is an evil, and I will bear it, because it is the will of God.

We must see every affliction allotted us by our heavenly Father, and in it must eye his correcting hand, and therefore must wait on him to know the cause wherefore he contends with us, what the fault is for which we are in this affliction chastened: what the distemper is which is to be by this affliction cured, that we may answer God's end in afflicting us, and so may be made partakers of his holiness. We must attend the motions of providence, keep our eye upon our Father when he frowns, that we may discover what his mind is, and what the obedience is we are to learn, by the things that we suffer. We must wait on God for support under our burthens; must put ourselves into, and stay ourselves upon the everlasting arms, which are laid under the children of God to sustain them, when the rod of God is upon them. And him we must attend for deliverance; must not seek to extricate ourselves by any sinful indirect methods, nor look to creatures for relief, but still wait on the Lord, until that he have mercy on us; well content to bear the burden until God ease us of it, and ease us in mercy (Ps. 123:2). If the affliction be lengthened out, yet we must wait upon the Lord, even when he hides his face (Isa. 8:17), hoping it is but in a little wrath, and for a small moment (Isa. 54: 7, 8).

2.2.6. We must expect the tidings and events of every day, with a cheerful and entire resignation to the divine providence. While we are in this world, we are still expecting, hoping well, fearing ill: we know not what a day or a night, or an hour will bring forth (Prov. 27:1), but it is big with something, and we are too apt to spend our thoughts in vain about things future, which happen quite differently from what we imagined. Now in all our prospects we must wait upon God.

Are we in hopes of good tidings, a good issue? Let us wait on God as the giver of the good we hope for, and be ready to take it from his hand; and to meet him with suitable affections then when he is coming towards us in a way of mercy. Whatever good we hope for, it is God alone, and his wisdom, power, and goodness that we must hope in. And therefore our hopes must be humble and modest, and regulated by his will; what God has promised us, we may with assurance promise ourselves, and no more. If thus we wait on God in our hopes, should the hope be deferred, it would not make the heart sick, no not if it should be disappointed, for the God we wait on, will over-rule all for the best; but when the desire comes, in prosecution of which we have thus waited on God, we may see it coming from his love, and it will be a tree of life (Prov. 13:12).

Are we in fear of evil tidings, of melancholy events, and a sad issue of the depending affair! Let us wait on God to be delivered from all our fears, from the things themselves we are afraid of, and from the amazing tormenting fears of them (Ps. 34:4).

When Jacob was with good reason afraid of his brother Esau, he waited on God, brought his fears to him, wrestled with him, and prevailed for deliverance! What time I am afraid, said David, I will trust in thee, and wait on thee; and that shall establish the heart, shall fix it, so as to set it above the fear of evil tidings.

Are we in suspense between hope and fear, sometimes one prevails, and sometimes the other? Let us wait on God, as the God to whom belong the issues of life and death, good and evil, from whom our judgment, and every man's doth proceed, and compose ourselves into a quiet expectation of the event, whatever it may be, with a resolution to accommodate ourselves to it: Hope the best, and get ready for the worst, and then take what God sends.

For Application.
First, Let me further urge upon you this duty of waiting upon God all the day, in some more particular instances, according to what you have to do all the day, in the ordinary business of it. We are weak and forgetful, and need to be put in mind of our duty in general, upon every occasion for the doing of it; and therefore I choose to be thus particular, that I may be your remembrancer.

1. When you meet with your families in the morning, wait upon God for a blessing upon them, and attend him with your thanksgivings for the mercies you and yours have jointly received from God the night past; you and your houses must serve the Lord, must wait on him. See it owing to his goodness who is the founder and father of the families of the righteous, that you are together, that the voice of rejoicing and salvation is in your tabernacles, and therefore wait upon him to continue you together, to make you comforts to one another, to enable you to do the duty of every relation, and to lengthen out the days of your tranquility. In all the conversation we have with our families, the provision we make for them, and the orders we give concerning them, we must wait upon God, as the God of all the families of Israel (Jer. 31:1). And have an eye to Christ, as he in whom all the families of the earth are blessed.

Every member of the family sharing in family mercies, must wait on God for grace to contribute to family duties, whatever disagreeableness there may be in any family relation, instead of having the spirit either burdened with it, or provoked by it, let it be an inducement to wait on God, who is able either to redress the grievance, or to balance it, and give grace to bear it.

2. When you are pursuing the education of your children or the young ones under your charge, wait upon God for his grace to make the means of their education successful. When you are yourselves giving them instruction in things pertaining either to life or godliness, their general or particular calling, when you are sending them to school in a morning, or ordering them the business of the day, wait upon God to give them an understanding, and a good capacity for their business. Especially their main business, for it is God that giveth wisdom. If they are but slow, and do not come on as you could wish, yet wait on God to bring them forward, and to give them his grace in his own time, and while you are patiently waiting on him, that will encourage you to take pains with them, and will likewise make you patient and gentle towards them.

And let children and young people wait on God in all their daily endeavors, to fit themselves for the service of God in their generation, you desire to be comforts to your relations, to be good for something in this world, do you not beg of God then a wise and an understanding heart, as Solomon did, and wait upon him all the day for it, that you may be still increasing in wisdom, as you do in stature, and in favour with God and man.

3. When you go to your shops, or apply yourselves to the business of your particular calling, wait upon God for his presence with you. Your business calls for your constant attendance, every day, and all the day, keep thy shop, and thy shop will keep thee; but let your attendance on God in your callings, be as constant as your attendance on your callings. Eye God's providence in all the occurrences of them. Open shop with this thought, I am now in the way of my duty, and I depend upon God to bless me in it. When you are waiting for customers, wait on God to find you something to do in that calling to which he hath called you; those you call chance customers, you should rather call Providence customers, and should say of the advantage you make by them, the Lord my God brought it to me.

When you are buying and selling, see God's eye upon you to observe, whether you are honest and just in your dealings, and do no wrong to those you deal with; and let your eye then be up to him, for that discretion to which God doth instruct not only the husbandman, but the tradesman (Isa. 28:26), that prudence which directs the way, and with which it is promised, the good man shall order his affairs; for that blessing which makes rich, and adds no sorrow with it; for that honest profit which may be expected in the way of honest diligence.

Whatever your employments be, in country business, city-business, or sea-business, or only in the business of the house, go about them in the fear of God, depending upon him to make them comfortable, and successful, and to prosper the work of your hands unto you. And hereby you will arm yourselves against the many temptations you are compassed about with in your worldly business; by waiting on God, you will be freed from that care and cumber which attends much serving, will have your minds raised above the little things of sense and time, will be serving God, then when you are most busy about the world, and will have God in your hearts, when your hands are full of the world.

4. When you take a book in your hands, God's book, or any other useful good book, wait upon God for his grace to enable you to make a good use of it. Some of you spend a deal of time every day in reading, and I hope none of you let a day pass without reading some portions of scripture, either alone or with your families; take heed that the time you spend in reading be not lost time; it is so, if you read that which is idle and vain, and unprofitable; it is so, if you read that which is good, even the word of God itself, and do not mind it, or observe it, or aim to make it of any advantage to you. Wait upon God, who gives you those helps for your souls, to make them helpful indeed to you. The Eunuch did so, when he was reading the book of the prophet Isaiah in his chariot, and God presently sent him one, who made him understand what he read.

You read perhaps now and then the Histories of former times; in acquainting yourselves with them, you must have an eye to God, and to that wise and gracious Providence which governed the world before we were born, and preserved the church in it, and therefore may be still depended upon to do all for the best, for he is Israel's king of old.

5. When you sit down to your tables, wait on God, see his hand spreading and preparing a table before you in despite of your enemies, and in the society of your friends; often review the grant which God made to our first father Adam, and in him to us, of the products of the earth (Gen. 1:29). Behold I have given you every herb bearing seed, bread corn especially, to you it shall be for meat. And the grant he afterwards made to Noah our second father, and in him to us (Gen. 9:3). Every moving thing that liveth shall be meat for you, even as the green herb; and see in those what a bountiful benefactor he is to mankind, and wait upon him accordingly.

We must eat and drink to the glory of God, and then we wait on him in eating and drinking. We must receive nourishment for our bodies, that we may be fitted to serve our souls in the service of God, to his honour in this world. We must taste covenant-love in common mercies, and enjoy the Creator while we are using the creature; we must depend upon the word of blessing from the mouth of God, to make our food nourishing to us; and if our provisions be mean and scanty, we must make up the want of them by faith in the promise of God, and rejoice in him, as the God of our salvation, though the fig-tree doth not blossom, and there is no fruit in the vine.

6. When you visit your friends, or receive their visits, wait upon God; let your eye be to him with thankfulness for your friends and acquaintances, that you have comfort in; that the wilderness is not made your habitation, and the solitary and desert land your dwelling; that you have comfort not only in your own houses, but in those of your neighbors, with whom you have freedom of converse; and that you are not driven out from among all men, and made a burden and terror to all about you. That you have clothing not only for necessity but for ornament, to go abroad in, is a mercy which, that we may not pride ourselves in, we must take notice of God in, I decked thee with ornaments, saith God, and put ear-rings in thine ears (Ezek. 16:11, 12). That you have houses, furniture, and entertainment, not only for yourselves, but for your friends, is a mercy in which God must be acknowledged.

And when we are in company, we must look up to God for wisdom to carry ourselves, so as that we may do much good to, and get no harm by those with whom we converse; wait on God for that grace with which our speech should be always seasoned, by which all corrupt communication may be prevented, and we may abound in all that which is good, and to the use of edifying, and which may minister grace to the hearers, that our lips may feed many.

7. When you give alms, or do any act of charity, wait on God, do it as unto him, give to a disciple in the name of a disciple, to the poor because they belong to Christ; do it not for the praise of men, but for the glory of God, with a single eye, and an upright heart, direct it to him, and then your alms as well as your prayers, like those of Cornelius, come up for a memorial before God (Acts 10:4). Beg of God to accept what you do for the good of others, that your alms may indeed be offerings (Acts 24:17). may be an odour of a sweet smell, a sacrifice acceptable, well pleasing to God (Phil. 4:18).

Desire of God a blessing upon what we give in charity, that it may be comfortable those to whom it is given, and that though what you are able to give is but a little, like the widow's two mites, yet that by God's blessing it may be doubled, and made to go a great way, like the widow's meal in the barrel, and oil in the cruse.

Depend upon God to make up to you what you lay out in good works, and to recompense it abundantly in the resurrection of the just; nay, and you are encouraged to wait upon him, for a return of it even in this life; it is bread cast upon the waters, which you shall find again after many days; and you shall carefully observe the providence of God whether it doth not make you rich amends for your good works, according to the promise, that you may understand the loving kindness of the Lord, and his faithfulness to the word which he hath spoken.

8. When you inquire after public news, in that wait upon God: do it with an eye to him; for this reason, because you are truly concerned for the interests of his kingdom in the world, and lay them near your hearts; because you have a compassion for mankind, for the lives and souls of men, and especially of God's people; ask, what news? Not as the Athenians, only to satisfy a vain curiosity, and to pass away an idle hour or two, but that you may know how to direct your prayers and praises, and how to balance your hopes and fears, and may gain such an understanding of the times, as to learn what you and others ought to do.

If the face of public affairs be bright and pleasing, wait upon God to carry on and perfect his own work; and depend not upon the wisdom or strength of any instruments; if it be dark and discouraging, wait upon God to prevent the fears of his people, and to appear for them, when he sees that their strength is gone. In the midst of the greatest successes of the church, and the smiles of second causes, we must not think it needless to wait on God; and in the midst of its greatest discouragements, when its affairs are reduced to the last extremity, we must not think it fruitless to wait upon God; for creatures cannot help without him, but he can help without them.

9. When you are going journeys, wait on God; put yourselves under his protection, commit yourselves to his care, and depend upon him to give his angels a charge concerning you, to bear you up in their arms when you move, and to pitch their tents about you where you rest. See how much you are indebted to the goodness of his providence, for all the comforts and conveniences you are surrounded with in your travels. It is he that has cast our lot in a land where we wander not in the wilderness, as in the deserts of Arabia, but have safe and beaten roads; and that through the terrors of war, the high ways are not unoccupied; to him we owe it, that the inferior creatures are serviceable

to us, and that our going out and coming in are preserved, that when we are abroad we are not in banishment, but have liberty to come home again; and when we are at home we are not under confinement, but have liberty to go abroad.

We must therefore have our eyes up to God at our setting out, Lord go along with me where I go; under his shelter we must travel, confiding in his care of us, and encouraging ourselves with that in all the dangers we meet with; and in our return must own his goodness; all our bones must say, Lord who is like unto thee, for he keepeth all our bones, not one of them is broken.

10. When we retire into solitude, to be alone, walking in the fields, or alone reposing ourselves in our closets, still we must be waiting on God; still we must keep up our communion with him, when we are communing with our own hearts. When we are alone, we must not be alone, but the Father must be with us, and we with him. We shall find temptations even in solitude, which we have need to guard against; Satan set upon our Saviour, when he was alone in a wilderness; but there also we have opportunity, if we but know how to improve it, for that devout, that divine contemplation, which is the best conversation, so that we may never be less alone than when alone. If when we sit alone and keep silence, withdrawn from business and conversation, we have but the art, I should say the heart to fill up those vacant minutes with pious meditations of God and divine things, we then gather up the fragments of time which remain, that nothing may be lost, and so are we found waiting on God all the day.

Secondly, Let me use some motives to persuade you, thus to live a life of communion with God, by waiting on him all the day.

1. Consider, the eye of God is always upon you. When we are with our superiors, and observe them to look upon us, that engageth us to look upon them; and shall we not then look up to God, whose eyes always behold, and whose eye-lids try the children of men.

He sees all the motions of our hearts, and sees with pleasure the motions of our hearts towards him, which should engage us to set him always before us.

The servant, though he be careless at other times, yet when he is under his master's eye, will wait in his place, and keep close to his business; we need no more to engage us to diligence, than to do our work with eye-service while our master looks on, and because he doth so, for then we shall never look off.

2. The God you are to wait on, is one with whom you have to do (Heb.4:13). All things, even the thoughts and intents of the heart, are naked and opened unto the eyes of him with whom we have to do; *with whom we have business*, or *word*, who hath something to say to us, and to whom we have something to say; or as some read it, to whom for us there is an account; there is a reckoning, a running account between us and him: And we must every one of us shortly give account of ourselves to him, and of every thing done in the body, and therefore are concerned to wait on him; that all may be made even daily between us and him in the blood of Christ, which balanceth the account. Did we consider how much we have to do with God every day, we would be more diligent and constant in our attendance on him.

3. The God we are to wait upon, continually waits to be gracious to us; he is always doing us good, prevents us with the blessings of his goodness, daily loads us with his benefits, and slips no opportunity of shewing his care of us when we are in danger; his bounty to us when we are in want; and his tenderness for us when we are in sorrow. His good providence waits on us all the day, to preserve our going out and our coming in (Ps. 121:8), to give us relief and succour in due season, to be seen in the mount of the Lord. Nay, his good grace waits on us all the day, to help us in every time of need; to be strength to us according as the day is, and all the occurrences of the day. Is God thus forward to do us good, and shall we be backward and remiss in doing him service?

4. If we attend upon God, his holy angels shall have a charge to attend upon us. They are all appointed to be ministering spirits, to minister for the good of them that shall be heirs of salvation, and more good offices they do us every day than we are aware of. What an honour, what a privilege is it to be waited on by holy angels, to be borne up in their arms, to be surrounded by their tents, what a security is the ministration of those good spirits, against the malice of evil spirits? This honour have all they that wait on God, all the day.

5. This life of communion with God, and constant attendance upon him is a heaven upon earth. It is doing the work of heaven, and the will of God, as they do it that are in heaven; whose business it is always to behold the face of our Father. It is an earnest of the blessedness of heaven, it is a preparative for it, and a preludium to it; it is having our conversation in heaven, from whence we look for the Saviour. Looking for him as our Saviour, we look to him as our Director; and by this we make it appear, that our hearts are there, which will give us good ground to expect that we shall be there shortly.

Thirdly, Let me close with some directions, what you must do, that you may thus wait on God all the day.

1. See much of God in every creature, of his wisdom and power in the making and placing of it, and of his goodness in its serviceableness to us. Look about you, and see what a variety of wonders, what an abundance of comforts you are surrounded with; and let them all lead you to him, who is the fountain of being, and the giver of all good; all our springs are in him, and from him are all our streams; this will engage us to wait on him, since every creature is that to us, that he makes it to be. Thus the same things which draw a carnal heart from God, will lead a gracious soul to him; and since all his works praise him, his saints will from hence take continual occasion to bless him.

It was (they say) the custom of the pious Jews of old, whatever delight they took in any creature, to give to God the glory of it; when they smelled a flower, they said, blessed be he that made this flower sweet; if they eat a morsel of bread, blessed be he that appointed bread to strengthen man's heart. If thus we taste in every thing that the Lord is gracious, and suck all satisfaction from the breasts of his bounty, we shall thereby be engaged constantly to depend on him, as the child is said to hang on the mother's breast.

2. See every creature to be nothing without God; the more we discern of the vanity and emptiness of the world, and all our enjoyments in it, and their utter insufficiency to make us happy, the closer we shall cleave to God, and the more intimately we shall converse with him, that we may find that satisfaction in the Father of spirits, which we have in vain sought for in the things of sense. What folly is it to make our court to the creatures, and to dance attendance at their door, whence we are sure to be sent away empty, when we have the Creator himself to go to, who is rich in mercy to all that call upon him, is full, and free, and faithful. What can we expect from lying vanities? Why then should we observe them, and neglect our own mercies? Why should we trust to broken reeds, when we have a rock of ages, to be the foundation of our hopes? And why should we draw from broken cisterns, when we have the God of all consolation to be the foundation of our joys.

3. Live by faith in the Lord Jesus Christ. We cannot with any confidence wait upon God, but in and through a Mediator, for it is by his Son that God speaks to us; and hears from us: all that passeth between a just God and poor sinners, must pass through the hands of that blessed days-man, who has laid his hand upon them both; every

prayer passeth from us to God, and every mercy from God to us by that hand; it is in the face of the anointed, that God looks upon us; and in the face of Jesus Christ, that we behold the glory and grace of God shining; it is by Christ that we have access to God, and success with him in prayer, and therfore must make mention of his righteousness, even of his only; and in that habitual attendance we must be all the day giving upon God, we must have an habitual dependence on him, who always appears in the presence of God for us; always gives attendance to be ready to introduce us.

4. Be frequent and serious in pious ejaculations. In waiting upon God we must often speak to him, must take all occasions to speak to him; and when we have not opportunity for a solemn address to him, he will accept of a sudden address, if it come from an honest heart. In these David waited on God all day, as appears by *verse* 1. Unto thee, O Lord, do I lift up my soul: to thee do I dart it, and all its gracious breathings after thee. We should in a holy ejaculation ask pardon for this sin, strength against this corruption, victory over this temptation, and it shall not be in vain. This is to pray always and without ceasing; it is not the length or language of the prayer that God looks at, but the sincerity of the heart in it: and that shall be accepted, though the prayer be very short, and the groanings such as cannot be uttered.

5. Look upon every day, as those who know not but it may be your last day. At such an hour as we think not, the Son of man comes; and therefore we cannot any morning be sure, that we shall live till night, we hear of many lately that have been snatched away very suddenly, what manner of persons therefore ought we to be in all holy conversation and godliness. Though we cannot say, we ought to live as if we were sure this day would be our last, yet it is certain, we ought to live as those who do not know but it may be so; and the rather, because we know the day of the Lord will come first or last; and therefore we are concerned to wait on him. For on whom should poor dying creatures wait, but on a living God.

Death will bring us all to God, to be judged by him; it will bring all the saints to him, to the vision and fruition of him; and one we are hastening to, and hope to be forever with, we are concerned to wait upon, and to cultivate an acquaintance with. Did we think more of death, we would converse more with God; our dying daily, is a good reason for our worshipping daily; and therefore wherever we are, we are concerned to keep near to God, because we know not where death will meet us: this will alter the property of death; Enoch, that walked with God, was translated that he should not see death; and this will furnish us with that which will stand us instead on the other side of death and the grave. If we continue waiting on God every day, and all the day long, we shall grow more experienced, and consequently more expert in the great mystery of communion with God, and thus our last days will become our best days, our last works our best works, and our last comforts our sweetest comforts: in consideration of which take the prophet's advice; Turn thou to thy God; keep mercy and judgment, and wait on thy God continually (Hosea 12:6).

THE THIRD DISCOURSE SHEWING HOW TO CLOSE THE DAY WITH GOD

PSALM 4:8
I will both lay me down in Peace, and sleep:
for thou, Lord, only makest me dwell in safety.

This may be understood either figuratively, of the repose of the soul in the assurances of God's grace; or literally, of the repose of the body under the protection of his providence; I love to give Scripture its full latitude, and therefore alike in both.

1. The Psalmist having given the preference to God's favour above any good, having chosen that, and portioned himself in that, here expresseth his great complacency in the choice he had made; while he saw many making themselves perpetually uneasy with that fruitless inquiry, who will shew us any good? Wearying themselves for very vanity; he had made himself perfectly easy by casting himself on the divine good will, Lord, lift thou up the light of thy countenance upon us: any good, short of God's favour, will not serve our turn, but that is enough, without the world's smiles: the moon and stars, and all the fires and candles in the world, will not make day without the sun; but the sun will make day without any of them. These are David's sentiments, and all the saints agree with him: finding no rest therefore, like Noah's dove in the deluged defiled world, he flies to the ark, that type of Christ, return unto thy rest, unto thy Noah (so the word is in the original, for Noah's name signifies rest) O my soul (Ps. 116:7).

If God lift up the light of his countenance upon us, as it fills us with a holy joy, it puts gladness into the heart more than they have whose corn and wine increaseth, verse 7, so it fixeth us in a holy rest, I will now lay me down and sleep. God is my God, and I am pleased, I am satisfied, I look no further, I desire no more, I dwell in safety: Or in confidence; while I walk in the light of the Lord, as I want no good, nor am I sensible of any deficiency, so I fear no evil, nor am apprehensive of any danger. The Lord God is to me both a sun and a shield; a sun to enlighten and comfort me, a shield to protect and defend me.

Hence learn, that those who have the assurances of God's favour towards them, may enjoy and should labour after, a holy serenity, and security of mind. We have both these put together in that precious promise (Isa. 32:17). But the work of righteousness shall be peace, there is a present satisfaction in doing good; and in the issue, the effect of righteousness shall be quietness and assurance for ever; quietness in the enjoyment of good, and assurance in a freedom from evil.

1.1. A holy serenity is one blessed fruit of God's favour; I will now lay me down in peace and sleep. While we are under God's displeasure, or in doubt concerning his favour, how can we have any enjoyment of ourselves! while this great concern is unsettled, the souls cannot but be unsatisfied. Hath God a controversy with thee? Give not sleep to thine eyes, nor slumber to thine eye-lids, until thou hast got the controversy taken up; Go humble thyself, and make sure thy friend, thy best friend (Prov. 6:3). And when thou hast made thy peace with him, and hast some comfortable evidence that thou art accepted of him, then say wisely and justly, what that carnal worldling said foolishly, and without ground, Soul take thy ease, for in God, and in the covenant of grace, thou hast goods laid up for many years, goods laid up for eternity (Luke 12:19). Are thy sins pardoned? Hast thou an interest in Christ's meditation? Doth God now in him accept thy works? Go thy way, eat thy bread with joy, and drink thy wine with a merry heart (Eccles. 9:7). Let this still every storm and command, and create a calm in thy soul.

Having God to be our God in covenant, we have enough, we have all; and though the gracious soul still desires more of God, it never desires more than God; in him it reposeth itself with a perfect complacency; in him it is at home, it is at rest, if we be but satisfied of his loving kindness; abundantly satisfied: There is enough in this to satiate the weary soul, and to replenish every sorrowful soul (Jer. 31:25). to fill even the hungry with good things, with the best things; and being filled, they should be at rest, at rest for ever, and their sleep here should be sweet.

1.2. A holy security is another blessed fruit of God's favour. Thou, Lord, makest me to dwell in safety, when the light of thy countenance shines upon me I am safe, and I know I am so, and am therefore easy, for with thy favour wilt thou compass me as with a shield (Ps. 5:12). Being taken under the protection of the divine favour. Though an host of enemies should encamp against me, yet my heart shall not fear, in this I will be confident (Ps. 27:3). Whatever God has promised me, I can promise myself, and that is enough to indemnify me, and save me harmless, whatever difficulties and dangers I may meet with in the way of my duty. Though the earth be removed, yet will not we fear (Ps. 46:2); not fear any evil, no not in the valley of the shadow of death, in the territories of the king of terrors himself, for there thou art with me, thy rod and thy staff they comfort me. What the rich man's wealth is to him, in his own conceit, a strong city, and a high wall, that the good man's God is to him (Prov. 18:10, 11). The Almighty shall be thy gold, thy defence (Job 22:25).

Nothing is more dangerous than security in a sinful way, and men's crying peace, peace, to themselves, while they continue under the reigning power of a vain and carnal mind: O that the sinners that are at ease were made to tremble: Nothing is more foolish than a security built upon the world, and its promises, for they are all vanity and a lie; but nothing more reasonable in itself, or more advantageous to us, than for good people to build with assurance upon the promises of a good God, for those that keep in the way of duty, to be quiet from the fear of evil; as those that know no evil shall befall them, no real evil, no evil, but what shall be made to work for their good; as those that know, while they continue in the allegiance to God as their king, they are under his protection, under the protection of Omnipotence itself, which enables them to bid defiance to all malignant powers; If God be for us, who can be against us? This security even the heathen looked upon every honest virtuous man to be entitled to, and thought if the world should fall in pieces about his ears, he needed not fear being lost in the desolations of it; much more reason have Christians, that hold fast their integrity, to lay claim to it, for who is he, or what is it, that shall harm us, if we be followers of him that is good, in his goodness?

Now, 1.2.1 It is the privilege of good people, that they may be thus easy and satisfied: This holy serenity and security of mind is allowed them, God gives them leave to be cheerful; nay it is promised them, God will speak peace to his people, and to his saints; he will fill them with joy and peace in believing; his peace shall keep their hearts and minds;

keep them safe, keep them calm. Nay, there is a method appointed for their obtaining this promised serenity and security. The scriptures are written to them that their joy may be full, and that through patience and comfort of them they may have hope. Ordinances are instituted to be wells of salvation, out of which they may draw water with joy. Ministers are ordained to be their comforters, and the helpers of their joy. Thus willing has God been to shew to the heirs of promise the immutability of his counsel, that they might have strong consolation (Heb. 6:17, 18).

1.2.2. It is the duty of good people to labour after this holy security and serenity of mind, and to use the means appointed for the obtaining of it. Give not way to the disquieting suggestions of Satan, and to those tormenting doubts and fears that arise in your own souls. Study to be quiet, chide yourselves for your distrusts, charge yourselves to believe, and to hope in God, that you shall praise him. You are in the dark concerning yourselves, do as Paul's mariners did, cast anchor, and wish for the day. Poor trembling Christian, that art tossed with tempests, and not comforted, try to lay thee down in peace and sleep; compose thyself into a sedate and even frame; in the name of him whom winds and seas obey, command down thy tumultuous thoughts, and say, Peace be still; lay that aching trembling head of thine where the beloved disciple laid his, in the bosom of the Lord Jesus; or, if thou hast not yet attained such boldness of access to him, lay that aching trembling head of thine at the feet of the Lord Jesus, by an entire submission and resignation to him, saying, If I perish, I will perish here; put it into his hand by an entire confidence in him; submit it to his operation and disposal, who knows how to speak to the heart. And if thou art not yet entered into the sabbatism, as the word is (Heb. 4:9), this present rest that remaineth for the people of God, yet look upon it to be a land of promise, and therefore though it tarry, wait for it, for the vision is for an appointed time, and at the end it shall speak, and shall not lie. Light is sown for the righteous, and what is sown shall come up again at last in a harvest of joy.

2. The Psalmist having done his day's work, and perhaps fatigued himself with it, it being now bedtime, and he having given good advice to those to whom he had wished a good night, to commune with their own hearts upon their beds, and to offer the evening sacrifices of righteousness, *verses* 4, 5, now retires to his chamber with this word, I will lay me down in peace and sleep. That which I chose this text for, will lead me to understand it literally, as the disciples understood their Master, when he said, Lazarus sleepeth, of taking rest in sleep

(John 11:12, 13). And so we have here David's pious thought when he was going to bed: As when he awakes he is still with God, he is still so when he goes to sleep, and concludes the day, as he opened it, with meditations on God, and sweet communion with him.

It should seem David penned this Psalm when he was distressed and persecuted by his enemies; perhaps it was penned on the same occasion with the foregoing Psalm, when he fled from Absalom his son; without were fightings, and then no wonder that within were fears; yet then he puts such a confidence in God's protection, that he will go to bed at his usual time, and with his usual quietness and cheerfulness, will compose himself as at other times: He knows his enemies have no power against him, but what is given them from above, and they shall have no power given them, but what is still under the divine check and restraint; nor shall their power be permitted to exert itself so far as to do him any real mischief, and therefore he retires into the secret place of the most high, and abides under the shadow of the Almighty, and is very quiet in his own mind. That will break a worldly man's heart, which will not break a godly man's sleep; Let them do their worst, saith David, I will lay me down and sleep; the will of the Lord be done. Now observe here,

2.1. His confidence in God; Thou, Lord, makest me to dwell in safety; not only makest me safe, but makest me to know that I am so; makest me to dwell with a good assurance; it is the same word that is used concerning him that walks uprightly, that he walks surely (Prov. 10:9). He goes boldly in his way, so David here goes boldly to his bed. He doth not carelessly as the men of Laish (Judg. 18:7), but dwells at ease in God, as the sons of Zion, in the city of their solemnities, when their eyes see it a quiet habitation (Isa. 33:20).

There is one word in this part of the text that is observable; thou, Lord, only dost secure me. Some refer it to David; even when I am alone, have none of my privy-counsellors about me to advise me, none of my life-guards to fight for me, yet I am under no apprehension of danger, while God is with me. The Son of David comforted himself with this, that when all his disciples forsook him, and left him alone, yet he was not alone, for the Father was with him. Some weak people are afraid of being alone, especially in the dark, but a firm belief of God's presence with us in all places, and that divine protection which all good people are under, would silence those fears, and make us ashamed of them. Nay, our being alone a peculiar people whom God hath set apart for himself, (as it is here, *verse* 8) will be our security. A sober singularity will be our safety and satisfaction, as

Noah's was in the old world; Israel is a people that shall dwell alone, and not be reckoned among the nations, and therefore may set them all at defiance, till they foolishly mingle themselves among them (Num. 23:9). Israel shall then dwell in safety alone (Deut. 33:28). The more we dwell alone, the more safe we dwell. But our translation refers it to God; Thou alone makest me to dwell safely. It is done by thee only! God in protecting his people needs not any assistance, though he sometimes makes use of instruments: The earth helped the woman, yet he can do it without them; and when all other refuges fail, his own arm works salvation; no the Lord alone did lead him, and there was no strange God with him (Deut. 32:12). Yet that is not all, I depend on thee only to do it; therefore I am easy, and think myself safe, not because I have hosts on my side, but purely because I have the Lord of hosts on my side.

Thou makest me to dwell in safety; That may look either backward or forward, or rather both: Thou hast made me to dwell in safety all day, so that the sun has not smitten me by day; and then it is the language of his thankfulness of the mercies he had received; or, thou wilt make me to dwell in safety all night, that the moon shall not smite me by night: and then it is the language of his dependence upon God for further mercies; and both these should go together; and our eye must be to God as ever the same, who was, and is, and is to come; who has delivered, and doth, and will.

2.2. His composedness in himself inferred from hence, I will both lay me down and sleep. They that have their corn and wine increasing, that have abundance of the wealth and pleasure of this world, they lay them down and sleep contentedly, as Boaz at the end of the heap of corn (Ruth 3:7). But though I have not what they have, I can lay me down in peace and sleep, as well as they. We make it to join, his lying down and his sleeping; I will not only lay me down, as one that desires to be composed, but will sleep as one that really is so. Some make it to intimate his falling asleep presently after he had laid him down; so well wearied was he with the work of the day, and so free from any of those disquieting thoughts which would keep him from sleeping.

Now these are words put into our mouths, with which to compose ourselves when we retire at night to our repose; and we should take care so to manage ourselves all day, especially when it draws towards night, as that we may not be disfitted, and put out of frame, for our evening devotions; that our hearts may not be overcharged either on the one hand with surfeiting and drunkenness, as theirs often are that are men of pleasure; or on the other hand with the cares of this life, as theirs often are that are men of business: But that we may have such a command both of our thought, and of our time, as that we may finish our daily work well; which will be an earnest of our finishing our life's work well; and all is well indeed that ends everlastingly well.

Doct. As we must begin the day with God, and wait upon him all the day, so we must endeavour to close it with him.

This duty of closing the day with God, and in a good frame, I know not how better to open to you, than by going over the particulars in the text, in their order; and recommending to you David's example.

1. First, Let us retire to lay us down: nature calls for rest as well as food: man goes forth to his work and labour, and goes to and fro about it, but it is only till evening, and then it is time to lie down. We read of Ishbosheth, that he lay on his bed at noon, but death met him there (2 Sam. 4:5, 6); and of David himself, that he came off from his bed at evening-tide, but sin, a worse thing than death, met him there (2 Sam. 11:2). We must work the works of him that sent us while it is day, it will be time enough to lie down when the night comes, and no man can work; and it is then proper and seasonable to lie down: it is promised (Zeph. 2:7). They shall lie down in the evening, and with that promise we must comply, and rest in the time appointed for rest; and not turn day into night, and night into day, as many do upon some ill account or other.

1.1. Some sit up to do mischief to their neighbours; to kill, and steal, and to destroy; in the dark they dig through houses which they had marked for themselves in the day time (Job 24:16). David complains of his enemies, that at evening they go round about the city (Ps. 59:6). They that do evil hate the light. Judas the traitor was in quest of his Master, with his band of men, when he should have been in his bed. And it is an aggravation of the wickedness of the wicked when they take so much pains to compass an ill design, and have their hearts so much upon it, that they sleep not except they have done mischief (Prov. 4:16). As it is a shame to those who profess to make it their business to do good, that they cannot find in their hearts to entrench upon any of the gratifications of sense in pursuance of it; say then, while others sit up watching for an opportunity to be mischievous, I will lay me down and be quiet, and do no body any harm.

1.2. Others sit up in pursuit of the world, and the wealth of it. They not only rise up early, but they sit up late, in the eager prosecution of their covetous practices (Ps. 127:2); and either to get or save, deny themselves their most necessary sleep; and this their way is their folly, for hereby they deprive themselves of the comfortable enjoyment of what they have, which is the end, under pretence of care and pains to obtain more, which is but the means. Solomon speaks of those that neither day nor night sleep with their eyes (Eccles. 8:16), that make themselves perfect slaves, and drudges to the world, than which there is not a more cruel task-master: and thus they make that which of itself is vanity, to be to them vexation of spirit, for they weary themselves of every vanity (Hab. 2:13), and are so miserably in love with their chain, that they deny themselves not only the spiritual rest God has provided for them as the God of grace, but the natural rest, which, as the God of nature, he has provided, and is a specimen of the wrong sinners do to their own bodies, as well as their own souls. Let us see the folly of it, and never labour thus for the meat that perisheth, and that abundance of the rich which will not suffer him to sleep; but let us labour for that meat which endureth to eternal life, that grace which is the earnest of glory, the abundance of which will make our sleep sweet to us.

1.3. Others sit up in the indulgence of their pleasures; they will not lay them down in due time, because they cannot find in their hearts to leave their vain sports and pastimes, their music, and dancing, and plays, their cards and dice; or which is worse, their rioting and excess, for they that are drunk are drunk in the night. It is bad enough when these gratifications of a base lust, or at least of a vain mind, are suffered to devour the whole evening, and then to engross the whole soul, as they are apt enough to do insensibly; so that there is neither time nor heart for the evening devotions, either in the closet or in the family; but it is much worse when they are suffered to go far into the night too, for then of course they trespass upon the ensuing morning, and steal away the time that should then also be bestowed upon the exercises of religion. Those that can of choice, and with so much pleasure sit up till I know not what time of night, to make, as they say, a merry night of it, to spend their time in filthiness, and foolish talking and jesting, which are not convenient, would think themselves hardly dealt with, if they should be kept one half hour past their sleeping time, engaged in any good duties, and would have called blessed Paul himself a long winded preacher, and have censured him as very indiscreet, when, upon a particular occasion he continued his speech till midnight (Acts 20:7). And how loth would they be with David at midnight, to rise and give thanks to God: or with their Master to continue all night in prayer to God.

Let the corrupt affections, which run out thus and transgress, be mortified, and not gratified; those that have allowed themselves in such irregularities; if they have allowed themselves an impartial reflection, cannot but have found the inconvenience of them, and that they have been a prejudice to the prosperity of the soul, and should therefore deny themselves for their own good. One rule for the closing of the day well, is to keep good hours: every thing is beautiful in its season. I have heard it said long since, and I beg leave to repeat it now, that

> *Early to bed, and early to rise,*
> *Is the way to be healthy, and wealthy, and wise.*

We shall now take it for granted, that unless some necessary business, or some work of mercy, or some more than ordinary act of devotion, keep you up beyond your usual time; you are disposed to lay you down. And let us lay down with thankfulness to God, and with thoughts of dying; with penitent reflections upon the sins of the day; and with humble supplications for the mercies of the night.

1.3.1. Let us lie down with thankfulness to God. When we retire to our bed-chambers, or closets, we should lift up our hearts to God, the God of our mercies, and make him the God of our praises whenever we go to bed. I am sure we do not want matter for praise, if we do not want a heart. Let us therefore address ourselves then to that pleasant duty, that work which is its own wages. The evening sacrifice was to be a sacrifice of praise.

1.3.1.1. We have reason to be thankful for the many mercies of the day past, which we ought particularly to review, and to say, blessed be the Lord who daily loadeth us with his benefits. Observe the constant series of mercies, which has not been interrupted, or broken in upon any day. Observe the particular instances of mercy with which some days have been signalized and made remarkable. It is he that has granted us life and favour, it is his visitation that preserves our spirits. Think how many are the calamities we are every day preserved from; the calamities which we are sensibly exposed to, and perhaps have been delivered from the imminent danger of; and those which we have not been apprehensive of; many which we have deserved, and which others, better than we are, groan under. All our bones have reason to say, Lord, who is like unto thee? For it is God that keepeth all our bones, not one of them is broken: It is of his mercies that we are not consumed.

Think how many are the comforts we are every day surrounded with, all which we are indebted to the bounty of the divine providence for; every bit we eat, and every drop we drink is mercy; every step we take, and every breath we draw, mercy. All the satisfaction we have in the agreeableness and affections of our relations, and in the society and serviceableness of our friends: All the success we have in our callings and employments, and the pleasure we take in them: All the joy which Zebulun has in his going out, and Issachar in his tents, is what we have reason to acknowledge with thankfulness to God's praise.

Yet it is likely the day has not past without some cross accidents, something or other has afflicted and disappointed us, and if it has, yet that must not indispose us for praise; however it be, yet God is good; and it is our duty in every thing to give thanks, and to bless the name of the Lord when he takes away, as well as when he gives; for our afflictions are but few, and a thousand times deserved; our mercies are many, and a thousand times forfeited.

1.3.1.2. We have reason to be thankful for the shadows of the evening, which call us to retire and lie down. The same wisdom, power and goodness that makes the morning, makes the evening also to rejoice; and gives us cause to be thankful for the drawing of the curtains of the night about us in favour to our repose, as well as for the opening of the eye-lids of the morning upon us in favour to our business. When God divided between the light and the darkness, and allotted to both of them their time successively, he saw that it was good, it should be so; in a world of mixtures and changes, nothing more proper. Let us therefore give thanks to that God who forms the light, and creates the darkness; and believe, that as in the revolutions of time, so in the revolutions of the events of time, the darkness of affliction may be as needful for us in its season, as the light of prosperity. If the hireling longs till the shadow comes, let him be thankful for it when it doth come, that the burden and heat of the day is not perpetual.

1.3.1.3. We have reason to be thankful for a quiet habitation to lie down in; that we are not driven out from among men as Nebuchadnezzar, to lie down with the beasts of the field; that though we were born like the wild ass' colt, yet we have not with the wild ass the wilderness of our habitation, and the desolate and barren land for our dwelling. That we are not to wander in deserts and mountains, in dens and caves of the earth, as many of God's dear saints and servants have been forced to do, of whom the world was not worthy; but the good Shepherd makes us lie down in green pastures: that we have not, as Jacob, the cold ground for our bed, and a stone for our pillow, which yet one would be content with, and covet, if with it one could have his dream.

1.3.1.4. We have reason to be thankful that we are not forced to sit up; that our Master not only gives us leave to lie down, but orders that nothing shall prevent our lying down. Many go to bed, but cannot lie down there, by reason of painful and languishing sicknesses, of that nature, that if they lie down they cannot breathe: Our bodies are of the same mould, and it is of the Lord's mercies that we are not so afflicted. Many are kept up by sickness in their families; children are ill, and they must attend them: if God takes sickness away from the midst of us, and keeps it away, so that no plague comes near our dwellings, a numerous family perhaps, and all well, it is a mercy we are bound to be very thankful for, and to value in proportion to the greatness of the affliction, where sickness prevails. Many are kept up by the fear of enemies, of soldiers, of thieves; The goodman of the house watcheth, that his house may not be broken through: but our lying down is not prevented or disturbed by the alarms of war, we are delivered from the noise of archers in the places of repose, therefore should we rehearse the righteous acts of the Lord, even his righteous acts towards the inhabitants of his villages in Israel, which under his protection are as safe as walled cities with gates and bars. When we lie down, let us thank God that we may lie down.

1.3.2. Let us lie down with thoughts of death, and of that great change which at death we must pass under. The conclusion of every day should put us in mind of the conclusion of all our days; when our night comes, our long night, which will put a period to our work, and bring the honest labourer, both to take his rest, and receive his penny. It is good for us to think frequently of dying, to think of it as oft as we go to bed; it will help to mortify the corruptions of our own hearts, which are our daily burdens, to arm us against the temptations of the world, which are our daily snares; it will wean us from our daily comforts, and make us easy under our daily crosses and fatigues. It is good for us to think familiarly of dying, to think of it as our going to bed, that by thinking often of it, and thinking thus of it, we may get above the fear of it.

1.3.2.1. At death we shall retire, as we do at bed-time; we shall go to be private for a while, till the public appearance at the great day; Man lyeth down, and riseth not till the heavens be no more; till then they shall not awake, nor be raised out of their sleep (Job 14:12). Now we go abroad to see and be seen, and to no higher purpose do some spend their day, spend their life; but when death comes, there is an end of both; we shall then see no more in this world, I shall behold man no more (Isa. 38:11); we shall then be seen no more; the eye of him that hath seen me, shall see me no more (Job 7:8); we shall be hid in the grave, and cut off from all living. To die is to bid good night to all our friends, to put a period to our conversation with them; we bid them farewell, but blessed be God, it is not an eternal farewell. We hope to meet them again in the morning of the resurrection, to part no more.

1.3.2.2. At death we shall put off the body, as we put off our clothes when we lie down. The soul is the man, the body is but clothes; at death we shall be unclothed, the earthly house of this tabernacle shall be dissolved, the garment of the body shall be laid aside; death strips us, and sends us naked out of the world, as we came into it; strips the soul of all the disguises wherein it appeared before men, that it may appear naked and open before God. Our grave clothes are night clothes.

When we are weary and hot, our clothes are a burden, and we are very willing to throw them off, are not easy till we are undressed: thus we that are in this tabernacle do groan being burdened; but when death frees the soul from the load and incumbrance of the body, which hinders its repose in its spiritual satisfactions, how easy will it be? Let us think then of putting off the body at death with as much pleasure as we do of putting off our clothes at night; be as loose to them as we are to our clothes; and comfort ourselves with this thought, that though we are unclothed at death, if we be clothed with Christ and his grace, we shall not be found naked, but be clothed upon with immortality. We have new clothes a making, which shall be ready to put on next morning; a glorious body like Christ's, instead of a vile body like the beasts.

1.3.2.3. At death we shall lie down in the grave as our bed shall lie down in the dust (Job 20:11). To those that die in sin, and impenitent, the grave is a dungeon, their iniquities which are upon their bones, and which lie down with them, make it so; but to those that die in Christ, that die in faith, it is a bed, a bed of rest, where there is no tossings to and fro until the dawning of the day, as sometimes there are upon the easiest beds we have in this world? where there is no danger of being scared with dreams, and terrified with visions of the night; there is no being chastened with pain on that bed, or the multitude of the bones with strong pain. It is the privilege of those, who while they live walk in their uprightness, that when they die they enter into peace, and rest in their beds (Isa. 57:2).

Holy Job comforts himself with this, in the midst of his agonies, that he shall shortly make his bed in the darkness, and be easy there. It is a bed of roses, a bed of spices to all believers ever since he lay in it, who is the rose of Sharon, and the lily of the valleys.

Say then of thy grave, as thou dost of thy bed at night, there the weary are at rest; with this further consolation, that thou shalt not only rest there, but rise thence shortly, abundantly refreshed; shalt be called up to meet the beloved of thy soul, and to be for ever with him; shalt rise to a day which will not renew thy cares, as every day on earth doth, but secure to thee unmixed and everlasting joys. How comfortably may we lie down at night, if such thoughts as these lie down with us? And how comfortably may we lie down at death, if we have accustomed ourselves to such thoughts as these.

1.3.3. Let us lie down with penitent reflections upon the sins of the day past. Praising God and delighting ourselves in him is such pleasant work, and so much the work of angels, that methinks it is pity we should have anything else to do; but the truth is, we make other work for ourselves by our own folly, that is not so pleasant, but absolutely needful, and that is repentance. While we are at night solacing ourselves in God's goodness, yet we must intermix therewith the afflicting of ourselves for our own badness; both must have their place in us, and they will very well agree together; for we must take our work before us.

1.3.3.1. We must be convinced of it, that we are still contracting guilt; we carry corrupt natures about with us, which are bitter roots that bear gall and wormwood, and all we say or do is imbittered by them. In many things we all offend, insomuch that there is not a just man upon earth that doeth good and sins not. We are in the midst of a defiling world, and cannot keep ourselves perfectly unspotted from it. If we say we have no sin, or that we have past a day and have not sinned, we deceive ourselves, for if we know the truth by ourselves, we shall see cause to cry, who can understand his errors? Cleanse us from our secret faults; faults which we ourselves are not aware of. We ought to aim at a sinless perfection, with as strict a watchfulness as if we could attain it: But after all must acknowledge, that we come short of it; that we have not yet attained, neither are already perfect. We find it by constant sad experience, for it is certain we do enough every day to bring us upon our knees at night.

1.3.3.2. We must examine our consciences, that we may find out our particular transgressions the day past. Let us every night search and try our ways, our thoughts, words, and actions, compare them with the rule of the word, look our faces in that glass, that we may see our spots, and may be particular in the acknowledgment of them. It will be good for us to ask, what have we done this day? What have we done amiss? What duty have we neglected? What false step have we taken? How have we carried it in our callings, in our converse? Have we done the duties of our particular relations, and accommodated ourselves to the will of God in every event of providence. By doing this frequently, we shall grow in our acquaintance with ourselves, than which nothing will contribute more to our soul's prosperity.

1.3.3.3. We must renew our repentance for whatever we find has been amiss in us, or has been said or done amiss by us. We must be sorry for it, and sadly lament it, and take shame to ourselves for it, and give glory to God by making confession. If any thing appear to have been wrong more than ordinary, that must be particularly bewailed; and in general, we must be mortified for our sins of daily infirmity, which we ought not to think slightly of, because they are returning daily, but rather be the more ashamed of them, and of that fountain within which casts out these waters.

It is good to be speedy in renewing our repentance; before the heart be hardened by the deceitfulness of sin. Delays are dangerous; green wounds may soon be cured, if taken in time, but if they stink and are corrupt, as the Psalmist complains (Ps. 38:5), it is our fault and folly, and the cure will be difficult. Though through the weakness of the flesh we fall into sin daily, if we get up again by renewed repentance at night, we are not, nor ought we to think ourselves utterly cast down. The sin that humbles us shall not ruin us.

1.3.3.4. We must make a fresh application of the blood of Christ to our souls for the remission of our sins, and the gracious acceptance of our repentance. We must not think that we have need of Christ only at our first conversion to God; no we have daily need of him, as our advocate with the Father, and therefore as such he always appears in the presence of God for us, and attends continually to this very thing. Even our sins of daily infirmity would be to our ruin, if he had not made satisfaction for them, and did not still make intercession for us. He that is washed, still needeth to wash his feet, from the filth he contracts in every step; and blessed be God, there is a fountain opened for us to wash in, and it is always open.

1.3.3.5. We must apply ourselves to the throne of grace for peace and pardon. Those that repent must pray, that the thought of their heart may be forgiven them (Acts 8:22). And it is good to be particular in our prayers for the pardon of sin; that as Hannah said concerning Samuel, for this child I prayed; so we may be able to say, for the forgiveness of this I prayed. However, the publican's prayer in general, is a very proper one for each of us to lie down with, God be merciful to me a sinner.

1.3.4. Let us lie down with humble supplications for the mercies of the night. Prayer is as necessary in the evening, as it was in the morning, for we have the same need of the divine favour and care, to make the evening out goings to rejoice, that we had to beautify those of the morning.

1.3.4.1. We must pray, that our outward man may be under the care of God's holy angels, who are the ministers of his providence. God hath promised, that he will give his angels charge concerning those who make the Most High their refuge, and that they shall pitch their tents round about them and deliver them; and what he hath promised, we may and must pray for; not as if God needed the service of the angels, or as if he did himself quit all the care of his people, and turn it over to them: but it appears by abundance of Scripture proofs, that they are employed about the people of God, whom he takes under his special protection, though they are not seen both for the honour of God by whom they are charged, and for the honour of the saints with whom they are charged. It was the glory of Solomon's bed, that threescore valiant men were about it, of the valiant of Israel, all holding swords, because of fear in the night (Song. 3:7, 8). But much more honourably and comfortably are all true believers attended, for though they lie never so meanly, they have hosts of angels surrounding their beds, and by the ministration of good spirits, are preserved from malignant spirits. But God will for this be enquired of by the house of Israel; Christ himself must pray the Father, and he will send to his relief legions of angels (Matt. 26:53). Much more reason have we to ask, that it may be given us.

1.3.4.2. We must pray, that our inward man may be under the influences of his Holy Spirit, who is the Author and fountain of his grace. As public ordinances are opportunities in which the Spirit works upon the hearts of men, and therefore when we attend on them, we must pray for the Spirit's operations, so are private retirements, and therefore we must put up the same prayer, when we enter upon them. We find, that in slumberings upon the bed, God openeth the ears of men, and sealeth their instruction (Job 33:15, 16). And with this David's experiences concur, he found that God visited him in the night, and tried him and so discovered him to himself (Ps. 17:3). And that God gave him counsel, and his reins instructed him in the night season, and so he discovered himself to him (Ps. 16:7). He found that was a proper season for remembering God, and meditating upon him; and in order to our due improvement of this proper season for conversing with God in solitude, we need the powerful and benign influences of the blessed Spirit, which therefore when we lie down we should earnestly pray for, and humbly put ourselves under, and submit ourselves to. How God's grace may work upon us, when we are asleep we know not; the soul will act in a state of separation from the body, and how far it doth act independent on the body, when the bodily senses are all locked up we cannot say, but are sure, that the Spirit of the Lord is not bound; we have reason to pray, not only that our minds may not be either disturbed or polluted by evil dreams, in which for ought we know, evil spirits sometimes have a hand, but may be instructed and quieted by good dreams, which Plutarch reckons among the evidences of increase and proficiency in virtue, and on which the good spirit has an influence. I have heard of a good man, that used to pray at night for good dreams.

2. *Secondly*, When we lay us down, our care and endeavour must be to lay us down in peace. It is promised to Abraham, that he shall go to his grave in peace (Gen. 15:15), and this promise is sure to all his spiritual seed, for the end of the upright man is peace; Josiah dies in peace, though he is killed in a battle; now as an earnest of this let us every night lie down in peace. It is threatened to the wicked, that they shall lie down in sorrow (Isa. 1:11). It is promised to the righteous, that they shall lie down, and none shall make them afraid (Lev. 26:6. Job 11:19). Let us then enter into this rest, this blessed Sabbatism, and take care that we come not short of it.

2.1. Let us lie down in peace with God; for without this there can be no peace at all; There is no peace, saith my God, to the wicked, whom God is at war with. A state of sin is a state of enmity against God; they that continue in that state are under the wrath and curse of God, and cannot lie down in peace: What have they to do with peace? Hasten therefore (sinner) hasten to make thy peace with God in Jesus Christ, by repentance and faith; take hold on his strength that thou mayest make peace with him, and thou shalt make peace, for fury is not with him. Conditions of peace are offered, consent to them; close with him who is our Peace; take Christ upon his own terms, Christ upon any terms. Defer not to do this; dare not to sleep in that condition, in which thou darest not to die. Escape for thy life, look not behind thee. Acquaint now thyself with him, now presently, and be at peace, and thereby this good shall come unto thee, thou shalt lie down in peace.

Sin is ever and anon making mischief between God and our souls, provoking God against us, alienating us from God, we therefore need to be every night making peace, reconciling ourselves to him and to his holy will, by the agency of his Spirit upon us, and begging of him to be reconciled to us, through the intercession of his Son for us; that there may be no distance, no strangeness between us and God, no interposing cloud to hinder his mercies from coming down upon us, or our prayers from coming up unto him. Being justified by faith, we have this peace with God, through our Lord Jesus Christ; and then we may not only lie down in peace; but we rejoice in hope of the glory of God. Let this be our first care, that God have no quarrel with us, nor we with him.

2.2. Let us lie down in peace with all men; we are concerned to go to sleep, as well as to go to die in charity. Those that converse much with the world can scarce pass a day, but something or other happens that is provoking, some affront is given them, some injury done them, at least so they think; when they retire at night and reflect upon it, they are apt to magnify the offence, and while they are musing on it the fire burns, their resentments rise, and they begin to say, I will do so to him as he has done to me (Prov. 24:29). Then is the time of ripening the passion into a rooted malice, and meditating revenge; then therefore let wisdom and grace be set on work, to extinguish this fire from hell before it get head, then let this root of bitterness be killed and plucked up; and let the mind be disposed to forgive the injury, and to think well of, and wish well to him that did it. If others incline to quarrel with us, yet let us resolve not to quarrel with them. Let us resolve that whatever the affront or injury was, it shall neither disquiet our spirits, nor make us to fret, which Peninnah aimed at in provoking Hannah (I Sam. 1:6), nor sour or embitter our spirits, or make us peevish and spiteful: but that we still love ourselves, and love our neighbors as ourselves, and therefore not by harbouring malice, do any wrong to ourselves or our neighbour. And we shall find it much easier in itself, and much more pleasant in the reflection to forgive twenty injuries than to avenge one.

That it should be our particular care at night, to reconcile ourselves to those who have been injurious to us, is intimated in the charge (Eph. 4:26). Let not the sun go down upon your wrath. If your passion has not cooled before, let it be abated by the cool of the evening, and quite disappear with the setting sun. You are then to go to bed, and if you lie down with these unmortified passions boiling in your breasts, your soul is among lions, you lie down in a bed of thorns, in a nest of scorpions. Nay, some have observed from what follows immediately, Neither give place to the devil (*verse* 27). That those who go to bed in malice, have the devil for their bed-fellow. We cannot lie down at peace with God, unless we be at peace with men: not in faith pray to be forgiven, unless we forgive. Let us therefore study the things that make for peace, for the peace of our own spirits, by living as much as in us lies peaceably with all men. I am for peace, yea, though they are for war.

2.3. Let us lie down in peace with ourselves, with our minds, with a sweet composedness of spirit and enjoyment of ourselves; return unto thy rest, O my soul, and be easy; let nothing disturb my soul, my darling.

But when may we lie down in peace? At night.

2.3.1. If we have by the grace of God in some measure done the work of the day, and filled it up with duty, we may then lie down in peace at night. If we have the testimony of our consciences for us, that in simplicity and godly sincerity, not with fleshly wisdom, but by the grace of God we have this day had our conversation in the world, that we have done some good in our places, something that will turn to a good account; if our hearts do not reproach us with a *diem perdidi**, alas, I have lost a day: or with that which is worse, the spending of that time in the service of sin, which should have been spent in the service of God; but if on the contrary we have abode with God, have been in his fear, and waited on him all the day long, we may then lie down in peace, for God saith, Well done, good and faithful servant; and the sleep of the labouring man, of the labouring Christian, is sweet, is very sweet, when he can say, as I am a day's journey nearer my end, so I am a day's work fitter for it. Nothing will make our bed-chambers pleasant, and our beds easy, like the witness of the Spirit of God with our spirits, that we are going forward for heaven; and a conscience kept void of offence, which will be not only a continual feast, but a continual rest.

2.3.2. If we have by faith and patience, and submission to the divine will reconciled ourselves to all the events of the day, so as to be uneasy at nothing that God has done, we may then lie down in peace at night. Whatever hath fallen out cross to us, it shall not fret us, but we will kiss the rod, take up the cross, and say, all is well that God doth. Thus we must in our patience keep possession of our own souls and not suffer any affliction to put us out of the possession of them. We have met with disappointments, in husbandry perhaps, in trade, at sea, debtors prove insolvent, creditors prove severe, but this and the other proceedeth from the Lord, there is a providence in it, every creature

---

* Conscience says to you: 'I wasted the day.'

is what God makes it to be, and therefore I am dumb, I open not my mouth: That which pleaseth God ought not to displease me.

2.3.3. If we have renewed our repentance for sin, and made a fresh application of the blood of Christ to our souls for the purifying of our consciences, we may then lay us down in peace. Nothing can break in upon our peace but sin, that is it that troubles the camp; if that be taken away, there shall no evil befall us. The inhabitant though he be far from well, yet shall not say I am sick, shall not complain of sickness, for the people that dwell therein shall be forgiven their iniquity (Isa. 33:24). The pardon of sin has enough in it to balance all our griefs, and therefore to silence all our complaints: a man sick of the palsy, yet has reason to be easy, nay, and to be of good cheer, if Christ saith to him, thy sins are forgiven thee, and I am thy salvation.

2.3.4. If we have put ourselves under the divine protection for the ensuing night, we may then lay us down in peace. If by faith and prayer, we have run into the name of the Lord as our strong tower, have fled to take shelter under the shadow of his wings, and make the Lord our refuge and our habitation, we may then speak peace to ourselves, for God in his word speaks peace to us. If David has an eye to the cherubims, between which God is said to dwell, when he saith, In the shadow of thy wings will I make my refuge (Ps. 57:1), yet certainly he has an eye to the similitude Christ makes use of, of a hen gathering her chickens under her wings, when he saith, He shall cover thee with his feathers, and under his wings shalt thou trust (Ps. 91:4), and the chickens under the wings of the hen are not only safe, but warm and pleased.

2.3.5. If we have cast all our cares for the day following upon God, we may then lay us down in peace. Taking thought for the morrow is the great hinderance of our peace in the night; let us but learn to live without disquieting care, and to refer the issue of all events to that God who may and can do what he will, and will do what is best for those that love and fear him; Father, thy will be done, and then we make ourselves easy. Our Saviour presseth this very much upon his disciples, not to perplex themselves with thoughts what they shall eat, and what they shall drink, and wherewithal they shall be clothed, because their heavenly Father knows that they have need of these things, and will see that they be supplied. Let us therefore ease ourselves of this burthen, by casting it on him who careth for us, what need he care, and we care too?

3. *Thirdly*, Having laid ourselves down in peace, we must compose ourselves to sleep. I will lay me down and sleep. The love of sleep for sleeping sake, is the character of the sluggard, but as it is nature's physic for the recruiting of its weary powers, it is to be looked upon as a mercy equal to that of our food, and in its season to be received with thankfulness.

And with such thoughts as these we may go to sleep.

3.1. What poor bodies are these we carry about with us, that call for rest and relief so often, that are so soon tired even with doing nothing, or next to nothing. It is an honour to man above the beasts, that he is made to go erect, it was part of the serpent's curse, on thy belly shalt thou go; yet we have little reason to boast of this honour, when we observe how little a while we can stand upright, and how soon we are burdened with our honour, and are forced to lie down. The powers of the soul, and the senses of the body, are our honour, but it is mortifying to consider how after a few hours use they are all locked up under a total disability of acting, and it is necessary they should be so. Let not the wise man glory in his wisdom, or the strong man in his strength, since they both lie for a fourth part of their time utterly bereft of strength and wisdom, and on a level with the weak and foolish.

3.2. What a sad thing is it to be under a necessity of losing so much precious time as we do in sleep. That we should lie so many hours every four and twenty, in no capacity at all of serving God or our neighbour, of doing any work of piety or charity. Those that consider how short our time is, and what a great deal of work we have to do, and how fast the day of account hastens on, cannot but grudge to spend so much time in sleep, cannot but wish to spend as little as may be in it: cannot but be quickened by it to redeem time when they are awake, and cannot but long to be there where there shall be no need of sleep, but they shall be as the angels of God, and never rest day or night from the blessed work of praising God.

3.3. What a good master do we serve, that allows us time for sleep, and furnisheth us with conveniences for it, and makes it refreshing and reviving to us? By this it appears, the Lord is for the body, and it is a good reason why we should present our bodies to him as living sacrifices, and glorify him with them. Nay, sleep is spoken of as given by promise to the saints (Ps. 127:2). So he giveth his beloved sleep. The godly man hath the enjoyment of that in a quiet resignation to God, which the worldly man labours in vain for, in the eager pursuit of the world. What a difference is there between the sleep of a sinner, that is not sensible of his being within a step of hell, and the sleep of a saint, that has good hopes, through grace, of his being within a step of heaven; that is the sleep God gives to his beloved.

3.4. How piteous is the case of those from whose eyes sleep departs, through pain of body, or anguish of mind, and to whom wearisome nights are appointed; who, when they lie down, say, When shall we arise? And who are thus made a terror to themselves. It was said, that of all the inhuman tortures used by those whom the French king employed to force his Protestant subjects to renounce their religion, none prevailed more, than keeping them by violence long waking. When we find how earnestly nature craves sleep, and how much it is refreshed by it, we should think with compassion of those, who, upon any account, want that and other comforts which we enjoy, and pray for them.

3.5. How ungrateful we have been to the God of our mercies, in suffering sleep, which is so great a support and comfort to us, to be our hinderance in that which is good. As when it has been the gratification of our sloth and laziness, when it has kept us from our hour of prayer in the morning, and disfitted us for our hour of prayer at night; or when we have slept unseasonably in the worship of God; as Eutychus when Paul was preaching; and the disciples, when Christ was in his agony of prayer. How justly might we be deprived of the comfort of sleep, and upbraided with this as the provoking cause of it; What! could ye not watch with me one hour? Those that would sleep and cannot, must think how often they should have kept awake and would not.

3.6. We have now one day less to live than we had in the morning; the thread of time is winding off apace, its sands are running down, and as Time goes, Eternity comes; it is hasting on; our days are swifter than a weaver's shuttle; which passeth and repasseth in an instant; and what do we of the work of time? What forwardness are we in to give up our account? O that we could always go to sleep with death upon our thoughts, how would it quicken us to improve time! It would make our sleep not the less desirable, but it would make our death much the less formidable.

3.7. To thy glory, O God, I now go to sleep: whether we eat, or drink, yea, or sleep, for that is included in whatever we do, we must do it to the glory of God. Why do I go to sleep now, but that my body may be fit to serve my soul, and able for a while to keep pace with it in the service of God to-morrow. Thus common actions by being directed towards our great end, are done after a godly sort, and abound to our account; and thus the advantages we have by them are sanctified to us;

to the pure all things are pure; and whether we wake or sleep, we live together with Christ (1 Thess. 5:10).

3.8. To thy grace, O God, and to the word of thy grace I now commend myself. It is good to fall asleep, with a fresh surrender of our whole selves, body, soul and spirit to God; now return to God as thy rest, O my soul, for he has dealt bountifully with thee; thus we should commit the keeping of our souls to him, falling asleep as David did with, into thy hands I commit my spirit (Ps. 31:5); and as Stephen did, Lord Jesus receive my spirit. Sleep doth not only resemble death, but is sometimes an inlet to it: many go to sleep and never awake, but sleep the sleep of death, which is a good reason why we should go to sleep with dying thoughts, and put ourselves under the protection of a living God, and then, sudden death will be no surprize to us.

3.9. O that when I awake I may be still with God; that the parenthesis of sleep, though long, may not break off the thread of my communion with God, but that as soon as I wake I may resume it. O that when I awake in the night, I may have my mind turned to good thoughts, may remember God upon my bed ,who then is at my right hand, and to whom the darkness and the light are both alike; and that I may sweetly meditate upon him in the night-watches; that thus even that time may be redeemed, and improved to the best advantage, which otherwise is in danger not only of being lost in vain thoughts, but misspent in ill ones. O that when I awake in the morning, my first thoughts may be of God, that with them my heart may be seasoned for all day.

3.10. O that I may enter into a better rest than that which I am now entering upon! The Apostle speaks of a rest, which we that have believed do enter into, even in this world, as well as of a rest which in the other world remains for the people of God (Heb. 4:4, 9). Believers rest from sin and the world, they rest in Christ, and in God through Christ; they enjoy a satisfaction in the covenant of grace, and their interest in that covenant; this is my rest for ever, here will I dwell. They enter into this ark, and there are not only safe, but easy. Now, O that I might enjoy this rest while I live, and when I die, might enter into something more than rest, even the joy of my Lord, a fulness of joy.

4. *Fourthly*, We must do all this in a believing dependence upon God and his power, providence and grace. Therefore I lay me down in peace, and compose myself to sleep, because thou, Lord, keepest me, and assurest me that thou dost so; Thou, Lord, makest me to dwell in safety. David takes notice of God's compassing his path, and his lying

down, as he observes in Psalm 139:3. He sees his eye upon him, when he is retired into his bed-chamber, and none else sees him; when he is in the dark, and none else can see him. Here he takes notice of him, compassing his lying down as his preserver; and sees his hand about him, to protect him from evil, and keep him safe; feels his hand under him to support him, and to make him easy.

4.1. It is by the power of God's providence that we are kept safe in the night, and on that providence we must depend continually. It is he that preserveth man and beast (Ps. 36:6), that upholds all things by the word of his power. That death, which by sin entered into the world, would soon lay all waste, if God did not shelter his creatures from its arrows, which are continually flying about. We cannot but see ourselves exposed in the night. Our bodies carry about with them the seeds of all diseases; death is always working in us, a little thing would stop the circulation either of the blood or the breath, and then we are gone; either never wake, or wake under the arrests of death. Men by sin are exposed to one another; many have been murdered in their beds, and many burned in their beds. And our greatest danger of all is from the malice of evil spirits, that go about seeking to devour.

We are very unable to help ourselves, and our friends unable to help us; we are not aware of the particulars of our danger, nor can we foresee which way it will arise; and therefore know not where to stand upon our guard; or if we did, we know not how. When Saul was asleep, he lost his spear and cruse of water, and might as easily have lost his head as Sisera did when he was asleep, by the hand of a woman. What poor helpless creatures are we, and how easily are we overcome when sleep has overcome us? Our friends are asleep too, and cannot help us. An illness may seize us in the night, which if they be called up and come to us, they cannot help us against; the most skillful and tender physicians are of no value.

It is therefore God's providence that protects us night after night, his care, his goodness. That was the hedge about Job, about him and his house, and all that he had round about (Job 1:10), a hedge that Satan himself could not break through, nor find a gap in, though he traversed it round. There is a special protection which God's people are taken under, they are hid in his pavilion, in the secret of his tabernacle, under the protection of his promise (Ps. 27:5); they are his own and dear to him, and he keeps them as the apple of his eye (Ps. 17:8). He is round about them from henceforth and forever, as the mountains are round about Jerusalem (Ps. 125:2). He protects their habitations as he did the tents of Israel in the wilderness, for he hath promised to create upon every dwelling place of mount Zion, a pillar of cloud by day, to shelter from heat; and the shining of a flaming fire by night, to shelter from cold (Isa. 4:5). Thus he blesseth the habitations of the just, so that no real evil shall befall it, nor any plague come nigh it.

This care of the divine providence concerning us and our families, we are to depend upon, so as to look upon no provisions we make for our own safety sufficient, without the blessing of the divine providence upon it, except the Lord keep the city, the watchman waketh but in vain. Be the house never so well built, the doors and windows never so well barred, the servants never so careful, never so watchful, it is all to no purpose, unless he that keeps Israel, and neither slumbers nor sleeps undertakes for our safety; and if he be thy protector, at destruction and famine thou shalt laugh, and shalt know that thy tabernacle is in peace (Job 5:22, 24).

4.2. It is by the power of God's grace that we are enabled to think ourselves safe, and on that grace we must continually depend. The fear of danger, though groundless, is as vexatious as if it were never so just. And therefore to complete the mercy of being made to dwell safely, it is requisite that by the grace of God we be delivered from our fears (Ps. 34:4), as well as from the things themselves that we are afraid of; that shadows may not be a terror to us, no more than substantial evils.

If by the grace of God we are enabled to keep conscience void of offence, and still to preserve our integrity; if iniquity be put far away, and no wickedness suffered to dwell in our tabernacles, then shall we lift up our faces without spot, we shall be stedfast, and shall not need to fear (Job 11:14, 15), for fear came in with sin, and goes out with it. If our hearts condemn us not, then have we confidence towards God, and man too, and are made to dwell securely, for we are sure nothing can hurt us but sin; and whatever doth harm us, sin is the sting of it; and therefore if sin be pardoned and prevented, we need not fear any trouble.

If by the grace of God we be enabled to live by faith, that faith which sets God always before us, that faith which applies the promises to ourselves, and puts them in suit at the throne of grace, that faith which purifies the heart, overcomes the world, and quencheth all the firey darts of the wicked one, that faith which realizeth unseen things, and is the substance and evidence of them: If we be acted and governed by his grace, we are made to dwell safely, and to bid defiance to death itself, and all its harbingers and terrors; O death where is thy sting? This faith will not only silence our fears, but will open our lips in holy triumphs, if God be for us, who can be against us?

Let us lie down in peace and sleep, not in the strength of a natural resolution against fear, nor merely of rational arguments against it, though they are of good use, but in a dependence upon the grace of God to work faith in us, and to fulfil in us the work of faith. This is going to sleep like a Christian under the shadow of God's wings, going to sleep in faith; and it will be to us a good earnest of dying in faith; for the same faith that will carry us cheerfully through the short death of sleep, will carry us through the long sleep of death.

For Application.

First, See how much it is our concern to carry our religion about with us wherever we go, and to have it always at our right hand; for at every turn we have occasion for it, lying down, rising up, going out, coming in; and those that are Christians indeed, who confine not their religion to the new moons and the sabbaths, but bring the influences of it into all the common actions and occurrences of human life. We must sit down at our tables and rise from them, lie down in our beds, and arise from them, with an eye to God's providence and promise. Thus we must live a life of communion with God, even while our conversation is with the world.

And in order to do this, it is necessary that we have a living principle in our hearts, a principle of grace, which, like a well of living water, may be continually springing up to life eternal (John 4:14). It is necessary likewise that we have a watchful eye upon our hearts, and keep them with all diligence, that we set a strict guard upon their motions, and have our thoughts more at command than I fear most Christians have. See what need we have of the constant supplies of divine grace, and of a union with Christ, that by faith we may partake of the root and fatness of the goodly olive continually.

Secondly, See what a hidden life the life of good Christians is, and how much it lies from under the eye and observation of the world. The most important part of their business lies between God and their own souls, in the frame of their spirits, and the working of their hearts in their retirements, which no eye sees but his that is all eye. Justly are the saints called God's hidden ones, and his secret is said to be with them, for they have meat to eat, and work to do which the world knows not of; and joys, and griefs, and cares which a stranger doth not intermiddle with. Great is the mystery of serious godliness.

And this is a good reason, why we should look upon ourselves as incompetent judges one of another, because we know not others hearts, nor are witnesses to their retirements. It is to be feared, there are many whose religion lies all in the outside, they make a fair show in the flesh, and perhaps a great noise; and yet are strangers to this secret communion with God, in which consists so much of the power of godliness. And on the other hand, it is to be hoped, there are many who do not distinguish themselves by any thing observable in the profession of religion, but pass through the world without being taken notice of, and yet converse much with God in solitude, and walk with him in the even constant tenor of a regular devotion and conversation. The kingdom of God comes not with observation. Many merchants thrive by a secret trade, that make no bustle in the world. It is fit therefore that every man's judgment should proceed from the Lord, who knows men's hearts, and sees in secret.

Thirdly, See what enemies they are to themselves, that continue under the power of a vain and carnal mind, and live without God in the world. Multitudes I fear there are, to whom all that has been said of secret communion with God is accounted as a strange thing, and they are ready to say of their ministers when they speak of it, do they speak parables? They lie down and rise up, go out and come in, in the constant pursuit either of worldly profits, or of sensual pleasures: But God is not in all their thoughts, not in any of them: they live upon him, and upon the gifts of his bounty from day to day, but they have no regard to him, never own their dependence on him, nor are in any care to secure his favours.

They that live such a mere animal life as this, do not only put a great contempt upon God, but do a great deal of damage to themselves; they stand in their own light, and deprive themselves of the most valuable comforts that can be enjoyed on this side of heaven. What peace can they have who are not at peace with God? What satisfaction can they take in their hopes, who build them not upon God the everlasting foundation? Or in their joys, who derive them not from him the fountain of life and living waters? O that at length they would be wise for themselves, and remember their Creator, and Benefactor.

Fourthly, See what easy pleasant lives the people of God might live, if it were not their own faults. There are those who fear God and work righteousness, and are accepted of the Lord, but go drooping and disconsolate from day to day, are full of cares and fears, and complaints, and makes themselves always uneasy; and it is because they do not live that life of delight in God and dependence on him, that they might and should live. God has effectually provided for their dwelling at ease, but they make not use of that provision he has laid up for them.

O that all who appear to be conscientious, and are afraid of sin, would appear to be cheerful, and afraid of nothing else; that all who call God Father, and are in care to please him, and keep themselves in his love, would learn to cast all their other care upon him, and commit their way to him as to a Father. He shall choose our inheritance for us, and knows what is best for us, better than we do for ourselves. Thou shalt answer, Lord, for me. It is what I have often said, and will abide by. That a holy heavenly life spent in the service of God, and in communion with him, is the most pleasant comfortable life any body can live in this world.

Fifthly, See in this, what is the best preparation we can make for the changes, that may be before us in our present state, and that is, to keep up a constant acquaintance and communion with God, to converse with him daily, and keep up stated times for calling on him, that so when trouble comes it may find the wheels of prayer going. And then may we come to God with a humble boldness and comfort, and hope to speed when we are in affliction, if we have been no strangers to God at other times, but in our peace and prosperity had our eyes ever towards him.

Even when we arrive to the greatest degree of holy security and serenity, and lie down most in peace, yet still we must keep up an expectation of trouble in the flesh; our ease must be grounded not upon any stability in the creature; if it be, we put a cheat upon ourselves, and treasure up so much the greater vexation of ourselves. No, it must be built upon the faithfulness of God, which is unchangeable. Our Master has told us, in the world you shall have tribulation, much tribulation, count upon it, it is only in me that you shall have peace. But if every day be to us, as it should be a sabbath of rest in God, and communion with him, nothing can come amiss to us any day, be it never so cross.

Sixthly, See in this, what is the best preparation we can make for the unchangeable world, that is before us. We know God will bring us to death, and it is our great concern to get ready for it. It ought to be the business of every day, to prepare for our last day, and what can we do better for ourselves in the prospect of death, than by frequent retirements for communion with God, to get more loose from that world which at death we must leave, and better acquainted with that world which at death we must remove to. By going to our beds as to our graves, we shall make death familiar to us, and it will become as easy to us to close our eyes in peace and die, as it used to be to close our eyes in peace and sleep.

We hope God will bring us to heaven; and by keeping up daily communion with God, we grow more and more meet to partake of that inheritance; and have our conversation in heaven. It is certain, all that will go to heaven hereafter begin their heaven now, and have their hearts there; if we thus enter into a spiritual rest every night, that will be a pledge of our blessed repose in the embraces of divine love, in that world wherein day and night come to an end, and we shall not rest day or night from praising him, who is, and will be our eternal rest.

FINIS.

APPENDICES

Appendix 1:
An Extended Outline For Scriptural
Prayer by J. Ligon Duncan III
(following Matthew Henry)

I. Address to God and Adoration of Him
Prepare to approach God by turning the mind totally to thoughts of Him.

A. We must solemnly address ourselves to that infinitely great and glorious Being with Whom we have to do, as those who are possessed with a full belief of His presence, and a holy awe and reverence of His majesty.

 1. And we should distinguish ourselves from the worshippers of false gods.

B. We must reverently adore God, as a Being transcendently bright and blessed, self-existent and self-sufficient, an infinite and eternal Spirit, who has all perfections in Himself, and give Him the glory of His titles and attributes.

 1. We must acknowledge His existence to be unquestionable and past dispute.
 2. Yet, We must confess His nature to be incomprehensible.
 3. And His perfections to be matchless and without comparison.
 4. And that He is infinitely above us, and all other beings.

Particularly in our adorations, we must acknowledge:

 a. That He is an eternal, immutable God without beginning of days, or end of life, or change of time.
 b. That He is present in all places, and there is no place in which He is confined, or from which He is excluded.
 c. That He has a perfect knowledge of all persons and things, and sees them all, even that which is most secret, with one clear, certain, and unerring view.
 d. That His wisdom is unsearchable, and the counsels and designs of it cannot be fathomed.
 e. That His sovereignty is incontestable and He is the Owner and absolute Lord of all.
 f. That His power is irresistible, and the operations of it cannot be controlled.

g. That He is a God of unspotted purity and perfect rectitude.

h. That He is just in the administration of His government, and never did, nor ever will, do wrong to any of His creatures.

i. That His truth is inviolable, and the treasures of His goodness inexhaustible.

j. And finally, that when we have said all we can of the glorious perfections of the divine nature, we fall infinitely short of the merit of the subject.

C. We must give to God the praise for the splendor and glory which He is pleased to manifest in the heavens.

D. We must give glory to Him as the Creator of the world, and the great Protector, Benefactor, and Ruler of the whole creation.

E. We must give honor to the three persons in the Godhead, distinctly; to the Father, the Son, and the Holy Ghost, that great and sacred name into which we were baptized, and in which we assemble for religious worship, in communion with the universal church.

F. We must acknowledge our dependence upon God, and our obligations to Him; as our Creator, Preserver, and Benefactor.

G. We must profess this God to be our God, and acknowledge our relation to Him, His dominion over us, and ownership of us.

H. We must acknowledge it an unspeakable favor, and an inestimable privilege, that we are not only admitted, but invited and encouraged, to draw near to God in prayer.

I. We must express the sense we have of our own lowliness and unworthiness to draw near to God, and speak to Him.

J. We must humbly profess the desire of our hearts toward God, as our joy and portion, and the fountain of life and all good to us.

K. We must likewise profess our believing hope and confidence in God, and His all-sufficiency; in His power, providence, and promise.

L. We must entreat God's favorable acceptance of us and our poor performances.

M. We must beg for the powerful assistance and influence of the blessed Spirit of grace in our prayers.

N.   We must make the glory of God our highest end in all our prayers.

O.   We must profess our entire reliance on the Lord Jesus Christ alone for acceptance with God, and come in His name.

II.   Confession of Sin and Declaration of Repentance
In this part of our work,

A.   We must acknowledge the great reason we have to lie very low before God, and to be ashamed of ourselves when we come into His presence, and to be afraid of His wrath, having made ourselves both odious to His holiness and obnoxious to His justice.

B.   We must take hold of the great encouragement God has given us, to humble ourselves before Him with sorrow and shame, and to confess our sins.

C.   We must therefore confess and mourn our original corruption in Adam, that we were the children of apostate and rebellious parents, and the nature of man is depraved, and wretchedly degenerated from its primitive purity and rectitude, and our nature is so.

D.   We must lament our present corrupt dispositions to that which is evil, and our indisposedness to, and impotency in, that which is good. We must look into our hearts, and confess, with holy blushing.
   1.   The blindness of our understandings, and their unaptness to admit the rays of the divine light.
   2.   The stubbornness of our wills, and their unaptness to submit to the rules of the divine law.
   3.   The vanity of our thoughts, their neglect of those things which they ought to be conversant with, and dwelling upon those things that are unworthy of them, and tend to corrupt our minds.
   4.   The carnality of our affections, their being placed upon wrong objects, and carried beyond due bounds.
   5.   The corruption of the whole man: irregular appetites toward those things that are pleasing to sense, and inordinate passions against those things that are displeasing; and an alienation of the mind from the principles, powers, and pleasures of the spiritual and divine life.

E.   We must lament and confess our omissions of our duty, our neglect of it, and triflings in it, and that we have done so little of the great work we were sent into the world about; so very little to answer the end either of our creation or of our redemption, of our birth and of our baptism; and that we have profited no more by the means of grace.

F.   We must likewise bewail our many actual transgressions, in thought, word, and deed.

1.   We must confess and lament the working of pride in us.
2.   The breaking out of passion and rash anger.
3.   Our covetousness and love of the world.
4.   Our sensuality and flesh-pleasing.
5.   Our security and unmindfulness of the changes we are liable to in this world.
6.   Our fretfulness, and impatience, and murmuring under our afflictions, our inordinate dejection, and distrust of God and His providence.
7.   Our uncharitableness towards our brethren, and unpeaceableness of our relations, neighbors, and friends, and perhaps injustice towards them.
8.   Our tongue sins.
9.   Our spiritual slothfulness and decay.

G.   We must acknowledge the great evil that there is in sin, in our sin, the malignity of its nature, and mischievousness to us.

1.   The sinfulness of sin.
2.   The foolishness of sin.
3.   The unprofitableness of sin.
4.   The deceitfulness of sin.
5.   The offense which, by sin, we have given to the Holy Ghost.
6.   The damage which, by sin, we have done to our own souls and their great interests.

H.   We must "aggravate" our sins (that is, we must intensify sin's wickedness in our heart's view) and take notice of those things which make our sins more heinous in the sight of God, and more dangerous to ourselves.

    1.   The more knowledge we have of good and evil, the greater is our sin.
    2.   The greater profession we have made of religion, the greater hath been our sin.
    3.   The more mercies we have received from God, the greater has been our sin.
    4.   The fairer warning we have had from the word of God, and our own consciences concerning our danger of sin, and danger by sin, the greater is the sin, if we go on in it.
    5.   The greater afflictions we have been under for sin, the greater is the sin if we go on in it.

6. The more vows and promises we have made of better obedience, the greater has our sin been.

I. We must judge and condemn ourselves for our sins, and concede ourselves liable to punishment.

J. We must give to God the glory for His patience and forbearance towards us, and His willingness to be reconciled.

K. We must humbly profess our sorrow and shame for sin, and humbly engage ourselves, in the strength of divine grace, that we will be better, and do better in the future.

III. Petition and Supplication

A. We must earnestly pray for the pardoning and forgiveness of all our sins. For the encouraging of our faith, and the exciting of our fervency, in this petition for the pardon of sin; we may plead with God,
   1. The infinite goodness of His nature, His readiness to forgive sin, and His glorying in it.
   2. The merit and righteousness of our Lord Jesus Christ, which we rely upon as our main plea in our petition for the pardon of sin.
   3. The promises God has made in His word to pardon and absolve all them that truly repent and unfeignedly believe his holy gospel.
   4. Our own misery and danger because of sin.
   5. The blessed condition which they are in whose sins are pardoned.

B. We must likewise pray, that God will be reconciled to us, that we may obtain His favor and blessing, and gracious acceptance.
   1. That we may be at peace with God, and His anger may be turned away from us.
   2. That we may be taken into covenant with God, and admitted into relation to Him.
   3. That we may have the favor of God, and an interest in his special love.
   4. That we may have the blessing of God.
   5. That we may have the presence of God with us.

C. We must pray for the comfortable sense of our reconciliation to God, and our acceptance with Him.
   1. That we may have some evidence of the pardon of our sins, and of our adoption.

2. That we may have a well grounded peace of conscience; a holy security and serenity of mind arising from a sense of our justification before God, and a good work wrought in us.

D. We must pray for the grace of God, and all the kind and powerful influences and operations of that grace.

1. We must pray for grace to fortify us against every evil thought, word, and work. Having been earnest for the removing of the guilt of sin, that we may not die for it as a crime, we must be no less earnest for the breaking of the power of sin, that we may not die by it as a disease; but that it may be mortified in us.

   a. And that the temptations of Satan may not overcome us.

2. We must pray for grace to furnish us for every good thought, word, and work, that we may not only be kept from sin, but may be in every thing as we should be, and do as we should do.

   a. That the work of grace may be wrought there, where it is not yet begun.

   b. That where it is begun it may be carried on, and at length perfected, and the foundation that is well laid may be happily built upon.

3. More particularly we must pray for grace.

   a. To teach and instruct us, and make us knowing and intelligent in the things of God.

   b. To lead us into, and keep us in the way of truth, and if in any thing we are in an error, to rectify our mistake.

   c. To help our memories, that the truths of God may be ready to us, whenever we have occasion to use them.

   d. To direct our consciences, to show us the way of our duty. and to make us wise, knowing, judicious Christians.

   e. To sanctify our nature, to plant in us all holy principles and dispositions, and to increase every grace in us.

      1) We must pray for faith.
      2) We must pray for the fear of God.
      3) We must pray that the love of God and Christ may be rooted in us, and in order thereunto, that the love of the world may be removed from us.
      4) We must pray that our consciences may be always tender, and that we may live a life of repentance.
      5) We must pray to God to work in us charity and brotherly love.
      6) We must pray for the grace of self-denial.
      7) We must pray for humility and meekness.

      8)   We must pray for the grace of contentment and patience, and a holy indifference to all the things of sense and time.

      9)   We must pray for the grace of hope; a hope in God and Christ, and a hope of eternal life.

      10)We must pray for grace to preserve us from sin, and all appearances of it, and approaches towards it.

4. We must pray for grace to enable us both to govern our tongues well, and to use them well.

5. We must pray for grace to direct and quicken us to, and to strengthen and assist us in, our duty, in the whole course of our conversation.

    a.   That we may be prudent and discreet in our duty.

    b.   That we may be honest and sincere in our duty.

    c.   That we may be active and diligent in our duty

    d.   That we may be resolute and courageous in our duty, as those who know that though we may be losers for Christ, we shall not be losers by Him in the end.

    e.   That we may be pleasant and cheerful in our duty.

    f.   That we may do the duty of every condition of life, every event of providence and every relation wherein we stand.

    g.   That we may be universally conscientious.

6. We must pray for grace to make us wiser and better every day than another.

7. We must pray for effectual support and comfort under all the crosses and afflictions that we meet with in this world.

8. We must pray for grace to preserve us to the end, and to fit us for whatever lies before us betwixt this and the grave.

9. We must pray for grace to deliver us from the fear and power of death, to prepare us for it, and to carry us well through our dying moments.

10.We must pray for grace to fit us for heaven, and that we may in due time be put in possession of eternal life.

11. We must pray for the good things of life, with an humble submission to the will of God.

a. We must pray to be preserved from the calamities to which we are exposed.

b. We must pray to be supplied with the comforts and supports we daily stand in need of.

12. We must plead the promises of God for the enforcing of all our petitions, put these promises in the form of an appeal, and refer ourselves to them.

IV. Thanksgiving for the Mercies of God

A. We must stir up ourselves to praise God by considering both the reason and the encouragement we have to praise Him.

B. We must be particular in our thanksgiving to God.
We must thank Him,
　　1. For the discoveries which He has made to us in His word of the goodness of His nature.
　　2. For the many instances of His goodness.
　　　　a. The goodness of His providence relating to our bodies, and the life that now is; and this,
　　　　　　1) First, with reference to all the creatures, and the world of mankind in general.
　　　　　　2) Second, with reference to us in particular.
　　　　　　　　a) We must give thanks that He has made us reasonable creatures, capable of knowing, loving, serving, and enjoying Him, and that He has not made us as the beasts that perish.
　　　　　　　　b) We must give thanks for our preservation, that our lives are prolonged, and that the use of our reason and understanding, our limbs and senses, are continued to us.
　　　　　　　　c) For remarkable recoveries from danger by sickness or otherwise.
　　　　　　　　d) For the supports and comforts of this life, which have hitherto made the land of our pilgrimage easy and pleasant to us.
　　　　　　　　e) For success in our callings and affairs, blessings in relationships, and comfortable places of abode.
　　　　　　　　f) For our share in the public plenty, peace and tranquility.
　　　　b. The goodness of His grace relating to our souls, and the life that is come.
　　　　　　1) We must give God thanks for His kindness to the children of men, relating to their souls, and their future state, and His favors to the church in general.
　　　　　　　　a) We must give thanks for His gracious design and provision of man's redemption and salvation, when he was lost and undone by sin.
　　　　　　　　b) For the eternal purposes and counsels of God concerning man's redemption.

c) For appointing the Redeemer, and gracious condescension in dealing with men on new terms, receding from the demands of the broken covenant of innocency

d) For the early and ancient indication of the gracious design concerning fallen man.

e) For the many glorious instances of God's favor to the Old Testament church.

f) For the wonderful and mysterious incarnation of the Son of God, and His coming into the world.

g) For God's gracious appointment of Christ, and His upholding of Him in His great work of redemption.

h) For His holy life, His excellent doctrine, and the glorious miracles He wrought to confirm His doctrine.

i) For the great encouragement Christ gave to poor sinners to come to Him.

j) For the full satisfaction which He made to the justice of God for the sin of man, by the blood of His cross, for the purchases, victories and triumphs of the cross, and for all the precious benefits which flow to us from the dying of our Lord Jesus.

k) For His resurrection from the dead on the third day.

l) For His Ascension into heaven and His sitting at God's right hand there.

m) For the intercession which He ever lives to make in the virtue of His satisfaction.

n) For the dominion and sovereignty to which the Redeemer is exalted.

o) For the assurance we have of His second coming to judge the world.

p) For the sending of the Holy Spirit to comfort and support us in the absence of Christ's bodily presence, to carry on His undertaking, and to prepare things for His second coming.

q) For the covenant of grace made with us in Jesus Christ, and all the exceeding great and precious privileges of that covenant, and for the signs and seals of it.

r) For the writing of the Scriptures, and the preserving of them pure and entire to our day.

s) For the institution of ordinances for the church, and particularly that of the ministry.

t) For the planting of the Christian religion in the world, and the setting up of the gospel church, despite all the oppositions of the powers of darkness.

u) For the preservation of Christianity in the world to this day.

v) For the martyrs and confessors, the lights of the church, and the good examples of those who are gone before us to heaven.

w) For the communion of saints, that spiritual fellowship which we have in faith, hope, and holy love, and in prayers and praises with all good Christians.

x) For the prospect and hope of eternal life, when time and days shall be no more.

2) We must give God thanks for the spiritual mercies bestowed on us in particular, especially if we are called with an effectual call, and have a good work of grace begun in us.

a) We must bless God for the strivings of His Spirit with us, and the admonitions and checks of our own consciences.

b) We must bless God if there be a saving change wrought in us by His blessed Spirit.

c) We must give thanks for the remission of our sins, and the peace of our consciences.

d) For the powerful influences of divine grace, to sanctify and preserve us, to prevent our falling into sin, and to strengthen us in doing our duty.

e) For sweet communion with God in holy ordinances, and the communications of His favor.

f) For gracious answers to our prayers.

g) For support under our afflictions, and spiritual benefit and advantage by them.

h) For the performance of God's promises.

V. Intercession and Supplication to God for others

A. We must pray for the whole world of mankind, the lost world; and thus we must honor all men, and according to our capacity do good to all men.

B.   For the propagation of the gospel in foreign parts, and the enlargement of the church, by the bringing in of many to it.

C.   For the conversion of the Jews.

D.   For the churches of eastern Europe, in their new freedom, that God would send revival by the Spirit and check the evil work of false prophets.

E.   For the churches throughout the world that are groaning under the yoke of Muslim tyranny. For God to check the growth of Islam.

F.   For the universal church, wherever dispersed, and for all the interests of it.

G.   For the conviction and conversion of atheists, deists, and infidels, and of all that are out of the way of truth, and of profane scoffers, and those that disgrace Christianity by their vicious and immoral lives.

H.   For the amending of every thing that is amiss in the church, the reviving of primitive Christianity, and the power of godliness, and in order thereunto the pouring out of the Spirit.

I.   For the breaking of the power of all the enemies of the church, and the defeating of all their designs against her.

J.   For the relief of suffering churches, and the support, comfort, and deliverance of all that are persecuted for righteousness.

K.   For all the nations of the world, especially the countries nearest us.

L.   For our own land and nation, which we ought in a special manner to seek the welfare of, that in her peace we may have peace.
   1.   We must be thankful to God for His mercies to our land.
   2.   We must be humble before God for our national sins and provocations.
   3.   We must pray earnestly for national mercies.
      a.   For the favor of God to us, and the tokens of His presence among us, as that in which the happiness of our nation is bound up.
      b.   For the continuance of the gospel among us, and the means of grace, and a national profession of Christ's holy religion.
      c.   For the continuance of our outward peace and tranquility, our liberty and plenty, for the prosperity of our trade, and a blessing upon the fruits of the earth.

d.   For the success of our endeavors for the reformation of manners, the suppression of vice and profaneness, and the support of religion and virtue, and the bringing of them into reputation.

e.   For the healing of our unhappy divisions, and the making up of our breaches.

f.   For victory and success against our enemies abroad, that seek our ruin.

g.   For all orders and degrees of men among us, all to whom we stand in any relation.

1)   For the leaders of our government, that God will protect their persons, preserve their health, and make their lives and government a public blessing.

2)   For public servants, ministers of state, legislators, ambassadors and envoys abroad, and all that are employed in the conduct of public affairs.

3)   For local government officials, magistrates, judges, and sheriffs in the various counties and corporations.

4)   For those who protect the public; police, firemen, paramedics, and other emergency workers whose own lives are often in harm's way.

5)   For all the ministers of God's holy word and sacraments, the masters of assemblies.

6)   For the universities, colleges, schools, and nurseries of learning. For all educational institutions, public and private.

7)   For the common people of the land.

M.   For the various ages and conditions of persons, as they stand in need of mercy and grace.

1.   For those who are young, and setting out in the world.

2.   For those who are old, and are of long standing in profession.

3.   For those who are rich and prosperous in the world, some of whom perhaps need prayers as much as those that request them.

4.   For those who are poor and in affliction, for such we have always with us.

5.   For our enemies, and those who hate us.

6.   For our friends and those who love us.

N.   We must pray, upon occasions of the cares, burdens, and afflictions of particular persons. Such as:

1.   We may pray with and for those that are troubled in mind, and melancholy, and under doubts and fears about their spiritual state.

2. For those who are under convictions of sin.and beginning to be concerned about their souls, and their salvation, and to inquire after Christ.

3. For those who are sick and weak, and distempered in body; that those who are sick, and in sin, may be convinced; those who are sick, and in Christ, comforted.

4. For those that are deprived of the use of their reason.

5. For sick children.

6. For families where death is, especially those which have lost a parent or parents.

7. For those women who are near childbirth.

8. For those who have recovered from sickness or are delivered in child-bearing, and desire to give thanks to God for his mercy.

9. For those parents whose children are a grief to them, or cause them worry.

10. For those that are in prison.

11. For condemned criminals who have but a little while to live.

VI. The Conclusion of our Prayers

A. We may sum up our requests in some comprehensive petitions as the conclusion of the whole matter.

B. We may then beg for the hearing and acceptance of our poor weak prayers, for Christ's sake.

C. We may then beg for the forgiveness of what has been amiss in our prayers.

D. We may then recommend ourselves to the conduct, protection, and government of divine grace, in the further services that lie before us, and in the whole course of our conversation.

E. We may conclude with doxologies or solemn praises of God, ascribing honor and glory to the Father, the Son, and the Holy Ghost, and sealing up all our praises and prayers with an affectionate Amen.

F. It is very proper to sum up our prayers in that form of prayer which Christ taught His disciples.

Appendix 2: Some Principles for Public Prayer
by J. Ligon Duncan III
(following Samuel Miller)

Those who regularly bear the solemn responsibility of leading the congregation in public prayer are here again encouraged to study and reflect on this important matter. The consistent devotional use of such helps as Matthew Henry's Method for Prayer should be a helpful aid in preparing for such an awesome privilege and duty. In the introduction Samuel Miller's Thoughts on Public Prayer has already been commended, but perhaps an enumeration of some of Miller's main principles and admonitions will whet the reader's appetite for more and prove useful in evaluating our own efforts in corporate prayer.

Miller detected the following common faults in the public praying of the church in his day and they remain applicable to our own.

Frequent Faults in Public Prayer

1. OVERUSE OF CERTAIN FAVORITE WORDS AND SET FORMS OF EXPRESSION. This can become monotonous if one leads in pastoral prayer week after week. Too much repetition of God's name ("Lord," "Father," "Heavenly Father," etc.) should also be diligently avoided. This is often simply a matter of habit and lack of forethought.

2. HESITATION AND APPARENT EMBARRASSMENT IN ARTICULATION. Long, awkward pauses and grasping for words detract from the power of public prayer.

3. UNGRAMMATICAL EXPRESSIONS IN PRAYER. Rules of grammar and syntax should be studiously observed lest our poor form of speech become a stumbling block to those congregated for worship.

4. A LACK OF ORDER AND CERTAIN IMPORTANT ELEMENTS OF PRAYER. Disorderliness is a distraction for people who are trying to pray along with the one leading in prayer. During our public worship every Biblical element of prayer (such as adoration, confession, thanksgiving,

petition, and intercession) should be employed. If there is only one comprehensive prayer in the service it should exhibit each part of prayer. If the various parts of prayer are divided into multiple prayers then each element should be given due prominence within the service. Corporate prayer which ignores or neglects any one of these elements is essentially defective.

5. TOO MUCH DETAIL IN PARTICULAR ELEMENTS OF PRAYER. We should aim for proportion between the various parts of the prayer.

6. PRAYING TOO LONG. Excessive length in public prayer should be avoided. "Long prayers are for the closet." In Miller's day, when attention spans were much longer than our own, he recommended 12-15 minutes at the most. The reader may judge what is appropriate for his own situation.

7. THE EMPLOYMENT OF ALLEGORICAL STYLE IN PRAYER. Overuse of highly figurative language is to be discouraged and simplicity of form commended.

8. INTRODUCTION OF ALLUSIONS TO PARTY POLITICS, AND PERSONALITIES IN PRAYER. These are serious faults in public prayer. On the matter of prayer and politics the wise and learned Dr. Miller, toward the end of his earthly course. said, "I resolved, more than thirty years ago, never to allow myself, either in public prayer or preaching, to utter a syllable, in periods of great political excitement and party strife, that would enable any human being so much as to conjecture to which side in the political conflict I leaned." With regard to alluding to specific personalities in prayer, it may be noted in passing that it is never appropriate to pray "at" someone in public worship.

9. USAGE OF UNSUITABLY AFFECTIONATE OR INTIMATE LANGUAGE IN PRAYER. The inappropriate use of amatory language (particularly when directed toward the persons of the Trinity) ought to be avoided in public devotions. This language, no matter how well-intentioned, often has the appearance of being artificial or quaint.

10. THE INJECTION OF COMEDY INTO PRAYER. The practice of indulging in wit, humor or sarcasm in public prayer is absolutely inexcusable and should not be tolerated.

11. USE OF PRAYER TO EXPOUND ON A POINT IN TEACHING. Miller says, "the excellence of a public prayer may be marred by introducing into it a large portion of didactic statement." The purpose of prayer is not to

provide an outline of the text, the sermon or some topic in Christian doctrine, but to lead sinners to the throne of grace.

12. CARELESS OVER-EMPHASIS OF DOCTRINES WHICH ARE PARTICULARLY REPUGNANT TO UNBELIEVERS. Those who are prone to discoursing on doctrine in their praying may also tend to be "studious of introducing, with much point, those doctrines which are most offensive to the carnal heart and which seldom fail to be revolting to our impenitent hearers." While no Scriptural doctrine should be deemed unsuitable for and excluded altogether from public prayer (even difficult and offensive teachings: the atonement, original sin, predestination, etc.) we should not become disproportionate in our emphasis or thoughtless in our language.

13. CASUALNESS OR OVER-FAMILIARITY IN OUR SPEECH WITH THE ALMIGHTY. The High and Holy One is often addressed with too much familiarity (and sometimes almost flippancy). This is both distracting and disturbing to devout persons and ought to be studiously avoided.

14. INAPPROPRIATE DISPLAY OF PASTORAL"HUMILITY." Many ministers, before they preach, are wont to confess their unworthiness to proclaim the gospel and abase themselves before God. Miller warns, "there is such a thing as expressing unseasonably and also as carrying to an extreme the profession of humility." Public avowal of our ministerial humility (even in the form of prayer) carries with it certain spiritual dangers for which we all must be on guard.

15. FLATTERY IN PRAYER. Anything even approaching flattery in public prayer is a serious matter. As Miller said, "flattery in any man and on any occasion is criminal." Yet, particularly when there are visiting dignitaries present in the congregation or preaching in the pulpit, this is a temptation to which ministers often succumb. We pray to God not to men. The Lord Almighty is our audience. Let us seek our approval of Him.

16. LACK OF A SENSE OF OCCASION. Some prayers so disregard the circumstances of the service, that they are virtually generic and would be as suitable for one occasion as well as another. Public prayer ought to be fitted for and appropriate to the circumstances of the service in which it is rendered.

17. LACK OF REVERENCE IN THE CONCLUSION OF A PRAYER. Often the sentences or words of a prayer are spoken in such a way which gives the impression that the one praying is more concerned about what he

must do following the prayer than he is with reverently addressing the Almighty. Our conclusions to prayer should be as worshipful as our beginnings.

18. EXCESSIVE VOLUME AND RAPIDITY IN PRAYER. Sometimes, as an expression of deep and ardent feeling, a person will pray very loudly and/or rapidly. Not only is this distracting in and of itself, but also makes it difficult for the congregation to follow along.

Characteristics of a Good Public Prayer

After his discussion of common weaknesses in public Prayer, Miller suggests a number of marks of suitable public prayer. The following synopsis is drawn from that discussion.

1. PUBLIC PRAYER SHOULD ABOUND IN THE LANGUAGE OF SCRIPTURE. This is one of the most essential excellencies in public prayer," said Miller. The language of the word of God is always right, safe, and edifying. Furthermore, in God's word there is a simplicity and tenderness which is very powerful and particularly suited to captivate the heart. Finally, it enables the listener to follow the prayer more easily.

2. PUBLIC PRAYER SHOULD BE WELL-ORDERED. Regular order is helpful to the memory of the one who is leading in prayer and assists the worshippers who are joining in it. Furthermore. it helps keep the prayer at a proper length. Of course, this does not mean that the same order must be used every time.

3. IT SHOULD BE GENERAL AND COMPREHENSIVE. Miller observes that "a suitable prayer" in the public assembly is dignified and general in its plan, and comprehensive in its requests, without descending to too much detail." This will better suit the prayer to the general petitions that need to be rendered up by the congregation as a whole.

4. IT SHOULD NOT BE TOO WORDY OR LENGTHY. This will involve care not to attempt to pray on too many topics, or in too great detail.

5. IT SHOULD BE APPROPRIATE TO THE OCCASION ON WHICH IT IS OFFERED. This is a Scriptural pattern, a help to the worshippers, and a good way to keep pastoral prayers from becoming too tedious or lengthy.

6. IT OUGHT TO CONTAIN A GOOD DOSE OF GOSPEL TRUTH. Without turning into a sermon, Miller suggests that "It is an important excellence in a public prayer that it include the recognition of so much gospel truth as to be richly in instructive to all who join in it, as well as who listen to it."

7. IT SHOULD MANIFEST VARIETY. There is so much that is suitable for inclusion in the petitions of corporate prayer in the Lord's church, that only laziness can lead us to pray over the same content, in the same pattern, week after week. A desirable degree of variety in prayer can be a great help to holding the attention of those worshippers who are seriously attempting to join in offering prayer to God.

8. IF PRAYER IS ROUTINELY CLOSED WITH A DOXOLOGY FROM SCRIPTURE, THE DOXOLOGY SHOULD BE VARIED. This practice was standard in Miller's day and is to be commended to the Christian public in our own.

9. IT SHOULD CONTAIN PETITION FOR THE ADVANCE OF THE GOSPEL. Miller says "a good public prayer ought always to include a strongly marked reference to the spread of the gospel, and earnest petitions for the success of the means employed by the church for that purpose."

10. THE NAMES OF THE LORD SHOULD BE APPROPRIATELY EMPLOYED IN THE VARIOUS PARTS OF PRAYER. Instead of simply employing one title of God throughout a prayer it is appropriate to change this title from one segment of prayer to another.

11. IT SHOULD BE MARKED BY THE SPIRIT AND LANGUAGE OF HOPE AND CONFIDENCE. "Our gracious covenant God loves to be taken at his word; to be firmly and affectionately trusted; to have his exceeding great and precious promises importunately pleaded; and to be approached as a willing, tender Father, not only 'mighty to save,' but ready and willing to save; more ready to bestow the gifts of his grace than earthly parents to give good things to their children" said Miller.

12. THE PRAYER AFTER THE SERMON SHOULD BE SOLEMN AND IMPRESSIVE. Miller suggests that "it ought to be formed upon the plan of taking hold of the conscience and the heart most deeply and effectually."

13. THE FREQUENT USE OF THE LORD'S PRAYER IS PROPER, BUT NOT MANDATORY. We should not feel constrained to use the Lord's Prayer every Sunday.

14. THE VOICE AND TONE IN WHICH WE OFFER PRAYER SHOULD BE SUITABLE TO THE SOLEMN ACTIVITY. "It is important to add, that the whole manner of uttering a public prayer should be in accordance with the humble, filial, affectionate, yet reverential spirit which ought to characterize the prayer itself throughout," said Miller. For a sinner to offer a prayer to Almighty God in a "pompous, dictatorial manner" is incongruous with our status as sinful men and the very activity of Prayer (which is an acknowledgment of our creaturely dependence and an exercise of humble reliance).

In conclusion, we may note Miller's pithy description of an acceptable public prayer. He said "Words 'few,' 'well considered,' and 'well ordered,' are the inspired characteristics of a good prayer."

Appendix 3: An Outline for Scriptural Prayer
by J. Ligon Duncan III
(following Matthew Henry)

I. Address to God and Adoration of Him

Prepare to approach God by turning the mind totally to thoughts of Him.

A. Solemn address to God.
B. Reverent adoration of God.
   1. Acknowledge His existence to be unquestionable and past dispute.
   2. Confess His nature to be incomprehensible.
   3. Profess His perfections to be matchless and without comparison.
   4. Grant that He is infinitely above us, and all other beings.

Particularly in our adorations, we must acknowledge:
   a. He is an eternal and immutable God.
   b. He is omnipresent.
   c. He is omniscient.
   d. He is all-wise.
   e. He is sovereign Lord and Owner of all.
   f. He is omnipotent.
   g. He is pure, holy, and just.
   h. He is just and fair in the rule of His creation.
   i. His truth is inviolable, and His goodness inexhaustible.
   j. Our adorations fall infinitely short of God's glory.

C. Praise God for the splendor and glory which He has manifested in the heavens.
D. Give Him glory as the Creator, Protector, Benefactor, and Ruler of the whole creation.
E. Give honor to the Trinity, distinctly; Father, Son, and Holy Spirit.
F. Acknowledge our dependence on and obligations to God as our Creator, Preserver, and Benefactor.
G. Profess God to be our God, and acknowledge our relation to Him, His dominion over us, and ownership of us.
H. Acknowledge what a favor and privilege it is that we are admitted, invited, and encouraged to draw near to God in prayer.

I.   Express the sense we have of our own lowliness, and unworthiness to draw near to God, and speak to Him.

J.   Humbly profess the desire of our hearts toward God, as our joy and portion, and the fountain of life and all good to us.

K.   Profess our believing hope and confidence in God, and His all-sufficiency; in His power, providence, and promise.

L.   Entreat God's favorable acceptance of us and our poor performances.

M.   Beg for the powerful assistance and influence of the blessed Spirit of grace in our prayers.

N.   We must make the glory of God our highest end in all our prayers.

O.   We must profess our entire reliance on the Lord Jesus Christ alone for acceptance with God, and come in His name.

II. Confession of Sin and Declaration of Repentance

In this part of our work,

A.   Acknowledge why we have reason to lie very low before God, to be ashamed of ourselves when we come into His presence, and to be afraid of His wrath: as sinners we are both odious to His holiness and obnoxious to His justice.

B.   Take hold of the encouragement God has given us, to humble ourselves before Him with sorrow and shame, and to confess our sins.

C.   Confess and mourn our original corruption in Adam, and the depravity of our nature which flows from it.

D.   Lament our present corrupt disposition to evil, and our reticence to and weakness in doing good.

    1.   The blindness of our understandings.

    2.   The stubbornness of our wills.

    3.   The vanity of our thoughts.

    4.   The carnality of our affections

    5.   The corruption of the whole man.

E.   Lament and confess our neglect of our duty.

F.   Grieve our many actual transgressions, in thought, word, and deed.

    1.   The working of pride in us.

    2.   The breaking out of passion and rash anger.

    3.   Our covetousness and love of the world.

    4.   Our sensuality and flesh-pleasing.

    5.   Our security and unmindfulness of the changes we are liable to in this world.

    6.   Our fretfulness, impatience, and murmuring in affliction, our inordinate dejection, and distrust of God and His providence.

    7.   Our uncharitableness towards our brethren, and poor relations with them.

8. Our tongue sins.
9. Our spiritual slothfulness and decay.

G. Acknowledge the great evil that there is in sin, in our sin, the malignity of its nature, and mischievousness to us.
1. The sinfulness of sin.
2. The foolishness of sin.
3. The unprofitableness of sin.
4. The deceitfulness of sin.
5. The offense which, by sin, we have given to the Holy Ghost.
6. The damage which, by sin, we have done to our own souls and their great interests.

H. Take notice of those things which make our sins more heinous in the sight of God, and more dangerous to ourselves.
1. The more knowledge we have of good and evil, the greater is our sin.
2. The greater profession we have made of religion, the greater hath been our sin.
3. The more mercies we have received from God, the greater has been our sin.
4. The fairer warning we have had from the word of God, the greater is the sin, if we go on in it.
5. The greater afflictions we have been under for sin, the greater is the sin if we go on in it.
6. The more vows and promises we have made of better obedience, the greater has our sin been.

I. Judge and condemn ourselves for our sins, and concede ourselves liable to punishment.

J. Give to God the glory for His patience and forbearance towards us, and His willingness to be reconciled.

K. Humbly profess our repentance of sin and engage ourselves, in the strength of divine grace, to be and do better in the future.

III. Petition and Supplication

A. Earnestly pray for the pardoning and forgiveness of all our sins.
To encourage us in this petition for the pardon of sin; we may plead with God:
1. The infinite goodness of His nature, His readiness to forgive sin, and His glorying in it.
2. The merit and righteousness of our Lord Jesus Christ, which we rely upon as our main plea for the pardon of sin.
3. The promises God has made in His word to pardon all them that truly repent and unfeignedly believe his holy gospel.
4. Our own misery and danger because of sin.

5. The blessed condition which they are in whose sins are Pardoned.

B. Pray that God will be reconciled to us.
1. That we may be at peace with God and His anger turned away.
2. That we may be taken into covenant with God.
3. That we may have the favor of God and an interest in his special love.
4. That we may have the blessing of God.
5. That we may have the presence of God with us.

C. Pray for the sense of our reconciliation to God and our acceptance with Him.
1. That we may have some evidence of the pardon of our sins and of our adoption.
2. That we may have peace of conscience and a holy security because of our justification before God and His good work in us.

D. Pray for the grace of God, and all the kind and Powerful influences and operations of that grace.
1. For grace to strengthen us against every evil thought, word, and work, and the Spirit's help in the mortification of sin.
2. For grace to equip us for every good thought, word, and work, that we may be and do what we should be and do.
   a. That the work of grace may be started where it is not yet begun.
   b. That where grace has is begun it may be carried on, and at length perfected.
3. More particularly we must pray for grace.
   a. To teach, instruct, and make us knowing and intelligent in the things of God.
   b. To lead us into, and keep us in the way of truth, and to rectify our mistakes.
   c. To help our memories, that we might remember the truths of God whenever we have occasion to use them.
   d. To direct our consciences, to show us the way of our duty, and to make us wise, knowing, judicious Christians.
   e. To sanctify our nature, to plant in us all holy principles and dispositions, and to increase every grace in us.
      1) For faith.
      2) For the fear of God.
      3) For the love of God and Christ to be rooted in us and the love of the world removed from us.
      4) For our consciences to be always tender and that we may live a life of repentance.
      5) For God to work in us charity and brotherly love.

6) For the grace of self-denial.
7) For humility and meekness.
8) For the grace of contentment and patience.
9) For the grace of hope; a hope in God and Christ, and a hope of eternal life.
10) For grace to preserve us from sin, and all appearances of it, and approaches towards it.

4. For grace to enable us both to govern our tongues well, and to use them well.

5. For grace to direct and quicken us to, and to strengthen and assist us in our duty, in the whole course of our conversation.
   a. That we may be prudent and discreet in our duty.
   b. That we may be honest and sincere in our duty.
   c. That we may be active and diligent in our duty.
   d. That we may be resolute and courageous in our duty.
   e. That we may be pleasant and cheerful in our duty.
   f. That we may do the duty of every condition of life.
   g. That we may be universally conscientious.

6. For grace to make us wiser and better every day than another.

7. For effectual support and comfort under all the crosses and afflictions that we meet with in this world.

8. For grace to preserve us to the end, and to fit us for whatever lies before us betwixt this and the grave.

9. For grace to deliver us from the fear and power of death, to help us die well.

10. For grace to fit us for heaven, and that we may in due time be put in possession of eternal life.

11. For the good things of life, with an humble submission to the will of God.
    a. To be preserved from the calamities to which we are exposed.
    b. To be supplied with the comforts and supports we daily stand in need of.

12. Plead the promises of God, put these promises in the form of an appeal, and refer ourselves to them.

IV. Thanksgiving for the Mercies of God

A. Stir up ourselves to praise God by considering both the reason and the encouragement we have to praise Him.

B. Be Particular in our thanksgiving to God.

We must thank Him,

1. For how He has shown us His goodness in His word.
2. For the many instances of His goodness.

    a.   The goodness of His providence relating to our bodies, and the life that now is:

        1)   With reference to all the creatures, and in general.

        2)   With reference to us (His people) in particular.

            a)   He has made us reasonable creatures, capable of knowing, loving, serving, and enjoying Him; not like the beasts.

            b)   For our preservation; our lives are prolonged, and we have continuing use of our reason, limbs and senses.

            c)   For remarkable recoveries from danger by sickness or otherwise.

            d)   For the supports and comforts of this life, which have made our earthly pilgrimage easy and pleasant.

            e)   For success in our callings and affairs, blessings in relationships, and comfortable places of abode.

            f)   For our share in the public plenty, peace, and tranquility.

    b.   The goodness of His grace relating to our souls, and the life that is come.

        1)   For His kindness to us regarding our souls, their future state, and His favors to the church in general.

            a)   For His gracious design and provision of man's redemption and salvation, when he was lost and undone by sin.

            b)   For the eternal purposes and counsels of God concerning man's redemption.

            c)   For appointing the Redeemer, gracious condescension toward fallen men, provision for the broken Adamic covenant.

            d)   For the early and ancient indication of the gracious design concerning fallen man.

            e)   For the many glorious instances of God's favor to the Old Testament church.

            f)   For the wonderful and mysterious incarnation of the Son of God, and His coming into the world.

            g)   For God's gracious appointment of Christ, and His upholding of Him in His great work of redemption.

            h)   For His holy life, His excellent doctrine, and the glorious miracles He wrought to confirm His doctrine.

            i)   For the great encouragement Christ gave to poor sinners to come to Him.

            j)   For the full satisfaction which He made to the justice of God for the sin of man, by the blood of His cross, for the purchases, victories, and triumphs of the cross, and for all the precious benefits which flow to us from the dying of our Lord Jesus.

k) For His resurrection from the dead on the third day.

l) For His ascension into heaven, and His sitting at God's right hand there.

m) For the intercession which He ever lives to make in the virtue of his satisfaction.

n) For the dominion and sovereignty to which the Redeemer is exalted.

o) For the assurance we have of His second coming to judge the world.

p) For the sending of the Holy Spirit to comfort and support us in the absence of Christ's bodily presence, to carry on His undertaking, and to prepare things for His second coming.

q) For the covenant of grace made with us in Christ, and all the privileges, signs and seals of it.

r) For the writing of the Scriptures, and the preserving of them pure and entire to our day.

s) For the institution of ordinances for the church, and particularly that of the ministry.

t) For the planting of Christianity in the world, and the establishment of the church, despite the oppositions of hell.

u) For the preservation of Christianity in the world to this day.

v) For the martyrs, confessors, lights of the church, and good examples of those who are gone before us to heaven.

w) For the communion of saints, that spiritual fellowship which we have with all good Christians.

x) For the prospect and hope of eternal life, when time and days shall be no more.

2) For the spiritual mercies towards those effectually called.

a) For the strivings of His Spirit with us, and the admonitions and checks of our own consciences.

b) For the saving change wrought in us by His blessed Spirit.

c) For the remission of our sins, and the peace of our consciences.

d) For the influences of grace in sanctification and perseverance.

e) For sweet communion with God in holy ordinances and the communications of His favor.

f) For gracious answers to our prayers.

g) For support under our afflictions, and spiritual benefit and advantage by them.

h) For the performance of God's promises.

V. Intercession and Supplication to God for others

A. Pray for the whole world of mankind, the lost world; honor all men, and according to our capacity do good to all men.

B. For the propagation of the gospel in foreign parts and the growth of the church.

C. For the conversion of the Jews.

D. For the churches of eastern Europe, in their new freedom, that God would send revival and check the evil work of false prophets.

E. For the churches throughout the world that are groaning under the yoke of Muslim tyranny. For God to check the growth of Islam.

F. For the universal church, wherever dispersed, and for all the interests of it.

G. For the conviction and conversion of atheists, deists, and Infidels.

H. For the amending of every thing amiss in the church.

I. For the breaking of the power of all the enemies of the church, and the defeating of all their designs against her.

J. For the relief of suffering churches, and the support, comfort, and deliverance of all that are persecuted for righteousness.

K. For all the nations of the world, especially the countries nearest us.

L. For our own land and nation, which we ought in a special manner to seek the welfare of, that in her peace we may have peace.

1. For God's mercies to our land.

2. Humble ourselves before God for our national sins and provocation

3. Pray earnestly for national mercies.

a. For the favor of God to us and the tokens of His presence among us.

b. For the continuance of the gospel among us, and the means of grace, and a national profession of Christ's holy religion.

c. For the continuance of our outward peace and tranquility, liberty and plenty.

d. For the success of our endeavors for the reformation and revival.

e. For the healing of our unhappy divisions.

f. For victory and success against our enemies abroad, that seek our ruin.

g. For all orders and degrees of men among us, all we stand in any relation to.
1) For the leaders of our government.
2) For public servants, ministers of state, legislators, ambassadors, etc.
3) For local government officials, magistrates, judges, and sheriffs in the various counties and corporations.
4) For those who protect the public; police, firemen, paramedics, and other emergency workers.
5) For all the ministers of God's holy word and sacraments. the masters of assemblies.
6) For the professors and teachers in universities, colleges, and schools.
7) For the common people of the land.

M. For the various ages and conditions of persons, as they stand in need of mercy and grace.
1. For those who are young and setting out in the world.
2. For those who are old, and are of long standing in profession.
3. For those who are rich and prosperous in the world, some of whom perhaps need Prayers as much as those that request them.
4. For those who are poor and in affliction, for such we have always with us.
5. For our enemies, and those who hate us.
6. For our friends and those who love us.

N. Pray, upon occasions of the cares and burdens and afflictions of particular persons.
1. For those that are troubled in mind, and melancholy, and under doubts and fears about their spiritual state.
2. For those who are under convictions of sin, and beginning to be concerned about their souls, and their salvation.
3. For those who are sick and weak; those who are sick and in sin convinced; those who are sick and in Christ, comforted.
4. For those that are deprived of the use of their reason.
5. For sick children.
6. For families where death is, especially those which have lost a parent or parents.
7. For those women who are near childbirth.
8. For those who have recovered from sickness or are delivered in childbearing, and desire to give thanks to God for his mercy.
9. For those parents whose children are a grief to them, or cause them worry.
10. For those that are in prison.
11. For condemned criminals who have but a little while to live.

VI. The Conclusion of our Prayers

A. We may sum up our requests in some comprehensive Petitions as the conclusion of the whole matter.

B. We may then beg for the hearing and acceptance of our poor weak prayers, for Christ's sake.

C. We may then beg for the forgiveness of what has been amiss in our prayers.

D. We may then recommend ourselves to the conduct, protection, and government of divine grace, in the further services that lie before us, and in the whole course of our conversation.

E. We may conclude with doxologies or solemn praises of God, ascribing honor and glory to the Father, the Son, and the Holy Ghost, and sealing up all our praises and prayers with an affectionate Amen.

F. It is very proper to sum up our prayers in that form of prayer which Christ taught his disciples.